THE SECOND CITY

C A Oakley

THE SECOND CITY

LUCEM LIBRIS DISSEMINAMUS

Blackie
Glasgow and London

Blackie & Son Limited
Bishopbriggs . Glasgow
5 Fitzhardinge Street . London . W1

© C.A. Oakley 1967

First published 1946
Second edition 1967
Third edition 1975

Designed by James W. Murray
Printed by Robert MacLehose and Company Limited
Printers to the University of Glasgow

Introduction

The Second City was published in 1946. In that and subsequent years it was reprinted six times. By the mid-nineteen-sixties the desirability of bringing the text up to date was very clear and this presented an opportunity to correct various omissions which had been noticed by readers and to make other amendments.

Approximately one-tenth of the text has been removed by 'streamlining' and it has been replaced by new matter. The most noticeable difference between the new book and the old is, however, in the illustrations. We waited for Mr. Joseph McAskie and the staff of the Mitchell Library to complete their indexing of the incredibly large number of periodicals issued in Glasgow during the Victorian and Edwardian eras, and we have procured from them many cartoons and caricatures depicting the contemporary scene.

As was observed in the *Introduction* to the original book we found it easy to write about the men of the seventeen-hundreds and early eighteen-hundreds because some bright old boys—in particular, 'Senex' (Robert Reid, 1773-1865), 'Alquis' (Dr. Mathie Hamilton, 1793–1869), Dr. John Strang (1795–1863), 'J.B.' (John Buchanan, 1802–78) and James Pagan (1811-70)—have left amazingly detailed and often amusing accounts of life in their day and, according to the tales they had been told as children, in the days of their fathers and grandfathers. In writing the earlier part of this book, we have merely gone through material which others—notably George Eyre-Todd—had gone through before us. The presentation is new. The matter is not.

Much of the book is devoted to the Victorians—the early Victorians, who lived in the age of progress and prosperity, who believed that they were making their way to an elysium on earth of perpetual content and happiness, and the later Victorians, who were less sanguine and less satisfied about their world, but who nevertheless lived in times of expansion and did not comprehend how very different things would be for the next generation.

The rest of the book is about the men and women of the twentieth century. This is no longer a new century. Indeed, it is two-thirds over, and some of us, who were born in its early years, now realize that to younger generations there is no longer an association between 'belonging to the twentieth century' and having a fresh outlook. A great deal has happened in the century—the Edwardian decade with its genial social life and angry political disputes, the horrible first world war, the noisy nineteen-twenties, when the Americans had the greatest of all industrial booms and this country had a general strike, the depressed and appeasing nineteen-thirties, the second world war and its aftermath in which we are still living. A writer in *Punch*, in 1940, wondered what her Edwardian mother would have said if she had seen her wearing her husband's flannel trousers, lying in mud on her stomach, squirting water at an incendiary bomb. Yet both mother and daughter 'belong to the twentieth century'. So, incidentally, does that daughter's daughter.

The book has a new title, *The Second City* now appearing in inverted commas. Glasgow is no longer the second city of the Empire (Commonwealth); but it held that distinction for approximately 140 years and we thought ourselves justified in continuing to use it, but within quotation marks—particularly as there is no certainty about which city is best qualified to take over the title from Glasgow.

UNIVERSITY OF GLASGOW   C.A.O.

Acknowledgements

I would like to acknowledge the financial assistance of the following bodies who have made it possible to publish this third edition: Burmah Oil Trading Ltd; J. and P. Coats Ltd; James Finlay and Co. Ltd; Stoddard Holdings Ltd; and the Isadore and David Walton Trust.

This drawing was made, as the costumes show, in the 1600s. The wall around the Bishop's (or Episcopal) Palace was 15 feet high. A lane ran between it and the Cathedral yard. The tower on the left was known as the West Tower and also as Bishop Cameron's Tower.

IN COMMON WITH THE OTHER PEOPLE OF PRESENT-DAY Great Britain, the people of the Glasgow district are of mixed stock. Their ancestors, who resisted the Romans with grim determination, were the products of a racial blend of Iberian and Alpine (central European) peoples, who had made their way at various times, probably by the western coast, to Scotland, and of an older people, whom they had overcome but about whom relatively little is now known. The Iberian element is clearly predominant on Clydeside; and, by being rather short, dark and swarthy, the people of Glasgow are probably very alike in appearance to their forebears, as the Romans portrayed them almost two thousand years ago. Perhaps the proportion of Scandinavian traits has increased, but only slightly in comparison with the changes which have taken place in the make-up of the people of the east coast of both Scotland and England and of the southern half of England, because the Iberian element is also predominant in the western Highlands and the Lowlands of Scotland, and in both Northern and Southern Ireland, which have been, and still are, the principal recruiting grounds for Glasgow.

Appearance is, however, perhaps secondary in importance to the characteristics acquired from environment—it is probably true to say of most people that they were 'made that way' rather than 'born that way'—and some of the Glasgow man's characteristics can be traced back to the hard struggle his ancestors, Picts, Scots, Britons and Angles, had in getting a living from the land. The soil and climate were not good for farming—although some parts, such as the Clyde Valley and Ayrshire, were very fertile—and they often had to fight strenuously to retain what little they had produced against marauders descending perhaps from the Highlands, particularly in bad years, or appearing quite unexpectedly by sea from Scandinavia. All of this tended, no doubt, to 'toughen' them, to steel them against misfortune, and to develop their possessive propensities. It also tended to divert their own attention to the sea where fish was abundant, and so promoted a restless rather than a 'settled' outlook.

Not Such a Bad Climate, Really

Climatic conditions have moulded the character of the Scot of the western Lowlands. Glasgow is thought, not only by the people of other parts but even by the people of Glasgow themselves, to have a severe climate. Certainly it is not kind to the farmer. But Glasgow has one of the best climates in Great Britain for factory work.

I

Glasgow's closeness to the sea makes snow a comparative rarity.
Glasgow is misty, but dense fogs, except occasionally in November,
are infrequent. The midlands of England have more snow and more fog
than Glasgow. It is protected from east winds—London and Sheffield
have more bitter winter weather than Glasgow. But Glasgow has, of
course, its own disadvantages. In particular, it is wet—not with
frequent drizzle in the Manchester sense, but with rainstorms of long
duration and severity—although other places in, for instance, south
Wales and Lancashire have a heavier rainfall as measured over the
year. So, although few realize it, has New York. It has comparatively
little sunshine in summer, and the grey skies of July and August tend
to make it depressing. But May, June, September and even October can
be splendid months. The people of Glasgow have never had to learn
what a hot August day in Birmingham is like, or a snowy January in
Nottingham, or an enervating June day in Plymouth, or a biting
February day in Newcastle.

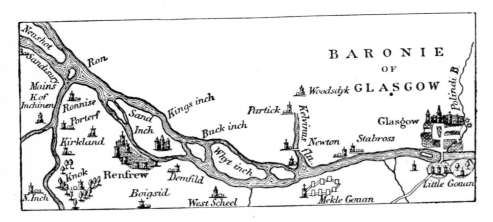

The Islands in the Clyde (1654)

The Old Bridge and the Shallow River

If Glasgow was known at all outside Scotland before 1650, it was as
an ecclesiastical city, with its cathedral founded in 1136 (on the site
of St. Mungo's Church of A.D. 543) and its university founded in 1451.
When the opening up of trade with the New World provided the
opportunity for creating a port on the west coast of Scotland—the
commerce of the country had previously flowed through ports on the
east coast, principally Aberdeen and Leith—the traders of Glasgow,
small business men and craftsmen, but astute and ambitious, converted
their quiet, academic little city into a port—or used Greenock as a port.

Glasgow had one great geographical advantage, an advantage to
which its antiquity—it has been described as the oldest town in
Scotland—is attributed. This advantage, which had led prehistoric
people to settle in the vicinity of its present-day Royal Infirmary, and
which later led the Romans to build their mid-Scotland wall with a
fort there, was the existence of shallows in the Clyde, by which the
river could be easily forded. The early history of Glasgow was written
around these shallows and around the bridges which were later built
across them. Throughout the centuries most of the people who came
to Glasgow did so as birds of passage, travelling between the western
Highlands and the western Lowlands. Partly for their convenience,
the cathedral authorities in 1345 constructed a bridge with eight piers
at the Stockwell shallows. This Old Glasgow Bridge, which was
relatively more vital even than Old London Bridge located over the
Thames shallows, was extended and altered in other ways from time
to time; but it was over 600 years old—so well were the old masons
masters of their jobs—when it was demolished.

2

This is the only sketch known to us showing the fording of the Clyde at Stockwell Street. The period is the 1720s. The adjacent Glasgow Bridge charged tolls and evidently much horse-borne traffic preferred to cross free by the ford.

Glasgow's life, until the Reformation, revolved around the cathedral. The Celtic holy men, who had chosen Glasgow as the centre of their dioceses, had their eyes not only on the convenience of being able to cross the river at Stockwell, but also on the protection provided against Norse raiders, who could not bring their ships through the shoals in the river, and who would have to march many miles inland from the Ayrshire coast before reaching the city. Those who grumble today about the port being so far up the river may well ponder on the reasons for its being where it is.

The cathedral was for some centuries a focal point of Christian culture in Scotland, and several of its bishops were appointed chancellors of the country. But the gradual development of trade with the Continent—particularly with Holland and Scandinavia—made the east of Scotland politically more important than the west. Edinburgh became the capital city, and St. Andrews the ecclesiastical centre, founding its university half a century before Glasgow. In 1600 the population was only 5000, and Glasgow ranked eleventh in taxable capacity among Scottish towns. It seemed to be slipping back at that time rather than advancing, and the life of the city was so thoroughly dominated by the cathedral that the bishop appointed the provost and magistrates. Glasgow was originally a burgh or barony, ruled by the bishop in his temporal right. Then it became a burgh of regality, the bishop holding authority on behalf of the king. When it achieved the status of a royal burgh in 1690, the council was answerable only to the king and Parliament. By 1660 Glasgow had become the second city of Scotland—and this in spite of a dreadful fire, spread over three days, which destroyed much of the burgh.

Although this rise was no doubt influenced by the new markets coming into being across the Atlantic, the first effects would seem to have been indirect, for the founders of Glasgow's shipping trade began by sending their 'smiddy coals, plaiding and herring' to ports on the west coast of Europe and the Mediterranean. This, then, is the century in which modern Glasgow had its beginnings, and it is significant that two legal corporations, the Trades House and the Merchants' House, received recognition in 1605. Members of the latter were the dignified and relatively wealthy wholesalers, exporters and importers. The traders were artisans and shopkeepers. The objective of both houses was combination, for professional, social, charitable and religious purposes. Both Edinburgh and Aberdeen were ahead of Glasgow. The first incorporated craft, the skinners,

3

goes back to 1516, and there were a dozen organized crafts by 1600.
Until the Burgh Reform Bill of the eighteen-thirties, these two Houses
shared the political and municipal authority of the city, and each
returned 'a full moiety of the town council' from its members.
That is to say, they took over the administration of the city's affairs
from the Bishop and his advisers and, for the next two centuries,
'ran the city'.

The enterprising Glasgow merchants, now sensing that opportunity
was knocking at their door, saw that it would be greatly in their
interest if the river could be opened to shipping. Even before their
time—in 1566—an attempt had been made to cut a navigable channel
through one of the worst sandbanks in the Clyde, at Dumbuck, but it
had failed. And so did all other efforts for many generations, and as
late as 1755 the river was still in a 'state of nature' and had been
'allowed to expand too much in width.' Nothing larger than barges
and small craft could make their way up the Clyde to Glasgow. Various
schemes were considered for building a harbour for ships trading
with the city but located near the mouth of the river and clear of
interference by people from the Royal Burghs of Dumbarton and
Renfrew. In the middle of the seventeenth century thirteen acres near
Greenock were bought, and Port Glasgow came into being, with the
first graving dock in Scotland. A hundred years later, when civil
engineering practice was more advanced, a method suggested in
1768 by John Golborne was adopted. The channel was cleared,
and large vessels began to sail to Glasgow. Port Glasgow became a
manufacturing town. Glasgow became its own port.

A New World Opens Up

The seventeen-hundreds began with Glasgow men in a black mood,
and they had no inkling of the astonishing change about to take place
in their fortunes. They had seen the first of the city's important
merchants, Walter Gibson, die in penury. Gibson had been 'the father
of the trade of all the west coasts' and responsible for building
the first quay in Glasgow—at the Broomielaw in 1688. The Glasgow
traders were feeling particularly bitter with the English at this time.
The colonies with which they wanted, and tried, to trade were English
colonies, and the Scots were sometimes not only warned off but
thrown off—not but that some, like the future merchant prince,
Daniel Campbell of Shawfield Mansion, were fully prepared to go
back and chance it again.

The legal obstructions put in their way seemed so great that they
looked favourably on a scheme propounded by William Paterson, the
Dumfriesshire man who had founded the Bank of England some years
before. His plan was to keep clear of the English (and French)
colonies, by creating a Scottish colony on the Isthmus of Darien
(Panama)—a brilliant conception, embracing trade with Pacific as well
as with Atlantic countries. Unfortunately, the district was disease-
ridden—as was learned again a century and a half later. The countries
already trading with the Americas, including principally England,
looked unfavourably on the new venture and did their best, quite
effectively, to wreck it.

The bitter resentment over the loss of many lives and half the
capital of Scotland was reflected in 1707 in opposition to the proposed
union of the Scottish and English Parliaments; although the resistance
of the magistrates and of the merchants was notably less ardent than
that of the populace. Riots ensued, and an attempt to break up the

The original Ramshorn Kirk in Ingram Street, built in 1720.

*Questions are sometimes asked about the 'piazzas'
described as a feature of Glasgow Cross in the mid-1700s,
but not seen in drawings of the period. Here is an explanation.
The colonades extended into High Street
and so were not in artist's pictures of the Trongate.*

Scottish Parliament in Edinburgh was initiated from Glasgow—but
without much official encouragement. Soon, however, the union
brought prosperity to Scotland and particularly to Glasgow. In 1707
Scotland had owned only 215 ships—Leith having 35 of them,
Glasgow 13, and the other Clyde ports 8. After five years the total
was 1123. The number of Leith's ships had grown to 45, Glasgow's
to 46, and those of the other Clyde ports to 149. Almost from the
moment of the signing of the Act of Union, and the withdrawal of the
barrier of the Navigation Acts, the Glasgow merchants seized the
new opportunities opened up to them, and began the great trade in
sugar and tobacco on which the fortunes of their city were to be
founded.

Glasgow's second thoughts on the desirability of the union led its
citizens to oppose the Old Pretender in the 1715 Rebellion, and to
raise a regiment of 500 to fight against him. Even stronger action was
taken against Bonnie Prince Charlie in the 1745 Rebellion—an
interesting point is that, while Glasgow was against the Young
Pretender, Manchester sided with him—and a regiment of 1000 men
was recruited. The prince's Highland Army descended on Glasgow
during its retreat, and held the city in custody for ten days, the towns-
people being forced to bear the cost of quartering and re-clothing.

The most important year in Scottish history during the eighteenth
century was probably 1723, although its significance was at first
greater on the east coast, and particularly in the Edinburgh district,
than on the west coast. In that year the Society of Improvers of

5

Knowledge of Agriculture was formed, with Cockburn of East Lothian—who introduced the turnip and the potato into Scotland—as its principal figure. Scotland was no longer to be a country of frugal living.

The turning-point in the business of the Glasgow merchants trading with the North American colonies and with the West Indies came in 1735. The merchants of Bristol, Liverpool and Whitehaven had not welcomed the Scottish merchants' incursion into their territory, and for almost thirty years after the union had thwarted them with vexatious lawsuits. In particular, the Glasgow merchants were charged with evading the payment of duty on the tobacco they were importing. After 1735, however, the Glasgow merchants came out 'on top'—partly due to their enterprise and ability, partly due to the French wars which closed the Atlantic off the south-west of England to shipping, and so diverted traffic to the northern ports. By 1775, when the Glasgow tobacco merchants were at the height of their prosperity, they were importing from Virginia, North Carolina and Maryland more than half of all the tobacco brought into this country, and much of the tobacco was sent from the Clyde to France and the Low countries. In 1771, just before the Revolutionary War, the Clyde imported 46 million tons of tobacco. Only 3 million remained in this country, most of the rest going to France. As the sugar trade was not far short of the tobacco trade in importance, the increase of wealth in Glasgow in the course of approximately half a century could be described as stupendous.

The Tobacco Lords

The men who created the tobacco trade with the American colonies did not belong to the landowners and the rest of the upper set. The latter financed the traders and put their sons in their businesses, even sending them to serve their apprenticeships on the plantations, but the first and second generation of tobacco lords were regarded as upstarts, and, while several rose to occupy important positions in the city, none was appointed provost. Every Glasgow child has heard stories about their haughty and arrogant ways, and about how, in the street, they brushed people from their path outside the Tontine Hotel with a sweep of their scarlet cloaks and a swish of their gold-headed ebony canes.

The best-known provost of the seventeen-forties and seventeen-fifties was Andrew Cochran, a sagacious and cultured man who is remembered as the provost called upon to deal with Bonnie Prince Charlie's impudent seizure of the city, and as the man who sub-

6

sequently procured from an unwilling parliament an indemnification for the exactions of the rebels. On a later occasion Andrew Cochran was asked to what he attributed the sudden rise of Glasgow, and he replied that it had been brought about by four young men of talent and spirit, who started at one time in business, without £10,000 between them, and by their success set an example to others.

There are many striking contrasts between these four men, all of whom became substantial land-owners. In each of them can be detected the strengths and weaknesses of the Glaswegian's character, and also those seeming inconsistencies which give personalities so much of their colour. Alexander Spiers, of Elderslie, and James Ritchie, of Busby, achieved respectability, and were highly regarded by the citizens. William Cuninghame, of Lainshaw, was perhaps less well placed, and poor John Glassford, of Dougalston, fell from grace.

Spiers (1714–82) had the largest business. He used his money wisely and, besides having a princely mansion and gardens in the city at the head of Virginia Street—like other city mansions it was a business house rather than a dwelling house—he acquired extensive lands at Elderslie, in Renfrewshire, on which his descendants still live. After his death his wife and daughters provided funds for charities administered by the Merchants' House—in which his portrait hangs—and he was thought of as a man who had spent his life well. Even as a speculator—and these tobacco lords made much of their wealth out of speculations on the price of raw tobacco—he was cautious. Calm and deliberate, he was an excellent example of one kind of Glasgow business man, and was held up to boys in the early nineteenth century to show what rewards earnest endeavour will bring.

Ritchie was more stolid even than Spiers, precise and dapper, although, as is often the way with even the dourest of Glasgow men, he could be distinctively jovial in his off-moments, and, while the man-in-the-street thought him cold and forbidding, his friends in the *Hodge-Podge Club* knew that he had another side.

In the early seventeen-eighties the American War of Independence wrecked the tobacco trade. Only one of the four great tobacco lords lived to see the crash, but he turned it to his advantage by acquiring all the tobacco he could lay his hands on. In this way William Cuninghame made an 'immense fortune'. Out of it he bought his country estate at Lainshaw, in Ayrshire.

Cuninghame has an interesting link with today, for in 1770 —he died in 1789—he built the most imposing tobacco lord's mansion in Glasgow. It was greatly admired by the citizens who, even fifty years afterwards, spoke of it as the finest urban house in Scotland. When town-planners in the eighteen-forties proposed to pull it down to join Ingram Street with Gordon Street, such an outcry was raised that the project was abandoned. Instead, the building was converted into the Royal Exchange, and there still stands—behind the massive Corinthian pillars and entablature added by the Victorians—William Cuninghame's mansion, once the architectural pride of Glasgow.

The family of the Cuninghames was perhaps not of the best, but it was ostentatious John Glassford (1715–83) who literally had his picture turned to the wall. In his day he was next in importance to Spiers as a tobacco importer and even more important as a ship-owner. His wrongdoing was dying in financial difficulties.

His misfortunes were not attributable to the American war—they came too early for that—but to bad speculation. He was more, however, than a speculator. He was a gambler, and had a saloon for games of chance built in an outhouse on his estate. Yet, in spite of his shortcomings, there was something about John Glassford which amuses and even appeals to us of today. He was thrawn, and, for instance, supported the American revolutionaries while his colleagues were very strongly on the government's side. He was a restless, ambitious man with a great desire to be in everything. But more important was the lead he gave in founding the industries of Glasgow. His name is better remembered, however, because 'Glassford Street', is so called because it runs through the grounds of his former house, which was incidentally the Shawfield Mansion.

It is sometimes said that the tobacco lords contributed little to the rise of the city. They made their money, spent it or lost it. Actually, the colonists' need for manufactured goods was so great and the opportunities were so apparent for filling the holds of vessels returning from the Clyde to America with goods for sale to the colonists that factories were established in Glasgow to manufacture many things, such as furniture, clothing, boots, wrought-iron tools and implements, glassware and pottery. This was, indeed, the beginning of the Industrial Revolution.

The most immediately important developments were taking place in the textile industry. The traditional Scottish fabric is linen, while that of England is wool. Keen rivalry grew up in the years after the union. Duties were imposed by Parliament, at the behest of the woollen manufacturers, to hamper the Scottish production of sheets, handkerchiefs, tapes and such things. They failed to achieve their purpose, however, and prompted the Glasgow magistrates and other leading men, particularly in the 1740–50 decade, to spend a good deal of money and much time in trying to foster the linen industry.

By 1748 Parliament had realized that Scotland was determined to build up its linen industry, opposition or no opposition. From then the policy was changed, and the Scots were helped instead of hindered. An Act was passed prohibiting the importing or even the *wearing* of

The Trongate in 1774. The Guard House is on the left, and the King Street well on the right.

French cambrics, and in 1751 a further Act encouraged weavers in flax and hemp to settle and to exercise their trades in Scotland. The British Linen Company, incorporated in 1746, also contributed greatly in expanding the industry and, until it restricted its business to banking, it not only provided manufacturers with capital and material, but also carried on an extensive linen trade of its own.

The linen industry swept through Scotland and, by 1772, there were 252 linen factories in the country. Although the industry settled in the east rather than in the west of Scotland, its importance to the latter was very considerable. Not only did it prepare the way for the cotton industry, but it was mainly responsible for creating the dyeing industry and, through it, the chemical industry. The first bleachfield and printworks for linen fabrics was laid out in 1742 at Pollokshaws, and by the end of the century there were no fewer than thirty printfields in the Glasgow district. The best-known company— William Stirling and Sons—began at Dalsholm on the River Kelvin, in 1750 to print handkerchiefs, but in 1770 they transferred their works to the Vale of Leven, where the water coming from Loch Lomond was plentiful and of exceptional purity, and created the great undertaking owned by the United Turkey Red Co., which survived until the nineteen-fifties.

Thus the general impression that the tobacco lords merely took out of the city whatever they could and contributed little or nothing in its evolution is mistaken. They brought industrial Glasgow into being, not only by putting up the money, but also by selling the goods manufactured. It is not without significance that the leading *industrialist* of the day, Provost Archibald Ingram, in whose memory a most elaborate bas-relief tablet was erected in the Merchants' House, was a brother-in-law of John Glassford.

Although Glasgow went on growing—the population had reached 28,000 by 1763—it was still a small place, and this has tended to obscure its rapidly increasing industrial importance. Where did the people come from who manned its factories? The answer appears to be that they walked into Glasgow every day from the neighbouring towns, such as Anderston, Finnieston, Partick and Govan, which have since been absorbed by the city.

The tobacco lords are so well remembered that the size of the sugar and rum trade, in which they did not participate to any extent, is usually overlooked. So is the fact that the Glaswegians of this century drank rum, not whisky, then regarded as a raw spirit. The importers of rum were often the very presentable sons of country gentlemen. Many had military rank. Consequently they played an important part in the vigorous social life of the eighteenth-century Glasgow. Furthermore they suffered less than the tobacco lords during the American Revolutionary War, although their sideline in the slave trade was badly affected, especially when France entered the war and shipping was disrupted. The most popular man in Glasgow during the seventeen-forties was one (he died in 1748) whose name is rarely mentioned today, Col. William McDowall. Unlike the tobacco lords, he was a Celt, and he came from the right people. Stationed with a brother officer, Major James Milliken, in the West Indies, they married two young women who had inherited great sugar estates, brought these ladies home to Glasgow, and founded the West India firm of James Milliken and Co. Jovial and carefree—he had married his fortune, not made it like Spiers and Glassford—Col. McDowall was the 'darling' of the city, and did much to shape its social and human qualities.

The great banking failure in Glasgow in the seventeen-nineties, discussed later in this chapter, was precipitated by the dreadful collapse of one of the largest of these West India houses, Alexander Houston and Co., whose partners, finding the times difficult, engaged in an astonishing and almost incredible attempt to corner the slave trade, which left thousands of African natives on their hands in the West Indies. There was no market for them, and they had to be fed, clothed and housed. The mortality among them tells its own tale.

During the prolonged war the tobacco lords lost not only their trade but also their investments. They had bought, or had become financially interested in, colonial estates so extensively that many papers signed by them are still to be seen, preserved in Virginia and in the Senate Library in Washington. It was appropriate that the government should send one of their number, Richard Oswald, a member of an Orkney family prominent in the city for almost a hundred years, to carry out the preliminary peace negotiations. Perhaps the Glasgow traders could have survived the disaster, by calling in their other investments. But they wilted under a new blow, when, within a few years, the Napoleonic Wars let loose in the Atlantic

In 1764 Glasgow was described as
'one of the most beautiful small towns in Europe'.
This is the view of the city's steeples
that delighted the traveller as he approached Glasgow Bridge.
The drawing was made by Robert Paul.
From left to right, the steeples are:
Hutcheson's Hospital (then in Argyle Street);
the old Ramshorn Church; Glasgow Cathedral;
the University (the 'Old College'); the Tron Church
(its steeple was later destroyed by fire
and replaced in an altered shape); the Tolbooth;
the Merchants' House; and St. Andrew's Church.

10

a host of French privateers, who brought much of the Jamaica trade to a standstill, as well as what was left of the American trade.

Twenty years later, when the wars were over, Glasgow was more interested in the newer branches of commerce than in the tobacco trade and the sugar trade, but both have survived. Indeed, when at the beginning of the twentieth century the great combine, the Imperial Tobacco Co., was created, three of the thirteen constituent firms came from Glasgow. Greenock is still a centre of sugar-refining, and some large refineries are still in production in that town. The Lyle of Tate and Lyle came from there.

A Beautiful Little Town

Glasgow in the eighteenth century was more than just a small town. It was a lovely town. Daniel Defoe spoke of it as the most beautiful little town in Great Britain, and others, including Tobias Smollett, shared his opinion. Its reputation was high as late as 1772, and well after that another visitor, Dorothy Wordsworth, wrote of it as a pleasant place. Perhaps it was rather like St. Andrews, Flemish in general conception, but with what might be described as a Highland

B

air. Even the original *Encyclopaedia Britannica*, published in Edinburgh in 1771, which dismissed Glasgow in six lines, did say that it was 'one the most elegant towns in Scotland'.

The university in High Street was perhaps the best building, for the cathedral, large and impressively plain, lacked distinction. A new church—St. Andrews, the tobacco lords' kirk, completed in 1756 and one of the six 'city churches'—was much admired, but the part of Glasgow which delighted visitors was Glasgow Cross. The buildings in its vicinity had colonnaded walks and the 'piazzas', as they were somewhat inaccurately termed, were the chief sight of the city.

The Tolbooth Buildings—the courts and gaol—were located at the Cross in 1626, and their steeple has been preserved. A first town house—the town council had met in various buildings at the Cross since 1400—was erected beside the Tolbooth Buildings in 1740, and later the Tontine Hotel was put adjacent to the town house. It was this small part of Trongate, stretching from the Tolbooth Steeple, at the foot of High Street, to the Tontine Hotel, which was, until Victorian times, the heart of Glasgow.

An indication of the size of Glasgow early in this century is given by its limitation to only eight streets—High Street, Drygate, Rotten-row, Gallowgate, Saltmarket, Bridgegate, Stockwell Street and Trongate. Then the merchants began to acquire ground, between High Street and what is now Union Street, for their *town* mansions and gardens. When Glasgow spread west along Argyle Street, new streets had to be built through these gardens, and the merchants—or their heirs—came out of the sale of their property extremely well. Many of the streets bear the names of these men of the eighteenth century, and while some, for instance, Cochran Street and Ingram Street, were so called because of the high regard in which the men were held, others were like Glassford Street in being named after the owners of the ground.

Glasgow Takes to Social Life

The ordinary Glasgow man had little thought during the seventeen-hundreds for pleasure. His life was simple and his living frugal. He did not work particularly hard, and judged by modern standards, he did not work particularly efficiently. But he was kept busy most of the day.

At six in the morning the post arrived by horseback from Edinburgh—until the early eighteen-hundreds the post from England continued to come to Glasgow through Edinburgh. When the mail was sorted, the postmaster fired a gun, and the citizens collected their letters. They returned to their houses, which were also their places of business, and breakfasted on parritch, herring or eggs, bannocks and small beer, possibly of their own brew. Then came the hours of commercial bargaining until noon, when 'the bells in the steeple of the Tolbooth rang out their merry tune', and they adjourned to their favourite tavern or coffee room for a 'meridian' (a tot of rum) and the exchange of news.

Dinner-time came between twelve and one. Shops were locked up and the merchants and tradesmen sat down to the meal accompanied by their apprentices. It was a homely meal composed of broth made chiefly of barley and green vegetables—few root crops were then available—followed probably by fowl or boiled salted meat or haggis or silver grilse from the Clyde. The beverage was a 'sma' gill'. The water   **12** for cooking and other domestic uses had been brought by the bare-foot servant lass from a public well.

The meal was not usually served in the house's single public room, as this was only used on special occasions, but in a room with 'enclosed beds' in which some members of the family slept at night.

No great hurry was taken over opening the shops and warehouses after dinner, for they would not be closed again until eight o'clock. After that, for about an hour, the taverns were busy, serving chiefly the particular kind of punch in which they specialized. Supper was taken in most homes shortly after nine. Family worship followed, and by ten o'clock most Glasgow people were in bed.

Glasgow now had a social set, and, while the wealthy merchants chiefly interested themselves in dining, wining and gambling, their offspring—and perhaps their wives too—had other ideas. Indeed, they had insisted on an assembly room being included in the new town house, and there every week a dance was held, beginning in the late afternoon and going on until eleven o'clock. Some informative and entertaining books have been written about the club habit which reached Glasgow in the mid-seventeen-fifties. Membership might be limited to fewer than a dozen men. Meetings would be in the back room of an inn, where a punch was prepared. The objects were partly

A favourite walk for Glasgow people in the 1700s and early 1800s was to Anderston or to Partick and back. Indeed, several of the Clubs, including the merchant's society of which Adam Smith was a member, used to meet at an Anderston tavern on Saturday afternoons, a bowl of 'Glasgow punch' (rum and citrus fruits) being prepared for each occasion. These two paintings by Thomas Fairbairn were originally published in 1849. The stepping stones are near the junction of the Kelvin and Clyde. One of the mills located on the banks of the Kelvin is on the left of the picture. Old Partick Bridge is in the background. At a damhead above this bridge were 'cruives' for catching salmon. The famous 'Wheat Sheaf Inn', seen in the lower painting, was located near the bridge, 'after a healthy ramble up and down the banks of the stream, the traveller obtained the comforting refreshment, mayhap entertained a fair companion, and debated with his fellows the position of the country at home and abroad, or sang a jovial stave'.

convivial and partly to enjoy good conversation. One of the longest lived was the *Hodge Podge* (1752), concerned with everything in general and with nothing in particular. The *Anderston* (1750) met in John Sharpe's hostelry in that village at 2 o'clock on Saturdays. It was founded by Professor Robert Simson, the mathematician, who left the college precisely at 1 o'clock and walked with slow and measured steps to Anderston, where he divided the immense tureen of punch equally between all those present. Adam Smith and Robert Foulis were members of this club. The *Morning and Evening Club* met at a High Street tavern at 7 p.m. and adjourned at 8 a.m. Although some hard drinking was done, this club's hours were really determined by the arrival of the morning coach bringing the London newspapers and the evening coach, in case it brought additional news. The names of some of the other clubs, particularly those established by the gay young dogs, make amusing reading. Several survived into the nineteenth century.

The Old Merchant's Hall, Bridgegate, as rebuilt in 1659. When the district degenerated into slums the building was demolished, but the steeple was retained and is one of the oldest structures in the city today.

The Merchants' Hall rather than the assembly room in the town house was, however, the scene of much of the city's social life. The Merchants' House had been rebuilt in 1659 near the Stockwell Bridge, 'in a most stately manner with a steeple 200 feet high'. For almost 150 years it was the principal place of meeting not only for the merchants and their friends, but was also the place for 'gay banquets and assemblies'. Indeed, had its surroundings not deteriorated early in the nineteenth century, it might still be in use. But the streets around 'the merry hall began to stink in the nostrils of the merchants'. and it was pulled down in 1818. The graceful tower was retained and still continues to look beautiful against the solid background of the Fishmarket. For almost 50 years the merchants avoided contamination by using other halls. They built a new Merchants' Hall in Hutcheson Street in the eighteen-sixties, but it was taken over by the Court House, and the present Merchants' House in George Square was opened in 1877.

By the middle of the century the taverns and inns were beginning to conform to the requirements of an important business city. The

14

first hotel was the Saracen's Head, in Gallowgate, opened in 1755 by Robert Tennent, the brewer. When the Edinburgh coach now carrying the mail as well as passengers arrived, they were met by two waiters with embroidered coats, red plush breeches and powdered hair. It contained a room in which a hundred people could be entertained at one time. The Black Bull Inn, in Argyle Street, was

built particularly for Highlanders in 1760, and marked the western boundary of the town as the Saracen's Head did the eastern end.

The Tontine Hotel, dated 1783, was, however, the first hotel which really catered for travellers. The Tontine buildings consisted of the hotel, a coffee room for subscribers, and an assembly hall. The eastern half had been completed by 1737 and the western half by 1760. They were bought by the Tontine Society in 1781 and converted into the hotel. The opening of the coffee room—actually a development of the recognized place for business deals—was a grand affair, and was inaugurated with the most splendid ball ever seen in Glasgow, 'at which no distinction of ranks was regarded'. Such was the popularity of dancing in the late eighteenth century that, after the passing of a decade, the Tontine assembly room was itself challenged by a competitor, and in 1796 lost its premier position to the New Assembly Hall in Ingram Street.

The dancing, according to 'Alquis', was confined 'almost to the walking of the minuet and *contredanse*, with Roger de Coverly, or

This is the only authentic drawing known to us showing the Glasgow merchants at the Tontine Hotel while its coffee room served as the Exchange. It is from a drawing begun by Robert Paul before his death in 1770 and finished by his friend, William Buchanan, who died in 1772. The date is at the outbreak of the American Revolutionary War. The picture was titled 'West Street, called Trongait'. The row of stone pillars can be seen, protecting the (unflagged) causeway. No shopkeeper or citizen of mean degree was allowed to loiter there. The merchants are all dressed in the black velvet of the period. The sentry box and the man at the wicket at the foot of the Tolbooth will be noted.

15

At an Assembly.

bab-at-the-bolster and the Highland fling. Waltzes, quadrilles, gallopades and polkas were not in fashion and practically unknown in Glasgow.' Ladies usually went to balls and concerts in sedan chairs, of which there was a great number in Glasgow, carried mostly by Highlanders.

Newspapers were dear and usually had only four pages. (The first to make its appearance, in 1715, was the *Glasgow Courant*.) Some of the tales which have come down to us about the way in which they were distributed may raise doubts about how dignified the merchants really were when by themselves—or perhaps, as most of these tales are about happenings after 1780, a deterioration of manners followed the passing of the great days of the tobacco lords. An instance is provided by the strange behaviour of Charles, the waiter in the Tontine coffee room in the early years of the nineteenth century. Charles was a wag. When the newspapers (about sixty in number) had arrived from the post office, Charles's custom was to make them into a heap, then rush into the middle of the room and toss them as high as the ceiling. 'Now came the grand rush and scramble of the sub-scribers, everyone darting forward to lay hold of a falling newspaper and soon a dozen or two of the subscribers were sprawling upon the floor, playing at catch-who-can. After this exhibition there came a universal laugh of the whole company.'

Books were expensive and scarce, but Glasgow was, even in those days, a relatively well-educated city, and private circulating libraries were distributing books by the middle of the century, the example

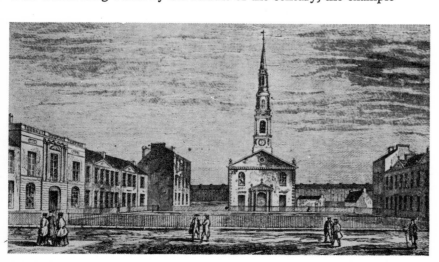

St. Enoch Square, seen from Argyle Street, in 1782. The building on the left was the Surgeon's Hall. St. Enoch Square is the site of the Chapel and Graveyard of St. Thenew, mother of St. Kentigern.

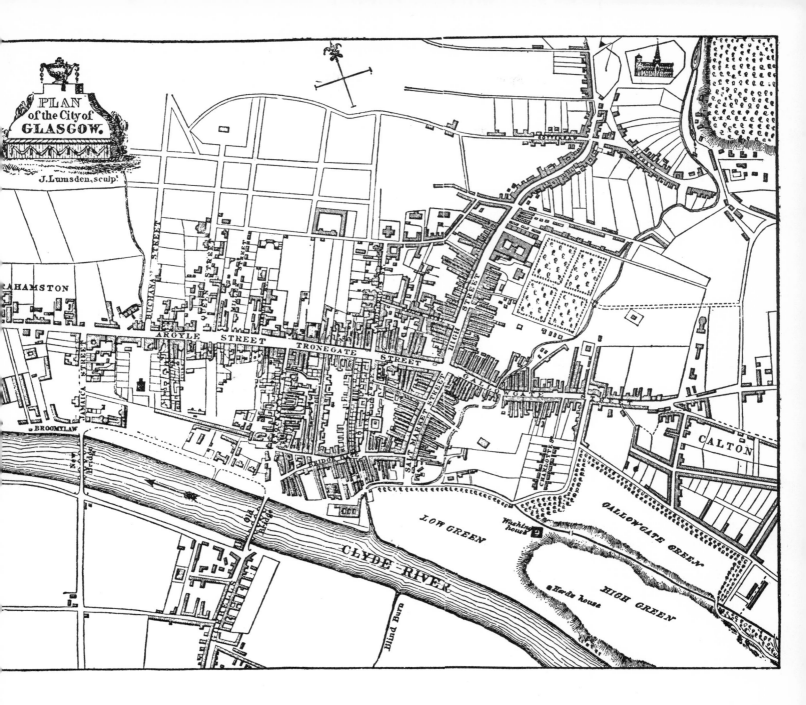

PLAN of the City of GLASGOW.

J. Lumsden, sculp.'

A map of Glasgow in 1783 published by John Mennons.
The Cross formed by the four principal streets
is clearly seen.

probably coming from Edinburgh, then establishing its position as the New Athens. In 1791 one of the Stirlings, of the textile printing firm, endowed a public library in Glasgow, and so takes his place among the first of many of Glasgow's industrialists who have made a substantial contribution to the public good out of their earnings.

In Glasgow, as in London, these good old Georgian days were, no doubt, delightful days—so delightful, indeed, that some of us in the harassing twentieth century, when reading about them, hanker after a return to yesterday. But, if we could be transported back, experiences might come our way which would be both disturbing and upsetting. Our noses, in particular, would be offended. 'Senex' has left an account of the state of the streets of Glasgow during his boyhood days—'most of the public thoroughfares were allowed to remain in a state of great filth. In many of them there were deep ruts filled with mire, and their gutters were made the receptacles of putrid accumulations. The streets were seldom swept or cleaned, except when the heavens kindly sent down a pelting shower of rain, which acted as the   **17** gratis scavenger-general of the city. Often a heap of dung was formed by individuals on the public streets, and allowed to remain there till it suited the proprietor to use it for manure, or to sell it to others for that purpose. This was particularly the case in by-streets and lanes, which seem at that time to have been little attended to by the public authorities of the city.'

The resentment of the merchants' policy in seeking to keep the public off the 'planestanes' in front of the town house and the adjacent buildings, where in the piazzas they transacted much of their business, is better appreciated when it is understood that this was the only part of the city in which the side-walks and roadways had any covering at all, other than that provided by nature. And when, in 1777, 'handsome flagged trottoirs, with curbstones', were laid down in Trongate and the Westergate (now Argyle Street) to Buchanan Street, this 'immediately became the fashionable mall of the city, the belles and beaux traversing the said range again and again at their pleasure'.

How well would the present-day Glaswegian mix with his ancestors of the late eighteenth century? He would find their conversation—when he understood it, for they spoke a braid Scots—refreshing, boisterous and at times witty. They would seem to him hearty and outspoken, rough and frank. But he would not like their appearance—misshapen, pock-marked, disease-ridden, gross, unclean. Their table manners would not meet with his approval; nor would some aspects of their general conduct, notably perhaps in not using handkerchiefs.

The Men of Learning

To what extent the Glasgow man of 1700 could be described as uncouth is debatable. That he had other attributes fifty years later is shown by the glorious record of the university at that time. Since the Reformation the cathedral had not taken a prominent part in the city's affairs, but the college was fostering the new intellectual life stirring throughout Scotland. It was, for universities of that time, quite large. Even at the beginning of the century it had 400 students. Half of them were not Scots, the closing of the English and Irish universities to dissenters having diverted to the Scottish universities many who might otherwise have gone elsewhere.

The great savant was Adam Smith (1723–90), a Fifer who entered Glasgow University in 1737, and held the chairs of logic and of

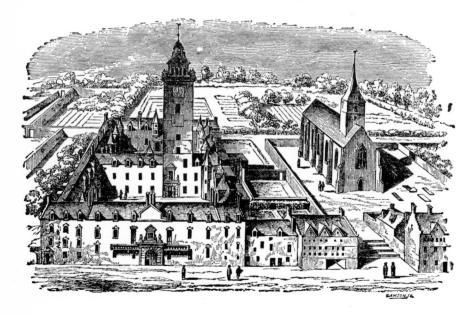

The Old College in High Street, showing the Outer and Inner Quadrangles, the College Open and the extensive College Gardens.

moral philosophy from 1751 to 1763. He had many discussions with the merchants in the Anderston Club and elsewhere—particularly, it is said, with Andrew Cochran—and their views and experiences undoubtedly influenced him considerably when he wrote his *Inquiry into the Nature and Causes of the Wealth of Nations*, perhaps the most important of all books on political economy and the most influential. By advocating the reduction of tariff barriers and other handicaps to free trade—and no one believed more in their reduction than the Glasgow traders—he originated the economic theory which dominated nineteenth-century commercial thinking almost throughout the world, that in a freely competitive market conditions will regulate themselves. His doctrine of *laisser-faire* is still deeply implanted in the minds of many Scottish business men. What has been described as the dead hand of Latin speech had been almost entirely removed from classroom and quadrangle by the middle of the century, and several other men of great distinction in their particular subjects occupied professorships—Robert Simson, for instance, 'the restorer of Euclid', William Cullen (chemistry and the practice of medicine), the Hamiltons, father and son, among the leading surgeons of their day, and the eloquent and progressive moral philosopher, Francis Hutcheson.

Adam Smith, from a Medallion by Tassie.

These men and their contemporaries encouraged and helped the Foulis brothers. Printing and type-founding were already established Glasgow trades when they began their work in 1741, and they were greatly indebted to Alexander Wilson, who was already making excellent 'Scotch type' in a foundry he had set up at Camlachie. Robert (1707—76) and Andrew (1712–75) Foulis bought and sold books of scholarship but, as the university was unable 'to get one sheet right printed' in Glasgow, they were encouraged to enter the printing business, specializing in learned works in Latin and Greek. By the beauty of their printing, choice of authors and accuracy of text, they were said to have 'converted the local press of what was but a small town into one of the most famous of the time, so famous that the books are everywhere known and esteemed, on the Continent no less than at home'. Examples are preserved in college libraries throughout Europe, and four are on permanent exhibition in the King's Library of the British Museum.

Robert Foulis gave much thought to ways of encouraging the appreciation of the fine arts, and in 1753 began his remarkable attempt to establish an Academy of Arts in Glasgow. He bought several hundred paintings abroad—unfortunately many of them fakes—and engaged continental artists to work in Glasgow. He received little public assistance in meeting his quite considerable outlays, but was helped by private patrons. The university put part of its new library at his disposal, and early in 1754 the academy opened—fifteen years before the Royal Academy of Art was founded in London.

Unfortunately, the academy became an obsession, particularly with Robert; the printing business took second place, and more and more money was poured into the new venture. In 1775, the year of Andrew's death, the academy closed, after an existence of over twenty years. A disastrous sale by auction followed and Robert died, while returning from London, a ruined man.

Scots have spread their love of learning throughout the world and if a list was prepared of all the universities, colleges and schools they have founded, it would be of considerable length. For instance, men from the Glasgow district were responsible in the later years of

19

THOMAS FAIRBAIRN

*The valley of the Molendinar with the Cathedral
and the Adam Brothers' Royal Infirmary in the background.
In the left foreground is the Town Mill.
The Molendinar rose in Hogganfield Loch
and was still an 'open rivulet' in the early 1800s.
It was spanned by no fewer than eighteen bridges.*

the eighteenth century for the establishment of two of the greatest
universities of North America—McGill University and Princeton
University. James McGill was born in Stockwell Street in 1744. He
was an arts student at Glasgow University before leaving for Canada
where he made his fortune. Many other Scots have followed his
example, in endowing this university of Montreal and its departments.
Princeton University was founded by West of Scotland emigrants to
New Jersey, Pennsylvania and Virginia, as a training college for the
Presbyterian Church. Its growth was achieved under the brilliant
presidency of John Wotherspoon, a Paisley minister who joined its
staff in 1786. Like McGill University, Princeton University still
maintains its links with Scotland.

The End of the Tobacco Fortunes

In the two decades between the outbreak of the War of American
Independence in 1775, and that of the Napoleonic Wars in 1793, the
fortunes of the tobacco lords vanished, like the delectable weed itself,
in smoke. Many of their companies survived and after a brief check
the manufacturing side of the business flourished. But the tobacco
lords and soon afterwards the Jamaica lords faded from the scene.

These wealthy merchants had experienced great difficulty in salting their profits away. They bought land at home, and it turned out to be a good investment. They established industries on Clydeside, with varying success. They financed the development of the colonies, and lost just about everything. But all this was insufficient, because the world expansion, which was to be such a blessing to their Victorian descendants, was far away. And there were moments when—as in 1775, soon after the war had begun—the Glasgow money market was 'quite glutted'.

They were much interested in banking. After a sharp struggle with the two old-established Edinburgh banks, the Bank of Scotland and the Royal Bank, several Glasgow banks were founded, 'to provide local banking facilities for meeting the monetary exigencies of the city'. They included the Ship Bank, with which the Dunlops, fathers of heavy industries, were associated; the Glasgow Arms Bank, with which Cochran, Spiers and Glassford were associated; the Thistle Bank, with which Sir Walter Maxwell of Pollok, and James Ritchie were associated; and the Merchants' Bank, established to serve the smaller merchants and tradesmen, the others being too 'aristocratic and superior'.

Grim times were to follow and in the dreadful year, 1793, the Arms Bank, the Merchants' Bank and a younger bank, Thomson's Bank, all closed their doors (although the Arms Bank subsequently paid its creditors in full), and the Thistle Bank, which had dealt chiefly with the West India trade, tottered without actually falling. One major bank alone, the Ship Bank, carried the well-being of the city on its shoulders, and it stood 'firm as granite rock while other banks foundered'.

The dominating figure in this bank, frigidly polite Robert Carrick (1737–1821), was a Lowland Scot of a type frequently depicted in plays and novels. A hard, joyless bachelor, he held on to the bank's purse strings and was much criticized for being unsympathetic. But he behaved during the crisis as other Glasgow men have since behaved during upheavals in many parts of the world—he kept his head and not only came through safely himself but brought a good many others through with him. His portraits leave no doubts, however, about why he was disliked. He must have seemed an awe-inspiring figure, with his solemn demeanour, his tall, lean figure, his olive-coloured coat with broad skirts down to his knees, his striped, woollen waistcoat of 'hotch-potch tinge', his drab breeches and his white stockings.

In the very early 1800s the district around the Cathedral retained much of the charm noted by visitors to the city. This drawing was made from Duke Street. The thatched roofs are particularly interesting.

H. M. URQUHART **21**

THOMAS FAIRBAIRN

This view of the Cathedral from Castle Street
shows the bell tower very clearly.
It was several centuries old,
although the year of its construction is not known.
It was substantial and was thought to have been planned
as a place of defence—for both the Cathedral
and the Bishop's Palace—rather than as a belfry.
The lower part was used as a chapel and a burying-place.
The storey above served as a prison.
The bell tower was pulled down by the mid-Victorians,
whether wisely or not will remain controversial.
The wonder now is that the Cathedral itself survived.

The old tobacco lords did not live to see their world collapse. Their companies were in the hands of second and even third generations. The records of the younger merchants at this critical time do not show up well under analysis, and Patrick Colquhoun (1745-1820), their leader, is, therefore, a particularly interesting figure, the more so because he was unquestionably one of the four or five greatest Glaswegians of the eighteenth century. Unlike their fathers, these young men were readily accepted into society—*they* were sons of landowners and had been reared in wealthy circumstances. They were well educated and had acquired some of the graces. They had tendencies which the older folk did not like—they were much criticized for being lax in church observation, for drinking and for swearing. They seemed as astute, enterprising and even tough as their fathers, but hard work appealed less to them, and many were perhaps more interested in investing their fortunes, or what was left of them, than in acquiring new fortunes by the sweat of their brows.

Pat Colquhoun, like other wealthy young Glasgow men of later generations, was really more interested in public affairs than in business. Having served his apprenticeship on the Virginian plantations, he returned to Glasgow in the seventeen-sixties and was soon regarded as a coming man. He was strongly opposed to the American revolutionaries, and was active in raising troops to fight against them —from the beginning of the war the Glasgow merchants smelt confiscation in the air. In 1782 he became provost—the best, it was said, since Andrew Cochran. In 1783 there came, when the war was reaching its unsuccessful close, his best-remembered achievement. This was in providing in Glasgow the first chamber of commerce in the British Isles, and the second in the Empire, the earlier chamber having been that of New York, where the Royal Charter is still displayed, He was chairman of the committee which built the Tontine Hotel with its subscribers' coffee room, described by Dorothy Wordsworth as the largest she had ever seen. Much business was done there over the next fifty years, and 'nothing else had so much effect in mixing the classes'.

Here in Pat Colquhoun, it would be thought, was the brilliant leader to guide the Glasgow merchants and manufacturers through

22

the many troubles which were to beset them in the early seventeen-nineties. But, in 1789, Pat Colquhoun heard, as many other successful middle-aged Glasgow men were to hear later, the call of London. He left his native city, at a time when it needed his help, and became a Londoner. It is true that he tried to assist some of the new Glasgow linen and cotton manufacturers by establishing a hall for them, where their fabrics could be auctioned, in imitation of the East India Company's sales; but it was a failure. Perhaps he was more interested in the tracts he was writing on public houses, in organizing the first soup-kitchens in London, or in forestalling Sir Robert Peel by several decades in founding a police force for the metropolis. Then he created the river police patrol, and conducted some experiments in education. He was a London *stipendary* magistrate for twenty years, and in 1814 published—he has been described as the first British statistician—his well-known treatise on the *Wealth, Power and Resources of the British Empire in Every Part of the World*.

A great man this Pat Colquhoun, and he well merited the marble slab erected in his memory in St. Margaret's Chapel, Westminster. Nothing was erected in his memory in Glasgow, for by 1820 he had been so long away that he was almost forgotten, even as a former provost.

The Argyle Street—Dunlop Street Corner
where Provost Murdoch's mansion was converted
into the Buck's Head Hotel.
In 1750 the two houses were outside the burgh boundary,
which was the West Port,
situated a few yards east of the scene
and a few yards west of Stockwell Street.

THOMAS FAIRBAIRN

King Cotton

Two very significant points about Glasgow in the seventeen-eighties often escape attention. In spite of the business depression, it was in this decade that Glasgow's population really began to grow. It leapt up from the 28,000 of the 'sixties, to 43,000 and then to 67,000. Many of the men who had supported Pat Colquhoun in founding the chamber of commerce, including David Dale, his vice-president, were not primarily merchants at all. They were textile manufacturers, and the goods they wanted to sell were not tobacco, sugar or rum, but linen and cotton fabrics.

23

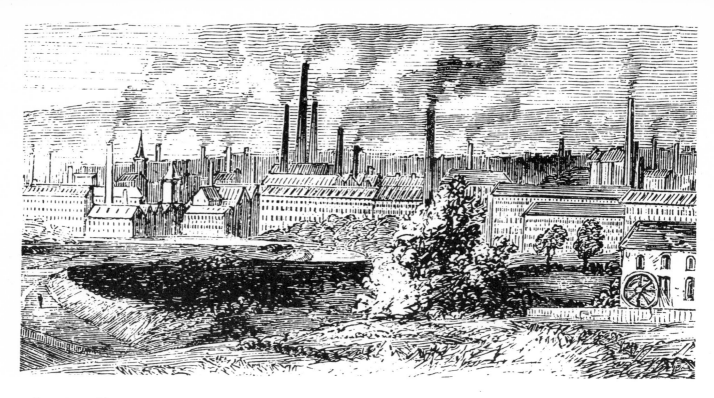

In 1780 a Glasgow linen weaver James Monteith, who had been mixing a fine, hard-spun cotton yarn with linen yarn in manufacturing cheap cambrics, made a revolutionary discovery. He found out how to weave an imitation Indian muslin, purely of cotton. It was both good and cheap. Such a secret could not be kept long, and soon other Glasgow linen manufacturers were following his example. The consequences were quite amazing, for a scramble developed to get into the new industry in which the misfortunes of the tobacco lords, the failure of the banks and even the trials of the wars were dismissed from the Glaswegian's mind as of secondary importance.

The immediate demand was for cotton yarn—weaving remained for some time a home-craft—and by 1787 no fewer than nineteen spinning mills had been built alongside fast-running Scottish rivers—to utilize the water power—most of them near Glasgow. New men came to the fore, and people poured in from the country districts to work in their new factories.

Old James Monteith had six sons. They all became cotton manufacturers, and three of them—the jovial John, the sedate James and the ambitious Henry—very prominent people in the city. The younger James was often spoken of as *the* father of the Glasgow cotton industry, partly because, during the trade paralysis in 1793, he established his own auction room in London and made a profit of, at least, £80,000 in five years. Henry Montieth (1765–1848) took a larger part in Glasgow life. He managed the family's original factory at Anderston. He was leader of the young manufacturers who broke the tobacco lords' exclusive right of attending certain assemblies— on one occasion a notice was placed on a pillar in the Tontine coffee room to the effect that if he attended another assembly, he would go out quicker than he came in. But Henry Monteith could not be held back, and he became provost twice—in 1815–16 and 1819–20, both difficult years. Thirty years before the idea of a weaver's son becoming provost would have been unthinkable.

Even Henry Monteith is little more than a name in Glasgow today. The other great figure of the cotton industry, David Dale (1739–

24

1806), prototype, according to some of his contemporaries, of Sir Walter Scott's Bailie Nicol Jarvie, is still a living figure. This really delightful character, son of an Ayrshire shopkeeper, built up a small business in Glasgow an an importer of Dutch and French linen yarns, when he sensed that manufacturing offered greater opportunities than selling. One year, 1783, was perhaps the most vital in his career. He had already become interested in cotton and particularly in Arkwright's spinning frame (1775). He was one of the Glasgow manufacturers—old James Montieth of Anderston was another—who invited the inventor to visit the city in that year. He addressed them and was, of course, well entertained; but David Dale wanted to make more use of him than just that. He took him to see some land near the Falls of Clyde at Lanark which, because of the water power available, seemed very suitable for a cotton-spinning mill. The two men went into partnership—which, by the way, did not last very long—and the historic mills still in active production were opened in 1786. With extensions they were by 1793 the largest of their kind in Great Britain, with 1300 employees, including many formerly destitute men and women from various parts of Scotland, whom Dale fed, clothed, housed and trained. He was perhaps *the* pioneer of industrial welfare, and inaugurated many of the schemes usually associated with the name of his son-in-law, Robert Owen, The memories of both men are still fresh in the town of New Lanark which they founded.

David Dale.

Arkwright, as a good Lancastrian, was rather unhappy about the assistance he had given David Dale, and he is reported as having told some of his fellow manufacturers, who were teasing him about having first made his living as a barber, that he had put a razor in the hands of a Scotsman who would one day shave them all.

By the end of the eighteenth century it was clear that most of the great new Scottish cotton industry was going to be situated in two counties, Lanarkshire and Renfrewshire. The humid atmospheric conditions of the west, so important for cotton manufacturing processes, were partly responsible. The older linen industry carried on in the east coast towns, while it was replaced to quite a considerable extent by the cotton industry in the west coast towns. The growth of the new industry during the next few decades can be best shown by quoting some figures. By 1800, according to one report, no fewer than 182,000 people were engaged in one way or another in the Scottish cotton industry, a great many being weavers still plying their craft in their own homes. Perhaps all their families were included in this total, as the wives helped in their spare time and the children filled the pirns. In 1834 the number of cotton factories in Scotland was 134, almost all within a circle of radius 25 miles centred on Glasgow. And the industry was to remain prosperous until financial disasters overtook it in 1857.

Where the Mechanical Revolution Began

The machinery for Glasgow's eighteenth-century industries was almost wholly imported—from England, Holland and France—and the first Glasgow millwrights learned their trade simply while undertaking repair and maintenance. Yet from this environment there emerged James Watt (1736–1819), the world's greatest figure in the history of mechanical engineering.

A Greenock youth, he developed, during his boyhood in his father's ship-chandler's shop, a keen interest in 'trying to make things go like clockwork'. Later he obtained a post as mathematical instrument maker to the university's physics department. He established a reputation as a 'universal mechanical expert', and in 1764 while repairing a model of an early steam engine, which was economically of little value owing to its very high consumption of steam, at least three-quarters of which was wasted, he thought of condensing the steam in a separate vessel which could be kept cold. In this way he could make the working of the engine continuous and safer, and bring about a very considerable saving in fuel consumption. Many people—and, incidentally, all mechanical engineers—believe that the Industrial Revolution started at that moment 200 years ago. After making other improvements, he took out a patent in 1769 and, the Birmingham engineer, Matthew Boulton, having invited him into partnership, other patents in 1773 which embodied many of the features of the modern steam engine. The first steam engines incorporating James Watt's ideas were used for pumping water out of mines—particularly the Cornish tin and copper mines—but before long they had a much wider field of application. For instance, although most of the new cotton factories had been located beside rivers to use waterpower, the majority changed over within a few years either partly or wholly to steam power.

Watt continued to have fairly close associations with Glasgow, but it is open to question whether Birmingham did not benefit more from his genius. Watt's engine, once it had been standardized, was manufactured there in the Soho Works, together with many of his later inventions, and the association of these two great men undoubtedly played no small part in making Birmingham the mechanical engineering centre it is today. Certainly, during the last decades of the eighteenth century, the works of Boulton and Watt were regarded as one of the wonders of the world, and were visited by engineers from every industrial country. In 1882 the British Association honoured Watt's memory by giving his name to the unit of electrical power.

Perhaps James Watt was lucky in having such a shrewd and sympathetic business partner as Matthew Boulton, for, although intellectually a giant, he was by temperament petulant and easily discouraged. A blot on his record is undoubtedly his treatment of the other great mechanical genius hailing from the Glasgow district of this period, the brawny, rugged William Murdoch (1754–1839). The son of an Ayrshire millwright, he was completely mechanically-minded. In 1777 he walked the 300 miles to Birmingham, hoping to persuade James Watt to employ him. It was Matthew Boulton who did so. Murdock—he changed the spelling of his name to suit the English—was better liked by the mine-owners than Watt, and became, according to Boulton, the finest engine erector he had ever seen. Murdock was an unambitious man, who stayed on as works manager with Boulton and Watt in spite of many attempts to persuade him to go elsewhere for a higher remuneration. His loyalty is the more remarkable as, but for Watt's opposition, he would undoubtedly have been successful in his experimental work on the steam loco-motive. His reputation today is chiefly centred on his discovery at Redruth, in Cornwall, of the use of coal gas as an illuminant. He was superintending the installation of pumping engines there. The flicker of the fire in his lodgings led him to put some coal dust in the bowl of his pipe, and then place this bowl in the fire. Soon gas began to come out of the mouthpiece, and Murdock found that it made a brilliant illuminant.

It is difficult today for us to appreciate the full significance of this

*The famous group, erected some years ago
in the centre of Birmingham,
showing the three creators of modern Birmingham.
Both James Watt and William Murdoch
were born in the Glasgow district.
Commenting on this recently,
the Lord Mayor said that it was Birmingham
that provided the opportunities for them to flourish.*

invention: gas as an illuminant. Glasgow took it up with enthusiasm and a Gas Light Company was formed in 1818. The young women of Glasgow are said to have been primarily responsible for urging on the lighting of the streets with gas, for they were now able to go out at nights without carrying lanterns and no longer had to be escorted. The Gas Company encountered considerable difficulty in getting their new illuminant installed in private dwelling houses, as the insurance agents threatened to increase their rates considerably to meet the dangerous risk of the houses blowing up. It was with great relief that they eventually received a written and much publicized application from six well-known personages, requesting the privilege of receiving the gas on moderate and reasonable charges.

After the examples set by Watt and Murdoch, the mechanical genius of Clydeside began to flourish on all sides, and some of the inventors gave Glasgow a flying start in the early days of the Industrial Revolution. The first man to operate the spinning mule by water power (William Kelly), the inventor of the scutching machine for opening and cleaning cotton fibres (J. Snodgrass), and several of the improvers of the 'practical power loom'—including John Bell (1794), Robert Miller (1796) and, in particular, Archibald Buchanan of James Finlay's Catrine Mill (1815 period)—all came from Glasgow. So, too, did J. B. Neilson, the inventor of the 'hot blast' process in making pig iron (1828), and while James Nasmyth, the inventor of the steam hammer (1842) was an Edinburgh man, his successors, including John Condie and William Rigby, who greatly improved the hammer, also came from Clydeside.

Many went to other parts of the country to start new businesses. For instance, the man who perceived the advantages possessed by the small town of Belfast, at the head of a magnificent waterway and with a rich agricultural hinterland, was a Glasgow man, William Ritchie, who went over from the Clyde in 1791 'with ten men and a quantity of shipbuilding material'. The most remarkable achievement of these

27

c

times is, however, associated with the farming district south of Glasgow. In the early days of the Lancashire cotton industry many young people went to Manchester from Kirkcudbright, on the Solway Firth. So well did some of them prosper than one, John Kennedy, became the leading figure in the industry, and in 1800 no fewer than three of the five great Lancashire cotton-spinning companies were controlled by men who had come from south-west Scotland. Manchester as well as Birmingham is greatly indebted to Scotland.

Clydeside's associations with the sea were so close that inevitably some of the young inventors turned their attention to ship propulsion. In 1788, a country millwright, William Symington, built a paddle ship, driven by a steam engine, which travelled across Dalswinton Loch at five miles an hour. In 1802 he constructed at Grangemouth the first paddle ship to be put to commercial use. She was the *Charlotte Dundas*, and towed barges in the Forth and Clyde Canal. Then, in 1811, came Henry Bell, the 'lucky amateur', who persuaded John Wood and Co., of Port Glasgow, to build the historic *Comet*, the first steamship to brave open waters. Bell made little from his enterprise, but he had the satisfaction of seeing, in the first ten years after the launch of the *Comet*, no fewer than 48 other steamships under construction on Clydeside.

The Broomielaw with the coming of the steam ships, seen from the south bank.

All of these early ships were made of wood, but Glasgow was not well placed for procuring wood. So her inventors began to experiment with iron ships, and in 1831 the first iron ship, the *Fairy Queen*, to be put into service was built by John Neilson and Co. at their Garscube Road foundry, transported through the streets accompanied by great crowds, and launched by steam crane at the Broomielaw. Thereafter, through all the transitions in shipbuilding and marine engineering during the century, 'wood to iron, iron to steel, paddle to single screw, single screw to twin screw, twin screw to multiple screw, and reciprocating engine to turbine engine, Glasgow ship-builders were to be in the front with exemplar ships'.

Not all of the inventors were engineers, however; some were more concerned with the chemical industry, then expanding rapidly in association with the textile industry. The most famous was Charles Mackintosh (1766–1843). While analysing refuse from the new gas works for by-products, he discovered how to dissolve indiarubber, then known as caoutchouc. He joined two sheets of fabric together with the rubber solution, dried them, and so produced the first piece

Netting salmon from the Clyde: Govan in the early 1800s. With the cleansing of the river fish are again able to go as far as Govan. But they would not be described as edible.

of waterproofed cloth. He became associated with the great Lancastrian chemist, George Hancock, and together they solved the many difficult problems involved in producing reliable waterproofed coats and sheets. Although Charles Mackintosh founded his waterproofing company in Glasgow in 1834, he later transferred his business to Manchester, and his factory, now owned by the Dunlop Rubber Co., has become one of the largest rubber works in Great Britain, covering many acres. His outstanding characteristic, apart from his genius as a chemist, was undoubtedly his persistence. At one time the opposition of tailors forced him to create his own company for retailing waterproofed garments, and through this company he inadvertently gave his name to the mackintosh coat.

Another of Glasgow's great industrial chemists, Charles Tennant (1768–1838)—Robert Burns's 'Wabster Charlie'—founded the St. Rollox chemical works, which became the largest of their kind in Europe. As owner of a bleachfield at Darnley, he had learned that a better method of bleaching linen was necessary than 'slow weathering' and, after carrying out many experiments with slaked lime and chlorine, he discovered how to make a bleaching liquor which did in hours what had previously taken months. The St. Rollox works were established to make his bleaching powder. They had the tallest chimney in Europe (436 feet), built in 1842; and then deposited vast amounts of white-grey waste around the factory which were to become one of Glasgow's greatest eyesores.

The caption to this drawing was 'A clear day at St. Rollox'.

Exploiting the Mineral Wealth of Lanarkshire

Coal has been 'worked' in Scotland since the twelfth century. The growing scarcity of wood brought about its use as fuel both in house and in forge by the end of the sixteenth century. Miners and other colliery workers were practically serfs, being 'thirled' for life by Acts, passed in the seventeenth century, to the mine in which they worked. (They were not alone in being treated so brutally—these were, for instance, the days of the press-gangs.) A collar was riveted to the miner's neck, stating the name of his mine-owner. The servile conditions were modified by an Act passed in 1775, but were not abolished until 1799. The practice of whole families, women and girls as well as men and boys, working in the pits continued for long afterwards.

Small mines had been opened in Glasgow itself—Camlachie, Carntyne, Govan, Gorbals, Haghill, Knightswood, Lightburn and Woodside have all had their pits—and parts of the city are honeycombed with centuries-old workings, many of which have not been traced. The Carron Company, the progenitor of the Scottish heavy industries, was located in 1760 near Falkirk, because supplies of coal and ironstone were at hand, and, incidentally, because water power could be obtained from the River Carron for driving the blowing engines. The company rapidly became famous—they had, when they cast the small cannons, known as carronades, used by Wellington at Waterloo, as many as 2000 employees—and inspired other potential manufacturers, notably Colin Dunlop, who founded the Clyde Ironworks at Tollcross, and William Dixon, a Northumberland miner, who came to Clydeside in 1770 to seek his fortune, assisted in building the Calder Ironworks, and in time acquired extensive interests in collieries, blast furnaces and malleable ironworks. The ironworks were founded at Calder and at Shotts between 1800 and 1802, largely because of difficulty in obtaining iron from Sweden. **29**

The Lanarkshire ironworks followed the line of the canal. William Dixon (2) founded 'Dixon's Blazes' in 1839.

In 1801 David Mushet, of the Clyde Ironworks, had discovered that a black material mined in the district and thrown away as 'wild coal' was really a valuable iron ore. Not much interest, however, was taken in this 'blackband ironstone' until after 1828 when J. B. Neilson, manager of the Glasgow Gas Works, while carrying out experiments at the Clyde Ironworks, discovered how to use hot instead of cold air for the furnace blast. At first stoves were used to heat the air but, when in 1840 a method was devised for heating the blast with waste gases from the furnaces, the 'hot blast' method was adopted as the most economical, and was soon being used at every furnace in Scotland and at most furnaces in England.

This interesting painting from the early Victorian era shows the 'hot blast' group. J. B. Neilson is on the left and J. Dunlop is fourth in from the left. Next to Mr. Neilson is Charles MacIntosh, presumably one of their financial backers.

From then the heavy industries were extensively developed in the district—to such an extent, in fact, that Clydeside has become, not altogether to its advantage, associated in the public mind with these heavy industries.

In 1827 the Scottish production of pig iron from 27 furnaces was 36,500 tons, out of the British total of 690,000. The rise during the next decades was steep: 1836, 75,000 tons; 1845, 475,000 tons; 1855, 820,000 tons; 1865, 1,164,000 tons. It seemed that the Glasgow district was destined to be the principal producer of pig iron in the British Isles.

Trading With the World

When, after the Battle of Trafalgar in 1805, the challenge to Britannia's rule of the waves was removed, the survivors of the old merchanting companies became interested once again in shipping, but with a changed viewpoint. Their predecessors had been primarily importers. They wanted to become exporters, and particularly exporters for the great new textile industry.

The Napoleonic Wars went on, however, for another ten years, and, when Napoleon attempted to destroy Great Britain's reviving European trade by an embargo through his Berlin Decrees, Kirkman Finlay (1773–1842), described as the 'beau ideal of a Glasgow merchant', was the leader of those who defied him, by organizing with skill and daring a steady flow of contraband trade in and out of the occupied countries. In 1812, also before the war was over, he challenged, in association with another prominent Glasgow merchant, James Ewing, the East India Company's monopoly of the Oriental trade, which had for over a hundred years kept Glasgow merchants out of some most attractive markets. So successfully did they conduct their opposition that the Company's exclusive rights were not renewed by Parliament. Almost at once Finlay sent a Clyde ship to Bombay, so pioneering the Eastern trade for Glasgow, and twenty years later he ventured even farther afield, by chartering the first vessel to go from the Clyde to China.

These Clyde ships rarely if ever ventured nearer Glasgow than Greenock. John Golborne's jetties and walls had done their work well, and even in 1775 the channel from the Broomielaw to Dumbuck was found to be almost eight feet deep. By the turn of the century this

JOSEPH SWAN

had been increased by dredging to ten feet—but the river was still narrow and winding, and few ocean-going ships, as distinct from shallow-draught coastal trade ships, were willing to sail up to Glasgow. In 1856 the depth at the Broomielaw was between seven and eight feet at low water. The epoch-making event in the history of Glasgow as a port—the opening of Kingston Dock, the first artificial dock—was still far away, although the decision to build it was taken in Kirkman Finlay's time, in 1840.

The Broomielaw in the 1820s, in the last years before the invasion by steam ships. The beautiful spire of Gorbals church was later destroyed by lightning.

The Multitudes Pour In

While the great new industries were growing, remarkable things were happening to Glasgow as a city. A table shows how the population increased:

1765 28,000
1780 43,000

1791   67,000 (*including the inhabitants of certain suburban districts, such as Gorbals, Calton and Anderston*)
1801   77,000
1811   101,000
1821   147,000
1831   202,000
1841   283,000 (*including suburban districts*)
1851   359,000 (*including suburban districts*)
1861   448,000 (*including suburban districts*)

In 1811 Glasgow realized that it was now not only larger than Edinburgh but larger than any other place in the country, except London. So it began to call itself the Second City (adding later of the Empire) and continued to do so until quite recently.

ANDREW DONALDSON

These old houses were still in High Street in 1817 when this picture was painted.

The picturesque little town of closes could not accomodate such numbers, and old houses, which had looked rather charming in their day, now became shockingly overcrowded. And some of the people who moved to Glasgow made matters even worse by being verminous in person and unclean in habit. Never was there such a breeding place for disease. Indeed, in 1831 and 1832 such severe outbreaks of typhus and cholera occurred that special ground had to be purchased for the burial of the victims.

Many now criticize those who attempted to grapple with the problem by building tenements, but it must be remembered that the tenement system, which had come to Scotland from central Europe through Holland, was already well established—witness, for instance, buildings in High Street, Edinburgh. Perhaps the greatest misfortune associated with these tenements is that they were so substantially built of stone that they remained standing, and were, for the most part, still quite sound structurally, malodorous and infested though many had become. So the conceptions of a hundred and more years ago about bedrooms, kitchens, water supply and sanitation were perpetuated, and conditions presumably acceptable to many of the people of those days—who had come from places which were perhaps even worse—had later to be accepted by people who knew and wanted better.

A comparison between the maps of Glasgow in 1778, 1795, 1808,

The original Hutcheson's Hospital in Argyle Street drawn in the 1820s.

1831 and 1848 shows how the expansion of Glasgow began. The first two centres of industrial development were, in the east end—Gallowgate, Barrowfield and Bridgeton—and in the west end, at Anderston. The city at first tended to move east—even in 1808 the newly-laid-out George Square was really too far west to be at its heart, while

JOSEPH SWAN

The spires of Glasgow seen in the 1820s from the east, looking over Glasgow Green.
The Nelson monument is in the foreground.

nowadays it, like Trongate, is too far east. With the growth of ship-building and the extension of the quay-sides, the swing then went in the other direction, and Glasgow for one hundred years moved west.

A glance at these old maps shows that, just as the new town in Edinburgh was well planned, so the new Glasgow was quite adequately laid out by those who tried to control the expansion of the city in the first decades of the nineteenth century. No town in Great Britain of comparable size shows so much evidence of careful planning, although unfortunately the streets in the centre of the city were not made wide enough, and most of the good work was nullified.

The planning of new Glasgow was begun by the city fathers in the 1780–95 period, aided by a building society organized by Dugald Bannatyne, secretary of the chamber of commerce—and last survivor of its original members—and, as Eyre-Todd says, the making of the new streets went steadily on. The layout of George Square with its adjacent streets, running to High Street and to Argyle Street, was decided on in 1782, many of the buildings being erected by Dugald Bannatyne's company as speculations. The Trades House was designed by Robert Adam in 1794, and is the oldest public building in Glasgow still used for its original purpose. The New Assembly Rooms in Ingram Street (where the General

33

A meeting in the Trades Hall in Glassford Street.

NORTHERN LOOKING GLASS

Post Office now stands) were built, as has already been mentioned, in 1796, partly to the design of Robert and James Adam, and became a centre of the city's social life for fifty years, besides providing accommodation for such worthy purposes as the first classes of the Commercial College (1845), and the discussion meetings of the Glasgow Athenaeum (1847).

The chief personage in the building of central Glasgow after the Napoleonic Wars was Dr. James Cleland. Although a builder rather than an architect, he prepared the plans for the new Grammar School and supervised the erection of St. George's Church in Buchanan Street. He was responsible during the hard years which followed the end of the Napoleonic Wars for several schemes to provide the unemployed with work. The most notable were the improvement of Glasgow Green, and the rebuilding of the Ramshorn Kirk.

Meeting the New Needs

The rapid growth in the population brought the city fathers many problems. The water supplies (apart from the polluted rivers, Glasgow drew its water from 300 wells), the schools, the medical services, the churches, the bridges across the river, the sanitary arrangements, all these were quite inadequate for the needs of over 100,000 people. None of the problems was completely solved. Some were not solved at all.

The pioneer in distributing water was an enterprising Perthshire man, William Harley, who dabbled in many things—a pleasure garden on Vauxhall lines in Blythswood Square, a hygienic dairy with 260 cows, a model bakery. In 1804 he arranged to pipe water from a near-by stream to large cisterns, built in Bath Street, near the present site of the Transport Offices—hence, incidentally, the name of Bath Street. From this centre, pony carts were sent all over the city, selling water at a halfpenny a stoup. Others followed his example, some inadvisedly drawing the water from the polluted Clyde; but one, the Gorbals Gravitation Company, showing splendid foresight by piping water into Glasgow from various lochs and streams in Renfrewshire.

The old Grammar School was coming in for a good deal of attention. It had been in existence near the High Street for over two hundred

D. SMALL

The Lady Well, near Duke Street,
as restored by the Merchants' House in 1835 and 1874.
There is no record of its foundation, but it is thought
to be one of three wells close to the Molendinar,
supplying users of the Cathedral:
St. Kentigern's Well inside the Cathedral,
the Priests' Well opposite the Cathedral,
and the Lady Well for the lower orders. The Lady Well was
one of the sixteen public wells in existence in 1726.
It was continuously used until 1820.

years, and its pedagogical methods had kept close to the classical tradition. When, in 1788, the town council put up a new building for the school near George Square, the rector was advised to choose subjects more in keeping with the requirements of a commercial city. He was reluctant to fall in with their wishes, and a prolonged struggle ensued. By the eighteen-twenties the growing number of pupils had made the construction of yet another school essential and, this having been done on an adjacent site in 1834, the town council changed the name to the High School, and insisted on its methods being entirely remodelled. This was perhaps unavoidable, as certain private 'English Schools', which had come into being (Glasgow Academy, Allan Glen's and Kelvinside Academy were founded rather later, in 1846, 1853 and 1878 respectively), and some of the parish schools, notably Hutcheson's Grammar School (founded in 1641), were attracting pupils away from the Grammar School.

An evening and very respectable class at Anderson's Institution in the 1820s. An interesting feature is the inclusion of women as well as men among the students.

By contrast, here is a class at the Mechanics' Institution. The artist seems to have gone out of his way to show it as a rough assemblage.

The College of Science and Technology in George Street in the mid-1890s. It shows the Andersonian University soon to be demolished to make way for the Royal Technical College, and now the University of Strathclyde.

Charles Dickens at the Grand Soiree in the City Hall for the opening of the Glasgow Athenaeum.

The buildings made available by the expansion of the Grammar School were put to excellent use in the evenings for technical education. In 1796 John Anderson, a remarkably brilliant but quarrelsome man, who had been Professor of Applied Physics at the university, died, leaving his fortune, which actually turned out to be not very much, for the establishment of a new university in Glasgow. He had long been interested in meeting the needs of industry, and had instituted in his classrooms courses of 'practical lectures' for mechanics, who were invited to attend in their working clothes and were excused from wearing the red gown. John Anderson is also regarded as a pioneer in teaching scientific subjects.

The town council, which had been sympathetic to him in his disputes with his brother professors, allowed the Andersonian University to be instituted, by means of evening classes in physics and chemistry held in rooms in the new Grammar School. Out of this university came the Mechanics' Institutes which spread throughout the country.

In 1827 Anderson's trustees acquired the old Grammar School buildings, and developed them during the Victorian era so successfully as a technical college that this was to become 137 years later the University of Strathclyde, located in the centre of the city.

The young business men also felt the need of education. They founded the Glasgow Commercial College (1845) and set out to 'fill the great educational vacuum between the Mechanics' Institute and the university', by providing classes. This led to the creation of the Scottish College of Commerce, now merged with the University of Strathclyde.

GLASGOW ATHENÆUM.
FIRST SOIREE.
TUESDAY, 28th December, 1847.
CHARLES DICKENS, ESQ., IN THE CHAIR.

36

On to the Theatre

Although dancing figured prominently in the social life of the city, theatre-going most certainly did not, Glasgow ministers being even more outspoken than those of Edinburgh in denouncing frequenters of the Devil's playhouse. A mob attacked and burned down a small wooden theatre built in 1752 near the cathedral. Another theatre was built in 1764 on the site of the present Central Station. On the opening night a crowd, at the instigation of a preacher in the street, rushed in and destroyed its interior. Repairs were made but the theatre had indifferent support and, after it was accidentally burned down in 1780, it was not replaced.

Its manager, John Jackson, formerly manager of the Theatre Royal, Edinburgh, was a determined man and he started again with another theatre—the Caledonian—in Dunlop Street, and after he had induced among others Mrs. Siddons in 1795 to appear in it, the public attitude changed, and the Theatre Royal, 'the most magnificent provincial theatre in the Empire', was built in Queen Street, just north of the Royal Exchange, by public subscription in 1804. For all its splendour—it cost £18,500—it did not do well, a 'succession of managers, all men of eminence in their profession', becoming involved in financial failure. The theatre was burned down accidentally in 1829.

The Dunlop Street theatre passed into the hands of an actor-manager, J. H. Alexander, who became one of the personalities of the town. In 1840 he made extensive alterations to the building, and changed its name from the Caledonian to the Theatre Royal. Its productions were scarcely of high quality—most of them were presented by 'stock companies' paid 'starvation wages'.

Although most of the 'better' people in Glasgow still had little use for theatricals, except at pantomime time, and the liking of the 'lower classes' was perhaps rather confined to melodrama at cheap

Queen Street shortly after the Napoleonic Wars.
On the left is the Cunninghame mansion,
now incorporated in the Royal Exchange,
and on the right is the Royal Theatre,
probably the finest theatre built in Glasgow in the 1800s.
It was destroyed by fire and not rebuilt.
Some of its underground rooms survived
and now serve as a wine merchant's vaults.

JOSEPH SWAN

Burning of the City Theatre in 1845.

Destruction of the Adelphi in 1848.

prices, there was in Glasgow in the 'forties quite a public for the theatre, particularly, it would seem, for opera. At the end of August 1845, a new theatre, the City, was opened by Anderson, 'the Wizard of the North', at the foot of Saltmarket, with Balfe's *Bohemian Girl*. But the City Theatre, like the other newcomers, the Adelphi and the Hibernian, was built largely of wood, and ten weeks later it was burned down in one of the most spectacular fires Glasgow had ever seen, flaming embers being carried by the wind as far as George Square.

A lecturer to the Royal Philosophical Society, in 1846, gave a rather grim account of the popular theatres of these times. 'Near the Saltmarket,' he said, 'four minor theatres have been located in wooden booths. The small admission fee of $\frac{1}{2}d.$ or $1d.$ fills them to overflowing every night. Fighting, brawling, pocket-picking, are usual occurrences. So little is a stand-up battle thought of, that the play goes on through all its acts. Sometimes there are sham fights for the purpose of picking pockets. The smallest booth holds 350, the largest 1000. Two have three performances a night, one has four and one five. On Saturday evenings the number of performances is nearly doubled. In addition to these dens of iniquity are five saloons in which dancing and music are entertainments. They are really supported by the sale of liquors.'

By 1849 the Adelphi and Cook's Circus had also been destroyed, and there had been a fire panic in the Theatre Royal (in Dunlop Street) in which seventy lives were lost. James Pagan, commenting on a decision by the owner of the wooden Hibernian Theatre to build a new theatre—the Queen's—of brick, expressed himself frankly. There will be 'ample room and verge enough for dishing up the penny drama for the delectation and improvement of the *canaille* and young Red Republicans of the Bridgegate, the wynds, Saltmarket, High Street, the vennels and the Havannah'.

Glasgow's First Men of Letters

The literary output of Glasgow men at the time of Edinburgh's greatness was a little disappointing and, although Robert Burns, the most illustrious of all Scottish writers, came from Ayrshire and was frequently in Glasgow, it was in the capital that his genius was recognized. However, the outstanding Glasgow poet,

38

Thomas Campbell (1777–1844), 'the Poet of Freedom', was of this period. No fewer than eleven of his poems are included in Palgrave's *The Golden Treasury*, and several, including 'Hohenlinden', 'Lochiel's Warning', and 'Lord Ullin's Daughter', have survived the passing of time. So has his song, 'Ye Mariners of England'.

During the eighteenth century and early nineteenth century other men of letters had close associations with the city. James Boswell and John Wilson (Christopher North) were students at the university, Tobias Smollett served his apprenticeship as a surgeon in Glasgow, and references to the city are included in both *Roderick Random* and *Humphry Clinker*. Joanna Baillie, the playwright and friend of Sir Walter Scott, went to school in Glasgow, and through her family connection with the London surgeons and anatomists, William and John Hunter, probably kept them in touch with the university of their student days, and influenced them in bequeathing their great collection to the university, so forming the Hunterian Museum. Sir Walter Scott himself was often in Glasgow, especially when collecting material for *Rob Roy*.

The Hunterian Museum and the College Gardens, drawn in the 1830s.

There were, of course, others, perhaps rather less well known— J. G. Lockhart, biographer of Sir Walter Scott, author of *The Lament of Captain Paton*, and the editor of the *Quarterly Review;* William Glen author of *Wae's Me for Prince Charlie;* Michael Scott, author of *Tom Cringle's Log;* Dugald Moor, author of *The Bard of the North;* Henry Glassford Bell, author of the poem, *Mary, Queen of Scots;* and Archibald Alison, Sheriff of Lanarkshire, author of the monumental *A History of Europe*, which Disraeli said 'proved that Providence is always on the side of the Tories!' In the 'thirties a later group used to gather in a 'snuggery' at the back of David Robertson's bookshop near the foot of Glassford Street. In this howff for poets, editors, clergymen and *literati* in general, William Motherwell, author of the ballad 'Jeannie Morrison', used to meet Alexander Rodger, the radical poet who wrote one of Glasgow's favourite songs, 'Behave Yoursel' before Folk', and William Miller, 'the laureate of the nursery', and author of:

> *Wee Willie Winkie*
> *Rins through the town,*
> *Upstairs and downstairs*
> *In his nicht-gown,*
> *Tirling at the window,*
> *Crying at the lock,*
> *'Are the weans in their bed,*
> *For it's now ten o'clock!'*

39

The Wars, Political Upheaval and Reform

The public attitude in Glasgow during the first years of the
Napoleonic Wars was confused, most men with liberal leanings being
well disposed towards the revolution. Pitt's government did not
carry the confidence of many people on Clydeside at that time.
Secret societies were set up and radical views openly expressed. But,
by 1797, Glasgow had made up its mind that Boney must be beaten
and, when his threat to invade Ireland was removed after the naval
victory off Cape St. Vincent, one of the new avenues leading from
George Square was called St. Vincent Street.

Later the city contributed materially both in men and in money
to the victory. Indeed, the great review of the troops on Glasgow
Green in 1804 was the occasion for a patriotic display, and was long
remembered. The Glasgow citizen volunteers for a time never went
to bed without having their muskets and regimentals at hand for
immediate use. They formed nine regiments, and were called out
several times on rumours of invasion. One of the heroes of the war,
Sir John Moore (1761–1809) of Corunna, was a Glasgow man, and
his statue was the first erected in George Square. He was the creator
of the modern infantrymen, and has been described as 'the finest
trainer of men the British Army ever knew'.

In the meantime the growth of Glasgow had gone on at an almost
fantastic rate. In the space of four decades almost one-quarter of all
the people in Scotland settled in urban conditions on Clydeside.
Most of them came to work in the cotton industry—an industry with
no traditions, good or bad. The employers had the minds of traders
—even of speculators. They had gone into cotton manufacturing to
make money, and many of them did not know much more about

*The central hall of the Royal Exchange
early in the 1800s, within a few years of its opening.*

40

managing and working in factories than the men, women and children who turned up at their gates seeking employment.

A strike at Henry Monteith's factory was followed by others. In 1799 the harvest failed, and Glasgow learned for the first time what happens when a large industrial town is deprived of a major part of its food supply. Recollections of the events of that year remained among the fireside tales of Glasgow folk for the better part of a century. But, although a bread riot occurred on 15th February, 1800, the city was really amazingly free from disturbance, much freer, indeed, than London, where times were also hard, and an attempt was made on the king's life. The Glasgow police force had its origin in this year, although for a long time the policemen were really watchmen, and, when there was trouble, a 'civic guard' was called out to help in maintaining order.

Most of the factory workers were uneducated and, in the squalor of the existing housing conditions, led an almost brutish existence. At times—as, for instance, in 1811, when shortage of raw cotton put many of them out of work—they were embittered. But usually they were bewildered rather than resentful. In more than a few homes the bread-winners were no longer the fathers, but the children, working perhaps a six-day week of thirteen hours a day. At the beginning of the century the hand-loom weaver had been relatively well-off, earning perhaps as much as fifty shillings a week—very good money for those days. But his wages fell steadily, until they were, in some instances, below ten shillings a week. Small wonder that whisky and gin—both crude spirits then—offered the only way of escaping insoluble problems. Rum was now comparatively rarely available because the war had cut supplies from the West Indies. As early as 1800 every twelfth house in Glasgow had become a drink-shop.

It was not until after 1815, when the war was over, that the new Glasgow encountered its first real political crisis. Unemployment was severe, and was aggravated by large numbers of men, disbanded from the fighting services, for whom no jobs were available. The war had lasted twenty years, and the industrial world with its belching factories to which these men returned was different from the one they had left. Their ways of thinking had changed too, for, although revolutionary France had been defeated, the motto, *liberté, égalité, fraternité*, was remembered. Much was being said about the rights of man, and several questions were becoming political issues, including the reform of Parliament and universal suffrage, cheaper bread and the repeal of the corn laws, and the right to join trade unions and to strike.

In spite of attempts by the town council in 1816 to organize relief, this was the year in which the Radical movement on Clydeside first attracted public notice, A crowd of 40,000—compare this figure with the city's whole population a few years before—assembled in Thrushgrove in October and passed resolutions demanding the redress of grievances. Rioting and other lawlessness continued through several troubled years. In 1817 a report of a secret committee of both Houses of Parliament referred to Glasgow as 'one of the places where treasonable practices prevail to the greatest degree'. And while this was happening more and more people poured into Glasgow seeking jobs in the factories.

The position worsened and, during the autumn of 1819, cavalry and a corps of special constables were on the streets every night, clearing what were described as crowds of idle populace, ready for riot. Matters came to a head on Sunday, 1st April, 1820, when the

41

threat of rebellion became real. Hardly a man in Glasgow went to work the next day, and many began to drill in the open.

Actually only desultory attempts at revolt were made, chiefly by weavers from outlying districts. Eighteen men were seized, charged with high treason, and tried in Edinburgh. Andrew Hardie, an ancestor of Keir Hardie, and John Baird were executed as the ring leaders, and the others were transported. James Wilson was tried in Glasgow, and was hanged and beheaded on 30th August, in the presence of 20,000 people in front of the jail at Glasgow Green. The next decade was quieter, although the feeling for radical reform remained as strong as ever. Indeed, Glasgow now had a very doubtful reputation, and, after Prince Leopold had declined the freedom of the city, the new king, George IV, paying, in 1822, the first visit of a reigning sovereign to Scotland since 1651, omitted Glasgow from his programme. In this year there was a riot during which a merchant's house was ransacked. One of the leaders of the riot was Richard Campbell, a weaver, who had been a police officer at an earlier stage in his career. Such a grave view was taken by the magistrates of his offence that he was sentenced to be scourged through the streets by the public hangman, Thomas Young, and then transported for a period of fourteen years. He was bound to a cart and was given twenty lashes with a 'formidable cat o' nine tails', at *each* of four stopping places—south of the Jail, at the foot of the Stockwell, at the head of the Stockwell, and at the crowded Glasgow Cross. Here, Peter Mackenzie says, he groaned before receiving the eightieth stroke and lamented his fate. Mackenzie who was himself one of the leaders of the reform movement in Glasgow, was less shocked by the affair than might be expected, and said 'this terrible example had the most salutary effect; it taught the mob that there was a power over them after all'. But there was never another public whipping through the streets of Glasgow.

Unemployment continued, and another 'year of short corn', 1826, intensified the necessity of relief. But change was in the air. In 1825 the right to strike was recognized. In 1829 the Catholic Emancipation Act was passed. The 'Reform General Election' took place in 1830, and a hundred thousand supporters of reform marched in procession through Glasgow.

In 1832 a great Liberal demonstration was held on Glasgow Green, and was attended by 70,000 people. Despite a good deal of feverish excitement, the proceedings passed off without violence or other manifestations of lawlessness. When news reached Glasgow that there had been a majority in the House for the Reform Bill, crowds gathered in 'the two Exchanges'—the Royal Exchange and the Tontine. An estimate was made that 900 were present in the Royal Exchange to hear the secretary read parts of Lord John Russell's speech. Rejoicing went on throughout the night, Provost Robert Dalglish's town house in West George Street being lit with 3000 gas jets with, as a centre piece, 'Let Glasgow Flourish'.

Trials & Sentences

Of the various Prisoners who have appeared before the bar of the Circuit Court of Justiciary, which opened at Glasgow, on Tuesday the 7th September, 1830.

GLASGOW, 7th Sept. 1830.

This day, the Circuit Court of Justiciary was opened here by the Right Hon. the Lords Gillies and Pitmilly, when, after an appropriate and impressive prayer, by the Rev. Mr. Forbes, the Court proceeded to try the following cases :—

John Smith, for breaking a lockfast place near Kirkintilloch; 14 years transportation.

Betty Ann Blar for breaking into the Burgher Meeting House. Campbell Street. on the 19th July, and stealing 2 bibles, and habit and repute a thief; 7 years transportation.

James Ewing, Paisley, for various acts of theft there; 12 months in Paisley Bridewell.

John Ross George Bertram, Peter Pollen, Alexander Donald, and Hugh M'Casker, for an assault and robbery in High Street, Paisley; 14 years transportation. They were all boys between 12 and 16 years of age, and used very unbecoming language on retiring.

Mary Connor and Mary Jones, theft in Craig's Court, Glasgow, on the 15th June last; Jones 14, and Connor 7 years transportation.

John Wemyss, for culpable homicide, near Port Glasgow; 7 years transportation.

Mary Hamilton, accused of child murder at Renfrew; libel not proven, and dismissed.

Catherine Macfarlane, theft of a watch in Paisley, on 25th May; 14 years transportation.

Thomas Thomson, William Dunnett, and Charles Cairns, the two first for housebreaking at Stobcross, Anderston, on the 8th March, and stealing various articles of apparel; also with another housebreaking; Cairns, for reset, was outlawed. The other two 14 years transportation.

John M'Dougall, accused of breaking a chest on board a vessel in Greenock. Dismissed.

Anty. Docharty, for 2 acts of fraud in Rutherglen and Glasgow; 7 years transportation.

Alexander Robbie, soldier, 72d regiment, for assault on Thomas Angel, police watchman, Paisley, on 25d May, was found guilty. Sentence delayed.

Alexr. Gillies and Thomas Quin. for breaking into a sloop at Greenock in June, and stealing several articles. Quin outlawed, and Gillies 14 years transportation.

Alexr. Adam or Adams, for theft of a purse with 11s 6d. on board the Toward Castle Steam Boat on the 3d June. Transportation for life. On leaving the bar he exclaimed, " Lang look'd for's come at last."

WEDNESDAY.—John M'Arthur, accused of rape at Port Glasgow. Goes to Edinburgh.

William M'Feat, porter, accused of murdering his own wife in Shuttle Street, Glasgow, on Saturday the 24th April last, pled Not Guilty. After the examination of a number of witnesses, the Jury returned a verdict of Guilty, and after a solemn address from the Judge, he was sentenced to be Executed on Wednesday the 29th September next, and his body to be given for dissection. The prisoner then said, " Before God and my Jury, and your Lordships, as I am doomed to die, I never touched that woman with any instrument, so help me God." He maintained the utmost composure throughout.

Martha Kean, for theft in Buchanan Street, Glasgow. 7 years transportation.

John Dalzei! and William Wright, for uttering base coin. 7 years transportation.

Crime and punishment in Glasgow, 1830.
From a Printer's Announcement now in the
Glasgow Room of the Mitchell Library.

This drawing comes from the same period as the one overleaf and shows that other people besides the merchants frequented the Cross. The 1830s were marked by the Reform Bill agitations.

NORTHERN LOOKING GLASS

1828. Glasgow pleasantries of the past— tormenting an old Jew with a pig's trotter.

*Urchins are trying to pull down
the statue of Sir John Moore, erected nine years earlier
They were unsuccessful,
the statue being in precisely the same position today.
George Square was used as a washing green then
and, judging from the pig to be seen on the left,
for other purposes too.
The building in the background is the North British Hotel.
Before it was given additional storeys,
it had a triangular feature,
as its twin building on the right still has.*

Afterwards, when the Bill was thrown out by the House of Lords, riots took place throughout the country, and a procession of 120,000 marched through Glasgow carrying banners inscribed, *Liberty or Death*. Later, the House of Lords gave way—the king had received protests from, among many others, the Glasgow Town Council, the Merchants' House and the Incorporated Trades—and the English and Scottish Reform Acts were both passed. The Reform of the Royal Burghs Act was approved in the following year, and a rather more democratic method of electing town councillors than nomination by a few institutions came into being.

43

D

Glasgow now became entitled to two Members of Parliament, and 7000 people had the right of voting at their election. The first Members chosen were the new provost, James Ewing, and James Oswald, of Shieldhall. And the following year Glasgow Corporation began to take its modern shape.

A domestic musical evening in one of these fine residential houses near St. Vincent Street.

New Year's Day 1828. Glasgow took little notice of Christmas Day.

These drawings are from 'The Northern Looking Glass', an illustrated periodical covering both Glasgow and Edinburgh (and one of the first ventures of its kind in the world). They all come from the late 1820s. Publication did not continue into the troubled 1830s. **44**

F. L. SWARBRECK

The Trongate in 1837 with
some of the merchants
gathering for a meeting
in the Tontine Hotel.

Awfu' weather.

NORTHERN LOOKING GLASS

Glasgow people
continue to be obsessed
with the poorness
of their climate.

Going to dinner in the Eighteen-twenties.
Sedan chairs continued in use until well into the century.

Roughs creating a disturbance at the departure of a London coach, 1824.

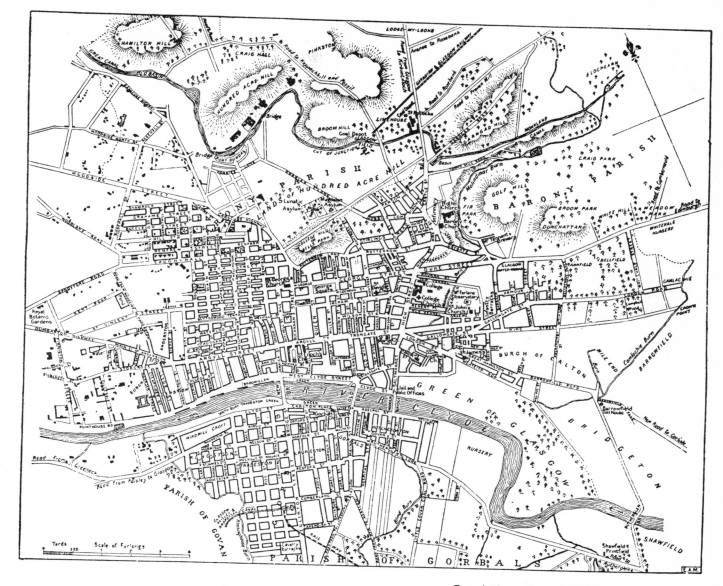

Central Glasgow had assumed its modern shape when this map was published in 1831 in Cleland's 'Enumeration of the Inhabitants of Glasgow'.

An Isolated Community

Anyone from the present day who happened to find himself back in the Glasgow of 1782 would not recognize the place. But if it were to 1832 that he was transported, he would have no doubts about where he was, and he would be able to make his way around the city quite well. Undoubtedly, however, one astonishing difference from the life of today would strike him. He would feel cut off from the rest of the country—as these notes show:

1678   *First stage-coaches to Edinburgh*

1749   *First regular conveyance between Glasgow and Edinburgh. Time taken, twelve hours. In 1758 this coach carried the mail*

1758   *First regular wagon connection (through Newcastle-upon-Tyne) between Glasgow and London. Time taken, seven days. This wagon also carried mail*

1763   *First Glasgow-Greenock stage-coach. Time taken, nine hours*

1780   *First Glasgow-Aberdeen wagon. Time taken, six days*

1781   *First Glasgow-Carlisle diligence to connect with London and other stages. Claim that journey to London can be made in four days*

1783   *First connection between Glasgow, Falkirk and Edinburgh by*

47

the Forth and Clyde Canal. Time taken, twelve hours.
(Construction had begun in 1768 but the crisis caused by the
American War delayed progress and the section to Bowling was
not completed until 1790)

1789 *Time taken by London mail reduced to sixty-six hours. (In 1819*
eight public coaches drawn by four horses and seven drawn by
two horses left Glasgow every week-day—one to London, five to
Edinburgh, three to Paisley, two to Greenock, and one each to
Hamilton, Kilmarnock, Ayr and Perth)

1842 *First connection between Glasgow and Edinburgh by railway*

1848 *First connection between Glasgow and London by railway*
through Carlisle

The London—Glasgow coach was always heavily laden.
Here it is parting company with the Edinburgh coach.

The Glasgow—Stirling stage coach
in the early years of the last century.

The fastest journey by road between London and Glasgow was
made in 1832 by a journalist bringing newspaper reports on the
division in the House of Lords on the second reading of the Reform
Bill. His time was 35 hours 50 minutes. The time normally taken by

48

The Paisley road was the scene of a disastrous explosion in 1830 when the boiler of a prototype steam omnibus blew up.

THE

Sons of Commerce,

AND

FAIR TRADER,

Coaches.

Messrs. LYON & FRASER

Most respectfully beg leave to announce to their friends and the public, that their Coaches will now run by RENFREW, at the following hours, viz.

From PAISLEY, at 10, half-past 10, 11, 12, 3, 5, and 7 o'clock.
From GLASGOW, at 12 noon, 3, half-past 3, 5, 6, 7, and half-past 8 evening.

Messrs. L. & F. trust these arrangements will meet with general approbation, the road being undoubtedly the pleasantest in the West of Scotland ; and, in consequence of its superiority, they will be able to run it in the same time as they did on the former one. Passengers not residing on the new line of road, and wishing to be taken up, the Coaches will call for them previous to coming to the Office ;—they therefore hope that a descerning public will still continue that support, which they have so liberally given these Coaches.

FARES AS FORMERLY.

PAISLEY COACH OFFICE, Mr. Lawrence's Shop, Cross.
GLASGOW COACH OFFICE, 159, Trongate.
RENFREW COACH OFFICE, Black Bull Inn.

Paisley, 19th May 1824.

J. Neilson, printer.

the mail then was 44 hours, a four-in-hand coach being used with 45 changes of horses—180 horses in all. The journey to London cost each passenger £40.

In February, 1848, the Caledonian Railway with associated railways actually ran a train—as a demonstration of what could be done—from Euston station to Glasgow in 9 hours 36 minutes, of which 46 minutes were taken up at halts.

Chartism on the Green

Life in general changed more in the eighteen-forties than in perhaps any other decade in Scottish history. The 'thirties ended on a sour note. By 1834 a good many Radicals were thinking that they had been duped about the Reform Act, and the banner, *Liberty or Death*, was unfurled again. In 1835 a great crowd went to Glasgow Green to listen to the Irishman, Daniel O'Connor, the Rev. Patrick Brewster of Paisley Abbey and George Miller, a son of the provost. A new political association, the National Radical, was formed, and a boycott declared of Whig and Tory shops. In 1837 a strike to keep the level of wages in cotton mills went on for fourteen weeks, and in the following January five of the strikers were prosecuted at the High Court, in one of the most often recalled—and most tragic—trials in Scottish history, for illegal combination, assault, fire-raising and murder. Four of the charges against them were found proven, and they were sentenced to seven years' transportation—not a severe sentence for those days. A great procession was formed to which seventy trade unions sent delegates, and support was given to the People's Charter, calling for universal suffrage, annual parliaments, vote by ballot, payment of members and equal voting districts. Chartist churches, Chartist shops, Chartist newspapers came into being. But then all sorts of side-issues were raised. Some wanted compulsory temperance too. Some, Home Rule for Ireland. Some wanted physical force to be used, and some were dead against it. Before long a good many of the supporters of the Charter were abusing, not the Whigs and the Tories, but one another.

Perhaps the formation of a Conservative Operatives' Association was a very significant portent of changes which were to take place in the next decade. Several hundred tradesmen signed a declaration that they 'would meddle not with those who are given to change, and would hold the Constitution of the Church and State in veneration'. And, when the next procession was made to the Green, the *Glasgow Herald* noted that the 15,000 who took part were 'a different and inferior class of tradesman from those who took part in the processions during the reign of terror. Indeed, many were in a state of intoxication.'

The Sordid Background

Rarely has Great Britain been so close to revolution as in those eighteen-thirties. Indeed, the brink was so often reached that continentals spoke of this country as the place where revolutions refuse to happen. Such were the social conditions of those times it is surprising that this particular revolution did not happen, at least, in Glasgow. In 1839 a report to Parliament on housing in Great Britain said: 'I have seen human degradation in some of the worst places, both in England and abroad, but I did not believe until I had visited the wynds of Glasgow that so large an amount of filth,

Stage Coaches. 66

DRYMEN, Mrs. Munn's, 38, Ingram Street, Monday, Wednesday and Saturday in summer, and Wednesday and Saturday in winter at 4 p.m.

DUMFRIES, Tontine Hotel and Black Bull Inn, at 5 a. m.

DUNBLANE. See Perth.

DUNDEE, Tontine Hotel, at 7 a. m.
Dundee, Black Bull Inn and Mail Coach Office, 64, Trongate, at ¼ to 7 a. m. and 1 p. m.

DUNFERMLINE, Croall's Office, 78, Trongate, at ½ past 8 a. m.

DUNTOCHER, Wylie & Lochhead's, 164, Trongate, at ½ past 4 p.m.

EAGLESHAM, Watt's, 161 and 163, Main street, Gorbals, Wednesday and Saturday, at 5 p. m.

EDINBURGH, Croall's Office, 78, Trongate, and Buck's Head, Argyll street, at 6 and 10 a. m. 12 noon, 2 and 4 p. m.
Edinburgh, Black Bull Inn, at ¼ to 6 a. m. ¼ to 10 a. m. ¼ past 12 noon, ¼ to 4 and ¼ to 6 p. m.
Edinburgh, Bain's, 64, Trongate, Perseverance, at 6 a. m. 12 noon, and 4 p. m.
Edinburgh, Mein's, 98 Trongate, Perseverance, at 6 a. m. 2 and 4 p.m.
Edinburgh, Tontine, at 10 a. m. and 2, 4 and 6 p. m.

FALKIRK, Croall's Office, 78, Trongate, and Mein's, 98, Trongate, at 2 and ½ past 4 p. m.

GARNKIRK AND GLASGOW RAILWAY CARRIAGES, See page 41.

HAMILTON, Mein's Office, 98, Trongate, at 9 a. m. 3 and 8 p. m. and 7 p. m. on Saturday.
Hamilton, Tontine Hotel, 4 p. m.
Hamilton, from Black Bull, at ¼ before 7 a. m. in summer only, and ¼ before 4 p. m.
Hamilton, Penman's, 74, Trongate, at 9 a. m. 12 noon, 3, 4, 5 and 8 p. m.
Hamilton, Hay's, 151, Gallowgate, at 5 p. m.
Hamilton, Ure's, 80, Trongate, ¼ past 4 p. m.

HOLYTOWN, Edinburgh Mail, 20 minutes past 12 noon, from the Black Bull Mail Coach Office, and 64, Trongate.
Holytown, Mein's Hotel, 98, Trongate, at 6 a. m. and 4 p. m.

IRVINE, Angus's, 144, Stockwell, 4 p. m. and Mein's Hotel, 98, Trongate.

KILMARNOCK, Bain's Office, 64, Trongate, ¼ before 7, ¼ before 11 a. m. and ¼ before 4 and 5 p. m.—Tontine Hotel, ¼ before 7, ¼ before 11 a. m. and ¼ to 4 p. m.—Black Bull, at 5, 7 and 11 a. m. 4 and 5 p. m.—Mein's, 98, Trongate, ½ past 4 p. m.

KILBRIDE, Perseverance, Mein's Hotel, 5 p. m.

Surprise is sometimes expressed about the number of stage coaches seen in drawings of the Glasgow Cross district. This page from the 1840 time-table provides an explanation.
The list includes 13 daily mail coaches (six to Edinburgh and two to London), several hundred stage coaches, seven local omnibuses and four railway trains a day to Airdrie.

A stage coach in Glassford Street near the Adam Brothers' Trades House.

crime, misery and disease existed in one spot in any civilized country.' Lord Shaftesbury, in the same year, said in his diary about Glasgow, 'Walked through the "dreadful" parts of this amazing city; it is a small square plot intersected by small alleys, like gutters, crammed with houses, dunghills, and human beings; hence arise . . . nine-tenths of the disease and nine-tenths of the crime in Glasgow; and well it may. Health would be impossible in such a climate; the air tainted by exhalation from the most stinking and stagnant sources, a pavement never dry, in lanes not broad enough to admit a wheelbarrow. And is moral propriety and moral cleanliness, so to speak, more probable? Quite the reverse.' In 1842 another report on the Sanitary Conditions of the Labouring Population was issued. 'It appeared to us that both the structural arrangements and the conditions of the population in Glasgow were the worst of any we had seen in any part of Great Britain. In the courts off Argyle Street there were no privies or drains, and the dung heaps received all the filth which the swarms of wretched inhabitants could give. We learned that a considerable part of the rents of the houses was paid by the produce of these dung heaps . . . The picture is so shocking that without ocular proof one would be disposed to doubt the possibility of the facts . . . Several women were found lying in a house under a blanket because others were then out of doors wearing all the articles of dress belonging to the party.' Elsewhere in the report a practice was noted of hawkers sharing their rooms with their horses, and instances were recorded of families having pigs and litters living with them in their rooms.

A stage coach setting out from the Tontine Hotel, 1834.

51

Theft and violence were prevalent. Many murders and a great many suicides took place. The citizens were advised not to leave their houses after dark in certain districts, the comparatively new east end being particularly mentioned. Factory accidents—'melancholy occurrences'—were dreadfully common, and accounts of utterly wanton cruelty were reported in the newspapers.

These were the brutal days in which street fighting was organized. As many as a hundred men and boys would meet each other armed with sticks and stones, and not disperse until the police—the police who until a few years before had been merely night-watchmen—had got the upper hand. Sometimes these fights were prompted by the most trivial of issues, but quite often they had, or at least pretended to have, a religious significance. This human misery aroused much sympathy and innumerable acts of kindness and help went unrecorded. Funds were created in the wills not only of substantial people but of others who had, in fact, little to leave. Often they referred particularly to vagrancy and broken homes. The names of these trusts make quaint reading—for example, MacAlpine's Mortification for poor men and women, the Glasgow North Parish Washing Green Society for providing comfort for old people living near the cathedral, and Old Maryhill Neighbourly Society for assisting old people.

(Many of the gifts were handed out almost indiscriminately. In 1874 the Trustees of Charities intervened and brought the

J. SCOTT

Hutcheson's Hospital was rebuilt in Ingram Street and had already become, in 1830 when this drawing was made, one of the city's features.

J. SCOTT

The washing green adjacent to the Cathedral, drawn in the 1830s.

Glasgow Charity Organization Society into being. Its aim was to organize charitable relief, to cultivate habits of thrift and to repress mendicity. Particular attention was given to assisting unemployed married men and to caring for the children of those in distress. A sewing room was opened 'for respectable women who had no other means of supplementing an inadequate livelihood'.)

The Irish Immigrant

At first the Irish had come in small numbers, but by the 'forties 50,000 were arriving annually, 'packed like cattle into filthy boats at fourpence a piece'. The movement was at its height in the years following 1846—that is, in the 'hungry 'forties', when the Irish potato crop failed in two successive years. The Irish Poor Law guardians were accused of solving their problems by decanting their destitute on Glasgow and Liverpool. In December, 1847, and the

An unusual view of the Tolbooth seen from the Gallowgate in 1830s.

J. SCOTT

George Square in the 1820s after railings had been erected. It had become the city's hotel centre.

JOSEPH SWAN

The Adam Brothers' Assembly Rooms in Ingram Street, the centre of the city's social life in the 1830s. Subsequently they were demolished to make way for the head post office and the central arch was re-erected at Glasgow Green.

J. SCOTT

The Royal Exchange in the 1820s shortly after its development and before the erection of the Wellington statue. This drawing shows very clearly how the Cunninghame mansion formed the principal part of the building.

The Broomielaw in the 1840s in the last great years of the sailing ships.

Another view of Glasgow Harbour in the 1840s.

first three months of 1848, nearly 43,000 Irish arrived in Glasgow, few bringing anything more than the clothes they stood up in. And among those who emigrated to the United States instead of to this country—by 1880 there were 1,000,000 native-born Irishmen in the United States—were many with black hatred in their hearts against those whom they thought of as their former oppressors. But perhaps Scotland and England came off rather worse than America in this transfer, for presumably the men with a little money in their pockets went 'off to Philadelphia in the morning', and those with nothing in their pockets made the short voyage across the Irish Sea.

James McNair writing, in 1850, on the antipathy of the working classes of Glasgow to the Irish, attributed it to the latter's willingness to take work at any price, 'to the injury and damage of our own townsmen'. He added, 'but with all this ill-usage and contemptuous treatment, they have wormed themselves among us'. No doubt in this is the source of the music-hall jokes—now rarely heard in this country but still, to some extent, current in the United States—in which the Scotsman is supposed to loathe the Irishman.

The hostility shown to the Irish immigrant had its origin partly in unwillingness to treat sympathetically the problem created by his different religion and by his lack of schooling. The west of Scotland had plenty of other problems to deal with at that time—unemployment, deplorable housing conditions, religious controversies between Protestant sects, accommodating the Highlanders who had poured into Glasgow after the clearances and had not settled down very readily in their new surroundings. 'The Irish may very well have seemed the last straw, even though they played an indispensable role at the bottom of the economic scale.' Further, the situation was aggravated by religious disputes, sometimes of a violent character, among the Irish themselves. The immigrants came both from the North and from the South of Ireland, and they brought the feuds of orange and green with them. For the most part, Glasgow preferred the Ulsterman, not only because he was a Protestant, but also because there was greater likelihood of his having learned a trade; but he was also an anti-reformer, and so was regarded with ill-favour by the Scottish Radical working man and by many members of the Liberal middle class.

An incidental consequence of the movement of people from the South of Ireland to Glasgow, with the accompanying increase in the number of Roman Catholics in the city, should be noted here. In 1878 the Pope restored the Scottish heirarchy, and the Most Rev. Charles Eyre was granted the dignity of Archbishop of Glasgow. This revival of an ancient office was badly received in some quarters, and a protest meeting was held on the Green against 'papal aggression'. The military stood by to deal with an emergency, but their services were not required.

55

The roof of the Tontine Hotel and Argyle Street, seen from the 'Cross Steeple', 1838.
The occasion would seem to have been a balloon flight (see foot of the Tron Church). A London stage coach is being loaded outside the hotel.
It will be noted that Hutcheson's Hospital had been moved from its original site in Argyle Street to the top of Glassford Street.

Looking north-west from Blythswood Square towards the 'new town' developing in the 1840s.

An Age of Building

Much building was going on in Glasgow at this time, particularly of the four-storey tenements which have since become the city's outstanding architectural feature. The centre of the city was also being much altered. For instance, a note in the *Glasgow Herald* of 1843 said that, since the meetings of the British Association held in Glasgow in 1840, the new public buildings erected had included the stations for the Edinburgh–Glasgow, Glasgow–Ayr, and Glasgow–Greenock railways, the Western Club, the Linen Bank, the Western Bank, the Union Bank, the Glasgow and Ship Bank, the Merchants' House, the City Hall, the Corn Exchange, the Gartnavel Lunatic Asylum, twelve Presbyterian churches and one Catholic chapel.

John Carrick gave his impressions of the changes taking place at that time. The demand for improved places of business, both for the merchant and for the manufacturer, could not be met in the

56

older parts of the city, chiefly because the subdivision of property in those parts—almost every shop and flat had a different proprietor—created too many problems for those who wished to extend and adapt the buildings. It was easier to go elsewhere, and a new business district around St. Vincent Street came into being. The Royal Exchange was opened, and became the merchants' meeting place. The Tontine coffee room fell on dull days, and eventually was abandoned. St. George's Church, in Buchanan Street, took the place of St. Andrew's Church as the kirk of the commercial city. The wealthier and better-paid people gave up their residences near Glasgow Cross, and went to live in the new and more fashionable localities, particularly the west end. Their old houses of five or six rooms, which had previously accommodated one family, were subdivided, one room being allocated to one family, 'and this without any change of structure to secure isolation'.

Soon after 1846, John Carrick went on to say, the town council began to acquire property in the districts known as the Wynds, and in the closes abutting on the High Street and the Saltmarket, and in the Gorbals; but it was soon felt that, although the council was rooting out wynds and vennels in the older parts of the city, the builders were just as busy constructing new ones, equally objectionable, in the modern parts.

Many of the wealthier people had no better understanding of hygiene than the other inhabitants of the city. In 1849 James Pagan

The Saltmarket in 1849, a reproduction of one of the paintings in the Old Glasgow collection at the Mitchell Library.
Until the construction of the first 'Jile Brig' across the Clyde in 1794, Bridgegate had been the principal street running south from Glasgow Cross.
It was the connection with the historic site of Glasgow Bridge at Stockwell Street.
During the 19th century Saltmarket increased in importance and Bridgegate became a secondary thoroughfare.

'We have no hesitation in pronouncing Glasgow
to be the most unhealthy city in the United Kingdom.
While the death rate in London averages 15 per 1000,
Glasgow reaches the enormous number of 32 per 1000'—
from a speech made at a congress on public health.

T. & R. ANNAN

28, Saltmarket about 1860.

remarked that, in certain parts of the west end, as little attention was being paid to sanitary arrangements as in the wynds and vennels. 'When we look at the filthy state of the mews lanes about Blysthwood Hill, surrounded on all sides by the dwellings of the rich, and with masses of decaying vegetable matter within a few yards of their houses, is it to be wondered at that, during the prevalence of the present epidemic of cholera, the malarious influence should have committed ravages in the very midst of wealth and comfort?' Later, he invited his readers to walk up Renfield Street, and to observe the lively stable-keepers actually laying manure on the thoroughfares to the right and left.

The promotion of railway schemes in the eighteen-sixties, referred to later, involving the construction of new stations, provided the town council with an opportunity to apply for a City Improvement Act—the pioneering slum clearance scheme in the United Kingdom —and in consequence they were able to sweep away some parts of the city in which people were huddled together to the extent of 1000 per acre, and in which 'hordes of the criminal classes sheltered in the dens and caverns of dwelling-houses in the narrow lanes and dark closes, rendering the localities notorious in the annals of robbery and murder'. Ninety acres in Trongate, Saltmarket, Gallowgate and the High Street were singled out as particularly bad, and, so quickly does time effect changes, the closes adjoining the Tontine buildings.

The Daft Year—1845

In the last decades of the eighteenth century coal and iron mine-owners made the vitally important discovery that, by laying iron rails to form a track, a road could be constructed covering many miles, on which wagons filled with minerals could be pushed by men or pulled by horses very quickly and with comparatively little effort. Several of these 'tramways' were built in Lanarkshire and Ayrshire. After a time the great Newcastle engineer, George Stephenson (son, by the way, of a Scot), thought that it would be even better to have the wagons pulled by a vehicle using steam power, and, in 1825, was responsible for building the first steam railway (from Stockton to Darlington), and, in 1830, the historic Liverpool–Manchester railway.

Locomotives were used in 1826 on the ten-mile mineral track in Lanarkshire, between Monkland and Kirkintilloch. As passengers were also carried, this has been claimed as the second railway line opened in Great Britain; but the date on which the Scottish railway system began is usually given as 27th September, 1831, when the Glasgow–Garnkirk railway was opened for passenger traffic. It had already handled mineral traffic for several months.

The second Glasgow railway also linked the city with mineral fields, this time in Ayrshire. The connection between Glasgow and Ayr was completed in 1840, and additions were made in rapid succession so that almost the entire Glasgow and South-Western Railway system was in existence by 1850. The third Glasgow railway —to Greenock—was opened for traffic in 1841.

Perhaps the most important date in the history of the Scottish railways was, however, 18th February, 1842, when the first train ran on the Edinburgh–Glasgow railway, between the Haymarket and Queen Street stations. The Bill authorizing its construction had been hotly contested in Parliament—the Forth and Clyde Canal Company being particularly active in opposition—and three years were taken

T. & R. ANNAN

A 'Close' in Gallowgate, 1868.

*The opening of the passenger service on the
Glasgow and Garnkirk Railway, 1831.
The view from Germiston Embankment
based on a photograph
by David Octavius Hill taken in 1842.*

Glasgow Cathedral with its old bell tower can be discerned on the right-hand side.

*The New Greenock and Ayr Railway Bridge
at King Street, Tradeston, in the 1840s.*

in getting it accepted. Once the railway had been opened to their mutual benefit, however, the two cities fell out, because both realized that, while it was very good to be in such close touch with one another, there was even more to be said for being in close touch with London. There was no dispute about one of the projected railways, which was to connect Edinburgh with London through Berwick and Newcastle-on-Tyne—that clearly was Edinburgh's affair, and it was opened by the North British Railway Company in 1846. But two routes by which Glasgow could be connected with Carlisle had been surveyed. One of them, by going through the Lanarkshire coalfield, could by a simple bifurcation in the Carstairs district be made to serve Edinburgh as well as Glasgow. The other would go much closer to the west coast, near the Ayrshire coalfield, and would pass through Kilmarnock and Dumfries. Glasgow favoured the latter, Edinburgh the former. The argument went on for several years, in and out of Parliament, and the decision was given in 1845 for the Lanarkshire route, in spite of a criticism that the steep rise over ten miles to Beattock Summit presented almost insuperable difficulties. The line was eventually opened by the Caledonian Railway Company in February, 1848—an indication of the manual effort involved is given in the statement that in August, 1847, no fewer than 20,000 men, 350 horses and two locomotives were working on the line between Carlisle and Glasgow.

In the passing of time both routes were developed, and the fastest trains are still going by Carstairs and Beattock. Actually, most of the railway systems proposed in the 'Daft Year', 1845, were built, but some—and in particular those affecting the north of Scotland— long after they had first been planned and companies floated. The West Highland line to Fort William was not opened until 1894.

The railways revolutionized British life. They created new towns— new industrial towns—and took away much of the importance from the old country towns—from Lanark, for instance. 'In 1840,' as Arthur Bryant has said, 'Britain was still regional in its outlook: by 1850 it was national.' Before long the stage-coach was to have a place only on Christmas cards, and the canals were to be neglected. The Forth and Clyde Canal had been, during its fifty years, a profitable venture, carrying 3000 ships a year and paying, in 1837, a dividend of 30 per cent. Its trade now dwindled rapidly although it was not closed for more than another hundred years.

It is interesting to note that Glasgow was the Second City for at least thirty years before it had direct railway connection with London. In the 'thirties and the 'forties, when the Industrial Revolution was well under way, and a great many business men travelled between the two cities, they had either to go to Ardrossan by train, then by ship to Liverpool, and then resume their journey by train—amazingly enough, this journey could be done in the middle 'forties, if the weather was good, in twenty-four hours. Or, if they were bad sailors, they could go by coach to Carlisle (ten hours), then by coach to Lancaster (six hours), and then by railway to London. The worst feature of this route was not the time taken, but the 'dreadful exposure encountered on the cold uplands of Lanark and on the fells of Cumberland'. And now, James Pagan said triumphantly in 1849, it is possible for a man to take an early breakfast in his own house in Glasgow and sup the same evening in London.

Four main-line passenger stations were built in Glasgow. Little controversy was occasioned about the location of two of them, and a great deal about the location of the other two. Queen Street Station

This remarkable aerial view of Glasgow, drawn in 1853, has a great many points of interest.

The first reaction on seeing the picture is a feeling of how little has changed in almost one hundred years.

But then significant points of difference are noticed. For instance, there are no docks—only quaysides.

The main railway station is south of the river, beside Jamaica Bridge. The north side of Sauchiehall Street is made up of gardens.

The open spaces north of Glasgow Cross are the College Gardens, the rectangular building with a dome being the Old Hunterian Museum.

Except for Port Dundas the areas adjacent to the Canal are undeveloped,

but Tennant's Stalk is already the outstanding feature in the northern parts of the city.

62

63

and Buchanan Street Station (1849) are situated just where they were built—Buchanan Street Station having been the Caledonian Railway's original terminal, the line to the South going through Coatbridge. But the location of the terminals of the two main lines to the South through Carlisle continued to cause much disagreement. The centre of Glasgow is—like that of London—north of the river. If these lines were to have stations near this centre, railway bridges would have to be built across the river. For many years the authorities would have none of this, and the two companies (the Caledonian and the Glasgow and South-Western) were compelled to locate their termini on the south side.

However, in the next decades their demand for stations nearer the centre of the city became so insistent that the opposition had to give way. The first major railway bridge across the river was built in the early 'seventies and led into St. Enoch Station, which, when it was completed in 1880, was regarded as the 'most imposing structure in Glasgow'. The Central Station of the Caledonian Company necessitated sweeping away a large but unsalubrious district adjacent to Jamaica Street, and the construction of yet another bridge across the river. The station was opened in 1879, and was extended on two later occasions, in 1890 and 1906.   The location of the goods stations

STRATTON'S GLASGOW

The Central Hotel was built in the 1880s and is still regarded as the City's leading as well as largest hotel. The hotel was originally erected on the site in Hope Street now facing it. After completion, however, a decision was taken to use this building for shops and offices, and to construct the hotel as part of the station. One of Glasgows' leading restaurants now occupies the section planned as the foyer and reception area.

also occasioned bitterness. As early as 1845, the university court first discussed with representatives of the railway companies a scheme for selling them the site of the university in the High Street, and using the proceeds for constructing new buildings in the Woodlands district. The university authorities were influenced partly by the inadequacy of the old college buildings to cope with the needs of the much larger city Glasgow had become, partly by the need for space for expansion and partly by the deterioration in the amenities of the High Street district. Those who resisted the move argued that this was the counsel of defeatism, and that the duty of the university was to remain in its traditional location, striving to restore the cultural standards in its environment. So strong was the opposition that the project was dropped, but, in the 'sixties, the deal was carried through.   64

T. & R. ANNAN

The Old College in the High Street.
This photograph was taken in the 1850s.
The removal of the University to the west of the city
had been advocated for some decades
and was to begin soon afterwards.

The university joined in the move west, taking with it part of the old building to be re-erected at Gilmorehill; and the College Goods Station came into being. The railway interests were never more than lukewarm for the scheme as they were developing a much more extensive site near Buchanan Street Station.

THE ADVISER

Being shown round Glasgow in the 1850s.

King Cotton Deposed

Although a considerable number of engineering works were established in Glasgow during these decades—the principal products included locomotives, textile machinery and sugar plantation machinery—the cotton industry continued to be the chief employer of labour in Glasgow. But, just as one American war, the War of Independence, wrecked the tobacco trade in the seventeen-eighties, so another American war, the Civil War, now wrecked much of the Glasgow cotton industry and involved some of its leading figures in financial difficulties.

Although the rapid construction of new cotton factories eased off after the 'thirties, the number of factories within 25 miles of Glasgow continued for some time to rise—from 134 in 1834 to 149 in 1850. Then the growth stopped, the figure being the same in 1860, just before the Civil War, as it had been in 1850. The peak of the industry

65

was reached in 1851, when 172,000 cwt. of raw cotton was imported by Great Britain from the United States, much of it into Glasgow. In 1864, after the war had been on for some time, the imports fell to 7000 cwt. Factories throughout the country were closed down or went on short time. Exports of fabric dwindled and markets were lost. The war ended, and raw cotton began to flow into the country again—and now, incidentally, in considerable quantities from other suppliers besides America, notably Egypt—but the Glasgow industry never recovered. It had no David Dale or Henry Monteith to give it fresh inspiration. The third and fourth generations of employers had lost interest. For a long time they had been fighting a losing battle—why 'losing' is still a controversial subject—with their rivals in Lancashire, and the troubles caused by continued labour disputes, by a financial crash in 1857, and by the Civil War irritated them rather than spurred them on. Then, too, the new shipbuilding and engineering industries were captivating them. They became 'mechanically-minded instead of textile-minded', and turned their attention to these fascinating industries, in which the work was so varied and interesting, the profits were so considerable, and the opportunities were so unlimited.

The exhibition referred to in this poster is the Great Exhibition of 1851.

Factories were allowed to decay, plant to become obsolescent, and then obsolete. Most of the factories saw the century out, however—there were still 114 cotton factories in Lanarkshire and in Renfrewshire in 1890. In the present century the decline has been rapid, and the charge is frequently heard that the west of Scotland spinning, dyeing and printing industries have been wrecked by Lancashire firms which first acquired them and then closed them down.

A comparison between the total numbers employed in the cotton industry at various times is apt to be misleading, as large numbers of independent hand-loom weavers are included in the totals for the earlier years, and whole families might be added because they all helped in the work. We have come across statements that as many as 200,000 people were engaged in the Scottish cotton industry in the 1812 period, and this makes the total numbers in the cotton factories in the 1860 period (35,000–40,000) and in 1938 (13,000) seem small.

An older and greater tragedy lies behind the hand-loom weavers' struggle in the early decades of the nineteenth century against the mass-production methods used in the new factories. From 1780 onwards the hand-loom weavers, working in their own homes, had turned their attention to cotton instead of linen, and had woven fine and delicate fabrics—chiefly plain muslins in Glasgow and fancy ornamented muslins in Paisley.

The first cotton factories established in the district were spinning mills, and their primary function was to supply the hand-loom weavers with yarn. Later, when the factories began to weave as well as spin, they took over these local specialities. Grey calico became even in those early days one of Lancashire's staple products, and it is interesting to note that from the beginning a considerable portion of the material sent to the Glasgow bleaching and print works came from Lancashire and not from local manufacturers—such was the importance attached to the purity of Scottish water.

Announcing the new ha'penny monthly magazine 'The Adviser'.

The Scottish fine-cotton weaver was by tradition one of the most prosperous of craftsmen. Many had been accustomed to working for perhaps only four days a week—Agnes Mure Mackenzie has reminded us that the Paisley weavers were keen gardeners and were particularly successful in cultivating carnations—and when they paraded on Sundays they were richly dressed. The power-loom came into commercial use after 1801—at first, mainly in Scotland—and the hand-loom weaver found his earnings falling. However, by tightening his belt, he managed to carry on for several decades, and, indeed, the excellent quality of the work done in Scotland made the drop in prices less catastrophic than in Lancashire. According to an estimate in the eighteen-thirties there were still almost 50,000 hand-loom weavers in the Glasgow district, but, as already noted, such figures must be accepted with qualifications. Paisley, at the height of its glory in 1834, made £1,000,000 worth of its exquisite shawls, and not one was woven on a power-loom. But within a decade the fall

Although Paisley shawls have not been made for a century, they are among the best remembered of all Scottish manufactured products.

in values was so steep that even the Paisley weavers could no longer make a living. A real Paisley shawl cost £20, and the customer had to wait six months for it. A printed imitation cost less than £5 and could be delivered in a fortnight. Distress was acute. No fewer than 28 societies were organized in the west of Scotland to encourage emigration to Canada and to the United States, and a co-ordinating body, the Glasgow Emigration Society, was formed to raise funds to assist men to go abroad. Thousands of hand-loom weavers left the Clyde with their families each year during these Hungry 'Forties, sometimes passing in the Firth of Clyde vessels bringing destitute Irishmen and their families to Glasgow, to join in the scramble for work, and so further lower the level of wages.

In spite of this there were still 10,000 hand-loom weavers at work in the west of Scotland in 1872, when they were described as a 'steadily declining remnant'. In 1875, the last of the Paisley shawl-makers were earning from four to five shillings a day but, in addition to their grossly inadequate earnings, fashions had changed, and they experienced difficulty in disposing of their wares even at incredibly low prices. Today there are scarcely a dozen hand-loom weavers in the Glasgow district, although, of course, those who make woollen fabrics are still quite numerous in the western Highlands and Islands.

One of the most interesting things about the failure of the cotton manufacturers to keep their industry prosperous is that they resisted the temptation to lower the quality of their products. Glasgow remained the place where the really good things were made, and, although few of the firms whose names were once well known are

THE CHRONICLES OF GOTHAM

The Glasgow policeman in this sketch, drawn in 1856, was described as one of the Tribe Hazy.

This amusing drawing is reproduced from the first issue (14th July, 1855) of the 'Glasgow Illustrated News',
a short-lived rival to the 'Illustrated London News'.
It is based presumably on the Crimea victory parade.
The point of the joke is that the portfolio, being honoured in this magnificent fashion, contains the drawings for the next issue of the magazine.
Interesting features of the drawing include the figure of Bailie Nicol Jarvie leading the parade;
in later decades he was replaced by St. Mungo, and nowadays few cartoonists use any traditional character to typify Glasgow.
It will be noted that the representatives of business on the right are carrying a banner
on which the device is used from the Merchants' House tower, a ship sailing around the globe.

still in existence, they include some, such as J. and P. Coats of
Paisley and James Finlay and Co.—Kirkman Finlay's company—
which are still among the most important of all Scottish industrial
undertakings.

A River of Shipyards

The success of Henry Bell's *Comet* led to several other steamships
being built, and one of them, the *Margery*—probably built by
William Denny of Dumbarton, although there is some dispute on the
point—was the first steam vessel to ply on the Thames and the first
to cross the straits at Dover. But little advance was made in steam
navigation until 1818. David Napier then began to adapt the steam
vessel for deep-sea traffic—for the Greenock–Belfast route—and was
successful in designing a ship, the *Rob Roy*, certainly built by William
Denny, which plied for two years, winter and summer, with 'perfect
regularity', and was then sold to serve as a packet between Dover and 68

THE CHRONICLES OF GOTHAM

*This revealing drawing depicts
the attitude collectors for philanthropies
adopted to the public in the 1850s.*

Calais. David Napier constructed the engines for his ships in his own works at Camlachie, and in 1820 designed the *Ivanhoe*, built by Scott's of Greenock, which ran between Holyhead and Dublin so satisfactorily that by 1822 the mail service was reduced 'almost to a certainty'.

His cousin Robert Napier (1791–1876), already an established engineer, turned his attention to steam navigation, and gradually took over the company's interests, David Napier retiring in 1822 after a short but brilliant career. His cousin continued in harness for almost fifty more years, and contributed more, perhaps, than any other man to the development of steam navigation. At the peak of his fame in the 'fifties, he was not only the leading mechanical engineer in Scotland, but one of the most influential engineers in the world. Painstaking in his attention to detail, he built thoroughly and, by continuing his active life until he was eighty-six, it was said he had been true to his guiding principle, for he had outlasted all his contemporaries.

In 1830 he joined a powerful shipping company formed by George Burns, who had been playing a lively part in the Belfast steamship trade since 1824, and by David McIver, the Liverpool shipowner. Napier supplied the steamers, most being built by John Wood and Co. at Greenock, and engined at his Vulcan Foundry. They were quite the finest steamships built up to that time, and some remained in service almost until the end of the century. In 1844 Robert Napier was partly responsible for procuring from Lloyd's a decision to grant the certification A1 to iron ships, and this greatly affected the future prosperity of the Clyde. Up to then the substitution of iron for wood had gone on slowly, Lloyd's reluctance to draw up 'iron rules' being largely responsible. Indeed, rather than convey the impression that the iron steamer was readily adopted, we should point out that it was not regarded with much favour until 1838, when Tod and Macgregor, of Partick, had a notable success with two iron steamers which, in spite of predictions to the contrary, 'combined all the advantages of timber ships, with others peculiar to themselves, particularly cheapness, durability, rapidity of construction, and light draught of water'. But progress in developing the shipbuilding industry was slow, and in the seven years, 1846–52, only 247 steam

THE CHRONICLES OF GOTHAM

*Collecting a grocer's subscription
before a parliamentary election in the 1850s.*

69

vessels were built on the Clyde. The steep rise in construction began
—significantly in the light of the comments just made on the decline
of the cotton industry—in the eighteen-sixties:

*Here is a detail from a panoramic drawing
showing the bustling life on the river side in 1858.
The artist is unknown.*

*Tonnage launched
on the Clyde*

1859	36,000
1861	67,000
1866	125,000
1871	196,000
1881	341,000

The Clyde had, by the time of Robert Napier's death in 1876,
achieved such an ascendancy that it was building one-third of all
British tonnage, and even then it had not nearly approached the
height of its triumph.

Two of Robert Napier's most important achievements have not
yet been mentioned. Both took place in 1840. First he procured, after
subtle coaxing, his first warship order from the Admiralty—
a significant happening in the history of the Clyde, for previously all
warship construction had been undertaken in the dockyard towns of
southern England. Then he and his two partners in the shipping
business, George Burns and David McIver, became associated with
Samuel Cunard in establishing the pioneer transatlantic steam-packet
fleet, the Cunard Line. It was the arrival of the Cunarder *Britannia*
at Boston on Independence Day, 1840, after a voyage from Liverpool
of 14 days 8 hours, which led to great rejoicings in the United States,
where it was realized that an era of commerce was opening which
would particularly affect the New World.

In 1842 Robert Napier became a shipbuilder as well as a marine
engineer, when he laid out the Govan shipyard. Here he constructed
many of the Cunard liners down to 1862, when he built their last iron
paddle-steamer the *Scotia*, and the *China*, the first Cunarder fitted
with a screw propeller instead of with paddle wheels. After 1851,
however, the Burns and McIver shipping interests, which were
accustomed to place all of their orders on the Clyde, showed an
increasing liking for J. and G. Thompson, also at that time of Govan,
and gradually this firm (now John Brown and Co.) established a close
association with the Cunard Company.

Next to the Napiers, the leading name in Victorian shipbuilding circles was that of the Elders, although in this instance the son, John Elder (1824–69), was even more distinguished than the father, David Elder. The latter was Napier's right-hand man for many years, and managed his engineering works. John Elder served his apprenticeship under his father. After getting experience in other parts of the country John Elder returned to Glasgow as Napier's chief draughtsman. Some years later, however, he had discussions with Charles Randolph, reputed to be the best millwright in Scotland, and in 1852 John Elder left Napier to form, with Randolph, a new company, Randolph, Elder and Co. Between 1853 and 1867 this company took out fourteen major patents for improving engines and boilers, and John Elder was spoken of as donning James Watt's mantle, because, by mastering the difficulties which had previously hindered the combination of high-pressure and low-pressure engines in steam navigation, he effected a saving of coal in the region of 30 to 40 per cent. He found shipowners at first unwilling to adopt compound

engines. But shortage of shipping during the Crimean War forced them to economize in coal, and in 1856 the Pacific Steam Navigation Company, which were particularly affected, as their ships had to make very long voyages, ordered compound engines from the young firm. A new era in marine engineering was thus opened. John Elder was also responsible for other modifications to marine engines associated with the replacement of paddles by propellers in ocean steamers. In the succeeding revolutionary period in marine engine design, many experiments were made, some quite startling.

This is the central portion of the panoramic drawing. It shows the second of the three Jamaica Street Bridges built by our ancestors in the course of one hundred years. All that we have managed to construct in our 20th Century is one bridge (the George V Bridge at Oswald Street). A particularly interesting feature of this drawing is the public water-cart in the right foreground.

71

As other marine engineers had done before them, Randolph, Elder and Co. became shipbuilders, and in 1861 they founded the shipyard now owned by the Fairfield Shipbuilding and Engineering Co. By 1870, it had become the largest private shipyard in the world, employing over 4000 men. John Elder, who had been in sole charge of the company since 1868, died while in London being treated for a disease of the liver. He was at that time giving much thought to ways of improving the strained relationship on the Clyde between management and work-people, and the feeling of calamity which spread through the city when it was learned that he had died—he was forty-five years old—is indicated by the closing of all workshops in the Govan district on the day of his funeral. It was said to have been attended by a multitude. The chair of naval architecture at the university was endowed in his memory.

Within a decade of his death serious labour disagreements · developed in the Clyde shipyards over a demand for an increase in wages. Whether he could have effected a settlement was always open to conjecture. Many thousands of workers stayed out from their places of employment throughout the late summer of 1871, and there was much distress in the city. With the approach of winter the men returned to the shipyards at their old rates.

WILLIAM SIMPSON

*Govan ferry and the site of the 'Fair Field' shipyard,
seen from Partick, at the mouth of the Kelvin,
in the late 1840s.*

72

Elder's company was taken over by a distinguished Admiralty naval architect, Sir William Pearce, and was reconstituted in 1886 under the name Fairfield. James and George Thomson had established their yard at Finnieston in 1845. They moved to Govan in 1851, where the second generation of Thomson's made such a reputation that further expansion was called for. During the 'seventies and the 'eighties they gradually transferred their activities to a place which had neither house nor railway accommodation'. When the move was completed, they had over 4000 employees, and their undertaking was probably larger even than Elder's. As the site they had chosen for their works had no name, they made one up. They called the place Clydebank. In 1899 their interests were acquired by John Brown and Co., with whom Clydebank will always be associated.

Tod and Macgregor, 'the fathers of iron shipbuilding on the Clyde', who founded their company in 1834, had to move their yard twice as the sizes of ships increased. Eventually they settled at Partick, where they built one of the first dry docks in the country. Barclay, Curle and Co. were founded by John Barclay at Stobcross in 1818, and moved to Whiteinch in 1855. In 1850 an Aberdeen shipbuilder, Alexander Stephen, who had yards also at Arbroath and Dundee, realized that the iron ship must in the passing of time oust the wooden ship; so, to be near the Lanarkshire ironworks, he transferred his interests to the Clyde, and twenty years later moved down the river to open the Linthouse Yard.

Many of the Clyde shipyards are not in Glasgow, They are located nearer the mouth of the river. Port Glasgow and Greenock have been described as 'the cradle of Clydeside shipbuilding'. The oldest firm, Scott's, was founded as long ago as 1711, and Lithgow's now head the largest group on the river. There are also smaller yards in which yachts, motor-boats, lifeboats, lighters, surf boats and barges are built. Comparatively few are recently established. Even by the middle of the Victorian era the Clyde had already become a river of shipyards.

The Most Diversified Industries in the Empire

New industrial firms were created in Glasgow during the 'forties and 'fifties in infinite variety. Many came 'out of the blue'—someone saw an opportunity and grasped it—but the part must be recognized which the shipbuilding industry played in bringing ancillary industries into being. A ship is self-contained, and has to carry not only all the equipment of a hotel but many other kinds of equipment too. And so encouragement was given for almost every conceivable sort of article to be manufactured on Clydeside. Some of the suppliers never became much more than ship-chandlers, but others, having satisfied the shipbuilders' needs, looked farther afield and began to open up new markets.

In every branch of industry, however, companies were founded and developed in the Glasgow district during this 'Age of Progress' which achieved national and even international reputation. They included: textiles (James Templeton and Co., carpets), publishing (Blackie and Sons; William Collins, Sons and Co.), beer (J. and R. Tennent), whisky (Black and White; Teachers; White Horse), pottery and earthenware (Verrefield and Britannia Potteries; Shanks and Co.), leather (W. and J. Martin), paper (Clyde Paper; Edward Collins and Son), tobacco (Stephen Mitchell and Son), chemicals

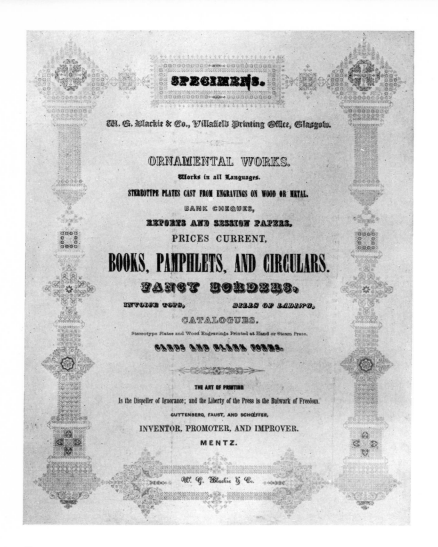

John and James White, chromes), rubber (George MacLellan and Co.), paint (Alexander, Fergusson and Co.), biscuits (Macfarlane, Lang and Co.; Gray, Dunn and Co.), confectionery (John Buchanan and Brothers).

Another influence was beginning to affect the industries of the city. Glasgow had become the metropolis of the North and was in many ways the focus of activity not only of Scotland but of Ireland and of the northern fringe of England too. That meant shops and warehouses; and, since the 1850 period, rivalry has gone on—fortunately of a fairly good-humoured character—between Glasgow and Manchester, at the heart of the vast Lancastrian manufacturing complex, as to which was to be the leading distributing centre outside of London. Warehouses have to be supplied with goods, and so other young Glasgow men were given a further incentive to take up manufacturing. The garment-making industry, employing many thousands of women on Clydeside, provides an instance of an industry which had its beginnings at this time and in this way. Small wonder, then, that James Pagan, when taking a stroll on a Sunday afternoon in 1849 around the Port Dundas-Dobbie's Loan district, was astonished at what he saw. 'On these few acres,' he said, 'have been established factories, colour works, chemical works, dye works, grinding works, mills for logwood, dye and bread stuffs, foundries, machine shops, potteries and soap works—presenting a view of manufacturing and curious industry which must be unparalleled in any other city of the world.'

In fact, during the century 1845–1945 it was claimed that almost every article manufactured in other parts of the world was also made somewhere in the Glasgow district. Sometimes too, when the statement was disproved over a particular item, it was found that this was being made elsewhere in Scotland, probably Dundee and Fife.

And who could be chosen as more typical of the industrialists of the age than James 'Paraffin' Young (1811—83), heir to the mantles of Charles Tennant and Charles Mackintosh? Born in poor circumstances, he served his apprenticeship as a cabinet-maker and took the opportunity of studying chemistry in the evenings under Professor Graham at the Andersonian University. Professor Thomas Graham (1805–69) himself was, by the way, one of Glasgow's greatest chemists and years later James Young had his statue included in the *melange* in George Square. Graham was so taken with the youth that he made him one of his assistants, and the pair soon left for London University, with which Graham's name is usually associated. An academic career did not, however, appeal greatly to James Young, and he went into industry. In 1843, while managing Charles Tennant's branch factory at Manchester, he was told that petroleum dripped from the roof of a coal-mine at Derby. The quantities of oil available were small, but James Young became interested in the phenomenon and, when in 1851 the manager of the Glasgow Gas Works told him of coal-mines in the Bathgate district from which much larger quantities of crude oil could be obtained, he returned to Glasgow to set up the first works in the West Calder district for mining shale and for obtaining from it crude oils and then paraffin, naphtha and lubricating oil. By the eighteen-seventies his own and other companies had established 65 works in the district. So began the world's petroleum industry.

The Merchant Venturers Overseas

The Scot has for centuries been a familiar figure throughout the world. There were, for instance, Scottish colonies in most of the trading centres of the Baltic countries, including Germany and Poland. But the Scot who went abroad in the sixteenth, seventeenth and even eighteenth centuries as a merchant, a soldier of fortune, a scholar, a packman, or a poet—the Admirable Crichton—was usually an east-coast man. The Scot the world knows today has his roots in the west coast. The grimy, thirsty, crotchety Scotch engineer, found in every port of the world, is a Clydesider.

Many references have been made to the remarkable part played by Scotsmen, particularly in the nineteenth century, in the expansion of the British Empire. The Caledonian, St. Andrew's and Robert Burns' Societies throughout the world run into thousands.

The most Scottish of the Dominions is, of course, Canada, for on three separate occasions—after the 1745 Rebellion, after the clearances from the glens, and after the collapse of hand-loom weaving—large numbers emigrated to Canada from western Scotland. Mackenzie, Fraser, Campbell and Douglas are the names of men who have taken a leading part in the Dominion's development, and both the Hudson's Bay Company and the North-West Company were predominantly manned by Scots. The sentiment in Toronto and Vancouver is still strongly Scottish. Australia is the most English of the Dominions, although a study of her history shows that Scots had quite a hand in her development—John Macarthur, for instance, the creator of both her wool trade and her wine trade, and

F

the two Scots who founded Western Australia, with its capital, Perth. New Zealand is more Scottish than Australia, a Scots colony having been established there with Dunedin as capital, and no one could doubt the nationality of Sir Donald Maclean, who smoothed out the relations between the emigrants and the Maoris, and of John Mackenzie, who put the agricultural economy on a sound footing.

The hazards, incurred by the eighteenth-century tobacco merchants in their voyages across the Atlantic and in their struggles with Indians and French on the eastern seaboard of the American colonies, seem almost trivial when compared with some of the adventures of the Victorian pioneers, an example being provided by a predominantly Glasgow concern. Allan Gilmour (1775–1849) was a young joiner who went into partnership in the timber business with two former school-fellows, John and Arthur Pollok. It was his job to get the timber. He explored unknown Canada, searching out possibilities for lumbering, and setting up (and manning) subsidiary companies where he thought fit. In one season he cornered all of the timber that came down the St. Lawrence (and on at least one other occasion all the timber coming from Norway). The Polloks had a worrying time arranging the finances of these enterprises, and incidentally in getting the supplies of stores needed for them. But by 1835 they had six Canadian subsidiary companies, and by 1853 further companies in Liverpool (shipping), New Orleans and Mobile. They became the largest timber importing establishment in the world, and were at one time employing 15,000 men. In 1838 the partners had a disagreement over a triviality, and the Polloks bought Gilmour out. He received £150,000 for the £1000 he had put into the parent company, and actually believed, with some justification, that, as the company was dealing in millions, this was an inadequate return. And then, as in the histories of so many other Glasgow companies, comes the unhappy sequel. By the 'seventies the parent company and all of its subsidiaries had sold out, except for a shipping company which continued its successful career—in Liverpool. Allan Gilmour was only one of many Glasgow men who roamed the world looking for business—and adventure—in the early years of the Victorian era. Few have left their stories behind them, but often a mention of a west of Scotland name in some out-of-the-world place will bring to light fading memories of remarkable achievements, once recorded in the ledgers and minute books of Glasgow trading companies, now themselves almost forgotten.

Scotland continues to export relatively more of her manufactured products, notably whisky, woven and knitted woollens and engineering articles, than the rest of the country. But how much of the spirit of the old merchant venturers survives today is sometimes questioned.

Two Companies Which Have Reached the Double Century

Some of the old trading companies are, however, still very active, although they may have undergone many changes in the passing of time. The most interesting series of links with great figures from Glasgow's past is to be found in the history of Connal and Co., now perhaps the largest storage and warehousemen in Scotland. They fit into the continuity here because they are descended from William Connal and Co., one of the leading firms in the first half of the Victorian era. They provide, too, a most remarkable example of the varying fortunes and activities of the old Glasgow merchanting

76

houses. The story begins with Provost Andrew Cochran's firm, Cochran, Murdoch and Co., which became William Cuninghame and Co., then Cuninghame, Findlay and Co., then Robert Findlay and Co., then Findlay, Hopkirk and Co., then Findlay, Duff and Co., then Findlay, Connal and Co., and in 1826 simply William Connal. The firm, at that time, had two specialties—sugar, a legacy from West Indian connections established by Findlay, Hopkirk and Co., and tea, 'which was Kirkman Finlay's doing. His mercantile genius', according to the history of William Connal and Co., published in 1894, 'gave Glasgow an astonishing position in the Eastern and China trade, and there was a time when tea came into the Clyde by cargoes, and the London mail came down crammed with tea-buyers from Mincing Lane to Connal's sales'. They established one of the clipper lines. It 'made famous passages but infamous dividends', and was sold eventually to the City Line.

In 1845, the firm changed its name again, William Connal taking two nephews into partnership, and making the concern William Connal and Co. He died in 1856, and in 1864 the business was split up.

This was partly a consequence of the enormous increase in the sale of Scotch pig iron after the introduction of Neilson's hot-blast process in 1828, coupled with the opening up of traffic by the railways. Lanarkshire became the principal supplier in Great Britain. At a meeting in Liverpool in the spring of 1845, the Scotch Pig Iron Association was formed, to operate along the same lines as the cotton market. Connals became the principal storekeepers and they issued warrants against the pig iron deposited with them. Manufacturers got their pig iron when they needed it, so they did not have to store it for themselves.

They did not obtain their pig iron direct, however, from Connals. The latter supplied it only to authorized dealers in warrants. Each warrant represented 500 tons and these warrants became marketable throughout the world. In the course of a day a warrant might change hands several times, the making or losing of money depending on the fluctuations of price. The iron merchants, headed by William Jacks and the Donaldsons, met every day in the Royal Exchange from 11 to 12 and from 2 to 3 to fix the current price, and the art of the speculators was at times of heavy demand to corner sufficient warrants to force up the price. It is said that 'quarter was neither given nor asked'. The fluctuations were, in fact, tremendous—for instance, in March, 1873 the price of pig iron was as high as £7.19s. By May of the following year it had dropped to £1.18s.

The huge stocks of pig iron in Connal's yards, sometimes over a million tons, were one of the sights of Glasgow. Since then the pig-iron side of the business has fallen off considerably, but new lines have been developed, such as oils and foodstuffs, and the facilities for financing, clearing and forwarding stocks of these various goods are still widely used. And so there flourishes in Glasgow today a company which comes directly from the original firm founded by Provost Andrew Cochran, and developed by one of the four greatest tobacco lords, William Cuninghame.

Many of the Scottish overseas enterprises during the early years of the Victorian era were concerned with India, Ceylon, Burma and China. Indeed, a toast given at the dinner in the Royal Exchange on the night of the Reform Bill celebrations shows how the merchants at the beginning of the 'thirties were thinking. It was that Glasgow's trading with the Yellow Sea should prosper. Broad Glasgow voices were to be heard in those days throughout the ports and business centres of Hong Kong, Shanghai, Rangoon, Bombay and Calcutta. The greatest of all Scottish trading companies—although it cannot be regarded as a Glasgow company—was that formed by Dr. William Jardine (1784–1843), a surgeon from Dumfriesshire, and by James Matheson (1796–1878), a Highlander. This was the company which opened up the China tea trade on an extensive scale and established the first warehouse in Hong Kong.

Unlike Connal and Co., the firm founded in the 1750s by James Finlay (1727–90)—Kirkman Finlay's father—has changed neither its name, James Finlay and Co., nor the general character of its business. It is quite the outstanding example of a successful Glasgow merchanting business continuing along established lines, suitably adapted to meet changing conditions. The company still operate their Scottish cotton mill at Catrine where they make such things as cotton sheets and towels. They have 'modernized the mill on several occasions', as in the eighteen-fifties, and being cut off in the early eighteen-sixties from their supply of raw cotton by the blockading of southern ports was a heavy blow. Their mills were completely closed for many months during which they gave their idle employees half-pay. For new outlets they turned to India, built large mills in Bombay and opened up trade in tea, indigo, jute and other commodities so successfully that they were known for the rest of the century as heirs to 'John Company' (the East India Company). They still carry on a large mercantile business with Asia and Africa through what is known as the 'Finlay group' of undertakings, and are, indeed, the largest manufacturers of some products, particularly those associated with tea, in the world.

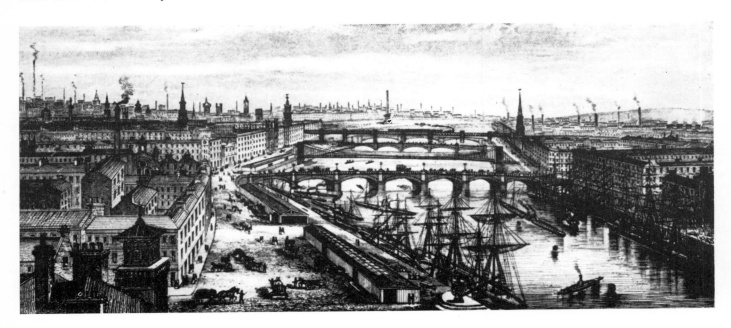

The Men Who Owned the Ships

In the early days the Glasgow merchants had to charter ships as they became available, but, when the port was developed and opportunities presented themselves, shipping lines were founded. The first shipping companies were engaged in coastal trade with Belfast and Liverpool. After some years of cut-throat competition, the firm of G. and J. Burns emerged triumphant. Like several others who founded shipping companies, the Burnses—George (1795–1890), who was interested in the formation of the Y.M.C.A. and was

Broomielaw viewed from the tower of the Sailors' House, 1870.

78

created a baronet in 1889, and James (1789–1871)—began as itinerant tradesmen, even as packmen, and made their first acquaintance with the sea by buying one small ship. The Burnses did this in 1823, and made themselves, within ten years, highly successful men.

George Smith (1803–76) was a small tradesman who conceived the rather quaint idea that it would be easier to sell soft goods in India than in the Highlands. He knew nothing about India, but, nevertheless, bought a small ship to open up trade with Asia. He soon came into conflict with the ship-brokers over their dilatoriness in loading his ship—and later ships—and, being brushed aside as insignificant, created his own organization for procuring cargoes. By guaranteeing strict punctuality, as well as by offering moderate freights, he secured the monopoly, after a few years, of the Calcutta trade, and then turned his attention to the Bombay trade. He was one of the steamship's strongest advocates against the sailing ship and, when in the 'seventies the Suez Canal opened up the new route to India, he stopped the construction of sailing ships and placed orders almost at once for four steamships. The passages of the sailing ships around the Cape of Good Hope had taken at least 79 days. The new route could be covered in between 31 and 33 days. One of his first ships had been named the *City of Glasgow* and, liking the idea, he named his succeeding vessels after other cities. So his company acquired the name, the *City Line*.

Several of the Glasgow-owned shipping companies were particularly associated in their early years with taking emigrants and others to the Dominions. The Clan Line (1845) of mail steamers to Montreal, for instance, was said to have played one of the principal parts in developing Canada. Much the same could be said about Patrick Henderson, a Fifer, who between 1865 and 1882 transported many thousands of emigrants to New Zealand and, incidentally, brought home the first cargo of frozen meat from New Zealand in 1882. The chief problem in the New Zealand trade was to get cargoes for the return journey, and this led the company to divert some of their ships to Rangoon for loads of teak logs and rice. Since then the firm's business has been chiefly associated with Burma, where they founded the Irrawaddy Flotilla Co., which, when Burma was over-run by the Japanese in 1942, had 650 vessels —one of the largest river fleets in the world.

Several companies came into being during the 'forties and 'fifties to run steamships regularly between New York and Glasgow, but by the 'sixties the Anchor Line was one of the few survivors. In their early days they had been engaged chiefly in the Mediterranean trade, but in 1857 they built a fine vessel, the *United Kingdom*, to compete with the Cunard Line, first on the route to Canada and in the 'sixties to New York, 'because the stream of emigration, then commencing in earnest, offered promising opportunities for the successful establishment of such a service . . . Much money, besides prepaid tickets, was sent over to Great Britain by successful emigrants to enable others to go to the New World.' By 1865, the company had established a weekly service between Glasgow and New York, and soon afterwards was recognized as one of the leading British shipping companies. In 1911, when these rivals, the Cunard Line and the Anchor Line, became associated with one another, each had about 20 vessels on the Atlantic route.

During the 'seventies and later several other well-known shipping companies were founded—the Glen Line to China, the Castle Line also to the Far East, and the Donaldson Line to Canada. Mention should be made also of the tramp-owning companies, of which there were more than fifty in 1919. Unfortunately the highly inflated prices paid for ships after the first world war led the majority of owners to sell their fleets, at excellent profits no doubt, but in few other respects to the city's advantage.

A Military Interlude

Expansion of trade is often accompanied in this competitive world with bloodshed and, during the 'fifties, Great Britain was involved in two wars. In one prestige was lost, and in the other gained. The Crimean War (1854–56) originated in a fear of Russian aggression in eastern Europe and in Asia, in the Liberal party's hatred of the 'Cossack Czar', and in the Tory party's desire for a military adventure. Dreadful incompetence was shown by all sides—in our own case partly because Wellington, during his many years as commander-in-chief, had been utterly stupid in resisting almost every attempt to modernize the army. Towards the end of the war, however, a new British general emerged—Colin Campbell (1792–1863). He was following in the tradition of his predecessor from Glasgow, Sir John Moore, but was born less 'near the purple'. In spite of his comparatively lowly place of birth—a carpenter's shop near Glasgow Cross—his mother had connections. She had him educated at the High School, and later sent to her brother, a Colonel in Hampshire. He served under Moore in Spain and was at Corunna. He was already middle-aged when a regiment of his Highland Brigade formed the 'thin red line' which prevented the Russians from storming Balaclava.

The Indian Mutiny followed within a year of the Crimean War. Palmerston sent him, as Britain's most trusted general, to relieve the position, and, as Jessie in the favourite Victorian ballad dreamed, the Campbells arrived in the nick of time to relieve the Lucknow residency. After the capture of the city of Lucknow, in March, 1858, the revolt was suppressed, although desultory fighting went on for some time. He returned to London as the general who had restored the reputation of the British Army. He was the man of the hour, and the country applauded when he was honoured as Lord Clyde.

The Glasgow Evangelicals

Nobody at the present time is really qualified to evaluate the part played by the churches in mid-Victorian Glasgow. We are incapable of seeing the Presbyterian and other churches through our grandfathers' eyes. To them the churches had an all-pervading place in the life of the community. To get an insight into the minds of our grandfathers, the biographies of 72 leading Glasgow men of the 'eighties, written by Andrew Aird, may be consulted. No fewer than 42 of the selected ones were ministers, and most of the others were apparently chosen because of their good works. The founder of the Allan Line, for instance, was no doubt a man whose contribution to temperance and other causes was outstanding; but we would probably have devoted more than two lines to his business career, including the Allan Line. And it is perhaps just a little difficult to stifle a feeling of irritation when a book on *How Glasgow can regain her prosperity* turns out to deal, not with an economist's theories on what had gone wrong with business and

industry, but with the spiritual salvation of the people of Glasgow. Indeed, as Glasgow was commercially almost at her peak, the argument would seem to be that sin had actually been a notable contributory factor.

One good aspect must be noted at once. In most parts of Scotland the comparable disputes to those which centred around nonconformity in England did not hamper social progress, as the bickerings which delayed the development of the scholastic system in the South certainly did. The Scots vehemently scolded one another, but were sufficiently realistic to prevent differences of opinion about theology getting in the way of social improvement. Although the Scot in late Georgian days had not—at least in some towns—been much more of a churchgoer than the Englishman, the Church had been relatively more important to him. In spite of his independent ways of thinking and of his comparatively high standards of education, however, the Scot was less successful than the Englishman during the eighteenth century in getting the life of his community on to a democratic footing. He had had no say in the choice of M.P.s, magistrates, town councillors and other functionaries, and popular institutions in which he could express his views on the affairs of the day were virtually non-existent. The Church provided the exception and, as the Scot has a liking for argument, it became the lively centre of collective life.

In 1814 Dr. Thomas Chalmers (1780–1847), a Fifer, was appointed by the Glasgow Town Council to be Minister of the Tron Church.

Glasgow Cathedral in the 1860s
with the Royal Infirmary in the left background.
In the foreground is the 'Bridge of Sighs',
leading to the Necropolis.

81

He held the office for eight years, until he became Professor of Moral Philosophy at St. Andrews University. His influence in those few years was profound. Not only did he attract large congregations, 'who hung as if spellbound upon his eloquent lips', and create religious fervour throughout the city, but he addressed himself to the great social problems which followed the Napoleonic Wars, and particularly to those arising out of acute poverty, neglect and complete lack of education. He engaged in poor relief by *voluntary* agency on a considerable scale, and set up between forty and fifty Sabbath Schools (which were, in fact, chiefly occupied in trying to give some education to children who had never attended any other kind of school). He was keenly supported by the town council, but his activities were frowned upon by his fellow ministers in the city, and the general session protested about them to the town council. Their action was to be reflected twenty years later, when the leading part in the disruption of the Church was taken by Chalmers and many of his most fervent supporters came from Glasgow.

The disruption of the Church was brought about by the feeling for self-determination, which the new rights they had won in the election of their Members of Parliament and their members of town and county councils had given the Scottish people. Attempts were made to persuade the government to draw up legislation, abandoning or modifying patronage and giving parishioners rights in the selection of their ministers. But the demands seemed to Peel's government inconsistent with the principles underlying Church establishment, and amendment of the existing laws was refused.

In May, 1843, Dr. Chalmers, Dr. David Welsh, the Moderator, and 200 others left the General Assembly in Edinburgh, were met by 300 others waiting outside, and went to another hall where the first General Assembly of the Free Church of Scotland was constituted, with Dr. Chalmers as Moderator. A third of the Scottish clergy followed him, giving up manses, stipends, prospects. Many students joined them, including three-quarters of the theological students at the University of Glasgow. Chalmers then demonstrated, what Glasgow knew already, that besides his other gifts he was a brilliant organizer, and within a few months the Free Church had become one of the dominant forces in Scottish life.

The effects of this moral act were far-reaching—on the Church itself no less than on the Free Church—and, although Parliament subsequently abolished the system of patronage, establishment itself had become an issue, and almost a century passed—the Church was reunited in 1929—before the breach was healed. One of the consequences was that discussions on theological questions took precedence over almost all others in every social group. The minutes of Glasgow Town Council, for instance, show that scarcely a meeting passed without some question about the churches being raised. For the next forty or fifty years the ministers formed much the most influential section of the community. The leading city men strove in taking office in their churches, and in participating in the benevolent and social reform movements with which they are associated. They also contributed substantially to the building of more churches.

During this period the declared outlook of many of the leading men of the day was almost as austere as that of John Knox himself. Indeed, when the provost, James Ewing, supported by the directors of the Merchants' House, conceived the idea of converting a small and attractive fir-covered hill near the cathedral into an

82

ornamental garden cemetery, to be called the Necropolis, they erected a monument to John Knox on its highest point.

The Ramshorn Church was taken down in 1824, and St. David's Church erected on its site. It is still usually called by its old name.

The word hypocrisy is often used when the Victorian's attitude to religion is discussed, and most must share G. M. Young's difficulty, when writing about the interminable rancours of Church and dissent in the nineteenth century—he was referring, of course, to England, but his remarks are no less applicable to Scotland—in keeping his temper over 'the stupid self-satisfaction on one side —the prurient self-righteousness on the other—the scolding, the melodrama, the self-martyrdom'. It is, indeed, hard to resist a feeling of aversion when reading, for instance, Peter Mackenzie's really dreadful story of how, on a Sabbath night in January, 1847, when the streets were covered with snow and 'a bitter, scowling east wind was mingled at intervals with gusts of sleet and rain', he found outside the House of Refuge an Irish family with seven children, all under ten, the mother in the last stages of consumption and the father standing beside them with 'mute but dejected countenance, sufficiently attesting the mental and bodily misery he was enduring'. With the help of the police the family was taken to the police station, where the woman died. The youngest child was gone already. Then Peter Mackenzie learned from the police that this tragedy was one of many, and had been brought about by starvation. The soup kitchens for the destitute were not allowed to be opened on the Sabbath.

On the whole, however, it must be said that the Victorian Church did much good in Glasgow—particularly for education and for the welfare of the poor—and had many splendid men and women associated with it. As evidence, there is the career of the most

83

famous churchman born in the Glasgow district, the 'prince of missionaries', David Livingstone (1813–73). Of Highland descent, he had a restless disposition and an inquiring mind. Immediately after he had been ordained—he had already qualified in medicine at the Anderson College, and studied applied science at the Technical College—he sailed for 'darkest Africa', where he spent most of his days, although he returned to this country on two occasions, and the opportunity was taken in the early 'sixties of presenting him with the Freedom of the City. He made several expeditions of discovery in central Africa. In 1849 he reached Lake Ngami; in 1851 he discovered the Zambesi; in 1855 he was the first white man to see the Victoria Falls. In 1866 he set out for Lake Tanganyika, and was presumably lost in the jungle. The story of how Stanley, the American journalist, went in search of him and of their dramatic meeting in 1871, when he was mortally ill with dysentery, is one of the best-known tales which has come down to us from Victorian times.

A final note about the Church in Victorian times. The general impression today is that everybody went to church. It is, therefore, a little surprising to learn that the average attendance of church-goers in Glasgow on one particular Sabbath was estimated in 1851 to be only 19 per cent of the population, and in 1881 to be 18·7 per cent. The number of churches in Glasgow and its suburbs in 1880 was 331, and the number of denominations was 31. The largest groups were: Church of Scotland, 78 churches; Free Church, 78; United Presbyterian, 64; Roman Catholic, 18; Congregational, 14; Scottish Episcopal and English Church, 13; Baptist, 12; Evangelical Union, 10; Plymouth Brethren, 8; Wesleyan Methodist, 7.

Thus the Glaswegian of Victorian times was less a churchgoer than is reputed. Perhaps the impression of prevailing general gloom has been spread by autobiographers, whose personal memories were too vivid of Church and Sabbath School all day, except for biscuits and tea at one o'clock and cold high tea in the evening. But, apart from the orthodox churchgoers, many other citizens turned out to hear the revivalists and, in particular, Moody and Sankey. The worthy mid-Victorian, having assured his place in this world, strove to do so for the next world too.

Schools For All

The feeling for education tended for several centuries to be stronger in Scotland than in England. Although both Oxford University (1249) and Cambridge University (1286) were founded earlier than the Scottish Universities—St. Andrews (1411), Glasgow (1450), Aberdeen (1494) and Edinburgh (1584)—it is noteworthy that no other English university of any kind was founded prior to modern times. From 1496 the sons of Scottish freeholders were compelled to attend the burgh (or grammar) schools, and from the days of John Knox the duty of providing elementary education for all children was admitted if not always enforced. The Scottish Education Acts of 1684 and 1696 required a school to be established in every parish, and during the seventeen-hundreds attendance was, in most places, including Glasgow, compulsory. In this century, too, another kind of school made its appearance in Scotland—the academy, or private grammar school, which was either socially exclusive or used what would be described today as a 'modern curriculum'. Well supplied by the Grammar School, the academies and the parish schools, there were very few children in Glasgow in, say, 1780, who did not receive a reasonably sound education.

The parish school system could not cope, however, with the rapid increase in Glasgow's size, and soon thousands of children were thronging the city streets, receiving no formal education at all. The comment already made on the work done by Dr. Chalmers and others in founding Sunday Schools in Glasgow brought out that the Sunday-School system was begun in the seventeen-eighties to provide urchins with scholastic rather than religious education. During the next fifty years the problem became steadily more pressing, and among the Glasgow men most impressed with the necessity for doing something to educate the children of the poorer classes was David Stow (1793–1864), then a young city merchant. He had already founded several Sunday Schools before he met Dr. Chalmers, and out of their many discussions emerged the idea of holding these schools on more than one day in the week. He received much assistance from his friends, and after a few years was able to organize a day school in the Drygate for one hundred pupils. As his activities extended, Stow realized the necessity for training people who wanted to become teachers, and in 1836 he took the step for which he is best known—the formation in Cowcaddens of the Normal School for the Training of Teachers.

Throughout the country the establishment of this college was regarded as 'beginning a new era in the science of education', and fourteen months later, when the Select Committee of the House of Commons was inquiring into education of the poorer classes, Sir James Kay-Shuttleworth described it as 'the most perfect school of this description' with which he was acquainted. Subsequently Stow was offered the first inspectorship of schools in Scotland, but declined, as 'I would not like to be paid for services in any shape, although I consider it right and proper that all special services should be paid'.

Glasgow children have played in the streets more than English children. They had few toys but there were plenty of traditional games, including singing games, to choose from. They resembled games played elsewhere, but the terminology was different—peeries and bools for tops and marbles, treel a gird for bowling a hoop and peevor for hop scotch. How good and bad for them this running loose might have been must remain a matter of opinion.

By the late 'fifties, almost all children in Glasgow were going to schools—overcrowded, under-staffed schools, but nevertheless schools—and, in keeping with the rest of Scotland, Glasgow was maintaining her interest in higher education. The proportions of school children receiving secondary education in the middle of the Victorian era are revealing. They were: Scotland, 1 out of 205 school pupils; Prussia, 1 out of 249; France, 1 out of 570; and England, 1 out of 1300. The ratio of university students to population in Scotland was twice that of Prussia and six times that of England.

The School Board system was created by the Scottish Education Act of 1872. Control of both parish and burgh schools was invested in School Boards, and the Scottish Education Department was created as the central authority to supervise the qualification of teachers, to inspect and to approve grants, and to arrange for the election of the School Boards. The first School Board for Glasgow was elected in March, 1873, and 'for long previous to that date the suffrages of the ratepayers were sought from all kinds of platforms,

'Dedicated with impatience to School Boards'. *This drawing is from a Conservative weekly that supported Disraeli and scorned Gladstone. The year is 1874.*

from use-and-wont to the most pronounced secularism'. The board had 15 seats, and for these 39 candidates presented themselves. Slightly more than half the qualified voters, 102,000, went to the poll. The compulsory ages for attendance at school—and compulsion this time really meant compulsion—were fixed at 5 to 13, and in 1883 the leaving age was raised to 14. As a contrast, it may be noted that the permitted leaving age in England was in 1880, age 10; in 1893, age 11; in 1899, age 12; in 1900, age 14.

The Greatest Surgical Discovery

The Royal Faculty of Physicians and Surgeons of Glasgow dates from 1599 when a charter was granted to Peter Low and Robert Hamilton. Its immediate object was the protection of the lieges from 'ignorant, unskilled and unlernit' men, For 250 years it acted as the supervisory authority of all medical practice in the west of Scotland, and it won in the early nineteenth century a 14-year law suit with the university on its right as the licensing body for surgeons. The founders of the Glasgow Medical School in the mid-seventeen-hundreds, William Cullen and Joseph Black, were both presidents of the faculty before going to Edinburgh to establish that great medical centre.

A tutorial class for Medicals in the Old College.

The Royal Infirmary, one of the largest hospitals in Great Britain, was founded beside the cathedral in 1792. Older 'hospitals' in the city, such as the St. Nicholas Hospital and Hutcheson's Hospital, were not hospitals as the word is used today, but places of rest for the aged poor and others in distress. The Royal Infirmary's origin was unique, for the prime mover in its establishment was not a medico but the professor of logic at the university, George Jardine. He was secretary of the Infirmary until 1815, and another non-medical professor, Meileman of natural philosophy, carried on after him, writing the annual reports from 1819 to 1826, and drawing up in 1824 the first proper financial statement. From the outset the infirmary was supported by the well-to-do of the city, its first benefactor on a considerable scale being David Dale.

The beautifully designed buildings of Robert and James Adam soon became inadequate for the needs of the rapidly growing city— in the early Victorian period the Infirmary was said to be receiving more factory accident cases than any other hospital in the country— and many extensions were made, particularly up to 1861. The move of the university from the High Street to Gilmorehill at that time, and the consequent necessity for providing facilities for clinical instruction near-by, brought to a head the proposal to build a new infirmary in the west end of the city. After various delays funds

86

were raised, and erection of the Western Infirmary began in 1871. In the next decade the third great Glasgow infirmary—the Victoria —had its beginnings on the south side of the city with pavilions opened in 1889. (In 1907 the immense task of rebuilding the Royal Infirmary itself was put in hand.)

Of the many famous men who have been associated with these and other Glasgow infirmaries, particular mention should be made of the Royal Infirmary, and of Robert Perry, who, while acting as fever physician, first distinguished typhoid from typhus fever; Sir Joseph Lister, who first began the antiseptic treatment of wounds with carbolic acid; Sir William Macewen, who did much of the pioneering work on brain surgery, and to introduce aseptic in contrast with antiseptic procedures; Dr. John Macintyre, who made the first use in a British hospital of X-rays for diagnosis; and Mrs. Strong, who inaugurated the systematic education of nurses.

Joseph Lister (1827–1912) is usually credited with having made the most important surgical discovery of all times. He was one of the many Englishmen who came to Glasgow in the Victorian era. He had become convinced, while house-surgeon at University College Hospital, London, that the dreadful scourge of the past, hospital gangrene, had its origin in a local germ infection. The recent introduction of anaesthetics had done away with much of the agony suffered on the operating table, but many, indeed most, patients were still unwilling, even when their need was most acute, to submit to the surgeon's knife—for they knew that, no matter how brilliantly the operation was executed, the chances of their wounds healing were relatively slight. Even the most skilful

The Royal Infirmary, the Cathedral, and the Barony Church in the 1830s with a water-cart in the foreground.

87

surgeons, it was said, had come to distrust their craft.

When Lister was appointed to the chair of surgery at Glasgow —he came to Glasgow via Edinburgh and later returned there— the Royal Infirmary was notorious. The public believed that there was a pestilence in it which killed the patients in the surgical wards. Throughout the country the whole hospital system was regarded with suspicion, but it was in this Royal Infirmary that Lister first demonstrated how the infection came, not as it had been supposed from the air, but from the surgeon's own hands and from his instruments. From that discovery he turned his attention to devising antiseptic methods, notably by putting dressings containing carbolic acid over wounds, and gradually brought about an entirely new approach in surgery which has been of inestimable benefit to mankind. 'At last it was possible to operate without fear of the consequences, and modern surgery was born.'

The City and the Public Utilities

The growth of Glasgow brought many problems to the city fathers and others responsible for organizing and administering the public utilities. The bridges across the Clyde, for instance, were all inadequate and had to be rebuilt. Their dates are interesting: Jamaica Bridge, which became *the* bridge, and is now often spoken of as Glasgow Bridge, 1772, 1836 and 1899; Old Glasgow Bridge at Stockwell Street, rebuilt as Victoria Bridge, 1854; the bridge to Glasgow Cross, the old 'Jile Brig', now known as Albert Bridge, 1794 and 1871; Rutherglen Bridge, 1776 and 1896; and Dalmarnock Bridge, 1821 and 1889. Of the lesser bridges the best known is probably the Suspension Bridge, which was completed in 1853, as a

Old Glasgow Bridge,
leading to Stockwell Street, in the early 1830s.
Already the new Jamaica Street Bridge
was carrying more traffic,
indicating that the city was moving west.

JOSEPH SWAN

Jamaica Street Bridge in the 1830s seen from the Broomielaw.

halfpenny bridge for foot passengers. The newest bridge, the George V, opened in 1927, is, along with the graceful Albert Bridge, the most handsome of the Clyde bridges, although Glasgow has been generally fortunate in their architecture and no Clyde bridge can be criticized as badly designed.

Perhaps the most important decision taken in those days was to stop the bridging of the Clyde at Jamaica Street. Accordingly, a ferry service had to be provided for the busier parts of the river, including all of the docks and shipyards. At first this service was developed by private enterprise; and later by the Clyde Trust and

Opening the Suspension Bridge,
regarded as a notable engineering feat.
A toll of one halfpenny,
was charged pedestrians for using it.

89

*Building Jamaica Street Bridge, 1895,
and demolishing the old Broomielaw Bridge,
described in the caption as the 'Heilan Cross',
a drawing by Muirhead Bone.*

by Glasgow Corporation. The great numbers of men who, at the end of the working day, attempted to cross the river on the ferry boats, created many problems. In 1861, an accident to the Partick ferry led to seven of Napier's employees losing their lives and, in 1864, no fewer than 19 men were drowned when the Finnieston ferry was upset by the surge of a passing steamer. Perhaps the most useful thing done by the Glasgow Underground Railway, or 'Subway', opened in 1896, was in linking Partick and Govan, and so taking much of the strain off the ferries.

Another reflection of the growth of the city and of the speeding up of life was provided by the many changes in the location of the Head Post Office. At the end of the eighteenth century it was at 51 Princes Street. It was very small, and when the West India mail arrived—once a month—'even the most eminent merchants attended the deliveries and pushed and scrambled at a little wicket window in a narrow close for possession of their expected remittances'. On one occasion Henry Monteith, before he became provost, and Robert Watson, who later became 'the first stockbroker in Glasgow, had a fair set to'. Between 1800 and 1876, when the foundation stone of the present building in George Square was laid by the Princess of Wales, the Post Office was located in no fewer than six different buildings.

One of the most far-reaching contributions of the city of Birmingham to the development of local government in this country was made when, under the leadership of Joseph Chamberlain, it embarked on its policy of buying local utility companies and administering their services through departments of the municipality. Glasgow was greatly interested in the Birmingham plan and followed it more closely than any other large city. The outstanding achievement of the municipality in the Victorian era was undoubtedly its provision of Glasgow's unequalled water supply. Until the 'fifties water was brought to Glasgow by private undertakings. In 1853 the Glasgow Water Company conceived the idea of tapping one of the Highland lochs near Glasgow, Loch Lubnaig, but their proposal was rejected by Parliament. In the

following year Glasgow Corporation sponsored a bill for bringing water by gravitation from Loch Katrine, 35 miles from the city. It, too, was defeated in Parliament, but, on being presented in slightly modified form, was passed in 1855. The scheme was carried forward, and the water was turned on by Queen Victoria, who had been much interested in the project, on 14th October, 1859. The works cost approximately a million pounds, and by 1880 were supplying, along with the Gorbals works, which the corporation

Cathedral Square in 1852.
The pony cart selling water
at a halfpenny a stoup is a feature of the picture.
Glasgow Corporation left the supply of water
to private enterprise until 1855.
The first proposal to bring water from the Highlands
(Loch Lubnaig) was advanced by the
Glasgow Water Company in 1853,
but the proposal was rejected by Parliament.
The building on the left is the Adam's Royal Infirmary,
built in 1792.
The Cathedral itself, which looks oddly small
in this painting, had just had its bell tower removed.
This was at the western end of the Cathedral,
towards which the artist was looking.
The church at the right was the Barony Church,
whose architecture, as described
by J. O. Mitchell in his Old Glasgow Essays, was 'dreadful'!
The Necropolis, although it is not prominent
in this picture, dates from 1832.

The Stewart fountain was erected
in Kelvingrove Park in the 1870s
to commemorate the Loch Katrine water scheme.
This drawing is of particular interest
because it shows the University tower without its steeple.

had acquired, 37 million gallons a day. Various extensions have since been made, and an adjacent source of supply at Loch Arklet has been drawn upon. The aqueducts are now capable of discharging 110 million gallons a day—Glasgow has no fear of drought—and the water is so soft and pure that it requires only straining instead of filtration.

There can be little doubt that this scheme was primarily responsible for ridding the city of cholera and typhus epidemics. In the cholera epidemic which swept through Great Britain in 1866—that is to say, after the water supply had reached Glasgow from Loch Katrine—only 55 lives were lost in Glasgow. This figure may be compared with the 4000 lives (1·4 per cent of the population) lost in the cholera and typhus epidemic of 1832, the 3800 lives lost in the Asiatic cholera epidemic of 1849–50, and the 3900 lives lost over a period of thirteen months in the scourge of 1853–54.

The town council was less successful in its first attempts to take over the city's gas supplies. Several rival companies to the pioneering Glasgow Gas Light Company had been established. After a dispute, which was taken to Parliament, the town council in 1869 acquired this company and also the City and Suburban Gas Company of Glasgow. New companies came into being, however, on the outskirts of the city, and quite a few years passed before Glasgow had a unified scheme of gas supply.

THE BEE

Glasgow, the Modern Andromeda, 1874
(based presumably on the famous mid-Victorian painting).

To most of us of the present time it seems puzzling that there was dilatoriness about arranging for the effective disposal of sewage. The Lanarkshire towns were not slow in using their rivers for the disposal of sewage, but, unfortunately for Glasgow, most of this sewage found its way into the Clyde above the city. In mid-Victorian days the Clyde, before reaching Glasgow, was receiving the drainage of 30 communities, totalling over 100,000 people. By the 'seventies the polluted condition of the whole Clyde Valley had become a scandal, and Glasgow, which established one of the

92

first sewage farms in the country in 1894, did an excellent pioneering hygienic job, not only in educating its own citizens but in educating the authorities of other towns.

One further civic enterprise of the period should be mentioned. Until 1846 the historic Glasgow Green was the only open space available in the city for general recreation. The westward trend made the establishment of a new park essential, and with fine foresight the town council engaged Sir Joseph Paxton, architect of the Crystal Palace, to plan three parks—for the west, the south and the east. He devoted his time particularly to the delightful west-end Park at Kelvingrove, which was opened in 1853. Queen's Park was completed in 1862, and Alexandra Park in 1870. To an overcrowded town they were quite invaluable. Incidentally, a suggestion was made in 1858 that a mine should be sunk in Glasgow Green, under which splendid coal is known to exist. This was to help pay for the new parks. East-end workers were indignant and offered to pay a penny in every pound they earned to save the Green. The project was abandoned.

So Glasgow went on expanding throughout the Victorian era. Vast areas of tenements were built and, as has already been remarked, built substantially. For the upper middle classes many 'freestone mansions of elegant architecture' were constructed. They began at

Glasgow Green
remained the city's principal park
long after this drawing
was made in the 1830s.

Blythswood Place and St. Vincent Street in the 1820s
were particularly smart and residential.
Some of the buildings seen in this engraving
are still in existence,
but they were being converted into offices by the 1850s.

JOSEPH SWAN

This print is from the Old Glasgow Room of the Mitchell Library. It shows Claremont Terrace in 1852.
The building where the omnibus is standing is now the Park Nursing Home. The Park Circus district was conceived in the 1830s as a New Town,
comparable to the New Town of Edinburgh. The 'pulpit steps' in the left background remain a feature of this part of Glasgow.

Crossing the River Kelvin
presented many problems
in the past.
This photograph, taken in 1870,
shows two bridges across the river
at Great Western Road.
Both were subsequently removed
when the present bridge
was built in 1891.

Charing Cross and eventually formed a belt almost three miles long
and in some parts a mile wide—reaching through Kelvingrove,
Hillhead and Dowanhill on to Great Western Road, up to
Anniesland. Coastal and other country towns, too, were taken
over by Glasgow people, and much building went on in
Milngavie, Helensburgh, Gourock and several Renfrewshire and
Ayrshire places to provide accommodation for 'commuters' from
Glasgow.

Glasgow's architecture of this period was often praised, and still is.
The compactness and 'correctness' of the building was admired,
even that of tenements now badly in decay. It was said that some of
the fine conceptions of eighteenth-century Glasgow continued
well into the nineteenth century. But the lack of variety, the
monotony, was criticized. The use of grey stone was splendid but
grey 'unrelieved' is dull. Why did Glasgow not use paint and
introduce colour on doors, around windows and elsewhere?

No one could pretend any longer that Glasgow was primarily
an ecclesiastic and academic city and, when the Lyon King of Arms
raised some objections to Glasgow's coat of arms, the opportunity
was taken to cut down the old motto. 'Lord, Let Glasgow Flourish
by the Preaching of the Word' became just, 'Let Glasgow Flourish'.

The Complacent Decades

In no other two decades has the character of the people of this
country undergone such changes as between the late 'forties and the
late 'sixties. In 1844 the country was sorely troubled. The threat
of revolution was still in the air—and indeed, as riots in 1848
showed, it was to linger for some time yet. Men spoke darkly then
of the satanic factories in which they had to work, and talked,
often openly, about burning them down. Most of them were less
concerned about whether the continued mechanization of plant
would bring about further wage cuts and unemployment than they
were about bad conditions, but some thought of the Industrial
Revolution as the most dreadful thing that had ever happened,
and wondered when the tragedy would reach its climax. Then
everything began to change. There was work for all, the Irish
included—few Glaswegians of today realize to what an extent their
city and its public services, and particularly their railways, were
built by Irish labourers. By the 'fifties the country was in its most
complacent mood ever. People thought that the secrets of nature
were at last being revealed, and were proud that Providence had
chosen their particular generation to confer such a blessing upon
mankind. They imagined that they would make things and do things
never dreamed of before. There would be progress everywhere,
and people would go on getting better, not only physically but
mentally too. The age of reason was at hand.

This was the time too when the professions associated with
commerce began to put their houses in order. The outstanding
example is perhaps the granting of a charter to the Institute of
Accountants and Actuaries in Glasgow. It was in 1855, one year
after a similar charter had been granted in Edinburgh. This was
described as the 'foundation of the accountancy profession in
the world'.

The Victorians were sentimental as well as self-assured in their
complacency. Consider, for instance, how Andrew Wallace
associated the introduction of gas lighting with the defeat of

Napoleon—'the art of war is a dark and gloomy art, fit only for nations lying in moral and physical darkness, and must inevitably disappear before the light of gas and civilization.'

There had been alarm in London when the Prince Consort pushed ahead with his project for holding an international exhibition in 1851. The good people thought of London filled with disreputable hordes from the Industrial North. There would be drunkenness, riot and worse. But when the hordes reached London, by cheap excursions on the new railways—many of them from Glasgow—they were found to be thoroughly decent chaps. The 'respectable working man' had arrived with the eighteen-fifties, and the well-to-do found him affable and friendly-disposed.

One of the most important influences in changing the Victorian way of life was the removal of the 'tax on knowledge' in the early 'sixties, which brought about a considerable reduction in the price of newspapers and a resulting increase in circulation. Even the *Glasgow Herald* itself had in the 'forties a circulation of only 3000. It was joined in 1847 by the *North British Daily Mail* (now the *Daily Record*), which later had the distinction of being the first daily newspaper published in Scotland. After the withdrawal of the newspaper tax, Glasgow had three daily newspapers, the *Herald,* the *Mail* and the *Morning Journal,* and almost twenty weeklies, including the *Courier,* the *Advertiser,* the *Citizen,* the *Times* and the *Penny Post* (a 'penny dreadful'), and some fortnightly and monthly periodicals. Incidentally, it may be remarked that old folk who accuse the modern press of sensationalism forget some of the papers of their own youth. Then came the evening papers, the *Citizen* in 1864, the *News* (which absorbed another evening paper the *Star*) in 1873, and the *Times* in 1876. And finally, there were the pawky weeklies, modelled on *Punch*—among the most characteristic features of later Victorian life. The *Bee* did not survive the eighteen-seventies. *Quiz,* much the best by modern standards, covered the eighteen-eighties and eighteen-nineties. *St. Mungo,* edited by Neil Munro had a short run in the mid-eighteen-nineties, and the *Bailie,* founded in 1872, had an existence of almost 60 years.

Throughout the Victorian era the middle class was dominant, more sober, more comfortable, more refined than ever before. It had grown so considerable in size that it had its own subdivisions. There were an upper middle class, a middle class, and a lower middle class. The respectable working man regarded himself as a member of the last of these groups, and some people who used to think of themselves as aristocrats now said, perhaps not quite sincerely, that they themselves were really members of the middle class. At the other end of the scale, there was a 'submerged tenth', the paupers, virtually unemployable, who were given some incidental charity, particularly by benevolent societies with a religious background. But such people did not fit into the mid-Victorian scheme of things. These Victorians were rugged individualists. Liberalism was at the height of its power and liberalism meant the protection of a man's right to do what he liked with his property, his labour and his time. Weaklings and failures had brought their misfortunes upon themselves, probably by addiction to alcohol and by laziness. The Victorian despised the sluggard and said so.

The early Victorian had every reason for supposing that his philosophy had brought him success. His trade and his earnings went on increasing—the annual exports of Great Britain doubled every ten years, and he believed that they would go on doing so indefinitely. Out of the sentimental side of his character came, however, an urge for social reform. He wanted to get the children of the working classes to school and their parents to church. State regulation—through the factory inspector, the school inspector, the poor-law inspector—put in an appearance once again. But there was still that confusion of thought which, as his critics have noted, ran throughout Dickens's works —the denunciation in the name of humanity of those who did nothing to improve social conditions, and the denunciation in the name of liberty of those who, in trying to improve them, infringed the rights of the individual.

Some of the vigorous radical reformers continued to be active and showed considerable administrative skill in putting the trade unions and the co-operative societies on a sound footing. The great craft unions all had their origin in the period immediately following the repeal of the Combination Laws in 1824, but they were somewhat shapeless until the late 'forties and the 'fifties, when men of outstanding ability began to organize them. The most prominent among the Glasgow trade unionists of this period was William Allan (1813–74), one of the founders of the Amalgamated Society of Engineers (which later became the Amalgamated Engineering Union) and its general secretary for over twenty years. In 1864, a Royal Commission was set up to inquire into the rights of trade unions, and in particular into the allegation that the unions fomented industrial disputes. Allan was a distinguished witness on behalf of the trade unions, answering a great many questions. The Royal Commission's findings led to a series of Acts being carried in the early 'seventies, which extended the legal powers of workers' organizations and placed them on a stable basis. The Webbs, in their *History of Trade Unionism*, have told how, by his methodical administration and his caution in handling the Society's funds, Allan did much to raise the status of trade unionism.

Robert Owen and the Co-operative Movement

So far reference has been made to several Glasgow men who went south to win fame and fortune; but, by the early nineteenth century, Glasgow was attracting able young men from other parts. Perhaps the best-known of these 'incomers' in the early decades of the century was the Welshman, Robert Owen (1771–1858). Making the acquaintance of David Dale when he came to discuss the purchase of the New Lanark Mills, Owen remained in the district, married Dale's daughter, and took over the management of the factory in 1800. At that time it had 1300 work-people, and in addition was employing between 400 and 500 pauper children. In the next two decades he created various institutions in his village community which were widely talked about, and in the 1824 period brought him more than 2000 visitors annually. Owen was at this time an excellent business man, and it is instructive to learn that, when he called a meeting in Glasgow of local cotton manufacturers to propose removing the import tax on cotton, he was warmly supported; but that, when he called a meeting to advocate the abolition of child labour, he did not get a seconder.

Unfortunately, Owen had many disputes with his partners, partly over what they regarded as his profligate way of living—Owen was far from being a religious man in the orthodox sense. In the late eighteen-twenties he sold his interest in the factory. After three

97

years spent in a rather unsuccessful attempt to establish a village community at 'New Harmony' in the United States he returned to this country and for a time participated in trade union activities. In the past he had created the Grand National Consolidated Trade Union, which at one time had, or was said to have, two million members. Then in the 'thirties he threw himself whole-heartedly into a project which was of more permanent value and which, more than anything else, made him one of the most important figures in the social history of his times. This was the furtherance of the co-operative movement.

An interesting and little-known fact is that the two oldest co-operative societies in the world are both situated within the 25 mile radius of Glasgow, at Lennoxtown, in Stirlingshire, and at Larkhall, in Lanarkshire. The centenary of the Rochdale (Lancashire) Equitable Pioneer Society was celebrated in 1944 as the starting-point of the co-operative movement which swept through the British Isles. But there are older societies, and Robert Owen derived from them many of the more practicable ideas he used when advocating the development of the movement so fervently.

The Habit of Thrift

The earnings of the working and lower-middle classes were meagre. The shadow of unemployment and the consequent lack of security were always present. During these decades, however, thrift became more than a necessity. It became a virtue. From all sides the bread-winners of the family were exhorted to acquire the habit of saving, although no one stood less in need of prompting to put something aside for a rainy day than the careful Scot, with his background of frugal living.

England.

Scotland.

NORTHERN LOOKING GLASS

The state of the money market, 1826, in the troublous years that followed the Napoleonic Wars.

One of the incontrovertible examples of the essential soundness of the Glasgow working man is to be found in the growth of the Savings Bank of Glasgow. It is the largest trustee savings bank in the United Kingdom, and has consistently kept ahead of its closest rival among other savings banks, the Birmingham Municipal Bank. The Glasgow Savings Bank was formed in 1836, after authority had been given for savings banks to invest their funds with the National Debt Commissioners. It was so well founded that its prosperity was only slightly affected by the later failures of the Western Bank and the City of Glasgow Bank. Indeed, the crisis year in its history came early in 1847—a pointer, incidentally, to the

98

privations suffered by the working classes in Glasgow during the 'Hungry 'Forties'. It was not only in Ireland that the crops failed.

The savings bank was intended for the 'small man'. Before 1891 no one could deposit more than £30 a year, or £150 in all, in it. This requirement has since been modified, but the fact that the savings bank has roughly half a million depositors shows that it is still essentially the institution to which the working man and his family entrust their savings.

The Friendly Societies, which played such a prominent part in Victorian life, were less concerned with personal thrift than with self-help among groups of people, who clubbed together to protect their mutual well-being. Originally these societies were just burial clubs. One of the greatest fears of the working man for many centuries was that, through lack of money, either he or members of his family would be disgraced by having to be buried by the 'parish'. Quite apart from feelings of shame at being dependent on charity, there were religious conceptions behind his desire to be 'decently buried', and much of the 'ceremony, mystery and romance', which were particularly associated with the ritual of the Friendly Societies during the Victorian era, were in their way relics of religious guilds. Their secrets were of an innocent character—many had, as their sole purpose, identification—and the annual parades of the societies, with their members dressed up in the vestments of their 'Orders', were entirely happy features of Glasgow's social life.

The societies' aims became something more than just 'to hold each other up', and they became 'mutual insurance societies of the poorer classes by which their members sought to aid one another'. They now provided, by voluntary subscription, for relief and maintenance of their members, and their families, during infirmity, old age and widowhood, for payment at the birth of their members' children and for their endowment later in life, and for relief in distressed circumstances. Many went further and covered loans, superannuation, pensions and even the promotion of scientific, literary and artistic interests. The seeds of trade unionism, of the building societies, and of the insurance companies are to be found in these Friendly Societies—perhaps also the Welfare State.

Social Life in the 'Fifties

Between 1845 and 1850 the last vestiges of Georgian social life disappeared. Victorianism came into full flood. The simplicity and grace of Georgian furniture and ornament were replaced by massive solidity and florid decoration. Families became larger—not because Victorian women had more children than their grandmothers, but because a much greater proportion were saved from dying in infancy or in early childhood. Paterfamilias saw himself as an enlightened elder guiding youth along the path it should go—but he cast an indulgent eye on a good deal of incidental fun. The holiday at the Clyde coast and the matinée at the Christmas pantomime both date from this time. People sang and danced throughout the Victorian era, and apparently with a great deal more gaiety than today. The waltz and the lancers came in the 'thirties, the polka and the schottische, the quadrilles and the galop in the 'forties. Above all, the polka was *the* ballroom dance of the Victorians—its vogue continued until the 'nineties—and it was most certainly neither dull nor strait-laced.

99

The Victorian mamma kept a close watch on her daughters, and in 1857 the respectable matrons of the city were shocked beyond words—or beyond polite words—by disclosures at the trial, for murder, of a twenty-one-year-old girl of good family; and, although the verdict was 'not proven', both the girl's father, a prosperous architect, and her mother were so prostrate that they were unable to attend the court at any time during the proceedings, and shut themselves away, with the other members of their family, at Bridge of Allan for the rest of their days.

The girl was Madeleine Smith. The man she was accused of killing, Pierre Emile L'Angelier, a handsome clerk from the Channel Islands, was admittedly her lover. In 1853 Madeleine, a beautiful young person, had completed her education at a genteel boarding-school in London. Two years later she was introduced to L'Angelier in Sauchiehall Street by a mutual friend. He pursued her and made an impression. Although she had no serious intention of marrying him, their relations were, for a time, intimate. Then an eligible suitor came along, and Madeleine wanted rid of her self-seeking friend. He showed no inclination to let the *affaire* peter out, and became a nuisance. On 23rd March, 1857, he died of arsenic poisoning. Amazingly candid letters from Madeleine were found in his room. She was arrested and charged with his murder.

The trial was almost the sole topic of conversation throughout Great Britain, and has become notorious. It has been the subject of books, plays and films. Never has anyone charged with murder been so cool and calculating—never an unguarded word, not even when her purchases of arsenic were admitted—as this Glasgow girl, deserted by her family, shunned, except for one brother, by her friends, and pre-judged a murderess.

F. Tennyson Jesse has suggested that she was born before her time. She had no outlet for her restless vitality, her intelligence, her individuality, her physical passion. 'As it was, she was born in that period of the world's history which was the most hopeless for a nature such as hers.'

Madeleine went to London after the verdict, and later to the United States, where she began a new life and lived on to be over ninety. The town house in Blythswood Square was incorporated in the Agricultural College. It is still there.

If the Victorian papa sniffed at this story of feminine frailty— for the question really was not whether Madeleine had been a sinner, but how much a sinner—his aplomb was disturbed a few years later, in 1865, when one of the city's leading medical practitioners, Dr. Edward Pritchard, of Sauchiehall Street, was condemned to death for poisoning his wife and mother-in-law. And he was disgusted when a great crowd turned out for the public hanging—the last execution of its kind to take place in Glasgow. Dr. Pritchard too has had books and plays written about him.

The fact is that there were more 'goings-on' in these mid-Victorian days than met the eye. Even in public, however, some kinds of 'high life' were freely indulged in, with a lot of drinking and over-feeding (perhaps not every vestige of Georgian days was gone, after all). For instance, when the Highland and Agricultural Show was held in Glasgow in 1844, the Show Dinner in the City Hall was such a great repast that it began at half-past five. This was followed next morning by a public breakfast in the Black Bull Hotel at eight, and by another dinner at two. On each occasion there was a feast of oratory as well as of food.

D. SMALL

D. SMALL

The middle classes devoured rounds of beef, roasted sirloin, mutton boiled and roasted, turkeys roasted and boiled, haggis, and cockie-leekie soup. The working classes had, of course, to be frugal —parritch for breakfast, with a little milk or small beer; Scotch broth and beef for dinner, or sheep's head and trotters, or salt herring and potatoes; and supper, usually a thin meal made up of left-overs.

Although more people went to the play than in the past, the theatre meant little to most of the citizens of Glasgow. The Theatre Royal, in Dunlop Street, was eventually destroyed by fire on the last night of the pantomime, 'Blue Beard', in 1863. Altogether, in various forms and under various names, it had been in existence eighty years, It was never a great theatre, but most of the leading actors and actresses over many decades appeared on its boards, and its patrons loved it dearly. Apart from the melodrama houses the only other theatre in Glasgow until the approach of the 'seventies was the

Two of Glasgow's famous hotels of the 1700s which survived well into the Victorian era. On the left is the Black Bull Hotel erected in 1758 by the Highland Society. It catered principally for Highland visitors. Above is the court of the Saracen's Head Hotel, sketched in the 1850s.

THE BEE

The fascinating drawing on the left is of the auditorium of the second Theatre Royal in Dunlop Street in 1856. This theatre was burned down. The drawing above shows the audience at the opera in the third Theatre Royal in Hope Street. Shortly afterwards it too was burned down. It was replaced by the present building.

Prince's, a converted exhibition hall in West Nile Street. It was founded in 1838 by a member of a leading London theatrical family, Edmund Glover. The performances were 'conducted with the utmost propriety'. The Prince's is said to have been the first theatre outside London to have stalls separate from the pit. The Western Club had a box booked permanently for its members.

Edmund Glover took over the management of the Theatre Royal in 1852 and 'scrapped Alexander's cheese-paring policy'. Some years after the destruction of the Theatre Royal William Glover, Edmund's son, transferred the royal patent to a theatre in the Cowcaddens. When it was burned down in 1879 he retired from management.

The music-halls were still in an elemental stage of development, boisterous and vulgar. They were, in fact, glorified public houses; but out of them was to come one of the features by which the later Victorian era is known to posterity. Sport was unorganized. Cricket was being played, although the Glasgow summer weather has never been quite suitable for the game. Most interest was being taken in rather brutal pastimes, notably pugilism. In the early days of the era great crowds used to gather outside the coaching hotels, to await the result of a prize-fight in which a Glasgow man had been taking part—this, incidentally, was not out of idle curiosity and local patriotism alone, for a good deal of money would be at stake. The nature of the contests is perhaps best brought out in a paragraph in the *Glasgow Herald* of 1839, announcing that 'Deaf Burke was disqualified for fighting foul. It will be remembered that it was this deaf blackguard who killed Simon Byrne, who killed Sandy MacKay of Glasgow'. The *Glasgow Herald* did not add, however, that MacKay had been killed in the 47th round, and Byrne in the 99th.

Almost all visitors to Glasgow in the eighteenth and nineteenth century commented on the way in which the people congregated in the streets, and listened to intemperate wits who indulged in 'droll speeches and harangues'. The congestion in their homes no doubt accounted for their unwillingness to spend much of their leisure time in them. Reference has already been made to the considerable number of 'soul-destroying drinking shops' which had been opened in Glasgow during the first decades of the nineteenth century. Taverns of a better kind, closer in mood to those of the last century, were also established, and for some decades were centres of social life. The leading tavern of the eighteen-thirty period was Jamie Begg's, located in Hutcheson Street near Argyle Street. 'Men of substance went there at night to discuss the topics of the day or special subjects, as well as Welsh rabbits, Finnan haddies and rationals.'

Various clubs were still meeting. The cholera epidemic in 1848 seems to have led to their breaking up, but new associations presumably were formed later in other places. Jamie Begg had not concealed from 'the more juvenile and flippant type' that he cared not to cultivate their connection, and perhaps, when they grew older and formed their own clubs, they were not inclined to give Jamie their custom.

Near by were three other taverns—Paul Spencer's, McArthur's and the Shakespeare 'Singing Saloon'. Paul, a former pugilist, was 'a good-natured lump of an Irishman', and was the first publican in Glasgow to sell 'half-pints'—previously some places served nothing under a quart, and two or three men often shared a tankard together. McArthur's was the howff of more studious people and, every night between 8 and 10 during the winter months, books were auctioned from a rostrum.

THE BEE

Glasgow's music-hall comedians of the 1870s. It will be noted that they do not include any 'Scotch comics'.

John Urie, in his reminiscences of the clubs of the 'fifties and 'sixties, recalled particularly the Garrick Club, which met in McLaren's Tavern in Dunlop Street, and the City Club, a literary club which later became the Burns Club. It met in the Bank Tavern in Trongate and among its members was Hugh MacDonald who, in the 'fifties, wrote the most popular book ever published about Clydeside, *Rambles Around Glasgow*. Members of the Garrick were associated with the theatre and the arts. Among them Urie mentioned: Alexander of the Theatre Royal; Anderson, the 'Wizard of the North'; Mossman the sculptor; and Sam Bough, then a scene painter and later Glasgow's leading portrayer in water-colours of its streets and buildings.

It is a reflection on the acumen of the well-meaning advocates of temperance reform that they tried to stamp out the drink trade by using their powers under local government to make places where drink was sold as uncomfortable and uninviting as possible. They did away most effectively with the places where people were accustomed to sit with their cronies at ease while drinking, and perpetuated the bare counter where drinks were gulped down, and where space could be readily cleared if a fight sprang up.

The reference to the City Club's decision to change its name to the Burns Club is a reminder that the Burns Supper, now a traditional Scottish feast, really dates from the centenary of the poet's birth, in January, 1859. No fewer than 872 Burns dinners were held on that evening—676 in Scotland, 76 in England, 10 in Ireland, 48 in the Empire, 61 in the United States, and 1 in Denmark. Over two dozen were in Glasgow, and the men of the city made up for any criticism which may have been directed against their grandfathers for slowness in recognizing Burns's genius. The greatest meeting was held under the chairmanship of Sheriff Sir Archibald Alison. The dinner began at 5, thirty speeches were given, and, according to the minutes, the proceedings came to an end at 11.30, 'when many of those present had become rather confused in their jollity'. There was, by the way, 'a brilliant assemblage of the fair sex' in the gallery, where they were sustained with a service of cake and wine.

The Glasgow Fair Holiday took on its present form during the 'fifties and 'sixties. The holiday itself is at least eight hundred years old. It ran for eight full days from 7th July. People from all parts of the west of Scotland gathered in the town to buy and sell things, to meet old acquaintances, and to see the shows provided by strolling players, acrobats, tumblers, singers and dancers. An eighteenth-century song, 'The Humours of the Glasgow Fair', gave an account of the festivities.

> *'Twas there the funning and sporting.*
>   *Eh, Lord! what a swarm o' braw folk;*
> *Rowly-powly, wild beasts, wheel o' fortune,*
>   *Sweety stan's, Maister Punch, and Black Jock.*

A note on what was happening on the Green when the Fair was in its prime would be perhaps interesting—say, in 1844, when it was described by the *Glasgow Herald* as 'the annual period when toil remitting lends its turn to play'. Miller's Adelphi Theatre and Cook's Circus have already been mentioned. During the Fair of this year the Adelphi gave performances 'by day as well as by night' of a spectacle about Aladdin. The entertainment at the Circus was characterized by 'chaste modesty'. There were also two collections of wild beasts, each containing performing elephants and lions, 'but neither are on the scale of splendour or extent to which the frequenters of Glasgow Fair have been accustomed in former years'.

'The grand staple of the Fair' was penny theatricals, taking place in four large booths, some of them capable of containing an audience of 1500. 'Pieces which have a touch of the horrible in them generally do best for the Fair, and accordingly mimic scenes of blood and treachery and rapine are served up pretty extensively.'

The *Glasgow Herald* had left also its impressions of the noise at the Fair. 'At times the scene on the Green is perfectly bewildering, at least to the ears—and amidst the blowing of trumpets, the skirling of the bagpipe, the crashing of the drums, the ringing of bells, the groaning of the showmen through their speaking-horns, the discharge of musketry, and the hum of the crowd, one might almost think that the pealing of a thunderstorm would pass unnoticed.'

THE GLASGOW HERALD COLLECTION

The writer added that the better order of the working classes, instead of gazing after childish and senseless sights, was making trips to the country or the coast. The great days of Rothesay and of Dunoon were beginning.

The Clyde Steamer became an institution, and for generations sailing 'doon the watter' was the supreme delight of Glasgow people and particularly boys, who were adept at distinguishing the ships by the colours and arrangement of their funnels. It began in the early eighteen-fifties, while Helensburgh and Gourock were still the Clyde's principal watering places. The most famous of the steamers were the *Columba* (1878 to 1935) and the *Iona* (1864 to 1935), but they were to some extent superseded by larger and more handsome

This is what Glasgow Fair looked like in the mid-1820s.
It was held on the outskirts of
Glasgow Green at Jail Square.
The Fair by this time had lost
some of the more pleasing qualities
of a country fair of previous centuries,
and was avoided by the best people and their families.

ships, beginning in 1901 with the first turbine steamer, the
King Edward. Rivalry between the captains was intense, particularly
as the paddlers raced from Craigendoran, Prince's Pier and Gourock
to Kilcreggan, Dunoon, etc. The size to which the business grew
is indicated by the number of steamers in the LMS fleet at the
outbreak of the second war—five turbine ships and eight paddle ships.

The Clyde steamers meant a great deal to many people.
Above is one of the most famous of the paddle steamers, the 'Columba';
on the right is the first turbine steamer, the 'King Edward'.
The opening of the Clyde season, April 1896, is shown below.

"GRENADIER"   "IONA"

A CLOSE FINISH
QUIZ   "IONA" OVERHAULS "GRENADIER"

The Dawn of a Doubt

The *Age of Progress* did not end in 1870—it is far from over even today—but the belief that things were going to get better and better, for ever and ever, was gone by 1870. For this loss of faith there are several explanations.

The belief had gone that the world would be willing to let Great Britain become the sole important manufacturing centre, and that other people would continue to buy our goods in return for their agricultural products and raw materials. Now it was clear that the United States were going to have a much larger population than this country, and that they had greater natural resources. Some day, it seemed, they must beat us at mass-production. But worse was the appearance of a European rival, Germany, who looked like beating us technically. And this rival was also upsetting the balance of power in Europe. The Germans had humiliated France and, although the Victorians did not have much kindly feeling toward the French—the Germans were still regarded as our cousins—they wondered if some day this able country, Germany, might turn on Great Britain. They felt that they would have to do something to get the army into better shape, and they were not too confident about the state of the navy either.

Then things were not so good at home. The failure of the Western Bank in 1857 (authorized capital, £4,000,000)—brought about by the inability of four leading firms to meet their debts to the bank, because of having been involved in a commercial crisis in the United States—had shaken confidence. There had been rumours, too, that the City of Glasgow Bank itself was in difficulties, but, after the directors had stopped payment for a few days, during which panic prevailed in the city and military assistance was sought from Edinburgh, all seemed to be well. The American Civil War upset things too. Not only had it caused some of the textile manufacturers and merchants severe losses, but the Southern States had incurred substantial debts which would have to be written off.

The reformers were restive again. It was as if—as G. M. Young has said—young Britain, now grown grey, began to redeem in the 'sixties the promise of its far-off fantastic youth. The Victorians were apprehensive when, in 1866, John Bright led a reformers' procession through the main streets of the city. Glaswegians had perhaps fresher memories of what a riot was like than people in some other parts. With that strange perversity, which so often leads Glasgow to be on its best behaviour when there is trouble elsewhere and to be truculent when others are peaceful, it had been the only city in which a serious disturbance had taken place during 1848–49—years in which revolutions were happening all over Europe, and a fear had been felt throughout the country that something might be attempted here too. On Sunday, 4th March, 1848, a disorderly mob ransacked shops in the city, the newly appointed superintendent of police having withdrawn his men within doors instead of going out to meet the miscreants. Large forces of military were brought into the city, especially on the Tuesday, when the mob proposed to stop the mills and dismantle the gas works. A crowd, which was about to attack Campbell's silk mill in John Street, was driven by the militia to the Green, where, after considerable bloodshed, six people were killed and several others maimed for life. In Glasgow no fewer than 10,000 special constables were sworn in within a week, and shortly afterwards a volunteer cavalry force was formed, which later became the Queen's Own Royal Glasgow Yeomanry.

Glasgow in the middle 'sixties still remembered that affair, but no disorders accompanied the passing of the Scottish Reform Bill in 1868, which greatly extended the numbers entitled to vote in the election of Members of Parliament (from 18,000 to 48,000). Three seats were allotted to Glasgow, although no elector was allowed to vote for more than two candidates. The three Liberal candidates, Robert Dalglish (of Dalglish, Falconer and Co., owners of the Lennoxtown Calico Printing Works), William Graham (of William Graham and Co., Cotton Spinners, Lancefield) and George Anderson (of Alex. Flather and Co., Flax Spinners, St. Rollox) were returned at the first election. An interesting sidelight on the state of the Glasgow textile industry at that time is contained in a note to the effect that the first two each employed 1000 workers in their factories, and the third 2000 workers. No textile work is undertaken in their districts today.

The election over, the people of Glasgow settled down, feeling that things were not so bad after all, when later in the year something else upset them. The Fenians reminded the citizens that not all of the Irish, who had by then settled down among them in such large numbers, were well disposed. Soon they caused serious trouble, and even by the late 'sixties they had attracted sufficient attention for Glasgow to come, according to Andrew Wallace, into somewhat unenviable notoriety.

ILLUSTRATED LONDON NEWS

The Prince and Princess of Wales
(later King Edward VII and Queen Alexandra)
laying memorial stones
at the site of the new University Buildings, 1868.

As against this, however, the laying of the foundation stone of the new university buildings by the Prince of Wales on 8th October, 1868, provided Glasgow with one of the greatest gala days in its history. A public holiday was declared, and 'all along the route from the Old College to Gilmorehill an immense concourse of people was thronged, and the loyal manifestations were frequent and hearty . . . The city was in a stir until a late hour, and numerous illuminations were made in honour of the occasion.' No doubt curiosity to see the charming Prince of Wales was partly responsible for the gathering and for the joyous scenes, but perhaps the most significant feature was that the event was associated in the public mind with education. Glasgow had come a long way since the days of David Stow.

107

Glasgow in North Britain

Until 1848, when the railway line through Carlisle was completed, the journey between Glasgow and London took so long and was so arduous that few people made it. Glasgow was the commercial capital of a part of the Empire in some ways as remote from London as Philadelphia had been, and much that happened in the political capital of the Empire meant little to the people in the north. Sometimes—as, for instance, when the American War of Independence wrecked her merchants' businesses, and when Boney threatened to invade the United Kingdom through Ireland—Glasgow took a lively interest in what was going on in Parliament. But usually London seemed far away. Centuries had passed without either the king or his leading ministers visiting, or being expected to visit, Glasgow.

In 1849 the queen and the royal family had paid the first of several visits to Glasgow, and soon after prime ministers and leaders of political parties in general began to come to Glasgow quite often, and to deliver important speeches in the City Hall. Hundreds and later thousands of Glasgow men travelled to London every week. The Crimean War, the Indian Mutiny, and the American Civil War affected Glasgow no less than other parts of the country. Londoners began to speak of Glasgow as if it were in England, and, while most Glasgow people disliked that, many fell into the habit of saying that Glasgow was in North Britain instead of in Scotland. Indeed, the leading Glasgow newspaper throughout the period—with the exception of the *Glasgow Herald*—called itself the *North British Daily Mail*.

The first royal visit to Glasgow since James I and VI (always excluding Bonnie Prince Charlie's uninvited stay) was made by Queen Victoria, accompanied by the Prince Consort and the Prince of Wales, on 14th August, 1849. The party came by steam yacht and drove across Jamaica Bridge into the city. The stone arch was built specially for the occasion and was demolished immediately afterwards. An arch of the same general pattern was built for a similar occasion in Dundee, but it was so admired that it was retained, and was demolished only recently to clear the approach to the new road bridge. The procession went by Argyle Street to the Old College, and then returned by Argyle Street and Queen Street to the new railway station, whence they went to Perth on their way to Balmoral. It was estimated that 40,000 people lined the streets, many of them choosing places near the Tontine Hotel.

Glasgow's hotel centre, George Square, in the 1860–70s. Above is the corner of the square with St. Vincent Place.
The hotels are the Waverley, the Crow (the original venture of the Cranston family), the Clarence and the Globe.
The building in West George Street beside the entrance to Queen Street Station is still in existence.
Particularly informative is the view of the North British Hotel. (below) Another floor was added later.
The new Bank of Scotland building can be seen on the left. It was built on the site of the Waverley and Crow Hotels.
The Merchants' House Building, in which the Chamber of Commerce is located, was erected on the site of the Globe and Clarence Hotels.

The railway to Edinburgh was the North British and that was the name of the hotel at each terminus.

Wider Still and Wider

Although some of the props of the industrial prosperity were giving way, the world expansion of trade was so great that the changes taking place in the national economy were largely overlooked. No other country was so active as Great Britain in opening up new markets, and during the thirty years the British Army fought more than a hundred wars and frontier engagements against the Afghans, the Zulus, the Hottentots, the Egyptians, the Chinese and the Sudanese, and always for the Empire, for Christian principles and, incidentally, for better business. The British people—including the Glaswegians —believed with Kipling that they had an imperial destiny.

We had little to do with the act that destroyed the feeling of kinship that had spread, following the 1851 Exhibition, through Europe itself. This act, which set Europe on edge and revived nationalism in some of its worst forms, was the seizure of Alsace-Lorraine by Germany in 1870. Yet the Victorians, up to the late 'nineties, regarded Russia, rather than Germany, as their potential enemy. For instance, a thriller, called *When Glasgow Ceased to Flourish*, published in 1884 to warn the country about the inadequate state of her defences, told of the horrors likely to follow the bombardment of Clydeside from the sea, and forecast that the deed would be done in the 'nineties by the Russian fleet.

The most spectacular overseas venture with which Glasgow was associated at this time began in 1871 when the Rangoon Oil Company was formed to refine and distil the crude oil to be found in Upper Burma. A few years later a Glasgow merchant, David Cargill, acquired the company's interests and despite 'continued obstruction' in Burma was able through his agents in Rangoon, of which Kirkman Finlay, a descendant of the famous Glasgow merchant, was head, to obtain further drilling and prospecting concessions.

The Irrawaddy Flotilla Company, another Glasgow venture, brought the crude oil down the river to the refinery until 1908, when a pipeline was constructed, 273 miles long. After 1904 David Cargill's son, (Sir) John Cargill, was chairman.

At the turn of the century the company was prospecting successfully in Iran, and in 1909 the Anglo-Persian Oil Company was formed. The Burma installations were deliberately destroyed in 1942 as part of the 'scorched earth' policy ahead of the Japanese advance. Compensation disputes led to a famous legal case. But the company's various associates and subsidiaries remained prosperous, notably in Pakistan and India.

In 1952, at the fiftieth annual general meeting of the company, as a limited liability company, the directors reported that the issued capital was almost £18 million and that the annual income had risen to over £10 million.

The First Generation of Real Democracy

Political change was still in the air in the late Victorian decades. The middle classes, which believed themselves inadequately represented in Parliament, and the working classes, which were scarcely represented at all, brought about by their vigorous representations two Reform Acts—Disraeli's in 1867, and Gladstone's in 1884—

Glasgow Green on a fine summer's Sunday evening in the 1890s.

and a great many electors were added to the constituencies. During
the last three decades of the nineteenth century the public took a
livelier personal interest in politics than ever before—for instance,
47,500 of the 57,900 electors in Glasgow voted in the 1880 General
Election. They were part, as Trevelyan has said, of the first generation of real democracy.

The Sixth City in Europe (or could it be Third?)

Glasgow continued to grow rapidly during the later Victorian years,
its population being:

1861	396,000	(also given as 448,000, including suburban districts)
1871	478,000	(also given as 565,000 including suburban districts)
1881	511,000	(also given as 704,000, including suburban districts)
1891	658,000	(with an additional 200,000 in suburban districts)
1901	762,000	(the population of Glasgow, including suburbs, was by this time in the region of a million)

In the 'nineties Glasgow was said to be the Sixth City of Europe
—the two largest cities by far being London, 3,800,000, and Paris,
2,300,000. Berlin and Vienna, each with a population of slightly over
1,000,000, and St. Petersburg differed little in size from Glasgow.

The Victorian era lasted a long time—over sixty years—and
millions of British people lived their whole lives without once singing
'God Save the *King*'. Amazing changes took place in these sixty years,
and the Glaswegian of 1899 was much more like the Glaswegian of
1939—to whom he was more closely linked in years—than like the
Glaswegian of 1839. It is a mistake, therefore, to speak of the people
of those sixty years as if they were of one generation. Mid-Victorian-
ism was certainly still to the fore in the 'nineties—see, for instance,
the memorials of the illustrious Glaswegians (that is to say, the
older men) of the period, who compared themselves to the Old
Testament prophets and tried with stern looks and flowing beards to
look like them. But this was the age, too, of Wilde and Beardsley and
Max Beerbohm, of Darwin and Huxley, of Bradlaugh, of Kipling, of
the new radicalism with left-wing leaders supported by 'intellectuals', such as Sidney Webb, William Morris, James McNeill
Whistler and Bernard Shaw, of scepticism, of licence, of 'perilous
triflings with the essential decencies', of feminism, of the Salvation
Army, and of the spread of trade unionism. At perhaps no other
time had there been such a difference between the points of view of
father and son—even more of mother and daughter—as in the gay
'nineties. And Glasgow was probably at its peak in this decade.

Glasgow in the News

Several happenings in Glasgow during the last thirty years of the
nineteenth century have lost little of their significance with the passing
of time. Perhaps the most important was the failure of the City of
Glasgow Bank in October, 1878. It was described by George
MacGregor as 'the greatest disaster that had ever befallen the
commercial community of Great Britain'. Its magnitude was such
that the business of the city was paralysed and the financial stability
of many Glasgow people severely tested. Yet, such was the spirit
of the merchants and the manufacturers of those days, that within
three years its 'evil results had been almost entirely overcome'.

The City of Glasgow Bank was founded in 1839, and catered

The City of Glasgow Bank in Glassford Street,
scene of Glasgow's greatest financial disaster
in the Victorian era.

particularly for small investors, branches opening in the evenings
to receive deposits. It appeared to be a prosperous undertaking
although, as already mentioned, doubts were expressed about its
soundness in 1857, at the time of the Western Bank's failure. The
directors at the annual meeting in June, 1878, reported that the
number of branches was now 133, that the deposits had risen to
£8,000,000, and that a dividend of 12 per cent would be paid. Some
weeks later stories spread in Glasgow about an application the bank
was said to have made to other banks for assistance, but few were
prepared for an intimation in the morning newspapers of 2nd October
that the directors had decided to close their doors. So great was the
surprise caused by this news that business in the city was practically
suspended throughout the day. Soon it transpired that an accountant,
appointed by the other banks to investigate the City Bank's affairs,
had advised that, as they were in such a bad state, no assistance
should be given. When the auditors appointed by the directors
estimated that the balance of loss, including the bank's capital, was
£6,200,000, the immensity of the disaster almost overwhelmed the
city. Collateral failures went on throughout the rest of the year, and
scarcely a day passed without an intimation that yet another Glasgow
commercial firm was bankrupt. Very little new business was done
in the city for months, but those who suffered most acutely were the
1200 shareholders of the bank itself and their families. Their liability
was unlimited and, when they met in the City Hall to agree to the
bank's voluntary liquidation, they knew that most of those present
were ruined men. A few days later the liquidators made a call of
£500 for each £100 stock, payable by two instalments, in an endeavour
to raise £5,000,000. So great was the sympathy felt in Glasgow for
these shareholders that Lord Provost Collins raised a fund to help
them in their distress, and collected £400,000.

The directors were arrested, and came for trial in the High Court at 114

QUIZ

The Sunday parade in Great Western Road.

Edinburgh in January, 1879. They were all men of good commercial standing. Some were prominent members of the Church, and this led to bitter attacks being made upon them. Indeed, those interested in changing standards of journalistic candour might find the Glasgow magazines and newspapers of the winter of 1878–9 informative. The indictment was formidable, and each was found guilty on some of the charges. Two directors were sentenced to eighteen months' imprisonment and the others to eight months. In the course of his remarks the Lord Justice-Clerk said that their mismanagement of the

115

funds was probably not actuated by desire or design of personal advantage but was committed, as they thought, for the benefit of the bank. The disclosure, however, that the bank had made large, unsecured loans to insolvent firms with which some of the directors were associated incensed the public. The liquidators, aided by a Relief Committee of the 'principal men in Glasgow, Edinburgh and Aberdeen', did their work thoroughly, and after two years had paid the bank's creditors 18s. in the £, an outstanding achievement which reflects well upon the integrity of the Glasgow business men of those times.

STRATTON'S GLASGOW

The Stock Exchange in the 1880s.

In 1888 Glasgow held the first of her four International Exhibitions. It was of considerable size—the attendance was 5,750,000—and was described as quite the finest exhibition ever held outside London. The main pavilion was located in Kelvingrove Park, approximately where the Art Galleries now stand, and the exhibition grounds stretched over the present Kelvin Way to Gray Street and up to the railings of the University. The architecture was Oriental in character —the Exhibition was known in Glasgow as Bagdad on the Kelvin— but its chief feature was a reconstruction on the Gilmorehill slopes of the Bishop's Castle. An archaeological collection was housed in it, and for the younger generation, who might have found this heavy going, a switchback was near at hand. It ran along the north bank of the Kelvin in front of the University grounds and, as nothing like it had been seen in Scotland before, gave many people—and not only youngsters—a great deal of pleasure.

Swimming galas were held in the River Kelvin, presumably less dirty than now, and sports meetings were held on the University rugby ground (where the Chemistry buildings now stand). Some of these meetings took place at night, the pitch being illuminated by 'Wells' Patent Lights'.

The Exhibition had a very considerable influence on the outlook of the city. It was the first time Glasgow had 'let itself go. No one had seen the like of it nor felt in his provincial bosom that intoxicating sense of being devilishly cosmopolitan.' The 'nineties were very different years in the city from the 'seventies and for that the Exhibition was in no small way responsible.

The Prince of Wales
entering the 1888 International Exhibition.

116

The architectural theme of the 1888 Exhibition was described as Oriental.

The bridges across the Kelvin at the 1888 Exibition.

The period was clouded by several disasters, the worst being the capsizing of the steamer *Daphne*, while being launched at the Linthouse Shipyard on 3rd July, 1883—a reminder that, in spite of the rapid progress being made in shipbuilding, naval architecture was still in its infancy. More than 200 workmen were on board, and 146 of them were drowned. The sight has been described as the most appalling ever seen in the city, and, as three weeks passed before the vessel could be raised and some of the bodies recovered, public concern could not be diverted to other matters.

Another reminder that the Industrial Revolution was still young

Progress and Poverty

A Cooling Luxury

A Transfer of Property

Sirens

Maternal Support

Harmony

Discord

QUIZ

came from a tragic occurrence in one of James Templeton's carpet factories, part of which collapsed during a gale, causing the deaths of 29 women and injuries to many others. An interesting point about this tragedy is that the firm accepted responsibility for compensation, and they were still making annual payments to elderly women who,

Glasgow Cross on a Saturday Night in June, 1884.

118

as girls of fourteen and fifteen, were hurt while in their employ seventy years before.

Beside these unlooked-for incidents must be placed an outrage by the Fenians, who, on 20th January, 1883, tried to blow up Tradeston Gasworks, Buchanan Street Goods Station and Ruchill Canal Bridge with dynamite. The Fenians were also blamed by the public for blowing up two gasometers at Dawsholm in 1890, but in this case the culprits were never traced, in spite of the offer of a substantial reward. Although they failed in their main objective, several people were severely injured and public feeling was greatly disturbed. In earlier years the immigrants from southern Ireland had been held in check—collectively if not individually. But now they were asserting themselves—and so were the Orangemen to keep them down. The Orangemen's leader, the 'happy bigot' Harry Alfred Long, was returned for twenty years at the School Board elections on the platform, 'No concession to Popery'.

In 1883 a movement was inaugurated in Glasgow which has spread throughout the world. Many attempts had been made in the past to devise social and other activities, capable of attracting youths and girls away from the bad company to be found on the streets.

QUIZ

Moral Philosophy (February) 1888.
Did you know that they had pin-ups in Queen Victoria's Day?

QUIZ

Juvenile Literature (July, 1884).
The book titles are: 'The Blood Stained Maniac';
'The Girl Fiend' or 'The Murderer's Curse';
'The Dead Man's Secret'; and 'The Fatal Spectre'.

Churchmen in Glasgow had not thought that the street characters, who abounded in days gone by and who could always raise a laugh with their cheek and their quick and often vulgar repartee, were good influences for the young. Over the century 1750–1850 there had been, for instance, Dougal Graham and George Gibson, city bellmen who wrote doggerel verse; Ugly James Dale, the city porter; Fesa, who spat on people's clothing when their backs were turned and earned a penny wiping off the mess; Major, a deformed singer, and Mary who danced to his music (both died in the cholera epidemic of 1832); Lang Tam, who raced the stage coaches; Hirstling Kate, a cripple who 'hirst' herself along on her knees; 'Rev.' John Aitken, a drunken street preacher; Daft Davie with an amusing lisp; Rab Ha' the glutton; Heather Jack who sang *Annie Laurie* and fell down on the roadway when he came to the line, 'I'd lay me doon and dee'; Old Malabar, a juggler; Hawkie, an abusive dwarf; and 'The Teapot', a newsvendor with a twisted body. It is a strange sidelight on our forebears' taste that several of these men and women were buried in the Cathedral or Ramshorn churchyards. The later Victorians, however, found them repulsive. They much preferred, for instance, a deeply religious cotton spinner, Mary Anne Clough, who established a Sunday School in the east end which John Burns, of the shipping company, and others used in 1867 as the nucleus for the Foundry Boys Religious Society, a much respected body which at one time had almost a hundred branches; and an enlightened philanthropist, William Quarrier, who established homes in Glasgow (1871) and Bridge of Weir (1878) for destitute boys.

Unfortunately a great many of the young people then running the streets looked on these religious societies as pious institutions, and would have nothing to do with them. In 1883, Lieut. W. A. Smith (later Sir William Smith), of the Volunteers (First Lanark Rifles), set up a Boys' Brigade in connection with Woodside Mission Sunday School. 'Its working details were on military lines; its objects were to aim at physical, mental and religious growth.' In spite of strong opposition, from those who thought that boys could not be taught discipline by military drill without encouraging militarism, the movement prospered. Within ten years 600 Boys' Brigade companies had been formed in the United Kingdom, and many collateral movements had begun in the United States, the Dominions, particularly Canada, Scandinavia and other parts of the world. At night B.B. bagpipes and brass instruments disturbed the quiet of residential streets throughout the land and on Sundays parades of boys, wearing jauntily perched pill-box hats, belts and haversacks, and carrying hymn books instead of dummy rifles, were to be seen in most towns.

The Boy's Brigade Inspection, Burnbank Sports Ground, Great Western Road. Spring Holiday, 1886.

QUIZ

In more recent times newer youth organizations have caught the public eye, but the continued strength of the pioneering body was shown in its Jubilee Parade, held in Glasgow in 1933, when 30,000 boys from all districts in the British Isles took part, besides representatives from many other countries. At that time the British

120

membership of the Boys' Brigade—which had amalgamated with the Boys' Life Brigade in 1926—was 112,000. It is now in the region of 134,000.

Getting about the City

Among the new things which came to Glasgow towards the end of the Victorian era were electric trams, electric lights and electric telephones —and, so far as the 'nineties were concerned, the most important were the electric trams.

As Glasgow grew bigger in size and people began to live farther away from factories, offices, shops and theatres, they were confronted with a new problem—how to get about. They were much more accustomed to walking than today but there can have been little enthusiasm for walking between, say, Govan, Paisley, or Rutherglen

The horse trams had made their appearance in Argyle Street by the early 1880s.

Bonnet Monday in Buchanan Street.

QUIZ

Farmers' Wednesday in St. Enoch Square.

QUIZ

Saturday night in the Trongate.

QUIZ

*This sketch, drawn in January, 1892,
depicts the muddy state of Buchanan Street.*

QUIZ

and Glasgow every day, particularly in the winter. Wealthy people
could, of course, follow the example set by the tobacco lords and
have their own carriages and attendants. Indeed, much ostentation
went on throughout the Victorian era about having a carriage of one's
own, and perhaps it still persists in showing off sumptuous automobiles. But most people had to get their transport in some other
way. Coaches for hire—one-horse cabriolets—first appeared on the
Glasgow streets in the eighteen-twenties, and the first omnibuses
came in 1834. They ran between the harbours on the river and on
the canals, Broomielaw, Port Dundas and Port Eglinton. In the early
'forties the noddies (with four wheels) and minibuses (with two

The Great Western Road Sunday Parade was still a great occasion in the 1890s.

Morning in Buchanan Street in the 1890s.

wheels) made their appearance. Each was drawn by one horse, and sometimes either these horses or their drivers indulged in reckless speeding. The magistrates thought it necessary in 1845 to draw up the first regulations for street transport.

Although the pioneer was Robert Frame, who in this year began to run buses between Bridgeton and Anderston, the outstanding figure in providing the Glaswegian with the means of getting about was Andrew Menzies (1822–73), who from 1849 onwards took over many of the city and suburban omnibuses, then running not only between places in the city but between places on the outskirts, such as Partick and Rutherglen. His most determined competitor, Duncan Macgregor, shared one idea with him. They painted their

A three-horse bus
at the Royal Crescent terminus in the late 1840s.
The artist was looking across Sauchiehall Street to
the hilly ground converted into the West End Park in 1853.

buses with the appropriate tartan. The buses were dreadfully un-comfortable things to travel in—outside the passenger was exposed to the weather, and inside, where the ladies travelled, there was no ventilation, and on wet days the floor was covered with damp, smelly straw.

Gradually the old cabs gave way to hansoms and four-wheelers, but so effectively did Menzies organize his buses and later his tramcars, that most Glasgow people travelled, as they do today, with their fellow-men in public vehicles. By the eighteen-eighties the interval between his buses on the Glasgow Cross and Anderston route was only $2\frac{1}{2}$ minutes. For many decades, however, a great deal of the travelling was done on the local railway lines—it is perhaps not fully realized even today what a large percentage of Glasgow people went to their work by train. Others were taking to bicycles—and for the rest, they did what their fathers and grandfathers had done. They walked.

Menzies was an enterprising man with a good publicity sense. In the 'fifties he ran 'holiday coaches from Glasgow to Glens Coe and Orchy and between Loch Lomond and Oban'. He was one of the first to realize how tram-lines would enable buses to run more quickly and, in particular, more smoothly. The laying of these rails in Glasgow streets was one of the most revolutionary steps in the city's history. It was, needless to say, warmly opposed. It was carried out in 1869–70 by the Corporation for the Glasgow Tramway and Omnibus Co., which Menzies had formed, with himself as managing director. The first tram, which was painted with the Menzies tartan, ran from St. George's Cross to Eglinton Toll on 19th August, 1872. But Andrew Menzies was not to see much of this revolutionary devel-opment, because he died the following year. The master mind behind the evolution of the tramway system was a solicitor, John Duncan.

In 1894 the Corporation did not renew the company's lease—a much-debated decision—and began to operate the system itself. At

A tartan bus in the 1860s at the terminus (Kelvingrove Street).
The West End Park appears to have extended to Sauchiehall Street at this time.

QUIZ

On the Cathcart Circle in the 1890s.

124

that time the company was carrying 54 million passengers a year. It owned 3,500 horses—stabling was an undertaking in itself—and the service was so frequent that the claim was made that on most of the routes 'at least one tramcar is always in sight'.

The new service functioned efficiently on its first day, 1st July, 1894. The citizens were delighted, and for a few days the takings were enormous. 'The cars were large and clean, the horses in their prime. The hours of drivers and conductors were reduced to a daily average of ten. The fares were, in many cases, reduced by half, and a half-penny fare was introduced for short journeys In these circumstances

Few drawings give such an impression of Glasgow's bustling life in the 1890s as this very detailed sketch of the Trongate.

125

Passengers on the
Parkhead and Kelvinside trams.

I.—FROM THE COUNTRY.

II.—TO THE MANNER BORN.

Crossing Buchanan Street in the 1890s.

*In this splendid photograph taken by T. & R. Annan
during the sunny summer of 1892,
there are many details of interest
to the student of Old Glasgow—
the horse-drawn traffic, for instance,
and the spire of St. Enoch Church
can be seen opposite the St. Enoch Hotel.*

HARVEY LAMBETH.

THE BAILIE

*The last car to Maryhill—
and the difficulty of arriving thereon with both feet.*

The small ship on the left is a 'Clutha'. These steamers operated to 1903, with in the peak year, 1891, 3½ million passengers.

P. TURNER

This splendid photograph was taken for the 'Glasgow Herald'
on the night when the Whiteinch Ferry made its last journey across the Clyde.
After the Clyde Tunnel had been opened, little use was being made of the ferry.

the inducement to walk practically vanished.' In 1900 the Glasgow Corporation tramways carried so many passengers that their numbers were one-fifth of the total number of passengers carried on all of the tramways of England and Wales. Arrangements were then being made for substituting electric haulage for horse haulage, the change-over being completed by 1902. Two interesting points about the arrangements made by the Corporation were the use of colours in addition to name boards to assist the public in picking out the routes, and the dark green uniforms in which drivers and conductors were dressed. Both subsequently became characteristic features of the system.

Two other ways of transporting people were in use at this time. After the disaster to the Finnieston ferry in 1864 the Clyde Trust first introduced larger, steam-powered ferries, and in 1884 it began operating a dozen small twin-screw passenger steamers, called Cluthas, after the Gaelic name for the Clyde, which took passengers from Stockwell Street Bridge to eleven landing-stages on the way to Whiteinch, a distance of $3\frac{1}{2}$ miles, for one penny. The full journey was done in 45 minutes. There was, it would seem, only one dis-advantage. The river stank! These small ships are still recalled by many Glaswegians with pleasure. Several had remarkable careers after they had been sold, the service having been abandoned when the electric tramcars brought about spectacular reductions in the times taken in travelling to Partick, Govan and Whiteinch. Much later, in the nineteen-sixties, several of the ferries were withdrawn when twin vehicular tunnels were constructed between Whiteinch and Linthouse.

Extensive tunnelling was done in Glasgow in the Victorian decades for the railway and the subway. This photograph, from the early 1890s, brings out the major character of the project, especially as the implication is that the whole of Argyle Street was dug up and that, after the tunnel had been completed, it was bridged over before the roadway was re-built on top.

129

In 1896, the Glasgow Subway Railway Company made a pioneering effort by running an underground cable-haulage railway in the western half of the city. Unfortunately, snags were encountered in constructing the tunnels, and the company, having spent £1,500,000, was never out of financial difficulties. The use of continuous rope haulage was scarcely satisfactory, but it was not until 1935, after Glasgow Corporation had taken over the system and electrified it, that the Subway, now called the Underground, was accepted by the public as a whole, and became a paying venture.

The early date of the electrification of the tramway service gives an indication of the steps being taken in the city in installing electric lighting, although, as in most other British industrial towns where gas supplies were well organized, progress in using the new illuminant was rather slow. Indeed, those who wish to draw a moral might contrast the readiness with which gas lighting was adopted in Glasgow at the beginning of the nineteenth century with the dilatoriness shown about electric lighting at the end of the century.

The first buildings to be lit by electricity in Glasgow were St. Enoch Station in 1879 and the head post office, where the workers showed such a preference for the new system (to the open gas burners to which they were accustomed) that electric lighting was adopted soon afterwards for London and other general post offices. The pioneers were John Munro, who lit Lord Kelvin's house at the University, and Henry and Sam Mavor. Street lighting began with a fizzy arc lamp outside the *Glasgow Herald* building and shop lighting at Cooper and Co.'s store in Sauchiehall Street.

In spite of this promising start, however, street lighting was not put in hand until 1893. Even in 1901, almost ten years after Glasgow Corporation had established its first generating station, there were fewer than 3000 domestic consumers of electricity in the city.

The Amateur Soldier—'Defence and not Defiance'

By 1859 the country was seriously alarmed over the militant temper the Third French Empire had been showing since the Crimean War. The hostile Paris press published threats about crossing the Channel and planting Imperial Eagles on the Tower of London—this, incidentally, helps us in understanding our great-grandfathers' attitude to the Franco-German War of 1870, and, in particular, their failure to perceive that Prussianism was the danger.

Concern was once again felt over the poor state of the country's defences, and attempts were made to revive the Volunteer Corps. In Glasgow, during February, 1859, a meeting was held of all surviving representatives of the Glasgow Light Horse of 1796 (one member was present), the Glasgow Volunteers of 1803, and the Glasgow Sharp-shooters of 1819. They resolved to set an example to younger men by forming a veteran rifle corps to be designated The Old Guard of Glasgow. (It was subsequently merged in the scarlet-coated 3rd Lanark Volunteers, drawn principally from the south side—the west-enders preferred the less gaudy 1st Lanark Volunteers.) Great enthusiasm was shown for the new project, and few at first cavilled at the government's edict that the country was not to be involved in expense. Several corps were formed. They were grouped in two battalions. Most were associated with groups of factories, and the employers agreed to meet the costs. Everything was 'novel, unorganized and ill-provided', but by October sufficient men were adequately drilled and equipped to form a guard of honour for

Queen Victoria, when she opened the Loch Katrine water-works—the first public appearance of any rifle volunteers in Great Britain.

That the movement had a greater hold in Scotland than elsewhere in the country is shown by the percentages of volunteers to the population:

	1861	1871
England	·63	·66
Wales	·66	·62
Scotland	1·12	1·43

During the 'sixties and 'seventies there were various phases of waning and reviving enthusiasm. The government gave greater recognition to the movement, by providing better equipment, by instituting proficiency examinations and by increasing grants. In 1881 sweeping changes were made in the organization of the army itself, territorial regiments with distinctive titles being instituted and the Volunteers were linked with them. The two groupings at Hamilton were: the Cameronians (Scottish Rifles), with which the 1st, 2nd, 3rd, 4th and 7th Lanarkshire Volunteers were included; and the Highland Light Infantry, with which the 5th, 6th, 8th, 9th and 10th Lanarkshire Volunteers were included. Some of their drill halls are still in existence.

The coming of age of the Volunteers was celebrated with a review by Queen Victoria at Holyrood on 25th August, 1881. This was the notorious Wet Review, still occasionally mentioned in the Press. A

Charing Cross and the Grand Hotel, 1888.
The terrace in the upper right section was Albany Place,
and some of the buildings are still in existence
behind the modern Sauchiehall Street.
The tree became a feature of Sauchiehall Street,
and was not removed until the first world war period.
The two joiners in front of the military parade
had nothing to do with it, but, being men of determination,
they were not prepared to get out of its way.

T. & R. ANNAN

'loyal array' of almost 40,000 officers and men paraded before the Queen in pelting rain. At one point the crowd could endure the discomforts no longer and broke up, so that the rear battalions and brigades had to make their way to the Queen through a dense mob. The experience brought about the death of a few of the men and the health of others was impaired. But the rest were made of sterner stuff, and continued until recently to hold an annual re-union.

One of the chief problems which faced the organizers of the Volunteers was how to maintain enthusiasm through four decades while the country's security, though challenged, was never seriously menaced. When, however, after the first reverses in the Boer War, a call was made on the Volunteers, the response was magnificent. Eleven special serving companies were formed in Scotland. They sailed for South Africa in February and March, 1900. Further corps, including a Medical Staff Corps, were created in 1901 and in 1902. As a good many Volunteers enlisted in the regular army in the early days of the war, the number of Scottish Volunteers who fought could not be determined, but was put at about 10 per cent of the enrolled force.

MUIRHEAD BONE—SCOTS PICTORIAL

Glasgow urchins play soldiers during the opening weeks of the Boer War.

After the war the Volunteers were recognized as having a definite place in the defence system of the country and, in 1908, they formed the nucleus of the new and more highly developed Territorial Army. Few even then, however, had any conception of the millions of amateur soldiers the country would have to recruit a few years afterwards.

Saturday Afternoons and the Sports Mania

By the second half of the Victorian era the 'Saturday afternoon off' had been recognized throughout British industry and although shop-assistants, among others, had to work longer hours, even up to 9 and 10 o'clock—Saturday night became the busiest shopping period of the week—a sufficiently large number of people were 'off the chain' by midday to give rise for the first time to the problem of what to do with leisure.

Some factory hands were almost illiterate and, perhaps reflecting their factory conditions, turned to brutal pastimes, such as bare-fist pugilism, cock-fighting, dog-fighting and worse. But gradually these activities were canalized into taking part in and attending athletic games. Soon the Glasgow man became so accustomed to going to football matches that working on a Saturday afternoon seemed to him worse morally than working on a Sunday.

By the 'nineties ministers and others were alarmed about the new mania for sport—which, with only slight justification, they were linking with the falling off in church attendances—and were asking if 'the intellectual was not giving way to the muscular'.

The first organized sport in Glasgow was cricket—it was being played by University students on the College green in 1790—but that was largely an echo of happenings in England. The senior Scottish club is Perthshire (1826-7) and the oldest club in Glasgow is the University (there is a record of the two clubs having met at Stirling in 1829). Cricket even at Lords has a village-green atmosphere, and such an atmosphere is not found in many places in Scotland, and particularly in its industrial belt. Then the game is too slow for the young Scot, and it has certain traditions which do not appeal to him. The wet weather is against it, although that is scarcely an important point, since the game did achieve considerable popularity in Glasgow in those early days. The pioneering club was the Caledonian, whose field was off Great Western Road, but later three clubs became prominent: West of Scotland, whose delightful ground at Partick really is comparable to many English county grounds, Clydesdale (1848), the oldest club in the Western Union League, who began at Kinning Park but later moved to Crossmyloof; and Poloc, whose ground is at Shawholm. Although cricket has more supporters in the west of Scotland than is commonly realized—occasionally Glasgow produces a Test Match player, like I. A. R. Peebles—and a big match at Partick may attract several thousand spectators, much of the keen competitive spirit of seventy years ago is gone.

The National Game

The team game with which Scotland, and particularly Glasgow, is connected in the public mind is Association football. In recent decades football has been established as the most popular sport in many countries, notably in Europe and South America, and with amazing frequency inquiries show that the trainers of the outstanding Continental and other teams were old Glasgow professionals.

Why of all games this one should have fitted in so well with the Glasgow temperament can always arouse discussion. Poetic themes have been woven to link, for instance, the characteristic feature of Scottish play—dribbling—with the agility acquired by small boys while controlling rubber balls 'stotting' at queer angles off the granite setts of the Glasgow streets. Probably, however, a sounder explanation is to be found in the delights of being able to outwit an opponent in close, personal contact. Hence the brilliance of the Glasgow footballer's outfield play, and his proneness to forget that the object in the game is for his side to score goals, rather than for him to show, after having beaten his opponent in the tackle, how he can turn round and beat him again—a failing which has moved strong men in crowds at international matches to tears and lesser men to profanity. Then, too, it must be remembered that football is exceptionally well suited to Glasgow's equable climate. Rarely throughout the year is it too cold or too hot to play football in Glasgow.

Three clubs have dominated the development of the game

in Glasgow—and, to a large extent, in Scotland—Queen's Park, Rangers and Celtic. Each has had its years of ascendancy, Queen's Park having been the pioneer—they were founded on 9th July, 1867, with rugby and cricket clubs as their model. This was so particularly in the early 'eighties, perhaps the most vital period in the game, when 'legislation brought order out of chaos'. The importance of the part taken by Queen's Park lay not merely in their getting a fine team together, but in formulating rules, in refusing to play other clubs who did not adhere to these rules, and in having been successful in getting their way. The rules were similar to those being adopted in England, and were intended to eliminate tactics then connected with the Rugby code, including handling, carrying, hacking and scoring by touch-downs.

Today, Queen's Park are best known for the stand they have made against professionalism. The club did not at first join the Scottish League, because it savoured of professionalism—the players of a well-known Glasgow amateur club actually went on strike on one occasion for better pay!—and for ten years kept apart from it, until 1900. But the club's achievement in being able to meet professional teams and to maintain season after season a reasonably good place in the league tables is nowadays regarded as a notable feature of the world of sport.

In the early days most of Glasgow's football was played on two parks—Queen's Park and Glasgow Green. Both Rangers and Celtic had their origin on the latter. Rangers are the older club, having been founded in 1872, originally for men from one of the West Highland districts. Their first ground was in Great Western Road, in the vicinity of St Mary's Cathedral. Then they leased the cricket ground formerly occupied by Clydesdale at Kinning Park, and in 1887 moved to Ibrox Park, near the shipbuilding burgh of Govan, with which their name has since been closely associated. It was at Ibrox in 1902, during an international match, that the worst disaster

SCOTS PICTORIAL

*This drawing shows the worst happening
in the history of Scottish sport until recently.
It was at the 1902 International match with England.
Part of the western terracing at Ibrox Park gave way,
There were 23 deaths, several hundred serious injuries,
several hundred lesser injuries.
The extent of the disaster
was not appreciated by the rest of the crowd,
and the game continued until time was up.*

The Football International with England, 1900,
in which R. S. McColl scored his 'hat trick'.
The game was played at Celtic Park and,
as a tribute to Lord Rosebery,
patron of the Scottish Football Association,
the team wore his racing colours, primrose and pink.

in Scottish football occurred; but in 1971 an even worse tragedy happened, also at Ibrox Park, when barriers collapsed on a stairway causing 66 deaths as well as 145 other casualties.

The story of the Celtic Football Club is perhaps just a little less distinguished than those of the other two clubs. But, on the other hand, it is possibly the more human. Celtic are sometimes criticized as having been mainly responsible for attracting the southern Irish Catholic football enthusiasts to themselves, and so causing the northern Irish Protestants to link up with Rangers. But, while admittedly one or two points are difficult to explain, the reason for the establishment of a Catholic club in Glasgow is quite readily comprehensible. Many clubs were established by religious and other bodies in the early days of football—for instance, the records show that in 1889 Celtic met in a Scottish cup-tie a team called the United Abstainers—and, before the days of professionalism, most clubs were composed of people drawn together by a common interest. For many years relations between the supporters of Rangers and Celtic were not bad. The trouble really began, according to William Maley, manager of the Celtic Football Club, when the 'brake clubs became the happy hunting-ground for the gangster, and religion became the common battleground . . . After that some games were played in a vile and abominable atmosphere.'

The great event in Scottish football, the annual international

135

match with England, was responsible for the largest gatherings of spectators in the history of the world's sport. It has also been responsible for Glasgow having no fewer than three of the finest football grounds in the world. The first international with England was played in 1872 on the West of Scotland cricket ground at Partick. This was the occasion when the whole Scottish team was composed of Queen's Park players. The result was a draw. The attendance of several thousand spectators encouraged the Queen's Park committee to go ahead with their plan for acquiring a ground of their own. Since then they have had three 'Hampden Parks'—the first, opened in 1873, being near Queen's Park Recreation Ground, the second, opened in 1884, is now occupied by the Third Lanark club, and the third, opened in 1903 and extended on various occasions since, is the recognized ground for the international matches with England. In 1937 it held 149,500 spectators, which was then a world's record.

Ibrox Stadium is almost as large as Hampden Park, and is, in some respects, the better ground. On 2nd January, 1939, it accommodated 119,000 spectators at a Rangers-Celtic match, the largest number at a league match in Great Britain. The capacity of Celtic Park is about 70,000 and, odd though it would seem to those who laid out the ground, this is too small to meet the needs of all those who want to attend international matches and cup finals.

Following Edinburgh's Lead

Many of the theories put forward to explain why the Scot played such a prominent part in the advancement of Association football break down because they do not explain why he has taken no less prominent a part in the advancement of the older kind of football, Rugby.

Rugby, in the middle of the Victorian era was probably fun, but as a game it must have had limitations. Certainly a great deal of brute strength was involved in the terrific scrummages of the period. How much ignorance—or skill—was also involved, we today can scarcely say. But the modern game took shape only when the players began to pass the ball, and in consequence three-quarters got clear of the ruck. This 'passing game' had its beginnings in Edinburgh.

Rugby football was brought to Scotland in the 'fifties to provide healthy exercise for schoolboys, and was taken up enthusiastically by the Edinburgh schools, notably Fettes and Loretto. When the schoolboys grew up and went, as so many of them did, to Oxford, they took their new 'passing' technique to the university, where it became known as the Oxford game It was soon adopted by most of the leading clubs in this country and in the Dominions, and revolutionized rugby football as a sport and a spectacle. Nearly all of the Oxford men who brought this about were Scots.

The close link between the schools and the senior teams has persisted in Scotland, many of the best teams being F.P.s—former pupils. Glasgow teams were soon the equals of Edinburgh teams, and in the 'seventies, Glasgow Academicals were regarded as the finest team in Great Britain. In the 'eighties the West of Scotland team, founded in 1865 and second to Edinburgh Academicals as the oldest club in Scotland, began to win championships occasionally, and in the 'nineties Clydesdale—now defunct as a rugby team—had a distinguished career. Few Glaswegians really resented the building of the splendid ground for international matches in Edinburgh, at

Murrayfield, and not in Glasgow. Formerly these matches were occasionally played in Glasgow, including one at Hampden Park.

Amateurism

The Highlander has always been interested in athletics—running, leaping, feats of strength, and so on—and in the remote past the chief of the clan was often the one who was most accomplished at putting the stone—it may be recalled that Bonnie Prince Charlie won the hearts of the Highlanders whom he first met by his accomplishment in this art. Games have been held regularly in Ceres, Fife, since 1314; others at Carnwath, Lanarkshire, and at Inveraray, Argyllshire, are almost as old. They were, of course, more akin to the Highland Games of today than to the modern sports meeting, and the contestants were, as they still are, professionals. In recent times these games have been linked in the public mind with Braemar, where they were established in 1832, and subsequently developed under the patronage of Queen Victoria. In central Scotland, however, athletics were fostered by men with a different point of view, and the Scottish Amateur Athletic Association, which was founded in 1883, has evolved along approximately the same lines as the Amateur Athletic Association in England.

Many of the men connected with the Association in its early days were rugby footballers. Athletics provided them with a summer-time sport. Just as rugby football was primarily an Edinburgh activity, so amateur athletics came into being in Edinburgh rather than Glasgow. Indeed, of the thirteen clubs affiliated to the Scottish Amateur Athletic Association in its first year only two, Glasgow Academicals and West of Scotland F.C., were from the west.

Scotland has produced few really great athletes but many have been good enough to win British championships. Athletic meetings in Glasgow attracted more spectators in the 'eighties and 'nineties than today. This difference is partly explained by the popularity of cycle racing at that time. As in England, relationships between the Amateur Athletic Association and the Cyclists' Union, the governing body for cycling, were not easy, and difficulties over the definition of amateurism cropped up. Cycle racing was associated with betting—bookmakers conducted their business at what were intended to be amateur promotions, and, as happened in other branches of sport which attract large attendances, some of the competitors were admittedly receiving presents and expenses from equipment manufacturers. A split occurred in 1895, and for a time a rival body to the S.A.A.U.—the Scottish Amateur Athletic Union—operated in the Glasgow district in association with cyclists' organizations.

Clubs were founded in various parts of the country and training was organized, although along happy-go-lucky lines in comparison with those adopted by Americans. In the meantime, however, rugby footballers had found in golf a summer pastime more to their liking and, apart from Glasgow University Athletic Club, the leading Glasgow athletic clubs of today, such as Bellahouston, Maryhill, Shettleston, West of Scotland, Victoria Park and Garscube, were primarily clubs formed for cross-country running.

Two Native Games and Some Others

Although Scotland has done at least her share in developing these various branches of sport, none had its place of origin north of the Tweed. Undoubtedly the game which the world regards as Scotland's own is golf, and St. Andrews, in Fife, is rightly regarded as its birthplace. Disbelievers have attempted to show that golf was derived from some game or other played in the remote past—such as the ancient Dutch ice-game of kolf—but golf is clearly a game which could have been conceived only by the men of the east coast of Scotland—a game which seems so simple and yet in practice is so difficult, a game which has to be played earnestly and grimly so that it takes on the atmosphere of a religion, a game beautifully adapted to the needs of men who want to go away and play by themselves, and yet who need the personal satisfaction of beating a bogey, a game suited only to those capable of battling with wind and rain, a game fit only for those who have all the mental attributes except a sense of proportion.

Golf was certainly being played in Scotland quite extensively in 1457, for it, along with football, was then banned as distracting the people's attention from archery, on which the future well-being of the country was thought to rest. James I, the first of the Stuart Kings (of the United Kingdom), was enthusiastic about golf and, when he transferred his household to London on becoming King of England as well as of Scotland, he, according to tradition, founded the Blackheath Golf Club. From the beginning, however, golf in Scotland has been something it is not in England and not in the United States—a game for all classes. The Royal and Ancient Golf Club at St. Andrews, where the code of rules was drawn up, was itself democratic in conception, and the game first made its appearance in Glasgow over two hundred years ago on Glasgow Green, part of which was set aside for golfers.

Golf is, in fact, one of the chief games of the people of Clydeside. They can play for next to nothing on municipal courses, they can join clubs a few miles from the city with an annual subscription of a few pounds, or they can go to the Ayrshire coast, where there are world-famous courses—at Prestwick, Troon, Turnberry and Western Gailes, for instance.

Many of the middle-aged and elderly men (and, incidentally, some of the women too) who do not play golf, play bowls instead, and here, too, Glasgow is well supplied with greens and is the home of champions. Bowls is, of course, a very old game, but nevertheless the modern game of bowls is so largely a creation of Scottish minds that it can be claimed with much justification as a native game. Indeed, in 1892, when a representative body met in Glasgow to appoint a central authority to draw up acceptable rules, they called it the Scottish Bowling Association, under the impression that English and Irish bowlers would willingly come under their jurisdiction. In that they deluded themselves, but the code of rules, the arrangements for rink and single-handed championships, and much else about the game are largely Scottish in origin.

The hills of the Cowal coast have looked down, so it is said, on regattas for centuries. The two world wars brought the glory of the Clyde Fortnight to its end. The great racing yachts with their towering canvas are rarely seen in the Firth now. But many people still recall the crowds on the esplanades at Gourock and Dunoon to see whether the *Britannia*, the *Thistle* or the *Shamrock* would pull it off this time. Almost all were Clyde-built and Clyde-designed, perhaps by the most famous of all specialists in this field, G. L. Watson.

SCOTS PICTORIAL

Golfing types
drawn by one of Glasgow's most famous cartoonists,
Tom Gentleman, in 1922.

138

Except for shinty, most of the other athletic interests of the Glaswegians have had their origin south of the border. In some of them, such as boxing and swimming, Clydeside has had quite a good record. Glasgow's need for a summer-time sport, capable of attracting large crowds, has still to be met, however.

Greyhound racing caught the public fancy. Several new stadiums were opened, and some football parks were adapted to meet the needs of the new sport. There can be no doubt that what attracts most of the spectators is betting and, although attendances have fallen off in recent years, it is still true that quite a lot of Glasgow people take quite a lot of interest in betting.

The Firth of Clyde has been famous not only for yacht racing but for yacht building. In the early decades of the twentieth century a dozen yards specializing in small craft were located on the banks. G. L. Watson was perhaps the best-known designer in the world. This is one of his yachts 'Gleniffer', built in 1899 for James Coats. At 496 tons it was the largest schooner afloat.

The Victorians Entertain Themselves

One of the outstanding differences between the Glaswegians of 1887 and of 1967 was that, while the former entertained themselves, the latter expected others to entertain them. Our grandfathers and grandmothers had a great deal of fun, and they had it—at least, if they came from the middle classes or from the upper working classes— in their own homes. True, a good many theatres, restaurants and saloons were opened in Glasgow during the 'eighties and 'nineties but, as in London, their patrons were relatively less numerous than their noise might have suggested. The 'midnight son' who caroused in Sauchiehall Street was quite exceptional and hardly typical of his generation.

139

J. J. Bell recalled his boyhood during the 'eighties among the 'bein and douce' inhabitants of the rather well-to-do suburb of Hillhead. There were evening parties in plenty—usually musical evenings or carpet dances. Talent, willing talent, had never to be sought on these occasions, and often at least half the company was prepared to contribute to the amusement, the women by playing 'drawing-room pieces'. As James Bone observed, at a house (or office) party every third man would sing or attempt to sing—even allowing for those who slipped off to the billiard room, located on the upper floor of many large houses.

The houses in which these parties were given seventy years ago still stand, perhaps sub-divided but still occupied by eminently respectable persons. They are quiet places today. Not many children; fewer domestic servants. No itinerant musicians or noisy coalmen. But, when walking that way on a mellow Glasgow winter's night, slightly foggy, slightly damp, imagination may play on what was to be seen and heard there not so long ago—windows ablaze, shrieks and gasps as an accompaniment to vigorous dancing, shadowy figures moving in porches and back gardens, pianoforte duets tinkling out quadrilles and lancers, perhaps even a quartette rendering the 'River of Years'.

Down Town in the 'Nineties

Glasgow had a few enthusiastic playgoers in the 'fifties and 'sixties, but the only resort regularly open to them was that rather second-rate Theatre Royal in Dunlop Street. With its destruction by fire in 1863, the old theatrical world of the city came to its end. Railway developments in connection with St. Enoch Station ruled out the reconstruction of the Royal, and in 1869 Messrs. Glover and Francis took over a music-hall, the Royal Coliseum built six years before

Glasgow's historic Theatre Royal was in Dunlop Street—one of the railway bridges on which St. Enoch Station was built replaced it. It was destroyed by fire on the last night of the pantomime in 1862. The Theatre's existence covered no fewer than 80 years. Most of the leading British actors and actresses over many decades appeared on its stage, and it was probably more loved by the people of Glasgow than any other theatre, before or since.

T. & R. ANNAN

There were still plenty of street musicians
in Glasgow in 1896.

in Cowcaddens Street, and called it the Theatre Royal. It too was
burned down, in 1879. Three years later it was reopened, only to be
badly damaged again by fire in 1895. Some months afterwards it
began its new career and survived until the nineteen-fifties, when it was
acquired by Scottish Television. The famous company, Howard and
Wyndham, founded by two actors, had its beginnings in the Theatre
Royal although they entered management first by buying an
Edinburgh theatre. They also became lessees of the Royalty Theatre
in Sauchiehall Street.

The other theatres, the Royal Princess's and the Grand, both
specialized in melodrama except at pantomime time. The leading
theatre of varieties was the Gaiety, advertised as the 'safest theatre in
Glasgow'. There were many other music halls in the city, most of
them small, and some just glorified public houses. Hengler's Cirque
was located in Wellington Street, on the site of the present post
office, and Newsome's Hippodrome and Circus was in Ingram
Street, near High Street.

It was in 1884 that a disaster happened in a small music hall—
the Star in Partick—which led to the introduction of stringent by-
laws. A cry of fire caused a stampede in which 14 people were killed
and 18 badly injured.

It is instructive to learn from this sketch
(22nd July, 1881) how estimable
and culturally-minded citizens
reacted to the first appearance
of Sarah Bernhardt in the Gaiety Theatre
(at special prices!).

141

The Gay Nineties in Glasgow
at the time of the opening of the
Empire Music-Hall.
It was considerably altered in the early 1930s,
and a new entrance built nearer Renfield Street,
but the fabric of the older theatre was retained.

At the end of the century the Glasgow theatres were: the Royalty (later the Lyric), home of comic opera and musical burlesque, then giving way to musical comedy; the Royal, described as the city's leading playhouse; the Grand, in Cowcaddens, where the west end went for its blood and thunder (burned down in 1917 and rebuilt as a cinema); the Royal Princess's for long *the* home of Glasgow pantomime and holder of a record run of twenty-two weeks; the Queen's Theatre, formerly the People's Palace, where the east end went for a noisy night out; the Scotia Music-Hall (later the Metropole); the Gaiety Music-Hall (being rebuilt at that time as the Empire); the Britannia, a tough music-hall near Glasgow Cross; and several other music-halls, including the Lyceum (at Govan) and the Tivoli (at Anderston). There were also Hengler's Circus (owned at that time by the Pooles), the Zoo-Circus (in Cowcaddens), and the Panorama (on the site of the present Regal Cinema, in Sauchiehall Street).

There were the last survivors of the penny geggies. They were still flourishing in the eighteen-eighties but were too unsophisticated to appeal in the Gay Nineties. They were little more than sheds with benches or hard seats. They specialized in 'adaptations' of current and famous plays. Horace Fellowes wrote that in his early youth he had been the violinist in an orchestra of three playing in a penny geggie in Clyde Street. "The company could go along to a play at one of the theatres, pick it up without benefit of script and produce it two days later."

D. SMALL

The orchestra at Mumford's 'geggie'
at the foot of Saltmarket, playing the audience in.
Many Glasgow people made their first acquaintance
with the theatre at Mumford's—
and that was something,
even if the fare was heavy melodrama.

142

There was much amateur talent and it had plenty of opportunities for expressing itself, not only at smoking concerts, soirees and amateur theatrical productions but at charity concerts. These were held during nine months of the year and for many purposes, such as sending a family to America. Competitions were frequent. There was keen rivalry between different parts of the town, and massive silver cups were awarded (and usually pawned the next day, to be used soon after for another competition). Most prizes never amounted to much more, however, than Balmoral bonnets and currant buns.

The Scotch comics had their beginnings in these concerts. W. D. Cocker wrote of them, 'they did not emblazon their names on the scroll of fame as an imposing galaxy of stars did later. They may have been equally talented—as a small boy I thought them uproariously funny—but they did not achieve more than a local reputation and too frequently a 'gey scrimp' measure of applause'. On Fridays the popular music-halls held amateur night, at which the behaviour of the audience seems at times to have been riotous. Jack Buchanan, the Glasgow Academy boy, made his first appearances on these occasions at the Panopticon, which must have been quite an experience. But before him were the first Scotch comics to make the grade—J. B. Preston, a gloomy comedian with a stentorian

The 'Scotch Comic' was late in turning professional.
The first Glasgow man to establish a reputation
was J. C. Macdonald,
to whom Harry Lauder paid tribute
as one of the men who had shaped his career.
His practice was to book a large hall
(here the City Hall in September, 1892)
and to engage other turns
to supplement his character studies.
Four are shown in the drawing.

QUIZ

AND SINGS
'I FEEL SAE AWFU' HAPPY.'

VIOLIN RECITAL BY THE GEDDES FAMILY.

MR W. F. FRAME AND SOME OF HIS CHARACTERS.

AND IMPERSONATES 'GENERAL JOCK.'

HE GIVES US 'TA-RA-RA-BOOM-DE-AY' (PARODY.)

IF YOU WANT TO GET YOUR HAIR CUT.

HERR B. SLOMAN. THE MAN BIRD.

MUSICAL DIRECTOR MR J^{AS} BOOTH

AGENT IN ADVANCE

MR MALCOLM MILLER.

JAPANESE ENTERTAINMENT BY KI-KI AND KO-KO

THE KORRIES MUSICAL ECCENTRICS. EDITH AND ERNEST

J.M.H.

TRIO - M^{DME} CRAIGIE, MR BOWIE, MISS ARNOLD.

QUIZ

J. C. Macdonald's rival was W. F. Frame,
seen here in the Queen's Rooms with his 'concert party'.
He made a fair reputation in English Music-Halls
as the 'Man U Know',
but his accent was considered too broad
for him to become a serious competitor of Harry Lauder.
The Queen's Rooms in the Park district were built in 1857,
but have not been used for entertainments
since the end of the first world war.

voice, J. C. Macdonald and W. F. Frame, who was acknowledged by Harry Lauder as his mentor.

Another star of the period was J. G. Burns who became the world's champion clog dancer in 1898. It was claimed that in the period 1870-1900 Glasgow produced more singers, dancers and song writers for the variety profession than any other city in the British Isles. The leading song writer, Jimmy Curran, was paid miserably by modern standards.

J. J. Bell wrote of the orchestral concerts of the 'eighties, transferred by his time from the City Hall to St. Andrew's Hall. He sat in a shilling seat on Saturday night. Each New Year's Day he went at noon with his family to the Choral Union's rendering of the *Messiah*. He also went to the 'bursts', organized by the Temperance Movement on Saturday afternoons. There he might hear the Pollokshields Philharmonic Orchestra or, in more popular vein, the Dennistoun Amateur Minstrels or their rivals, the Georgian Minstrels.

Few people now realize how great an influence the Temperance movement had on social life in Glasgow during the last decades of

144

the Victorian era. There was some hypocrisy, but the influence was for good and Glasgow was a more wholesome place in 1900 than in 1860. The movement had its origin in 1829 with an organization in Maryhill, out of which grew the Glasgow and West of Scotland Temperance Society; but it did not really make its presence felt until 1844, when the Scottish Temperance League was formed and Robert Kettle, a cotton manufacturer who had been a friend of Dr. Chalmers, became the leading advocate of abstinence. The society, which set out to attract people from the public-houses, particularly on Saturdays by holding cheap concerts, was the Glasgow Abstainers' Union. It adopted this policy in 1854. The desirability of providing an alternative to the pub was regarded throughout the Victorian era as a pressing need, and perhaps insufficient attention has been given to the fact that the problem was first solved, without the aid or encouragement of these well-intentioned people, in the early twentieth century by the cinema.

Other societies approached the temperance issue in different and, for the most part, less constructive ways. In 1856 a society for prohibiting the sale of intoxicating liquor was founded, and during the next decade its successor, the Scottish Permissive Bill Association, was very active organizing public opinion against the 'liquor traffic'. Another body with prohibition as its object, this time of American origin, the Independent Order of Good Templars, formed its Scottish Lodge in 1869, and opened over a thousand branches in Scotland. The Band of Hope Union followed in 1870, and set up over 650 juvenile societies in Scotland. On the other hand, this was the period in which songs were sung with gusto glorifying drink. Harry Lauder's 'Fou' the Noo' was soon to come into favour. So there was no unanimity of feeling in Glasgow about temperance.

Evening in Sauchiehall Street, 1897. (This drawing is by John Hassall.)

J. J. Bell made the interesting observation that there were relatively more people about in Glasgow late at night in the 'eighties and 'nineties than in the nineteen-twenties. Many banquets, dinners, balls and smoking concerts were held in the large new hotels and in the Waterloo Rooms during these late Victorian decades, and the magnificent Grosvenor Restaurant with its marble staircase, was being built to cater specially for social functions.

Most of the restaurants were still in the Argyle Street district, although the Bridgegate, where the first eating-houses had been established early in the century, was no longer in favour. But MacArthur's, with its red plush cubicles, automatic music and sixpenny ashet pies was in the Trongate, not far away, and so were Scott's and the Bank in Queen Street, Sloan's in the Argyll Arcade, Pie Smith's in Maxwell Street, the Silver Grill near the Argyle Street–Jamaica Street crossing—'where the French Renaissance began in Glasgow'—His Lordship's Larder in St. Enoch Square, F. and F.s and the Queen's in Buchanan Street, and the Corn Exchange in Gordon Street. These and various chop-houses, such as Joseph White's in Gordon Street and the City Commercial in Union Street, maintained many of the old traditions, such as serving sheep's head and pig's trotters on Wednesdays, and put in their windows such delectables as cooked sirloins of beef, lobsters and tubs of oysters. The Eagle Vaults, the Bodega and the American Bar in Jamaica Street were all much used in the 'nineties. The American Bar was conducted in proper style. It was 'where you got the bottle of Bourbon rye put down for you to help yourself, and pecked *ad lib* at cloves, olives, cinnamon bark and crackers'.

The growth of Sauchiehall Street as an entertainment centre

145

brought evening restaurants into being, notably Godenzi's, 'our Rathskellar', where late suppers of fish and pastries washed down with Chianti were served, and the restaurant in the Panorama, advertised as 'the place for a leisurely dinner'. In this district, too, some places had begun business on the lines of the Continental beer cellar, although they were not favoured by respectable people. The best known was the Garden of Eden—the Gaumont is now on its site—which is still spoken of by 'old-timers' because of an iron grille built around its stage to prevent inebriated and other patrons from clambering up from the floor. And, as the pubs themselves did not close until eleven, Glasgow might well have been a livelier place at midnight than it is today.

Most Glasgow people went home at midday for dinner. Such lunches as were taken by business men in the city were uninteresting meals. J. J. Bell spoke of his father having so little spare time, after he had written his letters and called at various offices to see the men with whom he did business—the telephone was in its early stages of development and little used—that he might not be able to eat until 4, when he would have a steak or a chop with boiled potatoes, perhaps followed by cheese. The Royal Exchange was no longer open from 7 a.m. to 10 p.m., serving meals of 'finnans and toddy'. In the passing of years the hours of opening were shortened, but even in 1887 they were 8 a.m. to 7 p.m.

The Glasgow tea-room arrived in the 'nineties, pioneered by two members of a family, the Cranstons, who had owned the Crow Hotel in George Square—where the Merchants' House now stands. Stuart Cranston began business in Argyle Street and in the Argyll Arcade, and Kate Cranston, one of Glasgow's personalities, began in Ingram Street. The Glasgow tea-room was to become famous. Many of the rooms were admirably decorated, and some had displays of framed pictures by first-class artists on their walls.

Light lunches have been served in these tea-rooms from the early days, and, by the turn of the century, according to J. H. Muir, the plain, unassuming Glasgow man had begun to 'tak his tea at denner-time and his denner at home insteid o' his tea'. Usually smoke-rooms were associated with the tea-rooms, and they were all-male affairs. They were packed between 11 and 12, and almost as full at 4, with

146

men who had slipped out to join their friends for twenty minutes.
How much business was done on these occasions, and how much of
the time was taken up with chatter, is itself debatable, but there was
no doubt that the Glasgow coffee habit—which spread throughout
commercial Scotland and much of England too—was responsible
for a very considerable reduction in 'drinking' during working
hours.

The self-service restaurant also had its origin in Glasgow. Over
a hundred years ago William Lang opened a new kind of dining-
room, whose customers were described by Neil Munro in *The Brave
Days*—prominent men from the Royal Exchange and its purlieus,
'even the Bains, Bairds, Dixons, Donaldsons, Ewings, Merrys and

*This Charles Rennie Mackintosh fireplace
was the main feature of the 'Dutch Kitchen'
in the basement of Miss Cranston's Argyle Street tea-room.*

*Here is a sketch made in 1903
of Stuart Cranston's smoke-room in Argyle Street,
described as 'the oldest of Glasgow smoking rooms'.
It will be noted that nobody
took his 'hard hat' off in these establishments.*

Lang's in Queen Street,
the first self-service restaurant, 1881.

Watsons,' all standing, balancing glasses of malt or milk, and browsing on assorted sandwiches. Shirley Brooks, while editor of *Punch*, wrote a eulogy on Lang's in the eighteen-sixties, which he published in that famous periodical. It is said that the 'honour system' of trusting the customer to state at the end of his meal what he had consumed—and to pay accordingly—began in this restaurant. The original Lang's was in Queen Street, but another restaurant was opened near the Stock Exchange, and this is the Lang's which was visited in late Victorian times by many purveyors from London, to see how the system was operated. Its site was nearer Renfield Street than Lang's present building.

As in most other large towns the Victorians fashioned the club life of the city, and it changed relatively little until the mid-nineteen-hundreds. But in Glasgow the largest and in some ways the finest of all the clubs, the Automobile (the Royal Scottish Automobile Club), did not establish its club house until 1909—and even then only in a small way. It admits women as well as men to membership —something which the Victorian would certainly not have done. It is unique, however, in being quite non-Victorian. The Western Club (1842) was perhaps in conception really late-Georgian. It has recently combined with the New Club (1869). The sites of both clubs were sold, and the Western Club now occupies smaller premises in Royal Exchange Square. The Conservative Club (1894) is impressive in size and jovial in temperament, while its appearance is not nearly so bad as J. H. Muir's description of it, as having the look of a store for sanitary appliances, would suggest. The Art Club (1886) has little to distinguish its exterior, but its lounge is the pleasantest in Glasgow. The most notable clubs to disappear altogether were probably the Liberal Club and the Constitutional Club, both founded in the eighteen-eighties. As in London and elsewhere clubs have changed their habits. Except for a little activity at the bar in the early evening, they are little used after lunchtime—and that gives rise to financial problems. Even the billiards and card rooms have become a liability instead of a financial asset.

St. Vincent Street 'Pavement Lawyers'
(This drawing was also by John Hassall.)

'The Centre of the Intelligence of England'

At a luncheon following the launching of the Czar's steam yacht, *Livadia*, in 1880, the Grand Duke Alexis referred to Glasgow as 'the centre of the intelligence of England'. This remark appealed enormously to the Glaswegians—though perhaps less disposed than today to resent the misuse of the word England—for it confirmed their assumption that intellectually they were ahead of the people of London, Manchester and Birmingham. And, as has been remarked

148

already, the average Glaswegian in the 'eighties and 'nineties really was better educated than the average Londoner.

Although most of the memoirs of University life at that time emphasize the importance of the leading lights in Arts and its associated Faculties, the great men of the College were really the scientists and the medicals. Some of the latter have been mentioned previously, but even Sir William Ramsay of Chemistry, Macquorn Rankine of Engineering and Sir John Harvard Biles of Naval Architecture must give way to the man who was probably the greatest applied scientist, and certainly the greatest physicist, of the Victorian era, William Thomson, Lord Kelvin (1824–1907). Professor of Natural Philosophy at the University for fifty years, he declined the Cavendish Chair at Cambridge three times, and brought to Glasgow almost every scientist of standing. He was honoured by many countries and, in 1902, became one of the original members of the Order of Merit.

He had an amazing grasp of physics—heat, light, sound, electricity —and coupled with a profound theoretical knowledge considerable inventive skill and remarkable mental nimbleness when dealing with mechanical contrivances. He had many contacts with shipbuilders and shipowners—he could not be accused of living in an ivory tower— and several of the problems with which he grappled were connected with the sea. Indeed, it was his work on submarine telegraphy which first made him internationally famous. He was responsible for many improvements in ship's equipment—in compasses, for instance, and in sounding apparatus. In his later days his steam yacht, the *Lalla Rookh*, was well known for the many social events as well as for the scientific inquiries which took place on it. His interests were not, however, confined to nautical apparatus. In his early days he did experimental work on electric lighting, and during his life his interests were to some extent diverted from thermodynamics to electrodynamics. In this connection he studied radioactivity and references are often made to his encouragement of the Curies during their experiments with radium.

Perhaps we may associate with the name of Lord Kelvin, which everyone knows, another name, Percy Pilcher (1867–99), which is almost forgotten. Percy Pilcher was a member of the staff of the Naval Architecture Department at the University during the early 'nineties. Becoming interested in aviation, he began to build gliders. In June, 1895, he made near Dumbarton the first flight in Great Britain of any kind of piloted heavier-than-air craft. He made many successful flights, improved the controls, devised the method of launching gliders still in use, fitted shock-absorbing steel springs, and

Lord Kelvin.

Percy Pilcher, a lecturer in naval architecture at Glasgow University, with his first glider, the 'Bat', in which he made the first flights in a heavier-than-air machine in this country. He was killed in 1899 during a trial flight.

designed the kind of undercarriage employed today for most aircraft. Indeed, he was the first to use landing-wheels. In 1899, while experimenting with a petrol engine attached to his glider, he made a trial flight at Market Harborough with one of his older gliders. A wire in the tailplane snapped, the glider turned over in the air, and he was fatally injured. As Nigel Tangye has written, 'had it not been for that accident, the honour of the first powered flight might have fallen to Britain and not—several years afterwards—to the Wrights and America'.

An architect's drawing of the new University buildings. The project for placing a clock in the tower will be noted. It led to much controversy and was subsequently abandoned.

Lord Kelvin was one of the men responsible for the transfer of the University from the High Street to Gilmorehill. The University has since grown greatly in size, its amenities have been immeasurably improved, its classrooms are larger, and its laboratories are more spacious. Furthermore, by occupying more and more of neighbouring Hillhead, the University has retained its unity—an asset possessed by few other large universities. The removal of the care-free student and his occasionally captious professor from the centre of the city ended most of the quibblings and feuds which used to make the town a little touchy in its dealings with the gown. On the other hand the University now seemed detached, remote, and this in due course led to the advocacy of a second university for Glasgow, but located near the city centre.

The buildings at Gilmorehill have a magnificent site, and no doubt a modern architect would have made greater use of the setting than Gilbert Scott. But the University, if undistinguished, is by no means bad, and its buildings are certainly the most photographed and sketched in the Glasgow district. They are massive and, while not free of Victorian embellishment, worse examples can be found, even at Oxford and Cambridge.

Perhaps the unique feature of the main block is the filigree spire on its tower. A controversy raged for several years over this tower, and those who have seen the architect's plans thank Providence that he was not allowed to carry out his own really dreadful conception.

150

A comparatively plain tower was built up to its battlements, and, after innumerable proposals had been made about how best to complete it, a tall spire composed mainly of ornamental tracery was adopted and finished in 1887.

As has already been noted, the Prince and Princess of Wales laid memorial stones at Gilmorehill in 1868. By then, construction was well advanced, much of the building stone having been procured within the grounds of Gilmorehill. The inaugural meeting took place on 7th November, 1870. Later, many extensions were made, the most notable in Victorian years being the erection of the Bute and Randolph Halls in 1888.

In 1892 the University admitted women to classes. Queen Margaret College, founded a few years before, became in effect a college of the University, Glasgow being among the first British universities to accept women students on equal terms with men students.

At the end of the century the University had 1700 men students and 350 women students. The total of over 2000 was thought large, but it seemed small in comparison with that of the men and women who matriculated after 1901. In that year Andrew Carnegie, the Dunfermline youth who had acquired great wealth in the heavy industries of the United States, set aside ten million dollars, yielding annually a return of 5 per cent. He directed that half of the income was to be applied to improving facilities in the four Scottish universities, and half to paying the whole or part of students' class fees. Afterwards more young people went to the universities. When, particularly after the first world war, other grants and aids to students became available, the number of students rose in some sessions to over 5000, and the University has since been among the largest in Great Britain.

The Dialectic Society, the chief debating society, is among the oldest student associations in the University, but it cannot rival in age the Medico-Chirurgical, founded as long ago as 1802. Dinners and balls —as distinct from 'informal hops'—played a larger part in university life fifty years ago than they do today. So did smoking concerts, and out of those held in the Scottish universities during the 'eighties and 'nineties came one of the most popular collections of songs ever published in Great Britain—the *Scottish Students' Song Book*. According to the men of that generation—who included Robert Horne, John Buchan, Henry Brailsford and William R. Pringle—they used to sing their choruses not only vociferously but tunefully as well. Incidentally, complaints in the press after every Rectorial Address indicate that these happy students were noisy on other occasions too. Indeed, several of them were fined in the Northern Police Court in 1896, following a clash with police, after those who had taken part in a torchlight procession had been refused admission to the Skating Palace in Sauchiehall Street.

J. L. Morison commented on the changing point of view from 1892. 'In contrast with the sentimental optimism of later student revolt, we were grimly rational in our social, intellectual and religious life. Innocent of hopes of any new Jerusalem of state-herded and spoon-fed masses, we learned to meet the world as individualistic, critical, hard-working servants of a community which we never called the State'. The professors themselves seemed men apart, imposing if isolated figures, most of whom continued the long obsolete practice of reading their notes at dictation speed—presumably a survival of the days when textbooks were too dear to be bought.

QUIZ

The Victorian students' liking for discussion reflected the general public's gregarious fondness for getting together in halls and listening to speeches and debates. Many societies and associations were formed and, as their funds accumulated, more than a few acquired their own premises. Some of their lecture halls are not very attractive by modern standards, and on the whole the modern generation does not rate them among its most valued heritages. Most are roomy, but they are dull, badly lit and badly ventilated. Their greatest defect lies, however, in their shockingly uncomfortable seating arrangements. It is, indeed, difficult to understand how our grandfathers could have sat through the long-winded orations of their day without marked physical discomfort. Perhaps they thought it worth while in the cause of mental 'improvement'. Much the finest of these buildings is that of the Institute of Engineers and Shipbuilders in Scotland but, although this association was founded in 1857, the present building is of relatively recent construction, 1908.

The Glasgow School of Painters

Next to her applied scientists the men who did most during the 'eighties and 'nineties to establish Glasgow's reputation as an

152

intellectual centre were her artists. Some decades earlier the first artists with national reputations to settle in Glasgow—Graham Gilbert and Daniel Macnee—were really members of Raeburn's great Edinburgh school, while Sam Bough, the best-known painter of the city, was an Englishman. Until the eighteen-eighties art in Glasgow was derivative.

The early attempts made by the Foulises to interest the people of Glasgow in the fine arts had been carried on by several others in the nineteenth century, although the artists did not always see eye to eye with their patrons, and on more than one occasion rival associations came into being. However, there were few years after 1821, when the first Institute of Fine Arts was founded, during which no exhibition of paintings by west of Scotland and other artists was held, under the auspices of the Dilettanti Society (1825), the West of Scotland Academy (1840), or the Second Institute of Fine Arts (1861), which later became the well-known Royal Glasgow Institute of Fine Arts.

Some of these associations attempted to carry on the work of the Foulises not merely by organizing exhibitions but also by acquiring paintings of exceptional merit. Remembering how the Foulises had

Muslin Street, Bridgeton, in the 1890s.
This was the outstanding feature at the Centenary Exhibition of the works of John Quinton Pringle (1864–1925).
Pringle, although on close terms with the members of the 'Glasgow School', was a figure apart.
He had a successful business as a craftsman optician and did not sell the paintings that he liked most, such as this one.
He is now described as a 'post-impressionist', and is said to have been born before his time.

The new Art Galleries, on the right of this picture, which opened on the same day as the 1901 Exhibition. The architectural theme of the Exhibition was Spanish Renaissance and was chosen to blend with the Art Galleries.

often been duped, caution was shown and sometimes suspicion went rather to extremes. This led to the loss of some excellent works of art acquired by Bailie Archibald McLellan. The Bailie, son of the man who is said to have saved the Trades House and the Merchants' House from extinction in the 'thirties after the Burgh Reform Act by developing their charitable and social activities, was greatly interested in aesthetic matters, and bought over a number of years a large number of paintings. Then he opened his McLellan Galleries in Sauchiehall Street in 1854, where the public could see his pictures for a small admission charge. Economically, this was scarcely a successful venture and, when on his death in the same year he bequeathed the Galleries and the collection to the city, many doubted the worth of the legacy. Disputes followed and, certain authorities having condemned the assemblage as containing many fakes, would-be purchasers were allowed to take their pick—and, as some of them knew their job, they procured genuine 'old masters' at bargain prices. Fortunately, the public attitude towards the collection gradually changed and, by the 'seventies, the Glaswegian was proud of his possession, then supplemented by several notable gifts.

So the great Glasgow permanent collection, now housed in the Art Galleries, began. It is undoubtedly the finest and most comprehensive municipal collection in the United Kingdom, and contains many world-famous paintings. A recent bequest, made by Sir William Burrell, a former Glasgow shipowner, has been valued at several million pounds. The location of the galleries in which the collection is to be housed has unfortunately been a matter of dispute over several years.

The Art Galleries collection is one of the glories of the city, but, so far as the world is concerned, greater importance might be attached to the rise of the 'Glasgow School' of painters in the 'eighties. Like most movements in art it began as a protest against

154

tradition. This particular revolt against the accepted standards of the Royal Academy of London—and, incidentally, of the Glasgow Art Club—had to take place somewhere, and perhaps Glasgow was the best place. The fashion in art in London and in the English provincial cities was set in those days—as it still is—by the Royal Academicians. The man whose works are bought by municipal galleries or by wealthy individuals is the man who is hall-marked. The Glasgow citizen is never much impressed, of course, by other people's appraisals—except when disagreeing with them—and he gave these young impressionists more encouragement than would have come their way elsewhere. And further, the greybeards of the Royal Scottish Academy, who had never thought much of the works of Glasgow artists—unless they had come in the first place from Edinburgh—were uninterested in the newcomers. So the Glasgow business man had another reason for wishing them well.

The Glasgow School of painters flourished for twenty years. It was not really a School, for it had no leader and no common idea, except perhaps in being influenced by the French School. Possibly Glasgow *Group* would have been a better designation. The members of the Glasgow School got on quite well with each other, and sometimes even assisted one another on their canvases. It is said that experts are able to detect more than one brush in some of the best-known examples of their work.

It is not possible to note here much more than their names, so we should call attention to a most charming and amusing description of the leading figures in the Glasgow School, given by Neil Munro in *The Brave Days*. The pioneers included: W. Y. MacGregor, a landscape painter who gave the initial impetus to the movement by gathering together men who shared his dislike of 'niggling finish and superfluous added facts'; James Guthrie, of whom a French critic said, when he was exhibiting in the Paris Salon, that they 'would gladly naturalize this foreigner so full of talent'; George Henry, who blended a vivid sense of colour with a liking for Oriental decoration; his *Galloway Landscape* was one of the most important paintings

George Henry's 'Galloway Landscape', one of the best-known pictures painted by members of the Glasgow School in the 1890s.

On a Clyde Steamer, July 1904,
painted by Leslie Hunter,
shortly after leaving the School of Art.

coming from the School, if for no other reason than for the controversy it aroused; E. A. Hornel, an Australian, whose style was so distinctive that the layman could identify his work at a glance; he was essentially a decorative artist in colour with a magnificent sense of form and space; John Lavery, an Irishman and a master of colour, who later became one of the world's leading portrait painters; in his auto-biography he described his early days as a poverty-stricken artist in Glasgow; Stuart Park, a latecomer to the School, whose 'soft focus' floral paintings with characteristic black backgrounds are greatly prized; James Paterson, a landscape painter, who was one of the first members of the School to win international recognition; Alexander Roche, who in his later days devoted himself chiefly to portraits, with 'a rare feeling for the beauty of colour and a peculiarly charming grace of line'; Macaulay Stevenson, a poet-painter of romantic, dewy landscapes; and E. A. Walton, who painted landscapes and figure-subjects in a decorative manner, with a 'fresh and delicious quality of atmosphere and light'.

Great men came in their wake—Sir D. Y. Cameron, Sir Muirhead Bone, William Strang and Leslie Hunter. The leading artists associated with the city in the period centred on the first world war were chiefly concerned with portrait painting—James Gunn and Cowan Dobson—and with commercial art—Martin Anderson (Cynicus), John Hassall, Maurice Greiffenhagen, George Whitelaw, Arthur Ferrier, Graham Simmonds and Warwick Reynolds.

The Golden Bough

In recent years the laurels have been worn by the Glasgow writers rather than by the Glasgow artists. Some of the leading authors, including John Buchan, Neil Munro, R. W. Service, J. J. Bell, James Bridie and A. J. Cronin, were born in the late Victorian days, but their work is on the whole more of the twentieth century, and is discussed later. With one exception the outstanding Scottish writers of the middle and closing decades of the nineteenth century, such as T. B. Macaulay, Andrew Lang, Thomas Carlyle, John Ruskin, Sir James M. Barrie, R. L. Stevenson, R. B. Cunninghame-Graham and Hector Hugh Munro ('Saki'), had little connection with Glasgow. Nor did Glasgow do much to rival Edinburgh as a publishing centre for magazines and reviews, particularly of the 'better type'. The *Quarterly Review*, the *Edinburgh Review*, *Blackwood's Magazine* and *Chambers's Journal* did inspire several Glaswegians to try their hand at editing periodicals, in particular the number of weeklies, bearing a resemblance to *Punch*, published in the period 1870–1914 was quite remarkable.

During the 'fifties and 'sixties it had seemed that Hillhead was going to be a literary centre but, of its promising young men, David Gray and Charles Gibson are now forgotten, and Robert Buchanan and William Black, who worked his native city into every novel he wrote, are little read. Most of the literary figures of the day visited Glasgow, however—nowhere were Dickens and Thackeray better received—and several followed the example of Scott in making Glasgow the scene of some of their stories—Sir James M. Barrie (who himself went to school for a time in Glasgow), for instance, in the first act of *The Little Minister*.

The outstanding Glasgow author of the late Victorian period was undoubtedly Sir James George Frazer (1854–1941). From Glasgow University he went to Cambridge and, after sampling several professions, turned to anthropology. In conceiving *The Golden Bough*, in which, by exploring legend and myth, he sought to give life a unity of purpose, he was greatly influenced by Herbert Spencer. But, besides being one of the leading savants of his time, he possessed that literary grace to make his work popular and so, by his 'generalizations upon his vast acquirement of knowledge, set the whole of mankind upon new paths of scientific inquiry'. *The Golden Bough*, originally published in two volumes, was so liked that Frazer had to go on adding to it and, between 1890 and 1915, its bulk increased to twelve volumes.

Of the famous men of letters who lived and wrote in Glasgow, Thomas De Quincey should be particularly mentioned. He had lodgings in various parts of the city in 1841–43 and 1846–47—according to J. A. Kilpatrick, in his *Literary Landmarks of Glasgow*, De Quincey merely kept books in most of these rooms and really stayed at 110 Rottenrow. Also Bret Harte, who was United States Consul from 1880 to 1885. Besides writing several of his stories about California while in Glasgow, he wrote *The Heir of the McHulishes*, in which he involved some of his characters from Roaring Camp in a rising of the clans, and a story about the city itself, *Young Robin Gray*.

The most famous Scottish cartoonist of the 1890s and 1900s was Martin Anderson ('Cynicus'). This is one of his earliest cartoons from 'Quiz'. Soon he began to draw his satires for picture postcards, which Harrap's published at six for fivepence. Most had a Radical slant. They were enormously successful and made a great deal of money.

Neil Munro represented as Para Handy.

SAINT MUNGO

I Have a Song to Sing

The Lowland Scot is too self-conscious to sing readily in public—
the Welshmen who accompany their rugby teams to Murrayfield
always impress the Scots in the crowd, not only because they sing
so well, but because they sing at all. Yet music has played an important part in Scottish life—chiefly perhaps in the Gaelic-speaking
parts—and the country as a whole is famous for the extent and
beauty of its folk-music. Much of the vernacular verse of the
Lowlands in more recent times has really been song, and some of it
has lyrical genius. During the last hundred years several collections
of old Highland songs have been made, and the work of William
Hamilton, Mrs. Kennedy Fraser and others in finding and
translating some of the loveliest old Gaelic songs, is one of
the contributions to world culture made by the people of the
west of Scotland in the last decades of the Victorian era and
in the Edwardian decade. Not only in song, however, has the Scot
created his characteristic music. Scottish dances and Scottish marches
are immediately recognized and liked throughout the Commonwealth,
Europe and the Americas.

*Patti singing in St. Andrew's Hall
in the 1890s.*

SCOTS PICTORIAL

The Glaswegian in Victorian days was fond of concerts, and, even
if the musical evenings in middle-class homes merely reflected the
ways of the English, the annual soirées which every industrial and
commercial firm gave for its employees had their own spirit, and
provided a field for native talent. The Saturday concerts, in the City
Hall and later in the St. Andrew's Hall, attracted large attendances.
At first the local orchestras were rather undistinguished, but they
prepared the way for the formation of the Scottish Orchestra in 1893,
'to foster the study and love of orchestral music in Scotland, and to
organize and maintain an efficient orchestra available for concerts
throughout Scotland'. The orchestra came into competition with
another, provided by the Glasgow Choral Union—successor to the
Glasgow Musical Association, founded in 1844 to perform 'the
Messiah of Handel on a scale proportionate to the greatness of the
work'. But an amalgamation was arranged in 1898, and the sponsoring
undertaking became known as the Choral and Orchestral Union of
Glasgow. Although concerts are given throughout Scotland, and

158

tours in England and the Continent have taken place, Glasgow is the home of the Scottish National Orchestra and provides it with its principal financial support. The orchestra has had distinguished conductors and leaders—Henschel, Wilhelm Kes, John Barbirolli and Warwick Braithwaite. The permanent orchestra numbers from 74 to 96 musicians and gives over 200 public performances a year. The musical director, Alexander Gibson, has been described as the outstanding British conductor under 50 years old of today. Glasgow also houses another famous orchestra, the BBC Scottish Orchestra. Perhaps, however, it is Glasgow's choirs that have attracted international notice—the Glasgow Select Choir, as long ago as 1878, and Sir Hugh Roberton's Glasgow Orpheus Choir, founded in 1906, which gave several command performances during its thirty years. Sir Hugh, although sometimes treated as a gifted amateur, did much to bring the Royal Scottish Academy of Music into being, and his services are commemorated there with a plaque in the Orpheus Room.

Two eminent musicians were born in Glasgow during the 'sixties, and both became pupils of Liszt. The better known in this country was Frederic A. Lamond (1868–1948), who was taught first by his brother, a Glasgow tutor, and then, after his exceptional talent had been recognized, at Dr. Hoch's Conservatoire in Frankfurt-on-Main. He completed his studies under, among others, von Bülow and Liszt, making his first appearance as a mature pianist in Berlin in 1885. His first piano recital in Great Britain was appropriately given in Glasgow in 1886, and later in the year he gave a recital in St. James's Hall, London, which Liszt himself attended. His subsequent career consisted chiefly in holding various professorships in Continental conservatoires and in taking part in tours to many countries. In his last years he returned to Glasgow, and, besides occasionally giving recitals, was associated with the Royal Scottish Academy of Music.

Eugene D'Albert (1864–1932) is still remembered in the city, chiefly, however, through his much-loved father, Charles D'Albert, composer of some of the most popular pieces of Victorian dance music, including the 'Sweethearts Waltz'. Eugene D'Albert went to the Continent for his training and studied under Liszt. After that, his career was very different from Lamond's. He specialized in composition, and wrote some of the best operas of this century. They were, however, German in conception and, although several have been performed in this country and in the United States, they have never really been popular outside the Continent.

Of the many other Victorian musicians born in the Glasgow district particular mention should be made of Hamish MacCunn (1868–1916), Professor of Harmony at the Royal Academy of Music, and Sullivan's successor as a conductor; and of Allan MacBeth (1856–1910), Principal of the Athenaeum School of Music (opened in 1890), conductor of the Glasgow Choral Union concerts, and composer of some of the later Victorian's favourite piano solos, part songs and cantatas.

The Hey-day of the Heavy Industries

The heavy industries of the Glasgow district were changed from the comparatively small undertakings founded by the Dunlops at the Clyde Ironworks and by the Dixons at Calder and Polmadie, to much larger concerns by the exploitation of blackband ironstone in Lanarkshire. Some Lanarkshire landowners almost suddenly became aware of the mineral wealth under their feet, and most of them tried to get their hands on this wealth with as little delay as possible. The outstanding example was provided by the Bairds—eight brothers brought up on a farm near Airdrie. They founded the Gartsherrie Ironworks in 1830, and had become, by the 'sixties, the largest makers of pig iron in Scotland. Everything they touched, it was said, turned to gold—and, incidentally, one of them, James, gave up some of that gold in 1873 when he made one of the largest bequests in Scottish history to be used in teaching the Gospel. It was for half a million pounds, a vast sum by modern standards.

Excellent profits accrued throughout the century, and bings went up all over the place. By the 'seventies Lanarkshire was mining 10 million tons of coal annually and, by the turn of the century, 17 million, besides another 5 million coming from Ayrshire and Dunbartonshire. After the 'eighties, however, the mining of ironstone did badly, and the Lanarkshire output fell steadily:

	tons of ironstone
1880	2,200,000
1890	700,000
1900	600,000
1913	590,000
1920	280,000
1929	25,000

There is still plenty of ironstone, blackband ironstone, in Lanarkshire. Unfortunately, it cannot be procured economically. But when the Victorian found that it was cheaper to import ironstone from Spain than to dig it up in Lanarkshire, he did not worry, for Scottish coal could be sent in the ships as return cargo, and so world trade would be fostered. Nor was he at first worried about the opening up of rival fields in Cumberland, supplying north-east England.

The west of Scotland continued to be the chief producer of iron in the United Kingdom until the last years of the Victorian era, when Cleveland took first place. But the production of Scotland's blast furnaces continued to rise until the nineteen-twenties, as is shown in this table:

	tons		tons
1788	6,000	1900	1,200,000
1823	31,000	1913	1,370,000
1843	250,000	1929	610,000
1861	1,040,000*	1937	495,000

This was roughly a third of the total British production.

In the early days of the industry the iron was 'wrought', the ductile iron being beaten, rolled, bent, twisted, welded and riveted to produce the many and varied articles needed for the new Iron Age. The factories engaged in this work were located mainly in the Coatbridge district. Steel is, however, preferable for most purposes to malleable iron and, when during the second half of the century new manufacturing methods were devised which greatly reduced its cost, steel rapidly ousted wrought iron. The Coatbridge firms were in the main unwilling to change their well-established processes— it is remarkable how conservative the most liberal-minded people can become after twenty or thirty years—and the new steel works grew up in another part of Lanarkshire, Motherwell, where the manufacturers relied from the beginning on imported pig-iron. By 1900 half the production of Scotch iron was made up of steel, and Sexton, writing

QUIZ

The Royal Exchange in its great days at the turn of the century.

on the wrought-iron industry, remarked, that 'the large forgings, which used to be the pride of Coatbridge, have completely disappeared and the mills now mainly roll small sections'.

A claim has been made—for instance, by Mayer in 1876—that the modern methods of manufacturing cast-iron pipes were evolved in Glasgow in the mid-Victorian period, particularly at the Phoenix and St. Rollox works, although subsequently the centrifugal process was developed elsewhere. Gradually a firm which had been founded near St. Enoch Square in 1862, A. and J. Stewart, achieved supremacy and became the largest manufacturers of butt and lap-welded tubes in Great Britain. In 1903 the assets of Lloyd and Lloyd of Birmingham were acquired, and one of the greatest industrial concerns of today, Stewarts and Lloyds, came into being. In spite of their developments elsewhere—including a partial transfer to Northamptonshire—they still have considerable interests in the Coatbridge-Airdrie district.

Although the steel production units shared in some of the difficulties experienced by the heavy industries in the years between the two world wars, the increase in steel production in Scotland has continued since the 'seventies:

tons of ingots and castings

1878	42,000
1883	230,000
1900	1,000,000
1912	1,400,000
1929	1,600,000
1937	1,900,000

161

In 1960, just before the new hot and cold strip mills came into production, the output of raw steel was 2,700,000 tons. The most famous of the Glasgow steel works are those of William Beardmore and Co., at Parkhead, developed on the site of the forge with which Robert Napier and many others had been associated in days gone by. William Beardmore, a London boy who had been brought up in Glasgow, entered the forge when fourteen, and rose to control its destiny. After 1879 he converted the works into a great concern, and in 1886 challenged Sheffield, then thought to be the only place in which armour plates could be forged. By 1900 the works covered 45 acres, and were described by Sexton as a 'steel works, forge and armour manufacturing establishment second to none in the country'. At this time the firm, under his son Sir William Beardmore, embarked on their policy of expansion—which eventually led to their becoming in 1918 the largest concern, as judged by the number of employees, there has ever been in Scotland—by buying Robert Napier's ship-building and marine engineering business at Govan and Lancefield, and by transferring it to Dalmuir.

The best-known name in the Scottish iron and steel industry today is Colville. David Colville founded his Dalzell Works at Motherwell

Locomotive design and construction was one of Glasgow's greatest engineering industries from the first years of the railways. The loss of virtually the whole of the industry since the second world war was generally regarded as a disaster for the City.

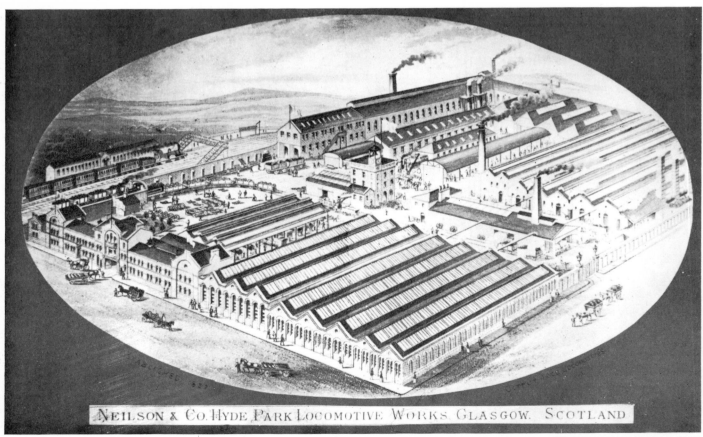

NEILSON & CO. HYDE PARK LOCOMOTIVE WORKS GLASGOW. SCOTLAND

in 1872 to make malleable iron, but in 1880 changed to steel production. His business grew rapidly and, such was the enterprise shown by these early steelmakers, David Colville and Sons had by 1900 the largest steel-producing plant in Scotland, employing over 2000 men. The expansion continued, among the works acquired being the Clyde Ironworks, near Tollcross, now entirely rebuilt, the Clyde Bridge Works at Cambuslang, laid down in 1888, the Glengarnock Works, in Ayrshire, laid down in 1884, and the Lanarkshire Works at Flemington, Motherwell, laid down in 1890.

Although the manufacture of cast-iron domestic goods—ovens, baths, rainwater pipes, and gas and water fittings—is most closely associated in the public mind with Falkirk, its importance within the boundaries of Glasgow is sometimes overlooked. One of the best-known of all Scottish manufacturing firms, Walter Macfarlane and Co., located their Saracen Foundry—originally beside the Saracen's Head in Gallowgate—at Possilpark, a northern suburb of Glasgow. They specialized in ornamental cast-iron work, and their elegant and astonishingly intricate gates, railings, balconies, lampposts, clock towers, fountains, bandstands—the dear old seaside bandstands—and other castings were in great demand during the last decades of the Victorian era and during the Edwardian decade, when they were awarded almost innumerable medals at international exhibitions. It is a quaint experience to be shown a typical example of French architecture—not necessarily in France itself but perhaps in Louisiana, in North Africa, or in South America—and to observe an imprint on, say, the elaborate railings of the veranda, indicating that they were made in Glasgow.

Walter Macfarlane's showroom in the 1880s. Much of the world's ornamental cast-iron work was made in Glasgow at this time.

A Pageant of Ships

During the last three decades of the Victorian era steamships were greatly improved in size, speed and luxury. The rise of the United States led to various shipping companies competing for the best 'ocean greyhound'; the development of the British Empire overseas encouraged the P. and O., the Cape, the Royal Mail and other lines to increase their fleets, new channel steamers were ordered to handle the numbers of passengers travelling to and from the Continent, the growth in the world's trade created demands for faster and more capacious cargo ships. In 1901 Robert MacIntyre was able to claim that, within the previous thirty years, the Clyde 'had contributed more famous vessels of the highest class than probably all the other shipbuilding rivers put together'. Further, the 'naval race' was on, and the Clyde was constructing battleships of the Royal Sovereign and Majestic classes, and warships of many other kinds. At the turn of the century opinion on the Clyde shared the fairly common view that the maximum size of the battleship had been reached, and that the future was with the fast armoured cruiser. Among smaller craft the Clyde had established its position as the centre for yacht-building, and palatial steam yachts were being commissioned by wealthy people who wanted to go to the ocean for change and rest.

The compound engines with whose design John Elder had been so closely associated, and which made it possible for steam to be used twice, were replaced by triple-expansion engines in which it was used for a third time—largely due to research work done on the Tyne, although the design actually adopted by the Admiralty was prepared by Dr. A. C. Kirk of Napier's. From this it was just a step to the quadruple-expansion engines, and Walter Brock of Denny's was particularly associated with the compounding. The effect of the

Shipping on the Clyde, 1898
from a drawing by the famous
'Evening Times' cartoonist, John Duncan.

stepping-up on the design of boilers was remarkable, and one of the most impressive achievements of the Victorian age was undoubtedly the increasing control obtained over steam. Dr. Kirk is due credit here, too, for he made some notable contributions to the design of the water-tube boiler. At the end of the century an initial pressure of steam on leaving the boiler of 180 lb. per sq. inch was demanded. Seventy years before, a pressure of 5 lb. was regarded as phenomenal.

It would be foolish to suggest that all of the inventions in naval architecture and in marine engineering at this time were made by Clydeside men. But a great many indeed were, and in the last decades of the nineteenth century the Clydeside designers were held in the highest regard. On the other hand, it would be churlish not to recognize the outstanding work of others, and particularly the Tynesiders.

A fanciful picture can be sketched of a pageant of Clyde-built ships sailing down the Clyde on the occasion, say, of the coronation of King Edward VII and derived from articles published then. First, there would be the ghosts of ships which had made history in their day but which had passed long ago into the hands of the breakers. At the head, of course, would come Henry Bell's *Comet*, and then perhaps the *Margery*, the first steamer to cross the Straits of Dover. There would be ships with remarkable stories, such as the long-lived *Industry*, a 10 horse-power steamer built in 1814 which continued in service until the 'seventies and the steamers with which 'dominion over the open sea was acquired', such as David Napier's *Rob Roy*, from the Glasgow-Belfast route of 1818, the *United Kingdom*, from the Leith-London route of 1826, and the first *City of Glasgow*, from the Glasgow–Liverpool route of the 'thirties. Perhaps, too, the *Sirius* would be included as the first steamer to cross the Atlantic. Although built in Leith, her engines were made on Clydeside. Some ships would be chosen for sentimental reasons—the *Leven*, for instance, for which Robert Napier built his first marine engine, the *Vesuvius*, the first Admiralty vessel which he supplied with engines, and the *William McCormick*, the first ship for which Randolph, Elder and Co. built the engines. Neilson's *Fairy Queen* of 1831, the first iron steamer, would be in the procession, and Tod and Macgregor's *Royal Sovereign*, from the Glasgow–Liverpool route of 1839, the first iron ship to steam beyond sheltered waters.

A proud place in the procession would be taken by the *Britannia*, the first ship of the Cunard Line, the pioneering steampacket fleet. Soon, however, it would be noticed that ships of almost all trans-ocean shipping lines had joined in the procession—Allan, Anchor, British India, Castle, City, Clan, Elder Dempster, Furness, Inman, P. and O., Royal Mail. There would be no end to their variety. In particular, the City steamers of 1850, *City of Glasgow*—the first transatlantic steamship built on the Clyde—and *City of Manchester*, might attract attention, for they were not only constructed of iron but were also screw-propelled. The days of the paddle-wheels were by then numbered, although the first Cunarder seen without them would be the *China* of 1862. Perhaps, as these ships are all phantoms, it would be possible to see through their shells into their engine-rooms, and Elder's *Brandon* would be commented on as the first ship effectively fitted with compound engines. The *Black Prince*, once the pride of the Clyde, an early 'iron clad' warship, would go down the river in the 1861 period, and beside her would be the *Erebus*, a remarkable armour-clad floating battery built by Robert

Napier for the Crimean War. Shortly afterwards some of the most attractive ships ever built on Clydeside, the China Clippers would scurry past, including the best known, the *Cutty Sark*, built at Dumbarton in 1869. In the next decade the most important craft would appear to be the *Hydra*, an armour-clad turret ship built by John Elder's Company in 1871, the *Propontis* of 1874 in which Dr. Kirk fitted a triple-expansion engine, and the *Parisian* of 1880, one of the first *steel* ships ever built.

Then would come the *Livadia*, the fantastic yacht built by Fairfield in 1880 for the Czar. Almost all of the leading naval architects in the world visited the yard during her construction, as it was claimed that Admiral Popoff, the designer, had, by making her 'turbot-shaped', succeeded in overcoming many stability and oscillation problems. However, the *Livadia* was doomed to end her days as a coal-barge on the Black Sea. The large number of ships being constructed on the Clyde at that time for foreign owners would be noticed. Warships for almost all of the maritime countries of the world, including the Japanese battleship *Asahi* of 1899, might be observed, and the seven ships built by Fairfield with which the Norddeutscher Lloyd began their career. Towards the end of the century, however, the relative increase in the number of warships being ordered by the Admiralty would be a significant feature. The *Ramillies*, the *Jupiter* and the *Terrible* would be there, as they were all constructed by John Brown's before the turn of the century, the *Ariadne* and several other first-class protected cruisers of the 1898 period, besides many torpedo-boat destroyers, and a remarkable medley of gunboats, tugs and troopers.

The largest ship built on the Clyde during the century would come towards the end of the procession. She was the *Saxonia*, built by John Brown's, and not handed over until 1900. She would be accompanied by several of the fine cross-channel twin-screw steamers built in the late 'nineties, including Denny's *Cambria* and Fairfield's *La Marguerite*, which could carry 6000 passengers. And then right at the end would come a special section made up of steamers that had won the Blue Riband on the North Atlantic racecourse. During the Victorian era this Riband was held by Clyde-built ships from 1840 to 1851, 1863 to 1872, 1880 to 1891, and 1892 to 1899. Napier's *Scotia* would be there, because, in 1863, she reduced the time taken for the crossing to nine days; Tod and Macgregor's *City of Rome*, which cut it to eight days; Elder's *Alaska*, which cut it to seven; and J. and G. Thomson's *City of Paris*, which cut it to six. The Fairfield-built Cunarders *Campania* and *Lucania* would be there too, for in the middle 'nineties they reduced the time to seven or eight hours over five days; but the five-day passage was not achieved during the Victorian era. And perhaps most significant of all would be the disclosure that at the end of the century the Blue Riband was not held by a British ship at all. The German-built *Deutschland* had—only temporarily—won the honour.

A New Generation of Mechanical Engineers

The Clydeside mechanical engineer of today is sometimes criticized for dwelling on such glories of the past. How much truth there is in this charge can be considered later; here our subject *is* the magnificent past, and we are fortunate in having beside us a detailed account of what the Scottish mechanical engineers were doing at the end of the Victorian era, prepared by Dr. Henry Dyer for the British

Three of the Clyde's most historic ships.
The 'Sirius', a wooden paddle steamer
little bigger than a tug,
was the first ship to cross the Atlantic
under continuous steam power.
This was in 1838.
The 'Cutty Sark'
(name taken from Robert Burns's 'Tam O' Shanter')
broke the China Clippers' record
in the early 1870s.
The 'Livadia', a yacht built for the Czar in 1880,
was perhaps the most fantastic ship ever built on the Clyde.

Association Meeting held in Glasgow in that great year 1901. It shows the Clydeside engineer, full of confidence and enterprise, striving to be first in making things for tomorrow.

Altogether about 80 mechanical engineering firms were mentioned, and half of them are still in existence. Many firms, now well known, are referred to as new-comers, and various groups of firms are mentioned as having made the Glasgow district famous for particular products. Most have already been noted in this book. Others included the manufacturers of sugar plantation machinery and machine tools.

The new-comers included two American concerns. The Singer Manufacturing Company, having in the late 'sixties decided to begin production in Great Britain, opened a factory in Bridgeton and, finding local conditions to their liking, prepared plans for building a great factory at Clydebank. This factory, dominated by an immense clock with a dial 26 feet in diameter, which became one of the features of the district, was opened in 1884, and within a few years was employing 7000 people. It is now one of the largest factories in the world making sewing machines.

In 1882, the boilers were ordered from another well-known American firm, Babcock and Wilcox. While installing the plant, the representatives of this company conceived an idea that they too should establish works in the Glasgow district. A temporary arrangement was made with the Singer Company for carrying on production in their premises, and within a few years 1000 men were being employed on a double-shift system. Their own factory was completed at Renfrew in 1897. The British concern has grown larger than the American.

Kelvin and Hughes were at that time Kelvin and White. The company had been founded by James White in 1849. When Lord Kelvin realized that he was capable of manufacturing the instruments he was devising in his laboratory, he became associated with the company. Lord Kelvin took out fifty patents, and the company were interested in most of them. Barr and Stroud, one of the leading British manufacturers of optical instruments, were also closely linked with the University. The firm had their origin in a response Professors Barr and Stroud made to an advertisement, issued by the War Office in 1888, for an efficient range-finder. Their first range-finders were made for them by Kelvin and White, but by the end of the century they had opened a workshop in Byres Road, near the University. Subsequently they moved their factory to Anniesland. Dobbie, McInnes had also been established by the end of the century—indeed earlier, for T. S. McInnes made his first commercial patent steam-engine indicator in 1886.

Other well-known engineering firms mentioned by Dyer were: G. and J. Weir, the pump manufacturers, whose '9½ acre works at Cathcart are lit throughout by electricity'; L. Sterne and Co. who had become 'the sole makers in Great Britain of De La Vergne refrigerators'; D. and J. Tullis, the laundry-machinery manufacturers, founded at Parkhead in 1891, who had just transferred their works to Clydebank to meet 'an ever-increasing demand'; Mavor and Coulson, the electrical engineers, who had recently moved to Bridgeton Cross, and whose directors were said to believe that 'there is no more promising field in the whole world for the applications of electricity to industrial purposes than that embraced by a circle of ten miles' radius round the City of Glasgow'; and David Carlaw and Sons, in whose Finnieston works remarkable progress was being made in

*The Umbrella
at Bridgeton Cross
in the early 1900s.*

devising printing machines for numbering transport tickets consecutively and absolutely accurately.

Although several of Glasgow's mechanical engineers of this period had international reputations, the most famous Glasgow engineer during the last decades of the nineteenth century was a civil engineer—Sir William Arrol (1839–1913). Beginning his career with general structural work in a small way, he founded in 1871 the business which is now Sir William Arrol and Co., and established works at Dalmarnock capable of handling large contracts. Becoming particularly interested in building railway bridges, he turned his attention to mechanizing drilling and riveting—so successfully, indeed, that part of his factory was kept busy making his patented riveting machines to supply most shipbuilding and iron-producing centres of the world. He was recognized as the leading British bridge-builder, and erected among others, the Forth Bridge, the Tay Bridge and the Tower Bridge in London, and also all the main viaducts and most of the swing bridges for the Manchester Ship Canal.

The Clyde Made Glasgow and Glasgow Made the Clyde

The rise of Glasgow was to quite a considerable extent attributable to its great advantage in having harbour accommodation for cargo and passenger ships only a mile from the warehouses of the commercial centre of the city. But the Clyde was, until the middle of the eighteenth century, just a small shallow river choked with silt. It has been dredged and deepened, and is to such a large extent man-made that it is now—between Glasgow and Greenock—an artificial waterway rather than a river. Its docks all had to be excavated and its quaysides built. Nature was far from kind, and although steam dredging dates from 1824, a very serious obstacle was found at Elderslie in 1854. A rock 8 feet below the water level, extending across the river and along it for almost 1000 feet, seemed to make further deepening impossible. After years of labour and at considerable cost, the obstacle was overcome, and by 1886 the rock was removed to a depth of 20 feet below the low-water level. The people of Glasgow could truly say that *they* had made the Clyde. During

169

little over fifty years they had dredged 58 million cubic yards of material from the river and its docks—by 1900 ten dredgers were constantly at work on the Clyde, and the sludge was being taken to the open sea in 22 barges—and had lowered the bed of the river on its whole length from central Glasgow by between 24 and 29 feet.

Glasgow's rights to use the river date from 1611 but the first Act of Parliament referring to improving the river was not approved until 1759 when the Clyde Navigation Trust was appointed. This body remained in being until December, 1965, when the Clydeport Authority was set up to oversee an area of 300 square miles, the largest of any port authority in the United Kingdom. Even in its last months it was considering further developments—a new dock at Shieldhall, new berthages at Meadowside and Yorkhill, and a new channel at Newshot Island, Clydebank (see map of the Clyde islands on page 2.)

The first of the tidal docks, the Kingston Dock, with 5 acres of water space, was opened in 1867. The Queen's Dock, with a water area of 34 acres, was completed in 1880, and large vessels floated where one of the largest cotton mills in Great Britain had stood. The Prince's Dock, with an even larger water area, was completed in 1900, and the Rothesay Dock at Clydebank was opened a few years later, in 1907, So prosperous was the harbour that, although 'mile after mile of wharfage was added and new docks were built, all that barely kept pace with the growing requirements of the shipping trade'. This is brought out in details of the increasing tonnage of goods being handled by the port:

	tonnage of goods
1860	1,200,000
1870	1,900,000
1880	2,700,000
1890	4,800,000
1900	7,200,000

Glasgow had, by the end of the century, become the third British port according to net registry—it was next to Liverpool and London. The leading shipping companies were:

	steamships	tonnage
CLAN LINE	41	80,000
ANCHOR	32	69,000
ALLAN	32	68,000
BURRELL & SON	27	58,000
MACLAY & MCINTYRE	47	52,000
CITY LINE	21	42,000
DONALDSON LINE	9	21,000
J. & P. HUTCHESON	11	14,000
	sailing vessels	
THE SHIRE LINE	27	40,000
THE LOCH LINE	16	24,000
THE PORT LINE	10	16,000
THE COUNTY LINE	9	16,000

Cotton's Successor

Woollen fabrics were made in the west of Scotland long before cotton fabrics, and, in spite of vicissitudes, the woollen industry carried on steadily, to become, in the course of time, larger and perhaps more important than the cotton industry, although the numbers of people employed in it seem small beside those employed by the cotton firms in, say, the eighteen-forties. The industry probably had its origin in Kilmarnock, where, as early as 1733, 'low-priced serges were made of our own wool partly for home consumpt and partly for the markets of Holland'. Carpets and caps were also being made, and in 1778 of the 146 looms in Kilmarnock 66 were working on carpets.

Carpet-making has since become the leading branch of the woollen industry in the west of Scotland, and James Templeton and Co. were, just before the outbreak of the second world war, the largest employers of industrial labour inside the city's boundaries. Fred. H. Young suggested that the Scots' hold on the industry was secured between 1824 and 1839, and that three inventions were partly responsible. Thomas Morton, a Kilmarnock engineer, found out how to make 3-ply fabrics, and they soon replaced 2-ply in carpet-making, not only because they were thicker and wore better, but also because they could be made in a greater variety of colours. In consequence the industry in Kilmarnock expanded rapidly, and by 1839 was providing employment for 1200 people. In Edinburgh, in 1832, Richard Whytock invented a new method of weaving carpets, dispensing with the 'dead frames of yarn' which had previously run through Brussels and Wilton carpets. His carpets looked rather like tapestry, and the manufacture of these 'tapestry carpets' became quite an important Scottish industry. As late as 1914 five Scottish factories were still making these carpets almost exclusively. In 1839 James Templeton found out how to apply the principle of chenille shawl manufacture in weaving Axminster carpets, and established the company which became the largest carpet-making firm in the British Commonwealth.

James Templeton's factory on Glasgow Green.
After endless disputes with the authorities
over its appearance,
the directors told their architect to reproduce a building
with an unquestionably high international reputation.
He chose the Doges' Palace at Venice, and there it is today.

In 1856 the Templeton factory was destroyed by fire, and production was transferred to a mill 'belonging to a cotton manufacturer who wished to get out of business'. This mill is still standing, although now used only as a yarn store. The growth of the undertaking led to the erection in 1889 of a second factory. As it faced Glasgow Green many discussions took place with the authorities about its appearance and the partners, having become exasperated at the frequent rejection of their plans, instructed their architects to copy the design of some building which was generally accepted as a masterpiece. And so the Doges' Palace of Venice came to be reproduced by Glasgow Green. This was the building which, as mentioned earlier, collapsed while being erected and caused the death of 29 weft weavers in an adjacent shed.

The policy of expansion was continued, more new factories being built. And here it might be appropriate to remark that one of the greatest periods of development was that between the two world wars. Probably the most reassuring sight in the Bridgeton Cross district during the depression of the early 'thirties was new Templeton factories in course of construction. Recently the company has built a large factory at the site of 'Dixon's Blazes'.

Comparatively few tweeds, blankets and scarves are now woven in Glasgow, although some of the older firms have survived, and the firm next in importance to James Templeton and Co., as weavers of woollen fabrics, is a comparative new-comer—William Hollins and Co., the Nottingham manufacturers of Viyella, Clydella and other yarns and fabrics. During the 'nineties they first became associated with the district when they placed orders for commission

On a clear July morning in 1905
T. and R. Annan took a famous series of photographs
from the University Tower.
This view, looking S.S.E., shows Kelvingrove Park
before it was divided by a thoroughfare, Kelvin Way.

weaving in Glasgow. Later they acquired factories, and eventually made arrangements for much of their weaving to be done in Glasgow. They have since expanded considerably in the west of Scotland.

Hand knitting was a source of income for the people of the west of Scotland over several centuries, and there are records showing that at the beginning of the eighteenth century people were 'extensively engaged in bonnet-making'. Knitting was gradually organized as a business, and by the middle of the Victorian era knitting machines were being used in making woollen underwear, as well as 'Scotch caps' and stockings. The foundations of the modern hosiery industry were being laid in the west of Scotland. It has grown since to considerable size.

The Chemical Manufacturers

The chemical factories, which were founded in the Glasgow district during the nineteenth century, were of two kinds. Some, such as Charles Tennant's own works (taken over in 1892 by the United Alkali Co.) and two other long-established undertakings, Alex. Hope, Junr. and Co. (1843), and R. and J. Garroway (1819), made industrial acids and alkalis, the raw materials which are produced in every large industrial centre because it is cheaper to make them locally.

Others made special chemicals—for instance, John and James White, founded in 1808 at Rutherglen (chrome and chromates);

This photograph, looking W.S.W., shows the site later occupied by Kelvin Hall.

Perry and Hope, of Nitshill (phosphoric acid and phosphates); the Cassel Cyanide Co., established in Glasgow in 1889, which revolutionized South African gold-mining—it is said that only five out of the fifty Rand mines could be profitably operated without the cyanide process; the Cartvale Chemical Co., of Paisley (distillation of wood to manufacture acetates); John Poynter and Macdonalds (animal charcoals, manufactured both in Paisley and in Greenock); and the British Dyewood Company, of Carntyne (grinders of dye-woods and preparers of liquid and solid extracts for dyers and printers). One of Glasgow's chemical industries—extracting iodine from kelp—not only came but disappeared in Victorian times, largely because it was found that potash salts could be imported at prices quite uneconomic for British manufacturers. The industry was founded in 1841, and by 1846 no fewer than twenty firms were engaged in it. By the end of the century their numbers had fallen to four. This was, unhappily, a foretaste of the future for many of these other chemical undertakings.

Much the greatest of the west of Scotland chemical industries —the manufacture of explosives—was, on the other hand, a comparative new-comer. In 1867 and the following years Alfred Nobel, the Swedish chemist and engineer, invented and patented dynamite—the first high explosive quite different from gunpowder— and then blasting gelatin and several other combinations. This placed his company, the Nobel's Explosives Company, in a dominant position for supplying explosives to the world's markets. In 1873 they selected the Ardeer district of Ayrshire for the largest of the works to be established in Great Britain. Its many sand-dunes were advantageous, because, by dispersing buildings over a wide tract of country, the effects of accidents could be localized. The presence of coal and iron near by, and the proximity of Ardrossan with its harbour on the Firth of Clyde were also convenient. By 1900 three branch factories had been constructed in the central Scotland belt, and the number of employees had risen to over 4000. So they were, even in those early days, among the largest employers of labour in Scotland.

Gains and Losses in the Industrial Field

Although Birmingham has been Glasgow's greatest rival among British towns, the industries of the two towns differ considerably in structure, Glasgow having been a place of large firms, while Birmingham was, and to some extent still is, a place of small firms. The multiplicity of Birmingham's interests is reflected in claims which have been made about the range of her products, but analysis last century might have shown that Glasgow's products were the more manifold. For this we have already suggested an explanation, the necessity for supplying ships with almost every kind of equip-ment. It gave the Glasgow manufacturers opportunities for turning their hands to an infinite variety of things.

As has already been shown, however, many of Glasgow's industries were in no way ancillary to shipbuilding, and a note on their condition—good or bad—at the end of the Victorian era should be included here.

The oldest Glasgow industry, soap making, remained throughout the nineteenth century one of the more important of the city's industries. In 1803 Charles Tennant had begun to make soap in his St. Rollox chemical works. After the sale of his company to the

United Alkali Co., a new soap-manufacturing company was formed
with the Ogstons, who were engaged in the industry in Aberdeen,
and a few years later a new factory was built at Renfrew. It was given
the old name of St. Rollox.

Little boot- and shoe-making survived, although two large new
factories were located in the district to engage in this branch of
industry, and the preparation of leather uppers and soles was carried
out quite extensively. Other branches of the trade took up the
manufacture of suitcases and furniture coverings, but it was for
leather driving belts that Glasgow became best known. Before the
coming of the individual electric motor in industry, they were used
throughout the world.

Printing and paper-making advanced with rapid strides during the
nineteenth century. Glasgow and Manchester vied with one another
as newspaper publishing centres, and the way was prepared for
Glasgow's unusual position in the nineteen-thirties of publishing four
morning papers, three evening papers and three Sunday papers. The
larger publishing and printing houses, William Collins, Sons and Co.,
Blackie and Son, and Robert MacLehose and Co. went ahead, each
generation adding something to their business.

Blackie and Sons' publishing offices
in Stanhope Street in 1892.
Their printing works, the old Villafield Press,
is immediately behind
and William Collins Sons and Co's offices and works
are diagonally opposite.

Several smaller concerns began printing books for London
publishing houses—Glasgow became one of the chief centres of
this branch of the industry, particularly for good-quality books—and
others specialized in printing stationery, cardboard boxes and posters.
George McCorquodale, an Argyllshire man who set out to locate
printing houses in towns likely to become railway centres, chose Glasgow
in 1854 for his second factory, and McCorquodale and Co. rose to be
one of the leading employers in the city. Some of Glasgow's products
were quite novel, and it is really surprising that this city, situated
in a Presbyterian country where Christmas has not been observed
officially as a holiday, should have become one of the largest centres in the 175

world for printing Christmas and other greeting cards.

Paper-making in the Glasgow district, although less in size than in Edinburgh, grew along with the printing industry to quite considerable proportions, and a novel claim made on behalf of one of the Lanarkshire mills was that it had become the largest manufacturer of rag blotting-papers in the world.

Very little is left of the famous Glasgow pottery industry. Ships brought the white china clay from Devonshire and had black coal as their return cargo. The original craftsmen came from the Netherlands, and Glasgow pottery was often described as delft ware.

OLD GLASGOW MUSEUM

GLASGOW ART GALLERY AND MUSEUM

The international reputation of the glazed domestic ware known as Glasgow delft was still high. Indeed, the annual import of Devonshire china clay through the Glasgow docks in the 1900 period reached 20,000 tons. The three largest companies were the Verrefield Co., the Glasgow Pottery Co., and the Britannia Pottery Co. They made 'ordinary white and decorated wares for table use, and fine china and ornamental ware of distinctive character, which had real artistic merit and for a time commanded high prices'. That was written in 1901, while the Verrefield Pottery was still in existence, although past its best, but while the industry as a whole was still flourishing— 'ships take Glasgow earthenware to every part of the world. It finds its way into almost every market, and is known over the globe.' One Glasgow firm made 20,000 'cheeny dugs' every week.

Several of the chemical industries were doing well, particularly the rubber industry, out of which came one of the great inventors of the late Victorian period, J. B. Dunlop. Son of an Ayrshire farmer, he was the first man to make a really practicable pneumatic tyre. That was in 1887. The cyclist benefited immediately, and within a few years almost everyone owned, or wanted to own, a bicycle. The later development of automobiles and aircraft was dependent on the pneumatic tyre, and it is appropriate that the company bearing Dunlop's name should now make large numbers of these tyres in the Glasgow district.

The paint and oil industry also went ahead in Victorian days, and attained considerable size. No fewer than 57 firms were engaged in it in the Glasgow district, 30 making principally paint and varnish, and 27 lubricating and other oils. This industry had an obvious link with shipbuilding and shipping, but many of its products had applications elsewhere, including the export market.

Glasgow, nowadays, is well known for manufactured foodstuffs.

176

Although Brown and Polson, the makers of cornflour and other commodities, are old-established—they came into being in 1842, and located their factory in Paisley to employ some of the unemployed men and women from the cotton-weaving industry—most of the leading makers of biscuits, oatcakes, confectionery, preserved meats and proprietary foodstuffs are of comparatively recent origin. More than a few had their beginnings in the very considerable number of small factories—often no more than back-room workshops—in which foodstuffs were prepared for sale to the public in days gone by.

The New Interest in Selling

During the last decades of the nineteenth century some keen young men began to ask themselves whether there was not more to be made out of selling things than out of manufacturing them. Sales methods in the past had usually been leisurely. Shops were clean and neatly if inconveniently laid out, with stocks plentiful but often in a state of confusion. Customers did not mind being kept waiting, for they were pleased to drop in for a chat, to buy anything the shopkeeper had to show, if it was to their liking, or to go away empty-handed if it was not. Most shopkeepers were honest, but unenterprising. There were some, however, who took in the gullible and gave them short change, and came out best in the bargaining which went on in stores where goods did not carry tickets showing their real prices. Then there were innumerable middle-men through whose hands merchandise passed, perhaps several times. Most of them did not exert themselves unduly to develop their businesses but each had a rôle to play in the passage of goods from manufacturer to customer. They made profits and led leisurely lives.

Actually, the movement for 'bigger and better businesses' had had its enthusiasts quite early in the century. For instance, William Dunn, of Duntocher, one of the prominent citizens mentioned by 'Senex', was among the 'progressive' shopkeepers. He was of humble origin—he began with a 'puny establishment' in Brunswick Street—and went on to acquire 'vast wealth'. He entertained lavishly—he is said to have given the best dinner parties in the Glasgow of his time—and was known for his charities. Perhaps that was why 'Senex' included him among the select few; but he had his defects, including a proneness to rush into litigation. Most of the anecdotes which have survived about him are scarcely complimentary.

The leading Glasgow shopkeeper of the next period was, undoubtedly, John Anderson. It is quite common nowadays for large stores to sell many different kinds of articles and, judging by the size to which some of them have grown, they have found it a profitable way of doing business. This practice is said to have been originated in Glasgow in 1845 by John Anderson, known as the 'universal provider'. A Perthshire man, he started in 1837 with a single-windowed drapery shop in the Gorbals. From there he moved to Jamaica Street, and included in his store a 'museum and waxwork, in which singing, entertainment and scientific lectures were given'.

He then moved to Argyle Street, taking the latest name of his emporium, the Polytechnic, with him, and set out on his bold plan of combining many different branches of trade under one roof. In 1849 he began selling books, and the Glasgow booksellers announced that they would boycott any publisher who dealt with him. But they did not understand 'buying in bulk', and he startled them by acquiring seven *tons* of the Religious Tract Society's publications.

In the following year he startled the grocery trade with a mass purchase of arrowroot. And in this way, coupled with frequent sales of remainders, he built up Anderson's Polytechnic, until it became the greatest store in Scotland.

An immense Jubilee banquet was held in St. Andrew's Hall in 1887 and was, incidentally, notable as the first large banquet in Glasgow to which women were invited. Among the many laudatory comments made on his career was a remark that 'the name of Anderson is not likely soon to disappear from the list of successful Glasgow warehousemen'. Less than fifty years later, however, the huge business was sold, the building pulled down section by section and replaced by an even larger building—in concrete—bearing quite a different name, Lewis's.

During the second half of the Victorian era the most successful men among the Glasgow distributors were probably the warehousemen. In the days before national sufficiency had been thought of, an almost insatiable demand came from the new countries, including those who were members of the Empire, for soft goods, furniture, household articles and many other things which they did not make for themselves. The Glasgow warehousemen used their opportunities well. They had the large industrial resources of the west of Scotland to call on, and the ships were at their door. They sent immense quantities of goods abroad, and were paid in part with the raw and other materials which their vessels brought back. During the 'eighties it was said of one Glasgow firm that, if they chose to call in all the money they were owed in Canada, they would have upset the financial stability of that Dominion. South Africa, too, was heavily involved with the Glasgow companies.

The leading families engaged in the business were the Campbells and the Arthurs. The firm of J. and W. Campbell was founded in 1817 by two young Stirlingshire farmers, James and William, who opened a small drapery business in the Saltmarket, chiefly for supplying handkerchiefs and pinafores to basket-women and hawkers. Soon they went into the retail and wholesale business in Candleriggs, where they set themselves against 'prigging'—that is to say, they put a price on every article, and would not make any abatement from it. So successful were their methods that by 1872, according to Jeans, 'a child of tender years can now be entrusted to make a purchase without the slightest risk of being overcharged or imposed upon'. They transferred their wholesale business in 1856 to Ingram Street, where it grew to very considerable size.

The most prominent member of the company in its early days was James Campbell (1790–1874), later Sir James Campbell, Lord Provost in the early 'forties. One of his sons, Henry, married a daughter of Henry Bannerman, a member of the leading firm of Manchester wholesalers, and by deed poll changed his name to Campbell-Bannerman. Early in the twentieth century, he became the first of Glasgow's two comparatively recent Prime Ministers.

James Arthur (1819–85), who founded Arthur and Co., was a Paisley man who showed extraordinary enterprise in opening up new markets. His statue was erected by his employees in the Cathedral Square. His son, Lord Glenarthur, was, however, partly through his political activities, the better known outside Glasgow. The firm still occupy their site in Queen Street, although they lost quite a considerable part of the original building during an air raid in 1940.

Glasgow warehousemen still send their soft goods to places throughout the world, but their representatives can no longer be

Sir Henry Campbell-Bannerman
(loquitor) "What a terrible time
I have had."

Glasgow has had two Prime Ministers in this century,
the first being Sir Henry Campbell-Bannerman,
a partner of J. & W. Campbell, warehousemen.
He was head of the Liberal Government after the Boer War.
This cartoon was drawn for 'The Bailie' in 1905
shortly after his appointment.

J. W. PHILLIPS

This drawing is from a little-known book, 'Glasgow in 1909'
and was sketched at the steps of the Royal Exchange.

regarded, as they were eighty years ago, as 'ambassadors of trade
and good-will with our kinsmen overseas'. Indeed, many are more
concerned with supplying the retail trade in the home market than
with adventuring into markets abroad.

The most famous figure in the history of the Glasgow distributive
trade was Sir Thomas J. Lipton (1850–1931). He was the son of
Ulster people who, during the 'hungry 'forties', had returned to
Scotland, the country of their ancestors. His father opened a 'wee
butter-and-ham shop' near 'Dixon's Blazes', getting most of the
produce from his acquaintances in Ulster. Young Thomas helped in
the shop, and when he was eleven formed a 'Yacht Club' for self-
made boats, which were sailed on the River Clyde near Glasgow
Green. After a period as office-boy in various Glasgow warehouses, he
went as a cabin boy to New York, where he worked for a time in a
prosperous grocery store. A desire to see his parents brought him
back to this country, and on his twenty-first birthday he opened a
retail provision shop of his own in Stobcross Street. Its amazing
success was chiefly attributable to two factors. He decided to cut
out the middle-man and, by buying direct from the Irish farmers,
was able to sell to the public at keen prices. And he had learned
in the United States the techniques of advertisement. He obtained
the services of an ingenious if crude commercial artist, and together
they devised series of posters which amused the people of Glasgow
and brought new customers. After opening one or two branches, he

founded a Lipton's Market at the corner of Howard Street and Jamaica Street and, partly by means of publicity stunts, greatly increased his business. Before long he had shops in most Scottish towns, and had begun establishing them in England too. His chief problem was how to get supplies. He advertised that his shops offered 'goods from every county in the Green Isle' but the Green Isle was unable to keep up with him, and he had to send his agents to Denmark, Sweden, Russia and elsewhere, 'practically with open cheque book'. It is an odd thought, in these days of intense international competition, that not so long ago some of these countries had to be persuaded to sell us their products.

During the 'eighties he added to his interests in the United States, and this indirectly prepared the way for the most important step in his career, his entry into the tea business. Again his plan was to cut out the middle-man, and within a year he was in Ceylon buying plantations. He was now becoming known for his Lipton's tea.

Perhaps his success in the tea trade was chiefly due, however, to his decision to prepare different blends of tea for different towns according to the chemical analysis of their domestic water. He was in no small way responsible for the great increase in tea drinking which began in Great Britain during the 'eighties, and for making tea a rival beverage to coffee in the United States.

G. L. WATSON

THE BAILIE, 1903

The world associates his name chiefly with the unsuccessful attempts of his *Shamrocks* to regain the America's Cup, and it is sometimes said that his happiest moment came when he was presented in New York with a magnificent cup for his 'never-say-die spirit'. But in his autobiography he says that the proudest day of his life came in 1923—when he was made a Freeman of Glasgow.

Howard Street, a short thoroughfare linking St. Enoch Square

Sir Thomas J. Lipton whose success in the tea trade was not quite matched in his attempts to regain the America's Cup. 'Shamrock II' shown here was designed for him by G. L. Watson and built in 1901 by Denny of Dumbarton. It came closest of all the contenders to winning the cup.

Sauchiehall Street, 1905.
Contrast the types with those of 1897, on page 145.

with Jamaica Street, has a unique place in the history of British multiple grocery stores, and particularly with the story of how tea was popularized, for it is associated not only with Lipton's first substantial move, but also with the foundation of Cooper and Co.'s Stores. The firm was created in 1871 by Thomas G. Bishop, Glasgow representative of one of the leading London tea houses. After setting himself up as a retail tea merchant, he took premises in Howard Court and, assuming one of his family names, began trading as Cooper and Co. He was a young man at the time—twenty-four years of age—and followed up his initial success by opening a branch in Sauchiehall Street in 1874, and another in Great Western Road in 1875. Besides extending his premises in Howard Street, he began to open branches not only in other parts of Glasgow, but in other towns in Scotland and in the north of England. In 1880, less than a decade after the founding of the business, he established his first branch in London. The branch in Liverpool, which grew to be perhaps the largest retail food store in the world, was begun in 1896.

Bishop, a man of vivid imagination, was always interested in new ideas. In the 'seventies he installed a field telegraph in his three stores, at Howard Street, Sauchiehall Street and Great Western Road, to put them in direct communication with one another. The Sauchiehall Street store was one of the first shops in Great Britain—perhaps it was *the* first—to be lit with electricity. The company were also among the first to install overhead cash railways in their shops—that was in 1886—and among the first to use commercial motor-cars for delivery purposes.

The point already made about retailers becoming manufacturers may be illustrated by this company. In 1878 they found it necessary to open a factory of their own in Howard Street. Before long they had to transfer it to a larger building. In 1894 they built their own bakery, near Eglinton Toll, and in the following year their own meat preserving factory, in James Watt Street. In 1913 they brought these branches together in a new factory in Bishop Street. In the meantime they had taken up many other lines, and in 1896 had built a factory in North Woodside Road. It was partially destroyed by fire in 1906, and was then replaced by a larger building.

The impression that a third famous concern—J. Lyons and Co., the largest catering undertaking in the world—had their origin in the Glasgow Exhibition of 1888 is not correct. This company began by

181

securing the catering contract for the Newcastle Jubilee Exhibition of
1887, and their success encouraged them to bid for and to obtain the
contract for the Glasgow Exhibition in the following year. Some of the
older people of the city still remember their Bishop's Palace tea-rooms
with waitresses dressed in Mary Stuart costumes—they were
known at the Exhibition as Lyons' widows. The profits made by
the company—'chiefly out of tea and bread and butter sold at
reasonable prices'—led them to found their tea-shop business in
London.

During the 'sixties another new development in distribution took
place and, as subsequent events have shown, it had considerable
significance. By then a large number of local co-operative societies
had come into being in England and in Scotland, and the formation
of a wholesale society to supply the various societies was advocated.
The Co-operative Wholesale Society was established in the north of
England in 1862, and in 1866 an attempt was made to associate the
Scottish societies with this Wholesale Society. Distance caused
difficulties, and in the following year the Scottish Co-operative
Wholesale Society was founded. Before long the Society engaged in
manufacturing as well as in marketing, and it has since become one
of the largest employers of industrial labour in Scotland.

A Well-Built City

When during our travels we hear disparaging remarks made about
the architecture of Glasgow we suspect that the detractors will not
be able to support their opinions with examples; and on occasion
we have eventually elicited the information that they had never been
in Glasgow at all, and were relying upon what someone else, a very
close friend, had told them. Glasgow is a comparatively well-built
city and authorities, including recently John Betjeman, have praised
it lavishly. Indeed, it is, next to Edinburgh and London, probably
the best built of all the large cities in Great Britain. Glasgow is
particularly fortunate in having few buildings embellished in the
extravagant way associated with the mid-Victorian period—Bothwell
Street contains the only really bad instance in the centre of the city,
although the appearance of the Art Galleries, in spite of their
beautiful setting, has also been criticized.

The most distinguished Glasgow architect of the early Victorian period was David Hamilton, whose works included the Western Club —a fine building in spite of its 'cold grey stone'—the Royal Exchange and the new Hutcheson's Hospital. Hamilton was a prize-winner in the competition for the design of the Houses of Parliament, but did not get the final award. The next of the outstanding Glasgow architects was Alexander Thomson ('Greek' Thomson), who was greatly interested in 'bizarre arrangements of Greek and Egyptian ornament', and used them in a novel and highly personal way. He specialized in churches—the number of churches of various denominations built in the Glasgow of his time is quite astonishing—and his St. Vincent Street U. P. Church was accepted as one of the sights of Glasgow. He was responsible for many other buildings in the city. Great Western Terrace in the Kelvinside district is his creation, and so, to a lesser extent, is Gordon Street.

The chief architect when central Glasgow was being rebuilt in the 'seventies was, however, James Sellars, who is perhaps best represented by the former New Club in West George Street. He designed St. Andrew's Halls which had magnificent acoustic qualities. Indeed, Caruso is reported as having said that he had never found anything better. The Halls were opened in 1877, having cost over £100,000, but they did not do well financially, and Glasgow Corporation were able to buy them in 1890 for £38,000. They were destroyed by fire in 1962.

The two most important buildings erected in the second half of the Victorian era were the University and the Municipal Buildings. Both are impressively massive and, although disparaged in the earlier part of the twentieth century, they are again being admired—particularly the Municipal Buildings which are beginning to attract visitors to the city.

Laying the foundation stone
of the Municipal Buildings in the mid-1880s.

The new Merchants' House building
was erected on the site of the Clarence Hotel in 1877.
This sketch was drawn in 1888.
Additional storeys have since been added
in the section where the Chamber of Commerce is located.

The Glasgow School of Art in Renfrew Street,
designed by Charles Rennie Mackintosh (1868–1928).
He was the greatest genius
among the Glasgow architects
of the nineteenth century.
The east wing, shown here, was completed in 1899.
The western half was completed in 1909
and was Mackintosh's finest achievement.
The building has since achieved world renown.

The necessity for adequately housing Glasgow's expanding administrative departments gave rise to many problems in the 'seventies. For several decades the city's affairs had been dealt with in buildings in Wilson Street. In 1874 an extension was taken up to Ingram Street but, so rapidly was Glasgow growing, that it was soon insufficient, and before long the decision was taken to use these buildings for the Justices' Court Hall, the Sheriff Court and other Courts. The attempt to make the small area bounded by Ingram Street, Glassford Street, Wilson Street and Albion Street the heart of the city was abandoned, and George Square was made the official centre of the city by clearing one side and erecting new municipal buildings there. During the earlier part of the Victorian era some of the city's leading hotels had been clustered around George Square—the North British Hotel alone remains. The first important step in changing the character of George Square was taken by the Merchants' House, when they acquired the site of the Crow Hotel and erected the new Merchants' House buildings in 1877. As has been mentioned, the tower of the old building had already been preserved, and a second model ship in full sail across the world was made to surmount the new buildings. The Chamber of Commerce transferred its headquarters to the Merchants' House buildings, leaving the Trades House in Glassford Street unique in still occupying its eighteenth-century premises.

The greatest genius among the Glasgow architects of the nineteenth century was undoubtedly Charles Rennie Mackintosh (1868–1928), but he was one of those unfortunate beings, born

The Room de-Luxe,
in Miss Cranston's Willow Tea-rooms, Sauchiehall Street.
It was the finest of her tea-rooms
and was built by Charles Mackintosh in 1903.
It is now Daly's Bridal Boutique.
The decorations were inspired by a Rossetti poem
beginning 'O Ye, all ye that walk in Willow wood!'
Unfortunately none of the Mackintosh tea-rooms
has survived in its original state.

before their time, who have to leave their native country before their talents are properly recognized. Perhaps he was unlucky in having won a measure of fame too early and too easily, for he became most outspoken in acid criticisms of his brother architects—'the traditional stylists'—and it was perhaps expecting too much of human nature that they would acclaim his revolutionary design in the 'nineties for the buildings of the Glasgow School of Art. Before that, however, the encouragement given him by Kate Cranston, who allowed him a free hand in decorating her tea-rooms, had brought him before the public. He was a brilliant decorator, and derived many of his patterns from the shapes of flowers and fruit. The modernist of his time, he designed all of the furniture and equipment for his buildings. His influence on other artists during the Edwardian period is to be seen in their periodicals, but he had to turn to the Continent to get scope for his talents, and particularly to Germany. And so the visitor, who looks up from Sauchiehall Street to the School of Art and dismisses it as Germanic in appearance, might ponder on the possibility of Germany having acquired that particular style from Glasgow. Incidentally, he was indebted for the opportunity to design this school to its famous director, Fra Newbery, whose aim was to achieve international standing for the school.

Where Glasgow Went Shopping

As the shipyards went farther and farther down the river, to Govan, Partick, Whiteinch, Scotstoun, Yoker and Clydebank, more and more people moved to live near them in the west and so the centre of the city itself also moved towards the west. Not only Glasgow Cross, but the newer George Square ceased to be the focal point of social and business life. By 1890 the centre of the city was in Union Street, although whether at the Argyle Street crossing or at the Gordon Street crossing was probably, even in those days, a point on which there was not general agreement.

No one now claimed that Trongate was one of the finest shopping streets in Europe, and Argyle Street had in some respects lost caste (although not in the volume of business done). Buchanan Street had maintained its position, but in face of robust competition from an ambitious rival, the upstart Sauchiehall Street. By then the central shopping district of Glasgow was well stretched, and the distance from Glasgow Cross, along Argyle Street, Buchanan Street and Sauchiehall Street to Charing Cross, with shops and side-streets all the way, was a couple of miles. Few people ever covered the whole distance, and it was remarkable how many men and women, who normally came into the city from the west through Sauchiehall Street, or from the south through Hope Street, were never at Glasgow Cross from one year's end to the next.

Argyle Street remained, however, *the* street of Glasgow. Nowhere else were the crowds so dense on Saturday afternoons and evenings, and nowhere else was so much money spent. Although it contained several large stores, one held the predominating position—Anderson's Royal Polytechnic. Much of the rest of the street has not changed greatly in appearance since 1900, or indeed earlier, although some impressive new buildings have been erected recently. Some of the buildings are very old, and an interesting few minutes can be spent, while standing at the Stockwell Street-Argyle Street crossing, in comparing buildings, particularly those in Trongate, with later additions.

Argyle Street on Saturday nights had a shocking reputation in the past. 'In 1889,' said Sir John Hammerton, 'Glasgow was probably the most drink-sodden city in Great Britain. The Trongate and Argyle Street, and worst of all, the High Street, were scenes of disgusting debauchery, almost incredible today. Many of the younger generation thought it manly to get "paralytic" and "dead to the world"; at least on Saturday there was lots of tipsy rowdyism in the genteel promenade in Sauchiehall Street, but nothing to compare with the degrading spectacle of the other thoroughfares, where there were drunken brawls at every corner and a high proportion of the passers-by were reeling drunk. At the corners of

Looking at the Trongate from Glasgow Cross in the early 1900s.
The large number of men who seem just to be 'hanging about' is noteworthy and is not readily explained.

SAINT MUNGO, 1905

'Young Glasgow'—according to our newspapers.

*The Tontine Buildings
were completely gutted by fire in 1912.*

the darker side streets the reek of vomit befouled the evening air, never very salubrious. Jollity was everywhere absent: sheer loathsome, swinish inebriation prevailed.'

There does not seem to have been much improvement in the following years. 'On Saturday nights,' said J. H. Muir (a collective pseudonym, by the way) in his *Glasgow in 1901*, 'Argyle Street held Saturnalia . . . A time of squalid licence, when men staggered out of shutting public-houses as out of a pit, and the street echoed to insane roaring and squabbles.' Argyle Street is still inclined to be noisy, but it is very much less drunken than in the past. Probably tradition has been partly responsible for keeping the street a Saturday evening promenade, because it had ceased to be an entertainment centre even by the beginning of the twentieth century.

If the Trongate's reputation in the past as a great shopping street is difficult to understand, no doubt can be felt over the claims made about Buchanan Street, built in the early decades of the nineteenth century as one of the handsomest streets in Europe. It still is, although it is a short street, and after crossing West George Street, loses its distinction. If only its architects had balanced St. Enoch's Square with something worthwhile at its north end!

'Glasgow has no leisured class,' J. H. Muir wrote, 'but she has a leisure hour, and if you wish to see her at her brightest, pass along Gordon Street and down Buchanan Street a little after noon.' Glasgow lunches rather later today, but, quite apart from that, the time to see Buchanan Street is the mid-afternoon. The people still look into the shop-windows of the substantial, long-established firms showing ladies' fashions, furniture, jewellery, toys, shoes and many other things, almost all good and rather expensive. Men's clothes, perhaps significantly, are more prominently featured in Buchanan Street than forty years ago. And the Argyll Arcade is still there— 'more spacious and pretty than the Burlington Arcade', said Muir. But, as in the past, it is the haunt of tourists and children. Men-about-town do not go there for their ties.

J. H. Muir called Sauchiehall Street the Piccadilly of Glasgow, with 'parks and terraces at the west end and theatres at the east end. It has,' he said, 'picture galleries, fashionable milliners, haber-dashers, court photographers, booksellers, universal providers, dealers in old furniture, and the necessary ladies' luncheon rooms at

Assafrey's and Skinner's. It is the brightest and gayest street in Glasgow, the only street of pleasure. It has more painted buildings and gilded signs than any other, and its sky-line is more irregular, piquant, and full of contrasts. English flower-girls cry their wares at Wellington Street in a foreign tongue. The Wellington Arcade is, however, given over to third-class businesses except for the German sausage shop with the appetizing still-life in the windows. And at the Renfrew Street end of the Arcade is the Soho of Glasgow with little squalid lanes, bright pubs and shady supper-rooms.'

Now this is almost unrecognizable as the Sauchiehall Street of

Buchanan Street (1902) showing the entrance to Argyll Arcade (the low building on the right).

Corporation horse trams in Sauchiehall Street at the turn of the century. The gentleman in the topper conveys an impression of Edwardian leisureliness.

*This photograph of Sauchiehall Street
was taken shortly after the lifting of the tram lines.
The appearance of the street is changing greatly,
and several of the buildings have since been demolished
to provide sites for taller blocks.*

today. It is still, however, the best-known street in Glasgow. Almost
everybody has heard of it. Probably the difficulty which the English
and, even more, the foreigners have in pronouncing *Sauchiehall* is
responsible. It seems to be one of those ridiculous things about the
Scots—or should we say the 'Scotch'?—like haggis and bawbees and
kilts and bagpipes—which amuse the simple-minded.

Sauchiehall Street was described as suffering from arrested development. The westward flow of the city was checked by the first
world war and in the nineteen-twenties and nineteen-thirties little
new building was attempted, except at the sites of the present
Regal Cinema and Locarno Dance-Hall. Some of the stores were one-
and two-storey shacks, that looked as if they had been knocked
together ever so long ago. Worse, however, there were two gaps,
given over to bill-posting. In one was a monumental mason's yard
and in the other a quite diminutive Sauchiehall Street mansion that
had survived for almost a century.

In 1938 one of the gaps was filled by the multi-storey Beresford
Hotel, which had a chequered career, and the other was in the
process of being occupied when this was written. Other major
projects were also under way. At the east end of the street both the
Lyric Theatre and the Empire Music-Hall had been replaced with

190

office blocks, one of great height. Perhaps—like Broadway or Piccadilly Circus—Sauchiehall Street looks best at night, when the theatres, music-halls, cinemas, dance-halls, hotels, restaurants and night clubs fill the street with light—garish but bright. For all its faults, Sauchiehall Street is very much alive.

Muir had practically nothing to say about Renfield Street, Hope Street and Bath Street. Clearly the growth in importance of what were to him secondary streets but are now main traffic streets is the most significant change which has taken place since his time. Perhaps Renfield Street has altered most of all. The Victorians believed that, in spite of this street's advantageous position in linking the Argyle Street and Sauchiehall Street shopping centres, its gradient would discourage the public from shopping in it. They were probably right in supposing that people avoid hills, but they failed to see how conveniently the street was placed for becoming an entertainment centre, and for linking up with Union Street and Jamaica Street as a major thoroughfare.

The construction of the George V Bridge brought Hope Street into the transport stream, and, as Neil Munro observed, the part of Hope Street which skirts the Central Hotel has become one of the busiest in the city. Muir was also not interested in that strangely neglected place, Bothwell Street. By providing the quickest connection between the Central Station and the Charing Cross district, it should have become more important than it is. Its construction was upset by the financial crises of the 'seventies, when grandiose schemes for its development were partly or completely abandoned. Apparently by 1901 it was dismissed as an unimportant street. But its day may yet come—a splendid office block was built in it during the late 'twenties, and more will follow. In the meantime, however, the tall buildings are going up in an adjacent and rarely noticed street, Waterloo Street.

The Queen Dies

Queen Victoria died on 22nd January, 1901. In recent plays and books elderly couples speak as if with her death their own lives—spent entirely under her sovereignty—had also come to their end. That Glasgow was less upset is shown by the reactions of theatre managers on this particular evening. The news of the Queen's death reached the city at about seven—an embarrassingly awkward time as, although the Queen's hours were known to be numbered, audiences were just assembling—they had paid their money at the box-offices—and it was clear that the attendances were going to be large. In St. Andrew's Halls, where one of the Choral and Orchestral Union's concerts was being given, the orchestra played the Dead March from Saul, and the audience dispersed. Other performances that stopped on hearing the news were: at the Royalty Theatre, George Edwardes's musical play *The Messenger Boy*, at the Royal *Aladdin*, at the Grand *Cinderella*, and at the Metropole *Bo-peep*. There was some confusion, however, at the Royal Princess's *Red Riding Hood*, at the Empire and Britannia music-halls, at Poole's Circus (set-piece *Deeds that Won the Empire*, and the latest and best animated photographs), at the Zoo-Circus (Juvenile Pantomime), at the Panorama *The Battle of Omdurman*, and at the *Savage South Africa* entertainment in the East-End Exhibition, Dennistoun. The performances had started, and the managements were not willing to lower their curtains without being sure of the authenticity of the news. Messengers were sent from one place of entertainment to another to find out what was being done, and in some houses the audiences were not asked to retire until the performances were almost ended. The newspapers on the following morning announced that the theatres would remain closed during the period of national mourning—but by the following day they were all open again. The *Glasgow Daily Mail* (formerly the *North British Daily Mail*) summed up the city's reaction to the news of the Queen's death as 'respectful silence'. Few people thought that their lives were over, that an era had closed or, indeed, that they would be involved in any real change. The Glasgow man—in spite of the drawn-out Boer War and some persistent disquiet about Germany and other Continental rivals— was in rather buoyant mood, and he was more confident about the future than his father had been thirty years before.

He was not really Victorian at all, for the 'nineties had been a decade of transition. Almost everything, if it was to attract his interest and support, had to be described as new—new freedom, new art, new poetry, new literature, new journalism, new restaurants, new ethics, new paganism, new naughtiness. The decade has been described as one of a thousand 'movements', some ephemeral, some still influencing ways of life today. He lacked his grandfathers' forthrightness, assurance, compactness, rigidity. He was not solid as they were—and his business was not solid as theirs had been. That, however, was not clearly discerned at the time, and the Glasgow man differed from his predecessors, of one hundred and of two hundred years before, in thinking that this time the new century was getting off to a pretty good start.

This photograph was taken in 1901 at Eglinton Toll, just before the opening of the Great Exhibition.

Into The Twentieth Century

To those of us who have lived our whole lives in the twentieth century much more seems to be happening than in any comparable period of the nineteenth century. Certainly the first sixty-five years of the twentieth century do not fall readily together into a single, coherent period. Several distinct phases are discernible.

The first, up to 1914, may be loosely termed Edwardian. It was really the concluding stage in an interval comprising the 'eighties and the 'nineties as well as the beginning of the twentieth century.

It was a nice time to live in—not so vigorous perhaps as the gay 'nineties, but jollier and less raucous. There followed the carnage of the first world war, which left Scotland with terrible losses and with many recriminatory thoughts. Another phase followed, 1919–39, which will probably be known in history as the Twenty Years' Truce or the Long Armistice. Even there sub-divisions are needed, for the roaring 'twenties were most unlike the doleful 'thirties, with their leaders groping for appeasement and muddled preparedness for another war, which people dreaded and tried to convince themselves would not come. The nineteen-twenties represent, however, a significant moment in Glasgow's story. The world had a trade boom—but, for the first time, Glasgow saw comparatively little of it. Eventually the second world war was declared, when this country was to have its finest hour—a war in which the people of Clydeside were subjected to severe air raids. It is virtually impossible for us to say whether the new era which began late in 1945 ended in 1956 with the Suez crisis or whether it still goes on. The consequences of today's happenings may not be fully appreciated in this century, and guesses about what future generations will think of us are in all likelihood wide of the mark.

The End of 'Splendid Isolation'

Whether people were quite so happy in Edwardian times as is often suggested is perhaps debatable, for the period was characterized by much squabbling over politics. The Victorians had left major unsettled issues and Glasgow was greatly concerned with some. The question of home rule for Ireland had now come up in earnest, and in 1914 almost brought the country to civil war, with Orangemen drilling in the open in Ulster and arms from the United States and Germany being smuggled into the South, not for the supporters of the old Irish Nationalists but for adherents to a Republican party. In Glasgow there were too many immigrants and the sons of immigrants from the North and from the South of Ireland for this turmoil to leave the city unmoved.

Militant feminism added to the tension, and one of the most astonishing episodes in recent social history was the organization of quite considerable numbers of women—drawn chiefly from the middle-classes—into groups of suffragettes for committing outrages on people and on property. There were two Glasgow High Court trials for arson at which, according to the *Glasgow Herald*, 'disturbances took place unparalleled in a Glasgow Court of Justice'. Missiles were thrown at the judges, and demonstrations by hundreds of excited women were held outside the courts. The social standing of some of them is indicated by that of the prisoners—each sentenced to eight months—at a trial for attempting to burn down a mansion at 6 Park Gardens. One was a well-known Edinburgh woman artist and the other the wife of the minister of one of Glasgow's leading churches. Headlines in the *Glasgow Herald* from 1912 to 1914 are quite startling: attempt to burn down Shields Road Station; bomb in the City Chambers; Kelly House at Wemyss Bay destroyed by fire (perhaps the worst of the outrages in this district); attempt to burn down a Gareloch mansion at Shandon; bomb in the Kibble Palace at the Botanic Gardens; destruction of a Rutherglen mansion; scene at the Repertory Theatre; bomb at Belmont Church; and, the last incident (8th July, 1914), bomb at the Burns Cottage, Alloway. Suffragettes also interfered with the Augustine Birrell

Rectorial at the University and students retaliated by destroying their headquarters.

The Conservative Government fell from power towards the end of 1905, and from then until well after the outbreak of the war the Liberals were in charge. The majority of Glasgow's M.P.s were Liberals, as is shown by the returns from the last election before the war, held on 8th December, 1910:

BLACKFRIARS AND	G. N. Barnes (Lab.)	4162
HUTCHESTOWN	A. H. B. Constable (U.)	2884
BRIDGETON	A. MacCallum Scott (Lib.)	4759
	W. Hutchison (U.)	3816
CAMLACHIE	H. J. Mackinder (U.)	3479
	J. M. Hogge (Lib.)	3453
	J. O. Kessack (Lab.)	1539
	W. J. Mirrlees (Suffragist)	35
CENTRAL	C. Scott Dickson (U.)	6888
	Prof. A. F. Murison (Lib.)	5907
COLLEGE	H. A. Watt (Lib.)	6291
	R. C. Glyn (U.)	5932
TRADESTON	A. Cameron Corbett (Lib.)	4800
	A. P. Main (U.)	3137
ST. ROLLOX	T. McKinnon Wood (Lib.)	9291
	A. R. Chamberlayne (U.)	7374

(The boundaries of the city had not at that time been extended to include Govan and Partick. In both of these constituencies the voters favoured radicalism in preference to the Unionist cause.)

While the people of Britain were pre-occupied with wrangles over home rule for Ireland, votes for women, trade union rights, reform of the House of Lords, tariff reform *versus* free trade (then thought to be perhaps the most fundamental of all political questions), health insurance (undoubtedly one of the most important social enactments of this time), old age pensions, land taxes, licensing, education, church disestablishment, army reform, imperial defence, local government, factory conditions, shop hours and labour exchanges—Germany came right into the open as the enemy of this country. Only those in the inner circle realized the seriousness of the menace, and, during the decade before 1914, our foreign policy was handled tactfully and with great skill. As long ago as 1905 Germany tried to gather the whole of Europe, including France and Russia, into an aggressive anti-British bloc.

In the few years before the declaration of war an entente was reached with France—the resulting military conversations took 100,000 British soldiers to France within a few days of the German invasion in 1914—and an agreement was made with Russia. The naval construction race with Germany was intensified, the army was reformed, the Territorial Force founded, and the Officers' Training Corps Scheme inaugurated. There were several 'scares', giving rise to incidental excitement about German spies. But, apart from some sensational fiction about 'the invasion of England', chiefly written for boys and for adults with boys' mentalities, the public were not greatly perturbed. They did not see that they were being forced out of the 'splendid isolation' in which this country had lived for almost a hundred years. In the meantime the Edwardian and early Georgian era went on its way contentedly, in spite of all the menacing troubles, and graciously.

Glasgow's Political Leaders

During the last seventy years Scotland has provided the country with many prominent figures—including six Prime Ministers. Indeed, Scotsmen were playing such a large part in public affairs in the concluding stages of the first world war that the question was being asked, *Where are the Englishmen?* and, while the Prime Minister himself at that time was a Welshman, a surprisingly high proportion of those around him were Scots. One explanation of the greater part the Scot has been playing in the affairs of the country— and in administering and managing large undertakings in the South— is that London is an increasingly attractive magnet for ambitious Scottish youths. Previously it was the wide world which called them, as is shown in the statement that more than 1,500,000 people have left Scotland since 1860—a disturbingly high figure for a country whose population has never been much more than five millions.

Two of the Scottish Prime Minsters were Glasgow men, both former students of Glasgow High School and Glasgow University. The first has already been mentioned—Henry Campbell-Bannerman (1836–1908), of J. and W. Campbell, the warehousemen. A brilliant scholar—he had a fine academic record—he became, while still young, Liberal M.P. for Stirling Burghs, and retained the seat for the rest of his days. His early political career was undistinguished, although his easy-going, good-humoured manner and his shrewdness were invaluable in healing splits. But, even as he took increasingly prominent places in the Party's affairs, few thought of him as a future Prime Minister.

T. P. O'Connor, his biographer, said that, if, when he was chosen to be Prime Minister, 'he seemed to be raised, honoured and magnified beyond his deserts, his rise was to be attributed to his having shown, through many years of stress and difficulty, extraordinary courage, tenacity and consistency. At first he had seemed the solid, typical, secular, phlegmatic Scotchman, but on closer inspection it was noticed that the phlegm was mixed with a certain dash of that *perfervidum ingenium Scotorum*, which is as much characteristic of his race as its caution and its sangfroid.'

Campbell-Bannerman was succeeded as Prime Minister by Asquith, who, although thoroughly English, had a close link with Glasgow, in that his wife was a great-granddaughter of Charles Tennant, the chemical manufacturer. The next outstanding Glasgow politician was a Tory. Sixteen years after Campbell-Bannerman left the High School, another boy, also destined to become Prime Minister, joined it as a pupil. He was Andrew Bonar Law (1858– 1923). Born in Canada, the son of a Presbyterian minister, he was brought to this country by relatives after his father's re-marriage, and through them eventually became one of the leading men in iron and and steel merchanting. Indeed, for a time he was the central figure in Glasgow's 'Iron Ring'. Although he lacked Campbell-Bannerman's academic brilliance, he took classes at Glasgow University and attended Gladstone's Rectorial Address in 1879. This greatly stirred his ambition, but his desire, as his biographer has recorded, was to emulate Gladstone in being Lord Rector of Glasgow University rather than in being Prime Minister. From then he took an active interest in politics, although he did not stand for parliament until he was forty-two. He then had a remarkable success in winning the Blackfriars (Gorbals) seat, for the only time in the Conservative

J. W. PHILLIPS

*Bonar Law, the other Glasgow Prime Minister in this century
besides Campbell-Bannerman.
In this sketch from 'The Bailie' in March, 1921,
he is seen as the Lord Rector of Glasgow University.
He recalled that as a student in the 1870s
he had heard Gladstone give his Rectorial Address
and had been filled with a desire to succeed him in later life.*

interest, and this brought him into prominence immediately. His
knowledge of industry became invaluable to the party, and he
followed Joseph Chamberlain as the leading advocate of tariff reform.
His aggressive if somewhat brusque platform manner made him
most acceptable to the party managers, as Balfour's leadership had
been thought lacking in vigour, and when the time came to choose a
successor to Balfour he was selected, in preference to better-known
candidates. He was the second business man—Campbell-Bannerman
being the first—ever to become Prime Minister, and the choice
caused surprise, not only because he was 'remote from the sentiment
and experience of traditional Toryism', but also because his social
background was entirely new to the party. One of his unusual
characteristics as the head of the Conservative Party was that of
being a 'teetotaller'—or perhaps we should say as the head of any
political party.

Bonar Law's chief services to the British Commonwealth were
during the first world war, when he consented to form the Coalition
Government, with Lloyd George as Prime Minister and himself as
Chancellor of the Exchequer and Leader of the House of Commons.
By then his temperament had mellowed, and he allowed the Prime
Minister to overshadow him, while retaining perhaps the controlling
influence in cabinet circles. Lloyd George said that 'without his
assistance I certainly could not have done my work in this war. A
more loyal, a more true comrade, I have never worked with, and a
more sagacious counsellor, I had never had the aid of.'

In the years immediately after the war Bonar Law strove to keep
the Coalition together and, incidentally, during this period achieved
his ambition of being Lord Rector of Glasgow University. When the
Coalition broke up he became Prime Minister, but his health was
poor, and he resigned after two hundred days, to die shortly after-

wards. So the way was cleared for Baldwin, and later for a second Coalition, this time with yet another Scot, Ramsay MacDonald. It is interesting to reflect on what would be the shape of the world today if Bonar Law had lived past his middle sixties. His policy would have been very different from Baldwin's.

We are much too close in time to these men to evaluate their place in history, but the possibility must be recognized of someone else, rather than Campbell-Bannerman or Bonar Law, being ranked as the greatest Glasgow politician of the early years of this century. That distinction might pass yet to a man who was never a cabinet Minister, J. Keir Hardie (1856–1915). He was not so much a member of the new Labour Party as its creator. Never an academic politician —he said he 'got more socialism from Burns than from Marx'— he became a labour agitator in his 'teens. In his early manhood he tried to organize trade unionism among Lanarkshire and Ayrshire miners, and the formation of the Scottish Miners' Federation in the 'eighties, with himself as secretary, was one of the outstanding achievements of his younger years. Barred as a trouble-maker from employment in many west of Scotland coal mines, he made his living by journalism, at first with Liberal journals, and later with more radical publications.

Most of his early writing was on industrial subjects, such as the 8-hour day, and unemployment, but he forced the Liberal Party to adopt more working-men parliamentary candidates. He was first recognized as a national figure in 1888, when he stood as a rival candidate to the official Liberal candidate at a by-election in mid-Lanarkshire and, in spite of much critisicm for splitting the Liberal vote, was himself only narrowly defeated. By that time he was convinced that the place for an advanced radical was not in the Liberal Party. He would stand against the Liberals and beat them. He became associated with Londoners who shared his views, and afterwards devoted most of his time to creating the Independent Labour Party in opposition to the Liberal Party—and to holding it together.

He died in 1915, unquestionably, his biographer William Stewart said, 'one of the victims of the war'. His funeral in Glasgow was attended by 'a great concourse of mourners', among them being his old friends, Bob Smellie, Cunninghame-Graham and Ramsay MacDonald. He was described as 'the best-hated and best-loved man in Great Britain'.

They were all in various ways products of the Sunday meetings which had been held on Glasgow Green since the eighteen-seventies and earlier. These meetings took place between 10 a.m. and 10 p.m. in summer and until dusk in the winter. Well-known orators had their own pitches and could attract audiences as large as 2000. Not all of them pontificated on political subjects. Theology came in for much attention too.

According to P. Walsh, 'the chief orators of the eighteen-seventies and later were John McGlynn, who began as a religious debator and later became a humorist; Tommy Weir, his chief opponent; Scott Gibson; and McMillan, a Social Democrat who stood all day advocating Socialism'. P. Walsh himself was known as the 'Lone Scout'. For 40 years he sold books and pamphlets. In his later years he specialized in selling the cartoons of Cynicus.

It was estimated that 100,000 people went to the Green every Sunday. In the troubled years after the first world war the right of assembly at the Green was withdrawn by bye-law (1922). By then,

197

however, the orators had found other pitches. According to W. D. Cocker, the leading haranguer in the early years of this century, Scott Gibson, established himself at the Wellington Street-Sauchiehall Street corner. His particular theme was that the workers should not allow the well-to-do to run the city. He created a sensation by challenging ex-Lord Provost Sam Chisholm, when he decided to resume his place in the Town Council, and defeating him. Some years later his stance was occupied by another Socialist, a young tailor called Emanuel Shinwell.

Glasgow Goes on Growing

The industrialization of the Continent brought about the expansion of other towns and deprived Glasgow of the position of Sixth City of Europe. Glasgow's rate of growth had slowed down. Indeed, including suburban districts, later brought within its boundaries, the population never rose much beyond one million. In 1931 it was 1,088,000, just sufficient to keep it ahead of Birmingham's 1,003,000.

During the second world war Glasgow's population did go higher because of people 'directed' to its armaments industries and others 'evacuated' from more heavily attacked towns, such as London. At one stage the population was put at 1,300,000. But after the war it returned to just over one million.

In the last Victorian decades and the Edwardian era the municipal area of the city was enlarged from 6000 to 40,000 acres. Since 1875 several struggles have taken place in parliamentary committees over the extension of Glasgow's boundaries, the representatives of the city contending that the residents of other districts enjoyed the privileges of Glasgow citizenship and should pay the appropriate rates. The most important amalgamations were made in 1891 (Govanhill, Pollokshields, Hillhead and Maryhill) and 1912 (Pollokshaws, Govan and Partick). Before it was absorbed Govan was the fifth largest burgh in Scotland.

The city in its expansion has now reached other places, including the ancient burghs of Paisley, Renfrew and Rutherglen, and some interesting prognostications have been made from time to time about its further enlargement. They were on the whole better received by the press of Glasgow than by the press of the other towns.

Living in One Room

Aberdeen was said to have, in proportion to its population, the largest number of really wealthy inhabitants in Great Britain. The explanation was, no doubt, that the Granite City is a nice place to retire to, and that a great deal of the wealth was really made elsewhere than in Aberdeen. Glasgow, too, has over the last two hundred years housed many wealthy men, and it is interesting to note how much of their money came from India and Eastern Asia. Glasgow housed these men well, as the many fine mansions in the Kelvinside, Maxwell Park and other districts around Glasgow show.

Next to them came the middle-class, even more sub-divided in Edwardian days than in mid-Victorian days. Most middle-class people lived very comfortably in tenement buildings, usually four storeys high, the flats containing from eight or seven rooms down to four or three. The rooms were characterized by spaciousness, high ceilings and wide windows, and were, in the opinion of the Glasgow middle-classes, infinitely superior to the rooms of the small terrace

A mid-Victorian upper-middle-class drawing room reproduced in the Old Glasgow Museum.

OLD GLASGOW MUSEUM

Also in the Old Glasgow Museum is this reproduction of a working-class room which illustrates clearly 'one room' living conditions.

houses in which their opposite numbers in England lived. After them came the working-class, the better-to-do of whom thought themselves quite well placed in tenements, adjacent to but smaller than those occupied by the lower middle-class, although they sometimes found it difficult to make satisfactory provision for sleeping the members of their families, particularly as they grew up—a large concealed bed in a recess in the sitting-room might be provided for the girls and one in the kitchen for the boys. The sanitary arrangements seemed inadequate, and in particular the closes smelly, damp and dirty, but they did not complain very much. It was what they were used to and in their way they liked it. The poorer sections of the working-classes did, however, complain about their lot, frequently and vociferously. And with good reason.

From the early eighteen-forties, when government and other reports on social conditions in Glasgow disturbed the public conscience, many attempts were made to house the working-classes better. In 1846 the Town Council decided to acquire the worst tenements and to destroy them—a policy it has followed at an increasing rate ever since. The City of Glasgow Improvement Act

A sketch drawn in the Central Police Court in 1900.

of 1866, in particular, was one of the most important pieces of
nineteenth-century social legislation. Even then, however, the real
significance of the problem was not appreciated, and it was not
until the recently appointed Medical Officer to the City, Dr. J. B.
Russell, began to make speeches during the 'seventies and 'eighties
on such subjects as 'Life in One Room' and 'The Children of the
City' that the extent of the prevailing degradation was perceived. Dr.
Russell showed that, in 1880, 25 per cent of the people of Glasgow
were living in houses of one apartment, that lodgers were living in
14 per cent of the one-room houses and in 27 per cent of the two-
room houses. Only 8 per cent of the people of Glasgow were living in
houses of five or more rooms.

In 1897, under another Act (Glasgow Corporation Improvements
and General Powers), seven congested and insanitary areas in the
central districts, covering six acres, were scheduled for demolition
and reconstruction, and warehouses, shops and tenements were
built on the cleared sites. Other powers, too, under the Working
Classes Act of 1890, were used to remove 'back lands' and to build
tenements for housing the poverty-stricken.

During the Edwardian period the problem became more acute and
for quite a different reason. In the past, tenement buildings were
looked on as a good financial investment—'put your trust in stone
and mortar'—but by the beginning of the twentieth century the
position was changing, partly, no doubt, because more had to be
spent on upkeep and on the provision of amenities. No longer were
massive tenements going up in the working-class districts. Indeed,
between 1902, when the Dean of Guild passed linings for 4600
houses of one, two and three apartments, and 1911, when the
total had fallen to 250, private enterprise lost interest in building
houses for rent by the working-classes—and, incidentally, not long
after it lost interest in building houses for rent by any other class—
hence some remarkable gaps to be seen in, for instance, the 'superior'
district of Hyndland, which looks as if someone in the years before
the first world war changed his mind suddenly and left as waste
ground perhaps one-eighth of what was clearly a well-planned scheme.
It is alleged that this change of mind was occasioned by Lloyd
George's budget of 1909–10, which put a 20 per cent tax on the
increment value of all heritable property, and was then described as

200

'the final stroke against all speculative building operatives'. The rating system of Scotland was also blamed and contrasted unfavourably with that of England. Putting such controversies on one side, however, the fact has to be recognized that for a period of 35 years practically no new houses were built in Glasgow by private enterprise for rent.

Under various housing Acts passed after 1919, by which local authorities could get subsidies from the government for erecting houses for working people, Glasgow Corporation began to build extensively. In 1945, however, it was said that although there were now 281,000 houses in Glasgow, another 100,000 were needed, some urgently. The Clyde Valley Regional Planning Advisory Committee estimated that in the whole district—some of which is included in Greater Glasgow—200,000 new houses were wanted, to provide accommodation for 800,000 people (estimated, by the Committee, to be 35 per cent of the area's population). Another aspect of the problem was that of general density. In parts of the Rutherglen Road district, for instance, it was given as 516 persons to the acre, and in parts of Scotland Street as 528 persons to the acre. This was said to be more than anywhere else in Great Britain.

Yet it must be realized that many of the people of Glasgow—like the people of central and other parts of Europe—prefer tenements to 'box-like' houses. William Bolitho and others could go on publishing pamphlets about housing on Clydeside, such as the *Cancer of Empire* (*1924*), and medical officers could go on saying that living in tenements was responsible for the death-rate being higher in Scotland than in England and Wales, but the policy of building more tenements was continued.

Then private building contractors and speculators began to create a new suburban Glasgow by constructing unit houses for sale. At first King's Park, Kelvindale and the other districts were disparaged, but now that their early bleakness has disappeared with the cultivation of trees and gardens they are much praised. Bus routes were extended into the new housing schemes and Glasgow people were intrigued at the new and strange names of districts coming into being. The first large blocks of service flats made their appearance in the nineteen-thirties and the sub-dividing of mansions and other big houses became common. With the virtual disappearance of domestic servants they had become unworkable.

An announcement that the Roman Catholic See of Glasgow was thought to comprise 450,000 Roman Catholics, caused some surprise as this was 50,000 more than Liverpool and 150,000 more than either Westminister or Salford. Such has been the remarkable movement of people into Clydeside during the last 150 years. In 1770 there were very few Roman Catholics in Glasgow. It would be a mistake to suppose, however, that almost all of these 450,000 people were descendants of or are themselves recent immigrants from the south of Ireland, although the majority of them probably were. Quite a number were of Italian stock, and George Blake selected them to show how European nationals flocked to Glasgow in the nineteenth century. They were all, in effect, camp-followers of the Industrial Revolution. The Italians worked hard for modest wages, saved their money, sent remittances home to their peasant parents and, if the luck was good, returned in the fullness of time to their native places. In some ways it seems odd that so many Italians settled in Scotland, where the summer is rather different from that of their sunny native land. Perhaps the mildness of the

QUIZ

The vagrant.
'Move on, move on', through streets everlasting,
flit Glasgow's vagrant population of the night.
'Move on' rings down the Clyde's muddy course
and must often sound like 'move in'.

201

climate appealed to them. Apparently many of those who emigrated from Italy in the second half of the nineteenth century thought that the Scots had a lot of bawbees to spend. They opened innumerable small shops, where they served ice-cream, peas-in-vinegar, fried fish and chips, and a confection known as a McCallum, a raspberry flavoured ice-cream. Their gaudy saloons with colourful names played an important part in the social life of the town, for they were very popular with young people in their 'teens—many a romance has begun in an alcove of a Café de l'Europe—and they provided the alternative to the pub.

Unlike the Italians, some other European nationals were readily absorbed into the life of the city—the Scandinavians in particular—and their children are unmistakably Scots. Even their surnames—slightly anglicized perhaps—are not regarded as unusual. But the names of the thousands of Polish and Lithuanian miners who came to Scotland in the 'nineties still seem queer and unpronounceable.

During this movement of people, a great many Scots left Glasgow. Apparently the prospects in their native city, which were so attractive to others, were not sufficiently attractive for them. Emigration to the United States was at its height in 1880, when the Anchor Line alone carried from Glasgow to New York 12,000 saloon and 50,000 second-cabin and steerage passengers (although a large number of these people were not Glaswegians, but had merely come to Glasgow to board ship). Another exodus followed the first world war. The numbers were smaller, but on this occasion a disturbingly high proportion were skilled craftsmen whom the city could not afford to lose.

The young Glasgow lad who gets a London appointment is often astonished at the ease with which his colleagues let him shove them out of his way. That does not necessarily mean that he is more intelligent than they are, rather that he is more ambitious, ruthless and hard-working, and that he has greater singleness of purpose. He is better at creating and taking opportunities. Many people do not like the Scot on the make—the Londoners of Georgian times, who took the first impact of the invasion of their city by young men from north of the border, expressed their antipathy—but the men with Scottish names who occupy high places today have 'got on' because they had something to offer which others had not. They had at least, to be able to hold down the positions they had shoved other people out of.

The most outspoken attack on the Scottish intruder was made in 1902 by T. W. H. Crosland in his *The Unspeakable Scot*. The Scot is to be be found everywhere—'to whatever department of activity one looks one finds therein, working his way up for all he is worth and by none too gentle methods, the so-called canny Scot. In journalism he has made himself more or less predominant. In banks, offices and manufactories he is to be found, as frequently as not, ruling the roost in the capacity of manager or overseer.' And the pity of it all, for 'his bumptiousness and uncouthness, his lack of manners, his lack of principle, and his want of decent feeling, have brought and will continue to bring their own reward'.

Among those who have replaced the departing Scots in Glasgow are the English. Their similarity to the lowland and east-coast Scots, and particularly to those of Scandinavian origin, is so marked, not only in appearance but even in name, that no estimate can be readily made of the number of people of English ancestry living in Scotland. There are more of them than there are people of Irish birth (if not ancestry) in Scotland. Whether this applies to Glasgow rather than to some other places, including Edinburgh, usually regarded as 'more English', is debatable but it does provide a pointer to one aspect of the movement of peoples, to and from, which is rarely commented upon. Crosland, for instance, had heard little about it.

The City With an Edwardian Air

The eighteen-nineties and nineteen-hundreds—particularly the latter—was a period in which many new blocks were erected in the business centre, and it has perhaps an Edwardian instead of a Victorian look. Unhappily, the narrowness of the streets makes it difficult to see some of these buildings properly and they are passed unheeded. They suffer also through the contiguity of diminutive, decaying buildings, perhaps over a century old. Recently a fair amount of demolition has been undertaken but the survivors are still remarkably numerous.

The two most notable public buildings erected in Glasgow in the Edwardian period were the Royal Technical College (now the University of Strathclyde) and the Mitchell Library. When the foundation stone of the Royal Technical College was laid by Edward VII in 1903, it was said to be the culmination of the remarkable work done for technical education in Glasgow since Professor John Anderson's 'practical lectures for mechanicians' in the seventeen-seventies, the pioneering Glasgow Mechanics' Institute, and the evening classes begun by Anderson's trustees in the Grammar School in 1827.

Almost every Glasgow engineer at some time in his career took classes at the 'Tech', and recollections of its teachers and of its students—many now distinguished in industry and commerce—form one of the chief topics of conversation when Glasgow men meet in distant places.

The Mitchell Library is another institution which holds a high place in the affections of countless men and women. As students, or just as young people keen to broaden their reading, they used its reference and magazine rooms, and found them invaluable. Hence the frequency with which it is mentioned in the auto-biographies of men of letters who had their origin on Clydeside. The Mitchell Library has played a larger part in the life of the city than many Glaswegians realize.

Andrew Carnegie (wearing cap) laying the memorial stone of the Mitchell Library in September, 1907.

It was founded with a bequest by Stephen Mitchell, the tobacco manufacturer, who left the residue of his estate to establish and endow a large public library in Glasgow. It was opened in 1877 in temporary premises at a corner of Ingram Street and North Albion Street. In 1889 it was transferred to Miller Street, and then in 1911 to handsome and extensive new buildings in North Street.

The immense red sandstone Telephone House near Bothwell Street is of later construction than the Edwardian period, but this is perhaps the point at which to mention the telephone services, if only to explain the significance of a tribute to Glasgow paid by the London *Times* in 1910—'The country has benefited largely by the more enlightened telephone policy of the last few years, and in bringing about this policy Glasgow has played no inconspicuous part.'

John Munro had been a pioneer in 1877 in using the telephone. As early as March, 1879, a telephone exchange was established by David Graham at 140 Douglas Street for members of the medical profession. The success of this exchange led to the establishment of further exchanges, covering the professions and businesses whose members found it most desirable to be in constant touch with one another, and so legal, stockbroking and commercial switchboards were added, the term Douglas Exchange being first applied, so it is said, to the switchboard of the 'Iron Ring'. Subscribers paid an annual fee of £15, which included a royalty charge to the Post Office, a court decision having been given that a telephone was a telegraph, within the meaning of the Telegraph Acts. Graham founded a second exchange, the Central, in Queen Street, but in 1881 his monopoly was challenged by the Bell Telephone Co. and by the Edison Telephone Co., both of which opened exchanges in the city. In May, 1881, they were all absorbed by the National Telephone Co., which operated throughout Scotland, Ireland and parts of England. By 1900 many people, including the Postmaster-General, thought that the service should be administered by the government, and, after political controversy, a compromise was adopted allowing municipalities to operate telephones.

Glasgow Corporation, which had already declined to let the National Telephone Company lay their telephone wires under the streets, immediately created a Municipal Telephone System to compete with the Company's. The only other important instance of a town having two systems was London, where one was run by the Company and the other by the G.P.O. In 1906 an agreement was made between Glasgow Corporation and the Postmaster-General, by which the G.P.O. took over the Municipal System, and for the next four years the government and the private systems continued to operate both in London and in Glasgow. Large concerns usually subscribed to both.

The Times remembered this in 1910, when the licence of the National Telephone Company was expiring, and agreements were being made between them and the Postmaster-General providing the foundations for the present service. Afterwards there was rapid expansion in Glasgow, a peak coming, rather oddly, during the years of the Depression, 1931 to 1935.

Although several of Glasgow's major industries decayed during the Edwardian era, this was scarcely heeded because of the widespread interest shown in the exciting new industries being opened up. The mood resembled that of the eighteen-sixties and eighteen-seventies when the cotton industry was cast aside in favour of engineering. Then, however, the engineering was of the kind described as heavy.

The R. 34 was the first airship
to make the double crossing of the Atlantic in 1919.
The hangar in which it was housed can still be seen,
close to Abbotsinch airport.
It was constructed by Beardmores.

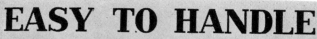

The Argyll car, here advertised in 1907,
was among the leading British cars in the Edwardian era.
The closure of the works in 1914
was for many years given as the outstanding disaster
experienced by Clydeside in this century.

Now it was much lighter and was focused on such products as motor-cars, aircraft and instruments. During the early years of this century no fewer than seven factories in the district were making automobiles —Albion (who later went over to commercial vehicles), Argyle, Arrol-Johnston, Beardmore taxis and Halley fire-engines, among others. Beardmore were also heavily engaged in the aircraft industry. At one stage in the first world war they were making three-quarters of all the aero-engines used by the Royal Flying Corps. They also made airships, including the R34, the first airship to cross the Atlantic.

'Ah Belang tae Glesca'

More people began to go to the theatres, the music-halls and the new cinemas. Dancing became less decorous and, while waltzes were written in the new tradition set by *The Merry Widow Waltz*, ragtime was ushered in with the cake-walk. Dances which Queen Victoria most certainly would not have liked—particularly perhaps the tango with its 'languorous music and sensuous rhythms'—were accepted on the ballroom floor. The character of popular songs changed. Indeed, to the younger generation the most important requirement of a tune was that they could tap their feet to it.

Musical comedies were pepped up, and the first snappy revues were produced in the theatre. Students of social changes noted that these innovations were coming from the United States and from the Continent, but they thought this country had only temporarily ceased to set the world's fashions in entertainment. Actually, the United States was challenging this country, not without success, in the only branch in which we retained our supremacy—the straight play. The Edwardian had other likings too; for instance, he participated in several crazes—diabolo in the parlour, billiards in the saloon, and roller skating in the rink.

In 1904 one of the most important events in the history of the theatre in Glasgow took place when the King's Theatre was opened by the company named after the actor-managers, J. B. Howard and F. W. Wyndham. It was essentially the 'West End Theatre' of the city, and many references were made in the newspapers of the time to the displays of smart evening clothes in its stalls and dress circle. Its special line was musical comedy. Its size reflected the growing demand for this kind of entertainment, and its stage equipment reflected the increasingly spectacular character of the productions.

An incidental consequence of the opening of the King's was that audiences at the smaller Royalty, also leased by Howard and Wyndham, and which had previously featured musical plays, fell off. So the way was prepared for its becoming in 1909 the Glasgow Repertory Theatre, under the direction of Alfred Wareing. No other venture had such enthusiastic adherents as the Rep, and it is remembered with much affection even today, in spite of its brief existence of only five years. A fine standard was set in the selection of plays, the works of new authors were tried out—week after week the representatives of London producers and dramatic critics from London newspapers came to Glasgow for the previews—and plays by Continental authors were given their first presentations in Great Britain.

The Theatre Royal was to some extent overshadowed by the King's Theatre except at pantomime time, F. W. Wyndham having acquired the title of King of the Pantomimes. An incidental point of interest about the Theatre Royal is that it was the first theatre outside London to permit smoking. That was early in the first world war.

The early cinemas were merely converted shops, in which a programme of perhaps seventy minutes' duration, made up of six or seven short 'comedies, dramas, interest and news', was shown, the prices of admission being threepence and sixpence, including perhaps a free cup of tea and biscuit in the afternoons. It was not, however, until the American film, *The Birth of a Nation*, had been shown in the Theatre Royal at *theatre prices* that the cinema was really taken seriously in Glasgow. By 1917 there were a hundred cinemas in Glasgow—much the highest percentage according to population in the country. Some newspapers suggested that housing conditions disposed the people of Glasgow more than those of other towns to frequent places of entertainment.

The chief cinemas in central Glasgow in 1918 were: The Picture House (now extended as the Gaumont) with its tea-rooms, equipped with fountains, gold-fish pool, and cages of singing birds; the New Savoy (formerly the Savoy Music-Hall); La Scala; the King's Cinema (formerly the Vitagraph, well-known for its commissionaire, Andra' Gemmel, one of the last of Glasgow's characters); the Electric Theatre (said to have been the first cinema in Glasgow); the De Luxe, near Charing Cross (the Vaudeville, also at Charing Cross, had recently closed); the Salon (in Sauchiehall Street, near Renfield Street); the Cinema House (now rebuilt as the Regent); Cranston's (now the Classic); the City (in Union Street); the Grand Central (in Jamaica Street); and the St. Enoch (in Argyle Street). The Picture House, opened in 1909, was for several years the leading cinema in Scotland, its Palm Court being one of the centres of the city's social life. It was described by R. W. Campbell in the successor to his *Spud Tamson* novels, when he located one of his incidents there, with a working-class mother taking her daughter to the Palm Court every week to mix with the 'fine folk'.

The music-hall was at its peak in 1912, and, as an example of the entertainment it was providing, a week in that year may be taken at random (it is the week beginning 8th April), noting what was on in Glasgow at that time. Since the turn of the century the Alhambra (perhaps the No. 1 Glasgow music-hall of its day), the Coliseum (the largest), the Savoy (built in 1911 to specialize in the 'better type' of programme), the Pavilion, and the Zoo-Hippodrome had all been opened. The Empress, the last of the pre-war music-halls, was constructed shortly afterwards. The Alhambra is the only survivor in what used to be one of the entertainment centres of the city, with its Waterloo Assembly Rooms (on whose site it was built) and the Royal Hippodrome (whose site is now occupied by the Post Office).

The press announcements for this week in 1912 were:

KING'S THEATRE *Sir George Alexander's Company in 'The Witness for the Defence'*

ROYALTY THEATRE (*The Repertory Theatre*) *'The Admirable Crichton'*

THEATRE ROYAL *Charles Hawtrey's Company in 'Inconstant George'*

ALHAMBRA *The Three Ragtime Boys (Hedges Bros. and Jacobson), Jake Friedman (the Dutch comedian and a company of thirty artistes in the musical extravaganza, 'The Dutch Corporal') and six other turns*

207

SAVOY *Ruth Vincent (the Covent Garden Prima Donna), George Ali (in the screaming playlet, 'Papa's Day Off'), and seven other turns*

EMPIRE *Fred Karno's stupendous attraction 'Perkins the Purser', Jack Pleasants (singing his latest success, 'I'm Twenty-One Today'), and six other turns*

COLISEUM *G. H. Chirgwin (the White-Eyed Kaffir), Elsie Southgate (the great violinist), and seven other turns*

PAVILION *Walter Passmore in the screamingly funny 'Sweet Williams', Wee Georgie Wood (the wonderful boy-comedian), and nine other turns*

PALACE (Gorbals) *George D'Albert (the popular bright and breezy light comedian), J. P. Ling (the mimic), and seven other turns*

OLYMPIA (Bridgeton) *George Gray in 'The Fighting Parson', and six other turns*

PICKARD'S PANOPTICON *(doors open at 6 a.m. during the Spring Holidays). Five turns, Fancy Fair and Laughing Mirrors*

METROPOLE *Arthur Hinton's famous play, 'His Indian Wife'*

PRINCESS'S *Wilson Barrett's famous drama, 'The Silver King'*

GRAND *Alex. Keith's sketch company in 'Where's Your Wife?', also Personality Films and Illustrated Songs*

LYCEUM (Govan) *The popular Scottish comedy, 'Wee Macgreegor'*

If Glasgow can be said to have ever attained a dominating position in any branch of entertainment, then that branch must be the music hall. A list of the players who came from Glasgow—almost all comedians—is quite astonishing. At the head is Sir Harry Lauder— one of the most successful comedians the world has ever known— and the others included Neil Kenyon, Nellie Wallace, Billy Bennett, Lily Morris, Naughton and Gold, and Jack Buchanan. (Stan Laurel, the film comedian, was another.)

Sir Harry Lauder was born near Edinburgh in 1870. After the death of his father, he worked for a couple of years as the family breadwinner in an Arbroath linen factory, and then joined an uncle, who was a miner at Hamilton, the town with which his name will always be associated. He developed an excellent voice, and passed on from local amateur concerts—including the Glasgow 'penny bursts', which he suggests took their name, not so much from the overeating of buns and the swilling of tea, as from the audience's habit of blowing up the empty paper bags and bursting them to signify both approval and disapproval—to semi-professional work with concert parties or as a deputy turn. On one occasion he took the place of J. C. Macdonald, then 'the King of Scots Comics', and the latter subsequently gave him much advice and helped shape his career. Sometimes he appeared in the north of England, and soon realized that 'it was utterly hopeless to break into England with purely Scottish dialect and words and idioms which nobody over the Border understood'.

His decision, in 1900, to try his luck as a 'pro' in London, was largely influenced by seeing Dan Leno perform at the Empire Music Hall. 'If Dan Leno,' he said to himself, 'can get a hundred pounds a week for singing London songs in Glasgow, I can get at least twenty for singing Scotch comic songs in London.' By this time he had acquired two popular songs—*Tobermory* and the *Lass o' Killiecrankie*—and he began to do well. One of his greatest triumphs followed in 1905, when he appeared in the *Aladdin* pantomime at the Theatre Royal. He then sang for the first time *I Love a Lassie*, a song which immediately became the rage, people travelling hundreds of miles to hear him sing it. Later, he added *She's Ma Daisy, Stop Yer Ticklin', Jock,* and *Roamin' in the Gloamin,* to his

"AM AWFA BUSY"

WAT MILLAR—THE BAILIE

Harry Lauder rehearsing for the Royal Pantomime of 1910. He had established his reputation there three years before, and this was his last appearance in pantomime. He had become one of the greatest of international Variety stars.

repertoire, and within a few years became the most popular vaudeville comedian in the world. He had personality, style and abounding good humour. But perhaps the chief characteristic which distinguished him from the other comedians of the day was that he really could sing.

A much-loved man, his appearance in Glasgow invariably aroused demonstrations of affection, but some nationalistic 'intellectuals' turned very critical of his career, saying that 'he made the Scot a figure of fun throughout the world', and it is difficult at times not to wonder, when a new acquaintance in the United States or in England asks something like, 'Hoo are yoo the noo ?'—or, indeed, for some unfathomable reason begins to talk about 'Glesgie'—whether Sir Harry was not partly to blame for this nonsense. On the other hand, his contributions to the well-being of his native land greatly outweighed any disservice he might have done. Indeed, it is possible that those who charge him with having made his country look ridiculous are, in fact, themselves doing just that by making such charges.

Although Sir Harry's name has been associated with most of the popular Scottish songs which have come out of the Glasgow district in this century, the best known was not his. It was Will Fyffe—internationally next in popularity to Harry Lauder—who told the world that he belonged to Glasgow. He, too, came from the east coast of Scotland, but, when the people of Glasgow learned that it was from Dundee that he hailed, they smiled indulgently over such an understandable pretence.

'Fun and Beauty on the Grand Scale'

Glasgow remembered her 1888 Exhibition with great pleasure and, when several members of its organizing committee and its general manager, H. A. Hedley, indicated that they were game for another one, the sequence was begun which led to further exhibitions in 1901, 1911 and 1938—so incidentally providing a most interesting link between the years before the first and second world wars. Each had its educational objects, but Glasgow liked to think of them as entertainment done in a big way.

The 1901 Exhibition had as its chief aim to illustrate the growth of art, industry and science during the nineteenth century. It was the largest exhibition held in Great Britain up to that time. The guarantee fund was £506,000, and the attendance was 11,500,000, including a record for the last day of 173,000. No call was made on the guarantors, the surplus being £40,000.

The architect, James Miller, who later designed the new Royal Infirmary, spread his buildings over 73 acres of Kelvingrove Park and its environs—the Exhibition was known in Glasgow as 'the Groveries'—the Machinery Hall being located where Kelvin Hall now stands, and a sports stadium, with grandstands, being laid out in the University grounds (now occupied principally by the Chemistry Department). Miller conceived the Exhibition in terms of the Spanish Renaissance—although Glasgow thought it more Oriental than Spanish in appearance. This choice was made partly to blend with the new Art Galleries, which were opened on the same day as the Exhibition by the Duke and Duchess of Fife. These red sandstone Galleries, which cost £250,000, were built partly with the surplus, £54,000, of the 1888 Exhibition, and contained 'the finest collection of pictures ever seen in Great Britain'. Most of them were

The 1901 Exhibition,
with the newly completed Art Galleries in the distance.
This exhibition was known as the 'Groveries'.

the property of the city, several Glasgow business men who had with great shrewdness bought pictures—Old Masters and new art—over a number of years, now bequeathing their purchases to the city.

The outstanding features of the Exhibition were its Industrial Hall with a great golden dome on which a Statue of Light floated, with only the great toe of her right foot resting on the dome; the Concert Hall, with a magnificent organ later transferred to the Art Galleries; the electric lighting and the electric lifts; a gondola in the Kelvin with two gondoliers from Venice; a 'Sunlight Cottage', showing how people were to be housed in the future; and some international pavilions, notably seven organized by the Russian Government as a gesture of friendship to Great Britain, but built so slowly that they were opened six weeks after the rest of the Exhibition. The cottage and a wooden bridge over the Kelvin, which once was 'a centre of enchantment, festooned with fairy lights', were retained, and are still to be seen from Partick Bridge.

The success of the Exhibition was in some ways remarkable, as it encountered several untoward happenings—the death of the Queen, the protraction of the South African War, and an outbreak of smallpox. On the other hand, the Clerk of the Weather was considerate, and there were prolonged spells of sunshine. Indeed, he treated all of the first three Glasgow Exhibitions kindly but the last most horribly.

Besides the football and athletic competitions at the Sports Stadium, cycle races were conducted on a quarter-mile track, boarded and banked, and motor-car tests were organized. In the latter, rivalry was keen between Glasgow's own Argyll, and the Darracqs, Daimlers, Wolseleys, and Lanchesters. Every evening the cars were on display, after their return from the 100-mile or 150-mile runs.

Competitions for motor-cars, beginning and ending at the Sports Stadium in the University were a feature of the 1901 Exhibition. The banked cycle track can also be seen.

The 1888 Exhibition had encouraged the railway companies to speed up the journey between London and Glasgow, and the time had been reduced to eight hours.[1] During the 1901 Exhibition several important meetings were held in Glasgow—including the annual meeting of the British Association, the celebrations associated with the ninth jubilee of the foundation of the University, and the congresses of various engineering and other technical institutions. All of this induced the railway companies to provide cheap excursion fares. They were very popular, and so the exhibitions brought many people from the south to the Second City, whose previous conceptions of what life was like in the north were perhaps strange and wonderful.

Above all, however, Glasgow remembered this glorious Exhibition because of the electric tramcar. Electric traction had been introduced

[1] Some other important dates in the history of the railway companies concerning Glasgow are: 1873, first British 'sleepers' (L.N.E.R.) London to Glasgow; 1874, first 'sleepers' (L.M.S.) to Glasgow; 1888, the route race to Scotland begun by companies operating on the west coast and the east coast. In 1895 the fastest journey on the west coast route to Aberdeen (L.M.S.) was done at an average of 63·3 miles per hour, while on the east coast (L.N.E.R.) an average of over 60 miles an hour was obtained, with six engine changes, the overall time being reduced from 11 hours 35 minutes to 8 hours 40 minutes; 1928, first British third-class 'sleepers' (L.M.S.) London to Glasgow; 1937, a regular daily service begun by the Coronation Scot (L.M.S.) between London and Glasgow, taking 6½ hours.

on the Mitchell Street–Springburn route on 13th October, 1898. No longer would Andrew Menzies have been able to say that, 'This is an equine world, run by men with horses as their servants and best friends'. The aim of the new manager, John Young, was to have the service all electric by the opening of the Exhibition. This was achieved, including the opening of a large generating station at Pinkston and the operating of no fewer than 332 cars. Few people walked to Kelvingrove in 1901.

The 1911 Exhibition was planned on a smaller scale than the other exhibitions. Its official name was the Scottish Exhibition of History, Art and Industry (Glasgow, 1911), and one of its objects was to raise money for the endowment of a Chair of Scottish History and Literature at the University. The guarantee fund was £143,000 and the attendance 9,400,000. Except for the opening day and the closing day, the weather was magnificent, and most Glaswegians in their memories associate the Exhibition with bright sunshine and gentle breezes. The end of the Exhibition on 4th November was quite remarkable, however, for a storm during the night took the tops off several of the leading buildings—including the Aviation Pavilion, whose roof was carried to Park Terrace—and destroyed one of the walls of the Palace of History.

Although built at Kelvingrove the Exhibition was located differently from the earlier Exhibitions. Its breadth was merely from Kelvin Way to Gray Street, but it stretched from Sauchiehall Street as far as Gibson Street. The Stewart Memorial Fountain in the park was its focal point, the architect setting around it his major palaces—of industries, history, fine arts, and machinery—the grand concert hall with 300 seats, and the conference halls. In other parts of

The 1911 Exhibition was planned on a smaller scale. This photograph of the bandstand and amphitheatre shows the manner in which the pavilions were placed to suit the park's configuration.

*This old-world 'Scottish Toonie'
with mercat cross and town crier
was a central point in the 1911 Exhibition.*

Kelvingrove were erected an old-world Scottish 'toonie', a Highland Village, a Pavilion on Old Glasgow, a Garden Club, an Aerial Railway, a Mountain Slide, a West African Village, and various side-shows. The chief Palace was that of History—it was modelled on the Palace of Falkland—and contained the most comprehensive collection of Scottish relics ever brought together. Good use was made of the River Kelvin, in which a cavalcade of model ships floated, but the great thrill was the aerial railway, which did a circular trip from the heights, where the Earl Roberts Statue now stands, to the University grounds—and went 130 feet above the Kelvin.

An interesting contrast has been observed between the songs most often sung at these Exhibitions. At the 1911 Exhibition the song was *Abide With Me*. The military bands and even some of the Continental bands—which included the Blue Hungarian Band— played it, and 'almost at once the vast throngs would take up the sacred tune and provide a vocal accompaniment. At such moments a wave of mass emotion seemed to sweep over the audience.'

The tune of which the crowds at the 1938 Exhibition could never hear enough was *The Lambeth Walk*. Although only 27 years had passed since the 1911 Exhibition, the circumstances had changed greatly. The new Exhibition was planned by men who remembered the last Exhibition with affection, but its principal object was not so much to provide fun and beauty on the grand scale, as to do Scotland a good turn. Robin Jay put it this way. 'Since 1911 the Second City has revised one or two of its articles of belief. The lean years have seen to that. It is even a little difficult to convince the young that less than thirty years ago fortunate citizens (and there were thousands) really felt in the heart of them that in Glasgow prosperity must last for ever.'

Only one exhibition on an international scale had been held in Great Britain between 1911 and 1938. That was at Wembley during the early 'twenties and, in spite of its many fine features it was financially a great failure. The promotors of the Empire Exhibition (Scotland) 1938 were bold, and the people of Scotland rallied behind them by guaranteeing over £750,000. Kelvingrove was too small to

213

accommodate their ambitious schemes, and a new site, of 175 acres, was chosen at Bellahouston Park. The focal point of the Exhibition, as planned by the architect, Thomas S. Tait, was a tower which rose like a gleaming silver pencil, 300 feet above Bellahouston Hill, itself 170 feet above sea-level.

The adjacent Amusement Park was equipped on a scale never equalled in Scotland, and was claimed in the Official Guide to be the 'biggest and most original amusement park in Europe'. Perhaps the outstanding features of the Exhibition apart from the Tower, were the beautifully proportioned United Kingdom Building, the acoustically perfect Concert Hall, and the cascades and fountains, particularly when lit at night. Architecturally the Exhibition broke from the 'wedding-cake' ornamentations of the past, and set new standards which, but for the outbreak of war in the following year, might have had a considerable influence on the design of public and other buildings in Scotland.

Approximately 13,500,000 people visited the Exhibition and the Stadium—364,000 on the last day, the largest attendance ever in the British Isles—and, as they gathered around the Tower at midnight, to hear a resonant broadcast voice declare the Exhibition at an end, the rain 'came down in buckets'. Almost everyone associates the Exhibition of 1938 with wind and rain, for the summer was the worst in the west of Scotland for almost one hundred years and, save for a bright opening spell, scarcely a day was without a downpour. In consequence a call on the guarantors—for the only time with a Glasgow Exhibition—was unavoidable. It was not heavy—three shillings and fivepence in the pound—and there can be no doubt that, had the Clerk of the Weather been better disposed, this, like the other exhibitions, would have been a financial as well as almost every other kind of success.

214

*The floodlighting
and water displays
of the Empire Exhibition 1938
were quite outstanding.*

*The focal point
of the Exhibition
was the 300-foot Tait's Tower.*

Interlude—A Murder Story

Patrick Hamilton chooses London as the scene for his gas-light melodramas, about murder in the unsubstantial, shadowy streets of winter's evenings at the turn of the century. But perhaps the Charing Cross district of Glasgow would provide a more appropriate setting. No fewer than four of the most publicized murders of the last hundred years were committed within a radius of half a mile of Charing Cross. Dr. Prichard, the last man hanged publicly in Glasgow, killed his wife and mother-in-law there. Jessie McPherson was murdered there in 1862. A footprint made on a floorboard by a bloody, naked foot—whose was it?—which played a large part in the trial of her alleged slayer, is still in the Police Museum. And note must be taken too of the Madeline Smith case. When, in 1857, the charge of murder against Madeleine Smith was found not proven, few people asked themselves, 'If she didn't kill L'Angelier, who did?' But when, in 1909, Oscar Slater was declared guilty of murdering Miss Gilchrist, many went on asking, 'But who really killed Miss Gilchrist?'

Miss Gilchrist was an old lady who lived with a maid, Lambie, in a flat at Queen's Terrace. She was timid, and had a premonition of being in danger. She arranged with a neighbour, Mr. Adams, that she would knock on the floor if in need of assistance. On the evening of 21st December, 1908, Mr. Adams became suspicious. As he approached the door he was joined by the maid, Lambie, who had been out buying a newspaper. She opened the door, a man came from the bedroom, passed them both 'quite pleasantly', and disappeared into the night. Miss Gilchrist had been brutally murdered. Her jewels seemed untouched, except for, according to Lambie, a diamond crescent brooch. But papers were scattered about the room, and the possiblity of the murderer having been in search of a document—and having found it—should be kept in mind.

Lambie's behaviour was so odd that suspicion immediately fell on her, and most students of the case think that she *must* have recognized the man who hurried past them. Possibly he had been in the flat before—otherwise, why did Miss Gilchrist admit him, as presumably she had done?—and from that point various theories can be evolved.

A few days later the police were told that a German Jew, Oscar Slater, had been trying to sell a pawn ticket for a diamond crescent brooch, and, when they found that he had already left by the *Lusitania* for New York, no one doubted that they were on to something. Unfortunately, for this theory, the brooch had no connection with Miss Gilchrist. But the police went ahead with Slater's extradition and charged him with the murder. This was too much for many people, and their doubts were increased when the evidence against Slater was found to consist chiefly of rather uncertain identifications by Lambie, now a witness for the prosecution, by a message girl who had been near the house when the murderer hurried past her, if it was the murderer who hurried past her, and by some people who had seen a strange man loitering in the street outside the house. Slater's case was rather inadequately handled, partly because his advisers thought there was something fantastic about his having been charged at all. Slater, who did not give evidence, declared from the dock following the verdict that he had never heard of Miss Gilchrist, that he was unaware of the existence

216

either of herself or of her jewels, and that he did not even know where she lived.

The verdict, which was by a majority—guilty, nine; not proven, five; not guilty, one—was no doubt greatly influenced by the Lord Advocate's vigorous concluding speech, in which he made great play of Slater's rather questionable career, in having lived by his wits—by gambling and dealing in jewels which it was alleged were not always honestly come by. Slater had spent most of his days in Glasgow in billiards saloons, and in the Motor and Sloper Clubs in India Street, and this disclosure too might have prejudiced the jury against him.

There was a public outcry, and the Secretary of State for Scotland decided that the death sentence should be commuted to penal servitude for life. Conan Doyle took up the case and pressed for a re-trial. Several other attempts were made to have the verdict re-considered, but for almost twenty years the authorities were adamant—and in this connection it should be remembered that their side of the story has never been told. What was behind their inflexible determination?

In 1927 another book on the trial was published—*The Truth about Oscar Slater*, by a Glasgow journalist, William Park—and some of the national newspapers revived the demand for the evidence to be gone over. It was at this time that Edgar Wallace, then at the height of his popularity, expressed his views. An American newspaper correspondent reported an interview with Lambie, now a married woman in Illinois, in which she admitted recognizing the man in the hall as one who had often visited her mistress, but added that, when she mentioned his name to the police, she was persuaded she had been mistaken.

Shortly afterwards Oscar Slater was released from Peterhead Prison on licence, but the demands for an inquiry, pressed by Conan Doyle, went on, and the Secretary of State for Scotland decided to remit all questions about the case to the Court of Criminal Appeal. Conan Doyle having guaranteed the costs of presenting Slater's case, it was put in the charge of some of the leading Scottish advocates. The surprises connected with the case were by no means over. Slater resented a refusal by the Court to allow him to give evidence. Without consulting his advisers, he wrote to the Lord Justice-General withdrawing the appeal, and informed the press of what he had done. This took some smoothing over, but eventually the trial went on, although Lambie refused to return to give further evidence.

The Court's decision was in Slater's favour, but on a legal point only—the Lord Advocate should not have been allowed to attack Slater's moral character, and the Judge had misdirected the jury on this point. Conan Doyle, although disappointed, said, 'we must be thankful for what we have got', and Lambie, in an interview with the American press, said simply, 'I am glad it is all over'.

Actually, the case was not quite over, for Slater's expenses at the appeal were £1500, and had still to be met. He had already, again through acting on his own instead of in consultation with his solicitors, got less compensation than he was due. An agitation to have the Government meet the costs of the appeal having failed, Conan Doyle found himself left to foot the bill.

Lambie has since died in the United States but this has not checked the flow of theories. The current explanation is that two men were involved, one a well-known city man who was looking for a paper concerning a will, and the other, an epileptic youth who got into an argument with Miss Gilchrist in another room and killed her before his friend could intervene.

The Citizen Army

Overlooking Kelvingrove Park at Park Circus is an equestrian statue which—at least, in silhouette—is among the best known in Glasgow. Because it occupies such a fine position it has come in for some criticism, for the soldier on the horse is Earl Roberts, whose name is little known to the younger generations, and the statue itself really commemorates no more than a phrase in a speech. But it was a speech which stirred Glasgow more than any other for generations and, as the *Glasgow Herald* said at the time, 'no other public man in recent years has had such a reception as the Glasgow people gave to the aged Field-Marshal'.

Earl Roberts addressed three meetings in Glasgow—one of them in the University at a special Honorary Graduation—on 6th and 7th May, 1913. He told his audiences that war was coming in Europe, and that 'Britain alone stands still, repeating the old watchwords, recklessly trusting to worn-out systems and discarded principles'. He pleaded for the formation of a Citizen Army which would be sufficient in numbers and efficiently trained to take part immediately in a war with Germany. An untrained man with a rifle, he declared, would be useless in modern warfare.

In St. Andrew's Halls, at the third of his meetings, the audience passed a resolution calling for legislative adoption of the principle of personal service in the Territorial Force. Actually, conscription was not adopted until well after the war had begun, but Lord Roberts, if he achieved nothing else in his old age, opened the country's eyes to stern realities. Or, at least, partly opened them.

The Grim Years, 1914-18

The first world war began in 1914. It took most of the British public unawares. In spite of Lord Robert's campaign they had gone on hoping that it would never happen. Many had supported Lloyd George in the early months of the year, when he denounced the folly of expenditure on armament, and most had shared in the common feeling, both in Great Britain and in France, that relationships with Germany were improving. Accordingly, when tension developed between Germany and Russia, following the murder of the Austrian Archduke, Franz Ferdinand, in Serbia on 28th June, the British public was irritated rather than alarmed, for its interests were focused on an attempt to solve the Irish problem by partitioning North and South Ireland, with a boundary running through Fermanagh and Tyrone. Indeed, up to 28th July it had seemed that war was going to be averted. The Kaiser himself supposed that a great diplomatic triumph was in the making. But mischief once begun is difficult to stop, and on 4th August Great Britain, in unity with the Dominions and the other members of the Empire, declared war on Germany.

Several days earlier, crowds had gathered outside the Glasgow newspaper offices to read bulletins on the situation. The naval reserves had already been called up, many coming from Glasgow. Confidence was felt in the power of the Royal Navy, already mobilized, to secure control of the seas. No fear was felt over the

long-threatened invasion of this country by the German Army, and few believed that the enemy would be able to make much of a stand against the combined forces of Russia, France and this country. Many thought that the war, if it did break out, would be over by Christmas. Later we learned that the Germans themselves thought so too, but they did not see themselves as the losers.

The Regular Army immediately went to France, where it was to earn undying glory as the Contemptible Little Army. The Territorial Army was called up and, having volunteered unanimously for service overseas, began intensive training. The 9th Highland Light Infantry (the Glasgow Highlanders) and the 5th Scottish Rifles were in France before the end of the year, being, with the London Scottish, the first battalions of the Territorial Army to join the British Expeditionary Force. They were followed soon afterwards by several other Glasgow battalions, although the 5th, 6th (Harry Lauder's Battalion), and 7th H.L.I., and the 7th and 8th Scottish Rifles went to Gallipoli with the 52nd Division, the Lowland counterpart of the 51st Highland Division.

Lord Kitchener, who had been appointed Secretary of State for War, told the people that the Regular Army and the Territorial Army would together represent only a small part of the army which would eventually be required of Great Britain. He asked for an additional 200,000 men and, as the country was not ready for conscription—it was not adopted until January, 1916—he called for

1915. The H.L.I. march down Sauchiehall Street into Renfield Street en route to France. This photograph has a detail of incidental interest as it shows the Salon Cinema, later replaced by a furniture store.

219

P

volunteers. Within a few weeks the famous poster of Lord Kitchener pointing directly at the public was everywhere insisting that 'Your Country Needs You'.

The stalwart in organizing recruiting in Glasgow was the Lord Provost, Sir Thomas Dunlop—along with his predecessor as Lord Provost, Sir Archibald McInnes-Shaw—and their efforts met with almost overwhelming success. Although quite considerable numbers of men went to the Navy and the Flying Corps, the majority went to the Army, and a reference to them may be taken as illustrative of Glasgow's record in the Fighting Services. In total Glasgow was said to have provided most of the men for 26 battalions. The best-chronicled were perhaps the 15th, 16th and 17th Battalions of the H.L.I., and many of the men were, as George Blake said, the rough, tough, occasionally turbulent and always warm-hearted children of mixed Lowland, Highland and Irish ancestry, who sang as they marched along, with a cocky wee swagger of the shoulders, side to side:

Ta-Ta, Bella ! I'll no' say good-bye
Although I'm leavin' Glesca wi' the H.L.I.

James Dalrymple, the manager of the Glasgow Corporation Tramways Department, took up recruitment with such enthusiasm that he was spoken of as the greatest recruiting agent Scotland ever produced. By using illuminated tramcars, bands and parades, open-air cinemas, and other forms of advertising, he was 'more or less the direct means of raising a brigade of artillery, two infantry battalions and five companies of engineers'. During sixteen hours on 13th September, 1110 employees of the Tramways Department enlisted in the 15th H.L.I. which, in spite of many changes made in its personnel during the war, will always be thought of as the Tramways Battalion.

TG

SCOTS PICTORIAL

Tom Gentleman's drawing
of an H.L.I. Sergeant, 1915.

The Glasgow Transport Offices
in Bath Street, 1915,
covered with
mammoth recruiting posters.

GLASGOW HERALD

The 16th Battalion also was closely associated with Glasgow Corporation, which in the beginning contracted to house, feed, and provide certain articles of kit for the two battalions. Originally it was recruited mainly from former members of the Boys' Brigade, its flags being presented by the Trades House.

The histories of these two battalions were written by Thomas Chalmers in the early 'thirties. The history of the 17th Battalion was written earlier, by J. W. Arthur and Ian S. Munro, and was published in 1920. This battalion's formation is dated from 3rd September, when the Glasgow Chamber of Commerce decided to raise it. It had at first four companies: A, recruited from the Royal Technical College; B, from the former pupils of the city schools; C and D, from the city business houses and trades. On 7th November the battalion paid a return visit to the city and marched through crowded streets, but 'hardly a cheer was heard. The men marched between banks of faces, in deep silence.' Unpleasant facts were at last being faced—and yet the delusion that the war was going to be short persisted. Early in 1915 members of this battalion were so concerned about the war being over before they reached France that they made representations for their training to be speeded up.

Almost everything, including khaki cloth, was scarce in the early months of the war, and for the first few weeks the recruits of the three battalions lived in their own homes, drilling and receiving instruction in the Territorial Force Association Halls. They received some kit on 19th and 20th September, and went to camp at Gailes in Ayrshire a few days later. They remained there until May, although the Chamber of Commerce Battalion had been transferred in October to rather more comfortable billets in Troon, so earning for themselves the nickname of the Featherbeds. In May the battalion went south, first to Shropshire and then to other parts, and in November—fourteen months after their formation—they crossed to France. They were in the trenches by Christmas, 1915, and lesser engagements took them on to the shambles of the Somme, beginning on 1st July, 1916, when in three days the casualties of the 16th Battalion alone were 20 officers and 534 other ranks. Indeed, Glasgow's losses at the beginning of this battle were so severe that on 8th July a memorial service was held in Glasgow Cathedral. In the dreadful days which followed the British casualties were 500,000 and the Glasgow casualty figures were commensurate. On 21st March, 1918, the British Army had an even greater trial, when it was called upon to bear the brunt of Ludendorff's tremendous final assault. The 15th and 16th Battalions were involved, although the 17th (and 18th) had by then been disbanded under a reorganization scheme.

Rather less has been written about the 18th Battalion than about the other three. It was a bantam battalion, recruited in March, 1915, and the 'wee fellas' were perhaps the toughest in the H.L.I. Stories are still told about them—for instance, about an occasion when a well-known police band accompanied them on a route march from Girvan to Ballantrae and, to the lively satisfaction of some members of the battalion, whose relations in the past with the police had not been entirely happy, did not last the pace. The 18th suffered heavy casualties and was twice—at the Somme and at Passchendaele—almost wiped out. It was subsequently reinforced by the de-horsed Queen's Own Royal Glasgow Yeomanry.

The colours of the 15th and 16th Battalions were carried into Germany after the Armistice, and were not deposited in Glasgow

A scene only too frequently seen in the Central Station during the first world war.

Cathedral, beside those of the 17th and 18th Battalions, until November, 1922. Altogether the H.L.I., which at the outset had two regular battalions, two special reserve battalions, and five territorial battalions, had thirty battalions during the war, some of them with second and third lines. In addition to those already mentioned, the 10th, 11th and 12th Battalions were largely composed of Glasgow men.

Next to the H.L.I. the regiment most closely associated with the city was the Cameron Highlanders. Towards the end of August, 1914, Lochiel (the Chief of the Camerons) launched a campaign at the request of Lord Kitchener, who had a high regard for the Regiment, to recruit several new battalions. His appeal was directed particularly to Inverness and North-West Scotland, but his letter to the *Glasgow Herald*—and a subsequent address to representatives of the Glasgow Highland societies—brought what the official history of the Regiment described as a response 'which surpassed every expectation'. James Dalrymple was particularly helpful, and had posters on all tramcars urging the desirability of joining Lochiel's Camerons. The glamour of the kilt proved an irresistible attraction, and a company of the 5th Cameron Highlanders, sponsored by the Stock Exchange, was soon filled.

The University then requested that students should be permitted to join a unit as a body, and a boisterous meeting was held in the Union, under the chairmanship of the Principal, Sir Donald MacAlister. 'So impatient,' says the official history, 'were the men to wear the Cameron tartan that they intimated their desire to enlist immediately, and it was with difficulty that they were persuaded to keep their clothes on their bodies and wait until the morrow for medical examination.' Between 200 and 300 students joined the 6th Cameron Highlanders, and it too was soon up to strength. Every night the men who had been accepted the day before marched to Buchanan Street Station to entrain for Inverness, and invariably they were headed by a piper. Neither the 5th (the Lochiels) nor the 6th (University and Stock Exchange) stayed long in the north, both

222

being transferred to Aldershot—the 5th sailed for France on 6th May, 1915, and the 6th soon afterwards—but the 7th, the 'Shiny Seventh'—so-called because of the great care given by all ranks to cleanliness and appearance—which was also largely recruited in Glasgow, spent some months in training at Inverness, and its memory is still preserved in that town. The 5th, 6th and 7th Cameron Highlanders formed part of the 15th Scottish Division—so, incidentally, did the 11th and 12th H.L.I.—which had a record almost unequalled by any other Division in the British Army, covering Loos, the Somme, Arras (1917), Ypres (1917), Arras (1918) and the German retreat. The Battalion was disbanded in the reorganization early in 1918, part being amalgamated with the 6th Battalion, and part forming a training battalion for the American Army. The 5th and 6th Battalions were not disbanded until late in 1919.

Thirteen men from the Greater Glasgow district were awarded the V.C. They were: 1914—Driver F. Luke (37th Battery R.F.A.); Lieut. H. May (1st Battalion Scottish Rifles); 1915— Pte. D. R. Lauder (1/4th Battalion Royal Scottish Fusiliers); 1916—Sgt. J. F. Erskine (5th Battalion Scottish Rifles), Lieut. D. Macintosh (Seaforths), Drum-Major W. Ritchie (Seaforths), Sgt. J. Turnbull (17th Battalion H.L.I.), Sgt. R. Downie (2nd Battalion Dublin Fusiliers), 1917— C.S.M. J. Skinner (K.O.S.B.), Sgt. J. B. Hamilton (9th Battalion H.L.I.), Sgt. J. McAulay (1st Battalion Scots Guards); 1918— Lieut.-Col. W. Anderson (H.L.I.), Sgt. D. F. Hunter (6th Battalion H.L.I.).

Less has been recorded about Glasgow's industrial contribution to the war effort than about the achievements of her men and women in the fighting services. The prevailing thought in 1919 was that there would never be another world war. The wish to get back to what the American President shortly afterwards called 'normalcy' was so predominating, that few were disposed to recall and to record what had been done in the factories during the last few exceptional years. Fortunately, Sir Muirhead Bone prepared a series of magnificent etchings depicting the exertions which had been made in the shipyards, engineering shops and munitions plants, and they will be a reminder to future generations of one of the greatest phases in the history of Clydeside. But it is only by chance that the student will come across such impressive items of information as that James Templeton and Co. converted a great many of their carpet looms to weave blankets for the Government Departments, that the machinery ran continuously day and night, and that, although they had never made a blanket before, they supplied during the war more than four million blankets, a larger number than any other firm in Great Britain. Nor will they read much about the adaptability shown by thousands of Glasgow women who went to work in the engineering shops. Sam Mavor in some of his incidental papers referred to the lessons which should have been drawn from this experience, but in the passing of time it was usually spoken of light-heartedly, even by the women themselves.

The *Glasgow Herald* in a supplement published in December, 1918, gave particulars of the achievements of the shipyards. Altogether thirty Clydeside yards and marine engineering works were mentioned, but a qualifying statement was made—'no figures can convey anything like an accurate impression of the activity that has prevailed or of the continuity of the process of turning out new ships, while there is no way of tabulating the immense amount of naval repair and overhaul work which has been done'. The three leading companies constructing vessels for the Royal Navy were: John Brown and Co. (the battleship *Barham*, and the battle-cruisers *Tiger*, *Repulse*, and *Hood*, the latter uncompleted at the end of the war); the Fairfield Co. (the battle-cruisers *Valiant* and *Renown*); and Wm. Beardmore and Co. (the battleships *Benbow* and *Ramillies*)—and an amazingly large number of light cruisers, destroyers, submarines, seaplane carriers, troopships, minesweepers and other craft. These and other yards also built many cargo and passenger ships for the Mercantile Marine. Indeed, at one time, when the U-boat menace was at its height, the outcome of the war seemed to hinge on the speed with which the Clyde could turn out new ships.

Subsequently some of the shipping companies published accounts of their accomplishments. A brief extract from Archibald Hurd's *History of the Clan Line in War* might give an impression of what they did. At the outbreak of war the largest Scottish steamship company, the Clan Line, had 56 vessels of 251,000 tonnage. They lost 28 vessels, but at the end of the war they had, so effectively did the Clyde shipyards undertake repair and replacement, 51 vessels of 261,000 tonnage. Their losses in personnel were heavy, 52 officers and 239 seamen. Their decorations included 1 D.S.O. and 6 D.S.C.s. Among their steamers sunk, two were by the German cruiser, *Emden*, in the Indian Ocean at the commencement of the war, and one was in the Atlantic in March, 1918, on a day when two others of their ships were also torpedoed, but brought to port. As in the second world war the enemy's main hope of success lay in the isolation of Great Britain from the rest of the world. His failure in both wars was largely accomplished by the heroism of the Mercantile Marine.

J. M. LOUDON

Glasgow's aircraft industry made a notable contribution during the first world war. Beardmore's were particularly prominent with their aero engines, but they also constructed airships. This is a fighter fuselage being assembled at Dalmuir in the 1916 period.

Many Glasgow industrial firms came out of the war with a greater variety of products than previously, and with enlarged and better-equipped workshops. One of them, William Beardmore and Co., whose energies had been almost prodigious, had employed almost 40,000 men and women in their various establishments in Glasgow, Dalmuir, Mossend, Coatbridge, Airdrie and Paisley, and in a forecast made about their products for the post-war world gave, besides those associated with shipbuilding and marine engineering and with heavy industries: locomotives and rolling stock; aeroplanes, airships and aero-engines; motor-cars; reciprocating and turbine machinery; and engines for crude or refined oils. This indicates that the Clyde engineering firms were forward-looking in 1918–19 and had little comprehension of the possibility of bitter disappointments lying ahead of them.

During the war the people of Glasgow, alongside those of the rest of Great Britain, had to accept many changes in their ways of living, and on the whole these changes were found more upsetting than the much greater changes to be made in the second world war—partly, no doubt, because many of them were quite novel and un-expected, and partly because the authorities who controlled so much of civil life during the second world war made fewer mistakes, having the experiences of the earlier war to draw on.

The comparatively easy-going Edwardian ways of living continued well into 1915 and even later—perhaps up to the Battle of the Somme (1st July, 1916)—and one of the first slogans of the war was 'Business as Usual'. By 1915, however, restrictions and other limitations on supplies were making their appearance. Hence, for instance, a *Punch* cartoon of the winter of 1915–16, in which an inebriated Glasgow tramcar passenger was alleged to be saying, 'I canna' jist bottom this. It's Seterday nicht an' this is the Clydebank caur, an' there's naebody singing' an' naebody fechtin' wi' the conductor.'

Germany declared her blockade of this country in February, 1915. Much of the submarine war was fought not far from the Firth of Clyde, and this gave rise to one of the most fanciful stories of the war. A U-boat commander was said, when taken prisoner, to have had in his pocket the counterfoils of two tickets for a concert given a few days before by Sir Thomas Beecham in St. Andrew's Halls. Voluntary rationing and meatless days in restaurants having been found inadequate, compulsory rationing was instituted at the beginning of 1917. The cost of living rose. The public were urged to contribute to war loans and to save coal. They had to supply particulars about themselves under a

The first women conductresses.
The posters on the car will be noted with interest.

BANTAMS FOR THE FRONT   3,000 WANTED

national registration scheme. They formed new interests—men, for instance, by growing vegetables in allotments, and women by knitting for the troops. Many women took jobs in the public services and in the munition factories. Glasgow played a pioneering part in this development, and was the first town to engage—in March, 1915—women tram-conductors. Some of the two million women who were by 1918 doing work previously done by men were alleged—usually by other women who had been unable to follow their example—to be earning fabulous wages, and comic papers published cartoons about girls from the shell-filling factories buying fur coats and grand pianos. In fact the emancipation of women had begun, and, in February, 1918, the vote was conferred on women over thirty. Skirts at once became shorter; hair was bobbed.

In one respect Glasgow was luckier than some other parts of the country. It was never raided by Zeppelins or by other aircraft, although on one occasion they were not far away, when they reached Edinburgh and dropped bombs on High Street. But the reduction of street illumination to a glimmer and the covering of windows with heavy curtains were a constant reminder to the people of Glasgow during the last winters of the war that this country had in some respects ceased to be an island.

The war ended, as it began, suddenly, and although, after 26th September, 1918, when Bulgaria asked for a truce, many had thought that the enemy's collapse must be near, few realized that the armistice was only two or three weeks away. The news that the war was over spread rapidly and by noon on 11th November almost all factories and offices were closed, and in the afternoon the city streets were more crowded than perhaps at any other time. At noon the Lord Provost, speaking in George Square from an improvised platform on a lorry, expressed 'the great joy with which Glasgow had received the glad tidings'. An aerial celebration of victory took place over the city—an appropriate favour, according to the *Glasgow Herald,* for Glasgow had provided the nation with a great Air Minister, in the person of Lord Weir, and was an important centre of the aeroplane industry.

The celebrations did not last long. The afternoon of 12th November turned cold and foggy, and, although many banquets and dances were held in the succeeding weeks, Glasgow had by 13th November entered the post-war world. Of later occasions, two in particular should be mentioned. On 8th May, 1919, Glasgow conferred the Freedom of the City on Sir Douglas Haig, the Scot who had been Commander-in-Chief of the British Armies in France, and, out of the discussions which took place at the time, came a Scottish institution, the Earl Haig Benevolent Fund. On 8th March, 1921, the Freedom was conferred on the Prince of Wales, when he came to Glasgow to open the short-lived Glasgow section of the British Industries Fair. He took the opportunity to pay the warmest of all tributes to the contributions made by Clydeside, saying that 'Glasgow's achievements in the war stir one indeed'.

During the Twenty Years' Truce

Many felt, when the second world war began in September, 1939, that the years since 1918 had lacked substance, and that a phantasmic existence of twenty years was coming to its end. History might dismiss the period, treating it as a time of truce, or perhaps even as a breathing space in what was really a long-drawn-out war. Surprise

226

might be expressed over the obtuseness of the people of the Allied nations, firstly, in forcing a severe peace treaty on the Germans and then in letting them evade its conditions, and secondly, in trying to carry out a foreign policy while discarding the armaments to support it. A few phrases will, no doubt, survive—such as, that the Frontier of Great Britain is now on the Rhine, and that the Bomber will Always Get Through—but posterity will probably be most puzzled to understand why the Allied nations re-armed at such a leisurely pace after 1932 when Japan defied the League of Nations over Manchuria, after 1933 when Hitler established Nazi rule in Germany, after 1935 when Mussolini attacked Abyssinia, or even after 1938 when the Munich Pact was signed.

This ineffectualness becomes comprehensible only when viewed against the fear which prevailed during most of the two decades. From 1921 to 1935 the shadow which persistently fell across Great Britain was cast not by warmongering among the nations but by unemployment. The decay of some of this country's basic industries, about the possibility of which statesmen had been worrying since the eighteen-fifties, seemed at last to be a grim reality. After a short post-war boom, business became chronically depressed. In 1921 approximately $2\frac{1}{2}$ million people were unemployed in Great Britain, and during the years which followed, up to 1929, while the United States was revelling in prosperity, the figure did not fall below one million. After that the Depression really set in, and by the end of 1931 the number of unemployed had risen to almost three million. Even then it was not evenly distributed throughout the country, the centres of the staple industries suffering worst—Clydeside, Tyneside, Cumberland, Lancashire, South Wales, Ulster, these were the districts in which most families were, at least in part, dependent upon 'the dole'. At no time between 1923 and 1939 was less than 10 per cent of the insured population of Scotland unemployed, and in the 1932 period the percentage rose to almost 30.

Life did not, however, move slothfully during the twenty years. Much important social legislation was passed, the franchise was extended, and in 1936—the year in which the country had three Kings—the worst constitutional crisis for years had to be faced. The general health of the country improved. The expectation of life increased. Rickets, which had been the cause of much dreadful disfigurement on Clydeside, was overcome, and the ragged, barefoot boy disappeared from the streets of Glasgow.

To some extent the public restraint was born of self-delusion. People were living in a fool's paradise while their economic world was collapsing about them—but most of them were enjoying themselves reasonably well. The post-war generation, in their desire to put the memories of the war behind them, had turned to dancing and enjoyed themselves during the evening with the Foxtrot, the Tango, the Charleston and the Black Bottom, swaying to American tunes played by dance orchestras in which saxophones took over from fiddles, and drums maintained the beat. The older dance-halls were enlarged, some changing their names to *palais de dance*, and new ones were opened in the city—the Plaza, the Waldorf, the Locarno, the Albert, and the Playhouse Ballroom—besides a couple of night clubs in Sauchiehall Street. It was said that there were over 50 dance-halls in Glasgow, providing an interesting comparison with London's total of 260. However, enthusiasm for dancing waned a little during the 'thirties—both the Waldorf and the Locarno closed down, the former permanently and the latter temporarily—and the

A selection of Tom Gentleman's 'Town Types', 1920–22.

GLASGOW

GREENOCK

PAISLEY

ROTHESAY

KILMARNOCK

MOTHERWELL
SCOTS PICTORIAL

227

cinemas in the centre of the town were replaced by more palatial buildings, including Green's Playhouse (which with 4400 seats was the largest cinema in Europe), the Regal and the Paramount.

On the other hand, vaudeville was on the decline, and several of the palaces of variety were transformed into cinemas. A most courageous venture in the early 'thirties, however, brought about the rebuilding of the Empire, described as the leading music-hall outside London. Along with the Pavilion, it upheld a tradition with which Glasgow is more closely linked. The theatre has kept its position much more securely in Glasgow than in most other British towns—and, incidentally, also in towns in the Dominions and the United States—where the cinema had tended to swamp all other forms of public entertainment. The Alhambra—built as a music-hall but now a theatre—the King's and the Royal all served Glasgow well. Indeed, the reputation of the Clydeside playgoer for discrimination led the promoters of many of London's plays, musical comedies and revues to give their productions a preliminary run on Clydeside. In consequence the Glasgow visitor to London often had difficulty in finding a theatre with a major presentation he had not seen already. It was in Glasgow, for instance, that Binnie Hale as Nanette sang *Tea for Two* even before New York had heard it, and Jessie Matthews went *Dancing on the Ceiling* before any other city had heard it. If Glasgow's taste for music-hall has been to some extent lost, it could be said to have been replaced by a preference for revue. This might be attributed particularly to the Half Past Eight shows first presented at the King's Theatre in the early nineteen-thirties. Every Glasgow theatre has since produced summer-time revues occasionally and three or four have been going on simultaneously.

But above all, Glasgow liked the cinema. Its Cosmo (1939) was the only cinema showing a specialized Continental programme which kept open throughout the war. Its Film Society (1929) is the oldest operating society of its kind in the Commonwealth and perhaps the world. Its International Amateur Film Festival (1932) attracted the largest audiences in the country. And its Scottish Film Council (1933) was first in creating a really large circulating library of educational and other 16 mm films.

Few better examples can be found of the way in which Glasgow men tend to forge ahead in the undertakings with which they become associated, than in this entertainment business. A Glasgow solicitor, John Maxwell, rose to be the chief of one of the greatest British circuits of cinemas, and in 1929 in his Elstree studios pioneered the production of British talking-films. Through him many other Glasgow men became associated with the making and showing of films. Another Glasgow man, John Grierson, founded the British documentary school—the one branch of the cinema in which Great Britain consistently led the world—and he, too, made opportunities for other young Glasgow men to take up this creative work.

In vaudeville a new coterie of Scots comedians came to the front— Tommy Lorne, Dave Willis, Jack Radcliffe, George West, Tommy Morgan, Jack Anthony, Alec Finlay, Peter Sinclair and many others, including among the women, Renee Houston, Jean Kennedy and Doris Droy. But only a few made reputations outside Scotland— some, indeed, never ventured south of Newcastle and Carlisle or west of Belfast.

In the middle 'twenties the most important building erected in

Kelvin Hall was burned down on 7th July, 1925 and was replaced two years later.

Glasgow was constructed by the Corporation. It was the Kelvin Hall, an exhibition hall with an area—170,000 square feet— approximately the same as London's Olympia, and all on one floor. It replaced an earlier hall burned down shortly after the war. Unfortunately, the section of the British Industries Fair intended for Glasgow did not survive—buyers apparently would not travel north, so providing a disturbing commentary on Glasgow's lost status. But many excellent trade exhibitions, including the Motor Show, were held in Kelvin Hall, besides the annual Christmas Carnival and Circus. During the second world war Kelvin Hall was converted into the country's chief factory manufacturing barrage and convoy balloons.

Posterity will certainly look on radio broadcasting as one of the most important developments of the two decades between the wars. Glasgow took up wireless with enthusiasm, and in 1922 many people made crystal sets to listen to an experimental transmitter (5 MG) working from a former hotel at 141 Bath Street. Their numbers increased considerably after March, 1923, when the first Scottish Studio of the B.B.C. (5 SC) was opened at 202 Bath Street. Among the claims which have been put forward for this studio are that it organized the first outside broadcast of opera (from the Coliseum in March, 1923), that it was the first B.B.C. station to broadcast a play (in August, 1923), and that it was the first to experiment in school broadcasting. After the growing Scottish staff had occupied various buildings in Glasgow, a controversial step was taken by the B.B.C.—shortly before the location, in 1933, of the Scottish transmitters near Falkirk—by transferring the headquarters to Edinburgh. Since then, however, a very large Broadcasting House has been built in Kelvinside—incorporating the old Queen Margaret College—and it was very fully used during the second world war.

The weekly and monthly journals, published in surprising variety and numbers during the nineteenth century, vanished, the *Bailie* and the *Scots Pictorial* being among the few which carried on until the nineteen-twenties before expiring. On the other hand, the Glasgow man was better supplied with daily newspapers, the *Glasgow Herald* and the *Daily Record* having been joined by the

Bulletin (in 1915) and by the *Scottish Daily Express* (in 1928). The three evening papers—the *Evening Times,* the *Evening News* and the *Evening Citizen*—all carried on. As several Sunday newspapers too were published in Glasgow, including the *Sunday Mail,* the *Sunday Post* and the *Scottish Sunday Express,* it could be claimed that no other town in Great Britain—not excepting London—was so well supplied with a *local* press.

Varsity Ygorra

An incidental consequence of the transfer of the University buildings from the centre of the city to, as some critics said, an ivory tower in the western outskirts was that, when the students, tiring of academic seclusion, came into town for jollification—a theatre night, for instance, or a tour of the hostelries—they did so *en masse.* Sometimes the citizens joined them in their light-hearted nonsense. Sometimes they did not see its funny side.

The student believed himself privileged and, being assured in his own mind that he was much loved by the populace, unquestioningly assumed his rights on these occasions. Usually he got away with it, and after 1921 his Charities' Week, organized in bleak mid-January, had, by bringing some of the colour and cheerfulness of the Continental carnival to Clydeside, increased his popularity.

No two generations of students are alike, bright ones and dull ones alternating. There is little sense of continuity, although each generation agrees that its successors are a pretty poor lot. James Bridie, in his *One Way of Living,* described the Glasgow student of his day—the late Edwardian period—as lively, violent, unprejudiced, friendly, noisy, sympathetic, moderate even in riot, interested, disinterested, intelligent, balanced, unaffected, chaste, adaptable, knowledgeable, humorous, companionable, wrapt like a mantle in common sense yet radiating poetry, downright, upright, a considerer of the lilies, a philosopher.

James Bridie's own generation was remembered particularly because of a riot at the Coliseum Music-Hall, in November, 1909. A magician, Walford Bodie, who had some pretensions to be a healer, had given offence to the medical profession shortly before coming to Glasgow and on his opening night delivered himself of slighting remarks on medical practitioners in general. The first house on the Thursday was packed with students, and there followed a terrific combat, terminated only when the magician was brought on to the stage to say something which was understood to be an apology. On the Monday five students appeared in the police court on charges arising out of the affair, but they were so well defended by 'two magnificent King's Counsel and some distinguished juniors', that the charges against three were found not proven, another was admonished, and only one was fined.

In 1919 another generation arrived at the University and earned for itself the reputation of being the rowdiest of all. Many of the men who returned from the war did not settle down readily in the classroom and in the laboratory. The University's own difficulties in handling them were made worse by a remarkable growth in numbers. In 1913–14 there had been 2900 matriculated students. In 1919–20 no fewer than 4200 matriculated. Staffs and accommodation were short, and uncertainty was felt about whether a policy of expansion would be justified, for the numbers might fall after a year or two. Actually, they rose to 5000, and extensions have been going

*The 'White' University car,
probably the most often recalled
of all tramcars,
at least in a sentimental sense,
1930s.*

on ever since, partly into the neighbouring suburb of Hillhead. No
one then thought, however, that 40 years afterwards Glasgow would
acquire a second university.

The Men of Letters

Among the many distinguished men and women who have graduated
from the University in recent times are more than a dozen who have
made their names by their writings. When the glories of the Glasgow
School of Painters began to diminish, the leading place was taken
by the authors, and the proportion of these men and women of letters
who served their apprentice days at the University is noteworthy.

In his day J. J. Bell (1871–1934) wrote popular books which had
enormous sales, and created for the world a Glasgow personality,
Wee Macgreegor, still remembered with affection. A son of J. T. Bell,
the tobacco manufacturer, he lived his early days in Hillhead, and
quotations were made earlier in this book from his *I Remember* and
Do You Remember ? In 1902 the *Glasgow Evening Times* published a
series of his sketches about a working-class family, the Robinsons,
and the English-speaking public took them to their hearts. In the
Edwardian years Wee Macgreegor—and a drawing by John
Hassall (who did much of his early work for Glasgow periodicals)—
was almost as familiar to the people of the United States and the
Dominions as to those of the British Isles. Bell was a kindly man,
and William Power has recalled that he never could resist an appeal
to lavish his wit and wisdom on meetings of church 'literaries', and
that his after-dinner speeches were carefully prepared, delightful
little masterpieces.

Wee Macgreegor was a little lad blessed with a taste for 'taiblet',
but cursed with a 'wake digeestion'. A boy of vivid imagination—
'Paw, I wudna' like to be a waux-wurk when I wis deid'—and
curiosity—'I want to see the ingynes'—encouraged by an indulgent
father—'aw the wean's fine, Lizzie'—to the despair of his mother—
'Magreegor, ye wud turn Solyman hissel' dementit'—especially when
indiscreet—'The wee camel's face is unco' like Aunt Purdie'—he got
into an awful lot of mischief, in too hastily assuming the emptiness
of a Corporation watering-cart he was hanging on. Wee Macgreegor
went on for a good many years. He joined up in the first world war,

Wee Macgreegor.

but his vogue had passed by then, and he will be preserved in public memory as a cheerful little lad, sometimes bewildered by the complexities of life, but always sounding off in his rich, Glasgow tongue.

Another Glasgow fictional character became a national figure for a time, 1916 to 1918, but, although in his day he was thought very funny, he has since been forgotten. Perhaps, if he had been conceived twenty years later, his creator, R. W. Campbell, would have been criticized in some quarters rather than praised for having created him. Wee Macgreegor had come from the upper working-class. Private Spud Tamson was of a much lower order. He was the 'heir-male of a balloon and candy merchant', his speciality being blowing up the balloons and blowing down the cornet. He was an 'impident keely, lean and wiry, with red hair, bachel legs and bleary een'. But he had the blood of Highland warriors in his veins, and in 1913 he joined the Glesca Mileeshy, along with the sons of many other 'tramps, burglars, wife-beaters and casuals'. He had been reared in the school of self-help, and no one took a rise out of him as he paraded in 'a pair of wide, ill-fitting tartan breeks, resembling concertinas, a red jacket, which hung like a sock, a white belt and a leather-bound Glengarry cap'. His adventures, farcical and heroic, are set in a period which seems quite remote. Perhaps the pages in the books about Spud's doings, which now arouse most interest, are those describing how the youth of Glasgow went to war in August, 1914, 'celebrating the Great Day and discussing how they would dispose of Kaiser Bill'. This was not strictly accurate, but at least not sufficiently inaccurate to be commented on when the book was published in 1916. Incidentally, its popularity has just been brought home to us by noticing that the edition of the book which we took from the shelves was issued in 1919 and was the sixteenth.

John Buchan, 1st Baron Tweedsmuir (1875–1940), could well be selected as the outstanding Glasgow man of letters of the twentieth century, and the relatively small part of his autobiography, *Memory Hold-The-Door*, devoted to his life in Glasgow might, for that among other reasons, be thought disappointing. Indeed, it is in some of the delightful books of his sister, Anna Buchan (O. Douglas), that the best insight into his life in Glasgow can be found. He was not born in Glasgow, and his family connections were with the Eastern Borders and with Edinburgh. He never forgot this. He came to Glasgow during his boyhood and lived in Pollokshields, then becoming a rival to the exclusive district of Kelvinside. He completed his scholastic education at Hutcheson's Grammar School, but, according to himself, was rather a carefree pupil. He found his first real intellectual interest at the University, which he entered when seventeen. Almost every day, he walked the four miles from the South Side to Hillhead. The road was ugly, but in retrospect it took on 'a changing panorama of romance'. He said that in his day (the early 'nineties) the Scottish universities still smacked of the Middle Ages, and he settled down as a 'diligent student, mediaeval in austerity'. He took some part, however, in corporate life, and recalls that in a rectorial fight he was manhandled by a red-haired savage, 'one Robert Horne, who later became Chancellor of the Exchequer'. He was fortunate in his tutors, and makes particular reference to Gilbert Murray, then a young man in his twenties, and to Sir Henry Jones, the Professor of Moral Philosophy, who had great influence on the social thinking of the country.

Encouraged to continue his studies by going to Oxford, he won a

RED POPPY

Spud Tamson returns from the war. The building on the right is Anderson's Royal Polytechnic later replaced by Lewis's.

scholarship. From then Oxford claimed him, and 'her bonds were never loosened'. It is difficult to resist the impression, while reading his autobiography, that he was planning his future in a coldly ambitious way, for at Oxford he made the acquaintance of the 'right people', and they did not forget him. He was invited to become one of the young men Milner was taking to South Africa on the conclusion of the Boer War, to shape the civil administration of the new Dominion. He did not stay long, however, and, after a short period at the Bar, joined one of his Oxford friends, Thomas Arthur Nelson, in his publishing business in Edinburgh. Their association continued for ten years, and during this time Buchan stood as a Conservative candidate for a constituency in the Borders. Throughout his life he had divided interests. Letters appealed to him. So did politics. And he arranged his affairs so skilfully that he was able to rise to the top in both. Between 1910 and 1922 he wrote a series of best-sellers, in the spirit of Scott and Stevenson, particularly of the latter, beginning with *Prester John* and going on through *Salute to Adventurers*, the *39 Steps*, and *Greenmantle* to *Huntingtower*. His services to the country during the first world war were notable, and in 1917 and 1918 he was Director of Information under the Prime Minister. By the nineteen-twenties he was recognized as one of the outstanding representatives of European culture, and many honours came his way—he was made a Privy Councillor, Chancellor of Edinburgh University, and, greatest of all, Governor General of Canada. He died in Canada, having worked hard at his post and having, in spite of ill-health, visited almost all parts of the Dominion. The Canadians saw in him the traditional Scottish student—'the iron discipline of self, the simplicity of habit, the methodical ordering of his own and other affairs'. Only in one respect did he disappoint the Canadians. They had expected him to have a Scottish voice. He no longer had that.

Neil Munro (1864–1930) did not make an international reputation comparable to John Buchan's, but some of his novels—such as *John Splendid*, *The Daft Days*, *Gillian the Dreamer* and *The New Road*— will undoubtedly live. Unlike so many of the other leading Scottish novelists of his day he hailed, not from the Eastern Borders, but from the Highlands. He was born in Inveraray, and some of the charm of his work was derived from his intimate knowledge of life in north-west Scotland. Having come to Glasgow in his youth, he spent the rest of his life on Clydeside, and in his autobiography, *The Brave Days*, he gives quite the most informative account of the city in the late Victorian and Edwardian period. Perhaps the part of the book most interesting to the student is, however, its foreword, by George Blake, written after Munro's death, in which he took as his theme that Munro was two men, a being of delicate sensibility, and a being gay and shrewdly observant of the world about him. 'His heart and genius were in the writing of romances; and yet his instinct and his talent were for journalism.' J. M. Reid has described his humorous *Para Handy* stories as easily the best things of their kind ever written in Scotland.

Several novelists of the period set some or most of their novels in Glasgow. Catherine Carswell, for instance, Dot Allan and Frederick Niven. The latter was described as being, next to the Orcadian Eric Linklater, the foremost Scottish novelist of the 'thirties. Of the novelists who later came into prominence, the best known was George Blake who also had a brilliant career as an editor. He wrote *The Shipbuilders*, the most widely read book about the Glasgow district published between the wars.

233

Congestion at Jamaica Street Bridge, period 1920.

Another novelist who established an international reputation was Dr. A. J. Cronin, a member of the remarkable generation which crowded into Glasgow University after the first world war. His first novel to attract attention was *Hatter's Castle*, set in the Vale of Leven, where over a century ago the Stirlings established their Turkey-red dyeing industry. His medical experiences were reflected in the Welsh backgrounds to *The Stars Look Down* and *The Citadel*, but he followed his *The Keys of the Kingdom* by returning in *The Green Years* more closely to Scotland and, in particular, to Clydeside. A television series, Dr. Finlay's Casebook, based on his stories won international success in the mid-1960s. An even later product of Glasgow University was Helen McInnes, who, writing from New York, crashed whole-heartedly into the ranks of the best-sellers with *Above Suspicion*, *Assignment in Brittany* and *The Unconquerable*.

It would be wrong to claim Glasgow origin for the Aberdonian John R. Allan, author of *Farmer's Boy*. But, while spending several years on the staff of the *Glasgow Herald*, he wrote some excellent pieces about the city. The best—and it is perhaps the best thing written about Glasgow between the wars—was his *A New Song to the Lord*. It is too long for quotation here, but an extract might give an impression of its quality.

'A man may see visions at Castle Kennedy. In Glasgow he will find the life that will bring those visions to life. Glasgow is ugly. It is dirty. But it is vividly romantic. From Park Terrace on a winter afternoon you look down into the heart of the city. The sun is falling red behind the smoke clouds. Dozens of tall chimney stacks, like the pipes of a devil's organ, throw rolling clouds into the sky. In the red smoke there is a vibration of immense activity. You are conscious of the drills battering in the shipyards, the dynamos humming in the power stations, trains shunting, engines roaring through steamy tunnels, women packing candles and men drawing molten iron from the furnaces, hundreds of shops selling tapes and scientific instruments to measure the stars, hundreds of restaurants where stout ladies drink afternoon tea, waited on by tired girls with headaches, studios where awkward youths are learning to dance and studios where artists are wishing they had never learned to paint, tramcars moving funereally

234

in a line down Sauchiehall Street and buses skidding madly round corners, tablemaids arranging delicate china in Pollokshields, and wheezy old wives buying kippers in Cowcaddens, banks, brothels and exchanges, some ending another day's business, some opening for a night of joy. It is ugly, it is dirty, but it is alive.'

The best-known Glasgow playright was James Bridie. Indeed, he was perhaps the most distinguished British dramatist of his time. His first play to be produced in London was *The Anatomist*, and it, like several others, including *A Sleeping Clergyman*, *Storm in a Teacup* and *Mr. Bolfry*, had a Scottish background. He also turned to the Bible for plots, and derived the story of *Tobias and the Angel*, regarded by many as his finest work. James Agate found both mischief and sentiment in his work, and described him as a descendant of Puck and Queen Mab. Others thought of him primarily as a satirist, cruel at times, but blessed with a rumbustious sense of fun.

Perhaps, however, it was in journalism that the Glasgow writer really came into prominence. T. W. H. Crosland in his *The Unspeakable Scot*, commenting on the large number of Scots working for the London newspapers and periodicals, said—and his intention was not to be complimentary—that, 'in Fleet Street, if you do not happen to possess a little of the Doric, you are at some disadvantage in comprehending the persons with whom you are compelled to talk'. He was referring to the days of Kennedy Jones, the Gorbals lad—about whom Neil Munro wrote in *The Brave Days*—who became Alfred Harmsworth's right-hand man, and who was, through *Answers*, the *Evening News*, and the ha'penny *Daily Mail*, to no small extent the creator of the vast Northcliffe organization, and of others, such as John Hammerton, recently arrived in London. The flow south of Scots reporters, sub-editors, special correspondents and others from Glasgow and Dundee—the latter often breaking their journey at Glasgow—went on throughout the century, and it is still true that a Scots voice will be heard within moments of entering Fleet Street. Why this predominance should have continued is scarcely debatable. The Scottish press offered greater scope than the English provincial press for the young reporter to learn his trade, and the lure of London is strong—particularly for the ambitious. Above all, the Scots journalist makes his way in Fleet Street presumably by his ability and by his diligence. Perhaps, of course, he is at times just a little more thrustful too.

Harder Times

Shipbuilding on Clydeside went on expanding throughout the Edwardian period, and the transfer in 1906 of the yards, boiler and marine engineering shops of Yarrow and Co. from the Thames to the Clyde, created what would be described today as a sensation. It even provoked London periodicals to publish cartoons about the drift north. Many famous ships were built—the *Lusitania* and *Aquitania* are perhaps the best remembered—but even more important was the increasing amount of Admiralty work carried out on the Clyde. Glasgow played a vital part in the naval race with Germany. Indeed, the launch of one of the new Dreadnoughts in 1910 was made the occasion for an important ceremony, during which Germany was told what she was in for, unless she mended her ways. The climax came during the first world war when, as has already been mentioned, Clyde shipbuilding was at 'full stretch'.

Q

"YARROW"

MERCANTILE MARINE

TORPEDO DESTROYERS ETC

WET NURSE CLYDE TO H M BRITANNIA

YACHTS

The transfer of Yarrow's shipyard
from the Thames to the Clyde in the early years of this century
gave the Glasgow people much satisfaction.

The end of the war found the industry in optimistic mood. So many passenger and cargo ships had been sunk between 1914 and 1918, that work for a large number of years, making up the wastage, seemed ahead. New yards were laid out, the most notable inside the boundaries of the city being that of the Blythswood Shipbuilding Co. at Scotstoun. But before long it was perceived that several Continental countries had become competitors and, instead of our building ships for Germany, France, Italy and Sweden, they were sending in quotations to build ships for us. Japan too was looking more like a future competitor than an ally. As late as 1929, however, the Clyde was building as much as 20 per cent of the world's new ships, but a large amount of business, which in days gone by would have come Scotland's way, was even then going elsewhere.

Also disturbing was the realization of the extent to which the rise of Glasgow since the eighteen-seventies had been linked with armaments. Now the war was over, the Admiralty had more ships than it knew what to do with. The country was hard up. There would never be another war. And so almost no orders for new naval vessels were placed. The inevitable slump followed, and a few years after the end of the war—in 1923—Clyde shipbuilding output was the lowest for several decades (180,000 tons against the peak of 760,000 tons in 1913). Then a recovery came, and the output by 1928 had climbed back to 600,000 tons, which, after allowance was made for the absence of Admiralty work, seemed rather good. But the Depression was around the corner, and it was catastrophic, the output for 1932 (66,000 tons) being the lowest since 1860, and that for 1933 (56,000 tons) even worse. These were the tragic years which Glasgow still cannot forget.

The shipbuilding industry created an organization called National

236

*A summer's day in Argyle Street
in the early 1920s.
The relative absence of traffic
is a remarkable feature.*

Shipbuilders' Security to carry out a rationalization scheme. Several
well-known Clydeside yards, including Beardmore's at Dalmuir,
Caird's at Greenock, and Henderson's at Partick, were closed and
dismantled, and their sites offered for sale. This scheme aroused much
criticism, and allegations came from other shipbuilding rivers,
particularly from the Tyne, that the rationalization was being carried
out in a way prejudiced in the Clyde's favour. To this the Company's
reply was that no shipyards were closed down unless the proposal had
first come from their owners; and the implication is that—rather as
George Blake has told in his novel, *The Shipbuilders*—faith in the
future of the industry was at that time stronger in Glasgow than in
some other places. The approach of the second world war changed
the position completely—by 1938 the Clyde's production had risen
to 440,000 tons—and during the critical war years the promoters
of the rationalization scheme were criticized on another score, as
having lost to Great Britain much valuable productive capacity
essential to her in time of war.

Intense feeling was aroused in 1931—when the Depression was
at its worst—by the suspension of work on No. 534 at Clydebank.
This Cunarder, now the *Queen Mary*, was the largest ship built on
the Clyde since the *Aquitania* in 1913. The shipping company proposed to leave her on the stocks until economic conditions improved.
This was a staggering blow to Clydeside, but it was not until 1933
that the Government gave a subsidy to assist her completion.
In the years before the war she had a keen struggle with the French
Normandie for the Blue Riband of the Atlantic and was holding it
when the second world war began. In the meantime another great
Cunarder, the *Queen Elizabeth*, of even larger size (84,000 tons) was
being built at Clydebank, and her amazing exploit in dashing without
trials across the Atlantic to New York in March, 1940, is one of the
most exciting stories in the history of Clydeside shipbuilding.

237

The suggestion that Glasgow was at its peak in the eighteen-nineties is likely to be strongly resisted by those who recall the liveliness and enterprise of the first years of the twentieth century, up to the outbreak of the first world war. But, while much interest was being shown in the new automobile and aircraft industries, some of the older basic industries, such as cotton, glass and pottery were declining rapidly.

In perhaps only one respect was the Edwardian Glaswegian greatly worried and this was about the Iron Ring's loss of influence. He knew from his father and his grandfather that for the whole of the Victorian era, seventy years of it, the heavy industries had been a major prop of Clydeside's prosperity. This decline really was alarming.

After 1860 a rival had been making inroads, and now these went deep. The Cleveland iron industry was based on Middlesbrough. The development of the Bessemer and Siemens processes of steel-making had rendered the non-phosphoric (or haematite) ores of Cumberland more suitable than the Lanarkshire ores. Before long Connals were issuing warrants for these as well as Scotch pig. But the north of England iron masters were less willing to allow Glasgow to be the central authority than the Lancastrians had been. They did not like the storage procedure and they preferred to have their dealings in pig-iron handled by the London metal market. No doubt there were clashes of strong personalities behind this switch.

By 1900 the commanding position of the Glasgow market was said to be definitely on the wane and between then and 1914 'one blow after another fell on the Glasgow market'. In 1913 one of the oldest Glasgow firms of iron merchants failed. The first world war put off the evil day. In 1919 a member proposed that the Association itself should be wound up. This was defeated but in 1924 some of the Association's funds were distributed among the members. The final dissolution was postponed from time to time. It came eventually on 4th April, 1934.

The most heartening thing about the iron and steel industries of the west of Scotland between the wars was the gathering together of several of the leading companies into compact and efficient groups. New plant was installed, a particularly interesting feature being the increase in the capacity created for dealing with modern alloys. But Lanarkshire was not the only British district engaged in the heavy

The 'Queen Elizabeth',
completed at Clydebank in the spring of 1940,
passing Erskine Ferry
on her dramatic dash—without preliminary trials—
to New York.
Subsequently during the war she carried,
along with the 'Queen Mary',
1,250,000 soldiers, chiefly Americans, across the oceans.

238

industries which had improved its working methods. Between 1929 and 1944—years of depression and war—the world's steel-making capacity was increased by more than 75 per cent. At least half of this new capacity was located in countries which before 1929 had been almost wholly agricultural. In some places, including India, Central Brazil and Eastern Turkey, evolution jumped over 500 years in one decade. The inevitable exhaustion of the Lanarkshire coalfield continued and between 1910 and 1939 the output was halved. No fewer than 77 mines were closed between 1929 and 1943.

There can be little doubt that the deterioration in the industrial position of the Glasgow district really began at the turn of the century, and was becoming worse in the nineteen-twenties. But a few comparatively good years in the late 'twenties—and they were only good comparatively—deceived most people of the district, and they did not realize that their affairs were going less than well. Six of those seven automobile factories mentioned earlier had either closed down or were soon to do so, locomotive building had gone into the doldrums, and the construction of aeroplanes and airships had stopped altogether. The once-thriving pottery industry was virtually dead, and the cotton-weaving industry was on the whole in poor shape. Indeed, the only leading industries which really advanced in employment capacity between 1924 and 1930 were the manufacture of hosiery—in which some notable successes were recorded—printing and paper-making, and the preparation of foodstuffs, drink and tobacco. And, although the percentage of the country's trade passing through the Clyde harbours was fairly satisfactory, an almost catastrophic fall was taking place in the tonnage of the Scottish-owned merchant fleet (from 4,600,000 tons in 1913 to 1,750,000 tons in 1939).

The awakening came with the Depression, and a *Report on the Position of Trade and Industry in Glasgow and the West of Scotland*, published by the Glasgow Chamber of Commerce in 1930, was followed by an *Industrial Survey of South-West Scotland*, prepared for the Board of Trade in 1932. They made gloomy reading, particularly as the second report forecast that there would soon be surplus male labour in the area of about 100,000. Even this was an underestimate, and in the year of the Report, 1932, approximately one-third of the insured population was unemployed. Then things began to get better, and by 1938 the munitions programme had re-absorbed many. Between 1939 and 1945 everyone who could do a job—whether he had factory experience or not—was kept hard at work. But in the minds of most workers the dread persisted that some day the bad times would come again, perhaps soon.

Books, pamphlets, articles on the industrial tragedy of Clydeside made their appearance in profusion during the 'thirties. Most of them set out—sometimes at considerable length—to prove that the heavy industries had passed their best—few allowed for the possibility of a second world war reversing this trend (and that in spite of Germany's unconcealed rearmament). Without exception, however, they were vague about how the situation was to be improved. Few of the analyses went deeply into the issue. Industry is not static, and Glasgow, more perhaps than any other large city, had weathered economic storms in the past. Twice previously her chief branch of commerce—the tobacco trade and the cotton industry—had collapsed; but new lines had taken their places, and she had gone on to be more prosperous than ever. So the basic question was why the new industries had not materialized this time?

History will probably have something to say about the alleged

Traffic problems had become so acute around Glasgow Cross in the early 1920s that a proposal was seriously considered for clearing away the Tolbooth buildings, with the tower. This was resisted, but the buildings had to go. They had replaced the original town house in the early part of this century, and so had little historical value.

lack of enterprise shown by Glasgow men during the twentieth century, and particularly during the nineteen-twenties. One explanation—and a very real one—was that a generation of the city's best young men had been lost in the first world war. The retention of the voluntary system of recruitment until 1916 had a most unfortunate consequence, in that it was these best young men who were lost in the futile slaughter during 1915 and 1916, while others, often of lesser calibre, came in only at the later stages or perhaps not at all.

It must be recognized too that Glasgow was unlucky. Many people did take an interest in new developments—for instance, in the use of the new yarn, artificial silk. And the results were sometimes unhappy. Apart from bad investments made in other concerns, Glasgow business men had reason to be disturbed over the very discouraging record of a company, Scottish Artificial Silks. In his summing-up at the trial in 1932 of several of its directors, for issuing a fraudulent prospectus, for fraud, for misappropriation of moneys and for uttering fabricated transfers, the Lord Justice-Clerk compared the case to that arising out of the failure of the City of Glasgow Bank in 1878. The sum involved amounted to £800,000. Two of the directors were found guilty of charges made against them, and one, a Lancashire cotton spinner who had been the sponsor of the scheme, was sentenced to penal servitude.

The plight of certain parts of the country—South-West Scotland, Tyneside, South Wales, and West Cumberland led the Government to appoint Commissioners for these districts, with powers to help them. There was a general reluctance, however, in the years before the second world war to display the sores of the Second City of the Empire to the world, by declaring it a depressed, distressed, special area. However, the boundaries of the Scottish Special Area were drawn so that a large industrial estate could be built between Glasgow and Paisley, at Hillington, by the Commissioner in conjunction with the Scottish Development Council, and this, the first major industrial project on Clydeside for almost ten years, seemed to augur better economic times.

Black memories have persisted of the poverty which prevailed in Glasgow during the nineteen-thirties. Some students have compared the shadow of the Depression that fell over Scotland to that cast by the hungry 'forties over Ireland. This is, no doubt, a considerable exaggeration, even though the Great Depression covered several more years than the Great Hunger. Another difference is that the latter drove the people from Ireland; the former brought back to Scotland many men who had chanced their arm in the United States or in Canada without permanent (if any) success—men who added to Scotland's problems instead of helping to solve them.

The City of Glasgow Society of Social Service had created a central register of the needy as long ago as 1909. The slump of the early nineteen-twenties brought the number on the list to over 100,000. In the early nineteen-thirties it threatened to attain astronomical proportions.

Cleaning Up Glasgow

In 1931 Captain (later Sir) Percy Sillitoe was appointed Chief Constable of Glasgow. Previously he had established a reputation in Sheffield as a 'gang buster' and in his autobiography he attributes his choice 'to the city being over-run by gangsters terrorizing other citizens and waging open war between themselves in the streets'.

The Glasgow Force was the largest in the country after London, with 1500 men. He adds that these men had to believe he would support them in the measures they took to quell troublemakers, and the general public had to be persuaded to side with the police.

Glasgow had been worried about its gangs of rowdy youths for many years but it was not until 1924 that, according to Captain Sillitoe, they came under the rule of 'hardened criminals'. In particular he had to deal with two notorious gangs in the Bridgeton area, the Billy Boys and the Norman Conks (from Norman Street, where many Roman Catholics lived). Both used hatchets, swords and sharpened bicycle chains in their conflicts. When fined they forced levies out of local shopkeepers.

The power of the gangs was not broken until one leader was given twelve months' imprisonment, from which he emerged 'a broken man', and another, fifteen years for culpable homicide.

Other problems he had to deal with were caused by the mass marches of unemployed which could have led to riots, and the activities of the I.R.A. who were using the city as their supply headquarters.

The most disturbing chapter in Captain Sillitoe's autobiography includes an account of his breaking the 'graft' ring among Glasgow bailies. In the course of his decade in Glasgow he was responsible for no fewer than five magistrates being sent to prison for corruption. He adds that the Rt. Hon. Tom Johnston, then Secretary of State for Scotland, warned him that if other people were detected and convicted it might be necessary to put in a Commissioner to act in place of the Corporation. If it can be said that Glasgow was at its peak in the eighteen-nineties, it was certainly far below it in the nineteen-thirties.

Red Clydeside

Glasgow originally got her bad name during the first world war. The trouble began in 1915, when Lloyd George (as Minister of Munitions), accompanied by Arthur Henderson, visited Beardmore's works, where, in his view, the delivery of heavy artillery was retarded by labour difficulties. Lloyd George wrote, incidentally, an account of some of his meetings, and they make interesting reading today, for several of the men later became prominent figures, including one whose fine, pleasant, open face was overlaid by a theatrical frown,

Trongate in the grim depression years at the beginning of the 1930s.

GRAINGER JEFFREY—RED POPPY

and another who, in spite of his perfect manners and soft tones, seemed a sinister influence. The almost complete absence of strikes on Clydeside during the second world war throws some doubt on the tact and skill with which these earlier disagreements were handled. They became worse in the shipyards in 1917. Several labour leaders, chiefly shop stewards, who, Lloyd George thought, 'felt they must justify their existence by searching out wrongs', were 'deported' from Clydeside. Unfortunately, when submarine attacks on the Mercantile Marine were at their worst, the belief was prevalent throughout the country that Glasgow shipyard workers were jeopardizing the winning of the war—and, indeed, the lives of their fellow-men—by holding up the construction and the repair of ships. Whatever might have been the rights and wrongs of those disputes of 1915–17, they undoubtedly prejudiced many people against Glasgow. The whimsical Wee Macgreegor ceased to be the popular conception of what a Glasgow lad was like. Something less pleasant took his place and has persisted since.

With the end of the war the trouble came to a head, and in January, 1919, a strike took place affecting many industries. Winston Chruchill in his account of the aftermath of the Great War said that the Government were seriously concerned over the situation on Clydeside, and he dealt with it at some length. Several issues were involved—unemployment, shortage of houses, high rents, and a demand for a 40-hour week. Mass picketing was resorted to, but the Government, under the Glasgow men, Bonar Law and Sir Robert Horne (then Minister of Labour), insisted on treating the strike as unofficial because it had not been countenanced by the trade unions. On 31st January, what the *Glasgow Herald* described as 'unprecedented scenes of violence and bloodshed' occurred in George Square, where a crowd had gathered to hear the Prime Minister's reply to the Lord Provost's request that he should intervene. A small occurrence caused the spark. Tramcars had difficulty in moving through the throng, and the police, in endeavouring to clear the way for them, came into conflict with some of the strikers. Batons were drawn, and eventually the Riot Act had to be read. Approximately 50 people

'That's richt, my Lord Provost',
says St. Mungo in this cartoon from "The Bailie" of **1924**.
'We'll hae' nae mair o' this scurrility.'
That was what they thought fifty odd years ago.

were injured, none seriously. On the following day armed troops and tanks moved into the city, but the storm was past and, within a few days, work was resumed throughout the district. Subsequently several of the leaders were charged with sedition. Eight, including David Kirkwood, were found not guilty but Emanuel Shinwell and William Gallacher were sentenced to five months' imprisonment.

Except for incidents in 1926 during the General Strike—incidents of a minor character in comparison to some which occurred elsewhere at that difficult time—there has not since been an industrial clash involving the police and a body of workers. The time lost by industrial disputes on Clydeside has also been surprisingly small in comparison with some other parts. It is Thamesside that is now known as Red.

Clydeside's reputation for being 'red' actually had its origin in politics, not in industry. It was at the General Election in 1922 that 'Glasgow went red', and some of the more advanced west of Scotland Socialist M.P.s became known as the Clydeside Group. Several have since published their memoirs. David Kirkwood, for instance, asked the rhetorical question, who were the Red Clydesiders? This was *his reply*— 'John Wheatley was the constructive mind; Thomas Johnston, the journalist; James Maxton, the evangelist; John Muir, the philosopher; William Stewart, the prose-poet; Neil McLean, the propagandist; and myself the engineer'.

Professor W. R. Scott, the economist, criticized them for allowing themselves to be spoken of in this way. Not only, he said, did they get Clydeside associated in the public mind with a political point of view, which, in his opinion, discouraged the establishment of new factories in their district, but, looking at the name from their own standpoint, he thought they should have remembered that no political creed, which becomes linked with one district, ever makes many converts in other districts.

The representations from Glasgow at the General Elections of this time were:

	1922	1923	1924
Conservatives	4	5	7
Liberals	1	0	0
Socialists	10	10	8

The names of the successful candidates at the December 1923 Election make an interesting contrast with those given on page 194 for the December 1910 Election.

BRIDGETON	*James Maxton (Soc.)*
CAMLACHIE	*Campbell Stephen (Soc.)*
CATHCART	*R. Macdonald (Con.)*
CENTRAL	*Sir William Alexander (Con.)*
GORBALS	*George Buchanan (Soc.)*
GOVAN	*Neil Maclean (Soc.)*
HILLHEAD	*Sir Robert Horne (Con.)*
KELVINGROVE	*W. Hutchison (Con.)*
MARYHILL	*J. W. Muir (Soc.)*
PARTICK	*A. Young (Soc.)*
POLLOK	*Sir John Gilmour (Con.)*
ST. ROLLOX	*James Stewart (Soc.)*
SHETTLESTON	*John Wheatley (Soc.)*
SPRINGBURN	*George D. Hardie (Soc.)*
TRADESTON	*Thomas Henderson (Soc.)*

The seats which changed hands at the October, 1924, Election were Maryhill (J. B. Couper, Con.) and Partick (H. B. Lindsay, Con.). Walter Elliot (Con.) took the place which became vacant at Kelvingrove on the death of W. Hutchison. In various Conservative and National Governments between the wars Sir Robert Horne was Chancellor of the Exchequer, Walter Elliot, Minister of Health, Minister of Agriculture and Secretary of State for Scotland, and Sir John Gilmour, Secretary of State for Scotland. A notable point about the 1924 Election was that, in the disaster which befell the Liberal Party, Herbert Asquith, the former Prime Minister, lost his seat at Paisley.

A month after the Election in December 1923, the first Labour Government was formed, with Ramsay MacDonald as Prime Minister, selected largely because of the support of the Glasgow M.P.s. Two Glasgow men held high office, Arthur Henderson as Secretary of State for Foreign Affairs, and John Wheatley as Minister of Health. John Wheatley was the Labour Party's expert on housing, and his death a short time later was regarded by both parties as a great misfortune.

For more than ten years after the majority of the parliamentary seats in Glasgow had been won by the Labour Party, the majority at the municipal elections continued to be held by a party known at first as Moderate and later as Progressive. But in a municipal election in November, 1933, the Socialists had an outstanding success. They had a net gain of 15 seats, and the previous Moderate majority of 21 votes was converted into a Socialist majority of 9 votes. In the next two years this majority was increased to 28 votes, and, except for a brief period in the late nineteen-forties when Sir Victor Warren was Lord Provost, it has since continued to be substantial.

Fewer changes took place in Glasgow in the remarkable parliamentary election of 1945 than elsewhere—the returns from Glasgow being, Labour (including the Independent Labour Party) 10, and Conservatives 5. In his broadcast comments on this election Walter Elliot observed that both the Labour and Conservative Parties had risen in Scotland with the decline of the Liberal Party. 'The new line-up in Parliament really took place in 1922. The hard, unyielding struggle has gone on since then, but the political tenacity has been great and changes have been slight.' In one industrial constituency, for instance, in 1935, 16,015 electors voted Labour and 13,053 voted Conservative; in 1945, 16,066 voted Labour and 13,489 voted Conservative.

Their Finest Hour

Posterity may agree that in 1940 and 1941 Glasgow, along with the rest of the country, had one of its finest hours. No one will say that Glasgow in 1938 and 1939 was at its best. Who was most to blame for the confusion and the anger prevailing at the time is a matter of opinion. The manufacturers were charged with being supine, the workers with being of uncertain temper, and the Corporation with being unhelpful in recruiting the Territorial and Civil Defence Services, and with being dilatory in approving A.R.P. schemes.

The industrialists were bitter with the Government for having located most of the new shadow factories in the south and midlands of England, and almost none in Scotland, and for fostering the expansion of engineering firms elsewhere, while doing little to increase the capacity available in the west of Scotland. This, too, is controversial, and a decision on who was principally at fault must remain for the judgment of posterity. At a meeting in the municipal buildings in 1938, Sir Kingsley Wood, as Air Minister, stated that the Government's policy was to regard Clydeside as the province of

R. EADIE

The City of Glasgow Bank building became Mann Byars warehouse, but it was taken over at the beginning of the war and was occupied by the production ministries— Admiralty, Supply, and Aircraft Production. The building has now been replaced by the largest Marks and Spencer store in Great Britain.

245

the Admiralty (in which comparatively little expansion was to be made) and the south and midlands as the province of the Air Ministry (in which the bulk of the expansion was to be made). The critics of Clydeside can show that Glasgow manufacturers were on the whole slower than their Birmingham rivals in looking for and in accepting Government contracts. One prominent Government official said that Glasgow men did not know what they wanted, and blamed everyone but themselves for not getting it. Nevertheless, an impression does remain that the English firms who doubled or trebled their capacity in the 1938–40 period—taking the opportunity of doing so at the taxpayers' expense—were willing to put their younger executives in charge of their new plant, and that the west of Scotland firms, who would not make any major extensions to their factories, or open new ones, denied to their younger executives comparable chances.

Soon after war was declared on 3rd September, 1939, it was seen that the second world war was going to be very different from the first. Most of the restrictions and controls of the first war had to be accepted again, but usually in a severer form. Indeed, the *Glasgow Herald* made this point in its edition some years later at the end of the German war, by contrasting the advertisements of goods for sale in its columns on 12th November, 1918, and on 9th May, 1945. Many things were on sale at the end of the first war which had disappeared altogether from the shops by the end of the second war. The black-out even preceded the outbreak of the war, and it was a very thorough black-out, particularly during the first few weeks, when there was no street lighting, and trams and buses had no interior lights. Children and old people were evacuated to country districts and, although many drifted back to the city, some were away from their homes for almost six years. The quantity of food available to the public, and particularly to those who took meals in factory canteens, was always ample, although variety was lacking, but the shortage of fruits, particularly oranges and bananas, was keenly felt.

Fuel was scarce— hence this queue for coke outside Tradeston Gas Works.

GLASGOW HERALD

Entertainments again had a boom, and queues outside cinemas in the evenings became as common as queues outside certain food shops during the day. At times supplies were very limited, particularly in the middle of the war, when cigarettes, matches, newspapers and many other things were all difficult to buy; but on the whole the home front was well organized, and the B.B.C., by providing news and programmes from early morning to midnight, in addition to its foreign broadcasts, was able to keep people in their houses contented and entertained in a way quite impossible in the earlier war. Indeed, in some respects—for instance, in appreciating music and art—

The Clydebank Blitz,
March 1941.

IAN FLEMING

public taste improved during the war. Transport services were reasonably well conducted, and, in the organization of its trams and buses, Glasgow Corporation was generally thought ahead of the rest of the country. Train services were curtailed, but were usually adequate. The memory of unbelievably crowded journeys at holiday time will, however, be among the most lasting of the war.

Although the first enemy air raid on the mainland was near Edinburgh, and the last warning of the approach of the enemy was sounded in Aberdeen, Glasgow, like the rest of the west of Scotland, suffered less from air raids than other ports, and particularly London and Liverpool. In view of the heavy traffic through the Clydeside docks, the enemy's policy in allowing this comparative immunity was puzzling, but it did demonstrate that Glasgow is much the most difficult of the large British cities to be attacked from the Continent. Apparently consumption of fuel was the deterring factor.

A balloon barrage protected Glasgow during the war, and occasionally a fog screen was put over the city. Gas masks were supplied to everyone, and during the first months most people carried them about, to their own and other people's inconvenience. Air-raid shelters were built, and baffle walls were put up outside many tenement closes. The first raid was a small one, and was made in daylight on 19th July, 1940, It was followed by a night raid

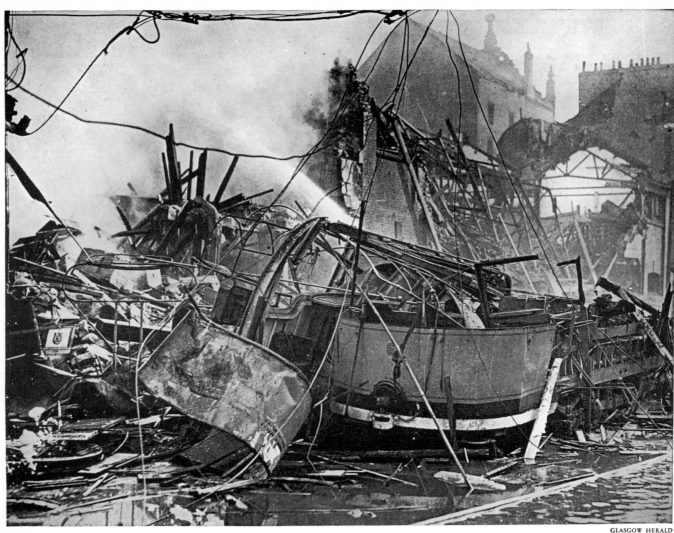

on 18th September, when a stick of bombs straddled George Square, missing, in a most remarkable way, all of the more important buildings there and also Queen Street tunnel which was presumably the target. A bomb during this raid set the cruiser *Sussex*, at Yorkhill docks, afire and, as there was considerable risk of her ammunition magazine exploding, the neighbourhood was evacuated, including the Royal Hospital for Sick Children.

A tramcar which took a direct hit in Nelson Street with heavy casualties. Incredible though it seems, this car was subsequently rebuilt.

In the spring of 1941 the only massed raids on Clydeside were carried out, and the loss of life was very heavy:

March 13–14–15: killed, 1083; seriously injured, 1602
April 7–8: killed, 64; seriously injured, 71
May 5–6–7–8: killed, 341; seriously injured, 312

Comparatively few of the casualties occurred inside the city's boundaries, the March raids being directed principally against Clydebank, and the May raids against Greenock. In Clydebank only 7 houses were entirely undamaged. All but 2000 of the population of 55,000 had to leave the town. Some had afterwards to travel 50 or 60 miles every day to their work; yet such was their fine spirit that 75 per cent of Clydebank's industrial production was resumed within two days. Perhaps the most frightening risk in the raids was, that blazing oil from the Admiralty tanks near Bowling (where 12 million gallons were stored) would flow on to the Clyde. No fewer than 500 men fought successfully to prevent this happening. After the raids 96 high-explosive bomb craters were counted on the site.

The last air raid on Glasgow was made on the night of 23rd March, 1943, when the loss of life was small, but one of 'Greek' Thomson's most admired churches was destroyed.

The City of Glasgow Fighter Squadron (No. 602) claimed the distinction on 16th October, 1939, of shooting down the first enemy aircraft over Great Britain. Its rival for the claim was the Edinburgh 603 Squadron which also destroyed a German aircraft. They were defending the Forth Bridge. It was one of the first squadrons raised in 1924 under the Auxiliary Air Force Order, members being drawn from the factories and offices of the district. Originally a bomber squadron, it was switched in 1938 to army co-operation, and shortly afterwards became a fighter unit. In 1939 it was designated to be a Spitfire squadron, and in 1940 went south to play an historic part over the English Channel in winning the Battle of Britain. Many other squadrons led by Glasgow men came into being—in the days before the war the squadron had a long list of candidates wishing to join—and, while a few of them were occupied in defending their native city, some went all over the world, protecting convoys to Russia, attacking U-boats in the Atlantic, joining in the Burma campaign, and eventually taking an active part on D-day in the landing on the Continent.

Quite the most vital as well as the most dramatic of the Clyde's duties during the war was that of being the country's chief port, assuming the functions of the naval bases of the south and east, which had been rendered unsafe by enemy bombing, and sharing with Liverpool the handling of 80 per cent of the merchant shipping coming to the country. Most vessels had to come to this country through the north-western approaches, which the Government insisted must be kept open, and many intended for Liverpool had at times to be diverted to the Clyde, when the Lancastrian port was under fire. A boom of steel net was carried across the Firth from the Cloch to Dunoon, harbour equipment was expanded, the river deepened and widened, and six deep-water berths were built by 5000 men in a new harbour at Gareloch, with a waterfront of $1\frac{1}{2}$ miles.

Most of the loading and unloading had to be done, however, while ships were at anchor, and a Clyde Anchorages Emergency Port was set up for this purpose, covering the estuary down to the boom and including Loch Long, the Holy Loch, and the Gareloch. A large number of barges and small coasting vessels were assembled to carry cargoes between ships and railheads, and 500 dockers were recruited from London to assist in the operations. During the six war years the net tonnage of vessels entering and leaving Glasgow harbour was 97 million, and the tonnage of war material and commercial goods handled was 52 million. The number of service personnel embarked was 2·1 million and disembarked, 2·4 million.

Much of the American Army and its equipment was landed at the Gareloch—and at another port built at Loch Ryan—and the rate of clearing the military stores, which included aircraft parts and vehicles, was claimed to have set up a world's record. The King and Queen, and the Prime Minister sailed at various times from the Gareloch. The largest naval and merchant vessels came to the Firth of Clyde—as many as four and five aircraft carriers were often there together, and once no fewer than eight battleships; on another occasion several hundred merchant ships, including 150 American Liberty ships, were at anchor in the Firth; convoys were made up; and warships and merchant ships of infinite variety were speedily repaired and supplied. One incidental aspect of the use of the Clyde

Posters in the Central Station, 1945.
During the second world war,
Glasgow had the reputation of being
the most hospitable large town in Great Britain.
When the American Red Cross Club closed in 1946,
a statement was made that during the previous months
over 90 per cent of the American Troops
spending their leave in Great Britain
had come to Glasgow.

harbours was that vast storage accommodation had to be created in the district. Within a radius of 10 miles of Glasgow docks enough food was stored to feed almost the whole of Great Britain in an emergency. Glasgow also handled the bulk of the British overseas mail, and in 1944 the bags of mail passing through the General Post Office were 600 per cent above the pre-war traffic. In June of that year the largest single dispatch of mail ever made from Great Britain went through Glasgow docks.

The *Queen Elizabeth* and the *Queen Mary* repeatedly returned to the Clyde, the first arrival being that of the *Queen Mary*, on 14th June, 1940, accompanied by the *Aquitania*, the *Empress of Britain*, the *Empress of Canada*, and other famous ships, bearing a great contingent of Australian and New Zealand troops, and escorted by the *Hood* and other powerful units of the Royal Navy. Before then, however, Canadian convoys had come to the Clyde, the greatest being that of 18th December, 1939, when the escort included the *Hood, Barham, Resolution, Repulse* and *Warspite*. Subsequently the two 'Queens' took 1,250,000 soldiers across the oceans—most of them Americans, who were landed at Gourock. On one occasion the *Queen Mary* transported 23,000 American soldiers across the Atlantic—a world's record passenger haul.

The convoy to Norway in May, 1940, sailed from the Clyde. So did most of the convoys to Malta, and later to North Africa. Many of the schemes for the D-day landings were worked out on the Clyde, much of the planning for the Mulberry Harbours being done in the Gareloch. Famous visitors came and went. Winston Churchill sailed from the Clyde on no fewer than four occasions to visit President Roosevelt.

Mention has already been made of the capital ships built on Clydeside during the war. The *Duke of York* and the *Howe* are battleships of the *King George V* class, and the *Indefatigable*, an aircraft carrier with a complement of 2000 officers and men. The *Vanguard* was the first (and only) battleship of an even greater class, and was launched by Princess Elizabeth in November, 1944. In addition to an unending stream from the 37 Clyde yards of cruisers, destroyers, anti-aircraft ships, submarines, corvettes, frigates, sloops, minesweepers, minelayers, depot ships, transport ferries and other Admiralty vessels, went landing-craft built by several shipbuilding

250

and structural engineering firms in large numbers for Combined Operations, some yards cleared in the past by National Shipbuilders' Security being used for that purpose. Towards the end of the war the First Lord of the Admiralty revealed that the production of merchant ships was roughly one-fifth greater than in the first world war. Altogether 1903 vessels were built, including the two battleships, four aircraft carriers and ten cruisers; 637 vessels were converted for war purposes and over 25,000 vessels were repaired, including on various occasions, 34 battleships, 202 aircraft carriers and 147 cruisers. Nor did all this represent the total of the Clyde shipbuilders' contribution to the war effort, for they were called upon to send executives and key-men to assist new yards in the United States, Australia, Canada and elsewhere to get into production.

The Clyde is so closely associated in the public mind with ship-building that no one has to be assured that great work really was done in the west of Scotland during the war. But few, even in Glasgow itself, realize that the contribution made in providing the requisites for war in the air was no less outstanding. In 1944 almost as many people (100,000) were working in Scotland for the Ministry of Aircraft Production as for the Admiralty. And, as most of the capacity for making aircraft and their equipment had been created since 1938, it was a notable achievement. Indeed, a factory covering 150 acres, built for Rolls-Royce, who employed 25,000 workers making and repairing Merlin aero-engines, was the largest factory, according to the number of employees, there has ever been in Scotland. The Ministry also brought to Scotland 24 firms, chiefly engaged in light engineering, who had their headquarters in England and had not previously manufactured in Scotland. All but a few decided to continue their production in Scotland after the war.

Perhaps the most important contribution the Ministry made to Scotland's economic future was the conversion of the small Prestwick and Renfrew airfields into major airports. Prestwick became one of the largest flying centres in the world, and was the chief terminal for transatlantic ferrying and transport operations, thirteen passenger services a day being organized between Prestwick and the United States. At Renfrew the Lockheed Aircraft Corporation, of California, assembled many thousands of American aircraft, brought by ships across the Atlantic in sections, and landed at the adjacent King George V Docks.

Many of Clydeside's engineering firms, and most of the iron and steel manufacturing firms, were organized under the Ministry of Supply to make tanks, guns, ammunition, and almost every type of equipment needed by the army. In particular, the west of Scotland was engaged in the manufacture and filling of explosives, a great factory being built at Bishopton only slightly smaller in size than the Rolls-Royce factory. Undoubtedly Clydeside's greatest achievement under the Ministry of Supply came, however, in 1944, in the almost predominating part it played in constructing and equipping the pierheads and other parts of the Mulberry Harbours for the invasion of Normandy. No fewer than 100 Scottish firms participated in the scheme—which was carried out in the greatest haste with a delivery date that had to be kept. The Clyde firms contributed 30,000 tons of fabricated steel to the enterprise. The choice of a special kind of dipper designed by Lobnitz and Co. of Renfrew for the pierheads had, incidentally, its origin in an investigation which followed a gale in the Bahamas some time before, when all craft were thrown ashore except a dipper dredger built by this company.

R

Most Glasgow people had unusual experiences during the war, in their own homes or in their factories. They also shared some with their fellow-townsmen, although censorship made it undesirable for the rest of the world to be told about them. Some were grim, such as the destruction of the French destroyer, *Maille Breze*, by an internal explosion off Greenock, with heavy loss of life among the crew, and a good deal of damage to the town. Some were exhilarating, such as the stationing for several weeks of the Chasseurs Alpins in Glasgow, quite the most picturesque troops ever seen in the city, their band creating a pleasant sensation when it paraded at an international match in Hampden Park. And some were intriguing, notably the baling out of Rudolf Hess, Hitler's deputy, over the Renfrewshire outskirts of Glasgow on 10th May, 1941.

Altogether about 150,000 men and women from Glasgow served with the fighting services during the war. Casualties were severe but, nevertheless, were little more than a third of those of the first world war. This indicates that on the whole less actual fighting was done, and in consequence fewer V.C.s were bestowed on Glasgow men. They numbered four, Sgt. John Hannah (R.A.F.), Lieut. Donald Cameron (R.N.R.), Pte. James Stokes (K.S.L.I.), and Flt.-Lieut. William Reid (R.A.F.).

Into the Welfare State

Most people except the very young know the date when the first world war ended. They are much less sure about the second world war. The fighting in Europe came to a halt rather indefinitely. The Allies marshalled their forces for the assault on Japan; but the dropping of two atomic bombs had a devastating effect on the enemy and V.J.-day came sooner than expected. Whether the war would have come to such a conclusion if the Russians had possessed an atomic bomb of their own must be decided by historians; but at the time the people of this country were blissfully unaware of this a possibility and they gave little thought to the horrors of nuclear warfare in the future.

The General Election results were declared on 27th July, 1945, between V.E.-day and V.J.-day. They were among the most remarkable in British history. The Tory party, led by Winston Churchill, obtained only 210 seats. The Labour party, led by Clement Attlee, obtained 390. Various explanations have been given, but on one point there is no dispute, Winston Churchill's defeat stunned our allies and enemies alike.

It was not in Glasgow that people switched their allegiances. Only one seat changed in the city, Walter Elliot losing Kelvingrove by 88 votes. The Glasgow Members after the election were: Bridgeton, James Maxton (I.L.P.); Cathcart, Frank Beattie (Con.); Central, James R. H. Hutcheson (Con.); Gorbals, George Buchanan (Lab.); Govan, Neil Maclean (Lab.); Hillhead, J. S. C. Reid (Con.): Kelvingrove, J. L. Williams (Lab.); Maryhill, W. Hannan (Lab.); Partick, A. S. L. Young (Con.); Pollok, T. D. Galbraith (Con.); St. Rollox, William Leonard (Lab); Shettleston, John McGovern (I.L.P.); Springburn, John Forman (Lab.); Tradeston, J. Rankine (Lab.).

The change of Government had some very beneficial consequences for Glasgow. Forecasts of labour unrest, based on happenings in 1919, proved unwarranted. Strikes on Clydeside during the years following the second world war continued to be of a minor character—and, incidentally, have been since. But that appellation 'Red Clydeside' sticks. 252

The vital decisions of these times were taken in foreign policy, and decades will pass before an assessment can be made of the effects of the Government's decision not to take the lead in forming the Common Market but to hasten the winding-up of the British Empire. It seemed that one crisis came on the heels of another—over the emergence of Red China, the admission of immigrants to Israel, the revolts in Egypt, the Berlin blockade, the ferment in the Middle East, the explosion of an atomic bomb by Russia, and the war in Korea.

Much of this had comparatively little impact in Glasgow where greater interest was taken in the Government's struggle against the economic aftermath of the war. The war had been won; now the bill was to be paid, particularly to the Americans who as in the years after the first world war were both exasperatingly churlish and incredibly generous. Rationing did not come to an end. Instead it was more severe. Fair shares for all seemed to mean precious little for anyone. Austerity was in full bloom. Then, in the first months of 1947, came the torments of the worst winter in this century. During the 'great freeze-up' electricity and gas supplies were not only 'shed'; sometimes they disappeared altogether. Glasgow people grumbled a lot, and the Minister, Emanuel Shinwell, came in for hard knocks. In actuality, Clydeside suffered much less than most other parts of the country.

The Government went ahead with its plans for the Welfare State and for nationalizing chosen industries, such as electricity and gas supplies, coal, iron and steel. The National Health Service was launched. All of this greatly exercised politically inclined Glaswegians, but the issue which concerned the public most was, unquestionably, more and better housing. Although many people left the comparative safety of Clydeside for their homes in the south, their departure seemed to make few houses available. A serious problem was caused by the activities of 'squatters' (not noticeably drawn from the ranks of ex-Service men). They took occupation of houses in Great Western Road and Park Terrace. They invaded churches. They entered Maryhill Barracks and the Press Club. A group of 30 families settled down in the Grand Hotel. Eviction was, for some reason, not always readily effected, and groups were still living in disused air raid shelters seven and eight years after the end of the war.

The desperate situation was high-lighted with such press announcements as that 667 applications had been received for one particular house. The extent to which the Rent Restriction Act was beneficial to Glasgow will be debated for many years—property-owners have strong views about it—and it was the erection of a great many temporary houses (intended to last 20 years, more or less) which offered an immediate if inadequate solution. The city engineer said that no fewer than 200,000 new houses would be needed eventually.

In spite of all these worries, including the devaluation of the pound by 30 per cent, Glasgow was an exciting place to live in during these post-war years. New industries were being established by American, Continental and English companies on a scale which a decade before would have seemed quite beyond human expectation. Six more industrial estates were being developed within the city's boundaries; several more in the vicinity. A new town was to be built at East Kilbride. Imaginative plans were drawn up for re-developing the whole of Glasgow and the Clyde valley.

253

Entertainment boomed. The theatres continued to stage many pre-London productions. The new Citizens' Theatre was well established. Cinemas had queues every night. Football matches drew great crowds. Dance-halls were packed by the younger generations.

A particularly memorable year was 1949. The first of the four Scottish Industries Exhibitions was held in the Kelvin Hall and displayed to an enthralled public the new things Scotland was manufacturing; furthermore a surplus of £47,000 was made. The Saint Mungo Prize, awarded in 1946 to Sir William Burrell for his magnificent gift of art treasures to the city, was presented this year to Sir Steven Bilsland for his efforts to diversify Scottish industry. (It has since been given to: 1952, Bailie Violet Roberton; 1955, Mrs. Mackenzie Anderson; 1958, John D. Kelly; 1961, Rev. Nevile Davidson; and 1964, Rev. Tom Allan.)

There were other signs of changing times. The Royal Exchange, centre of so much of the city's commercial life for over a century, was bought by the Corporation for conversion into libraries. It seemed that the pendulum which had swung from Edinburgh to Glasgow in the early years of the nineteenth century was swinging back again. Perhaps this was merely a consequence of the highly successful Festival of Music and Drama. Perhaps it had a deeper significance. But, whatever the explanation, there was cause for real concern in the decision of the French and West German Governments to transfer their consulates to Edinburgh. The Second City was, indeed, being down-graded.

Trepidation on the South Side

During most of 1946 people living on the South Side were perturbed by two grim murders committed on 10th December, 1945, in the small railway station of Pollokshields East. Did this give a preview of the post-war world ahead of us? At 7 in the evening a young man with a soft hat pulled over his eyes, gangster-fashion, entered the office, flashing a Luger pistol and shouting, 'This is a hold-up.' The middle-aged clerkess screamed, and he shot her. While dying she went on screaming and the 15-year-old office boy came forward to protect her. He too was shot and died later in hospital. A porter came up and he was shot, but not fatally. He did not regain consciousness until the murderer had fled. The booty was just over £4.

The bullets provided the only clue. Army camps, dockland haunts, dance-halls, public houses were searched without result. No whisper of a name came up from the underworld. Everyone who was thought might have brought home a Luger gun, licensed or unlicensed, was visited. The ballistic tests were all negative.

Ten months later, while the C.I.D. were still ferreting out unlicensed guns, they learned that Charles Brown, a 20-year-old railway fireman, possessed a gun, and a call was made at his mother's house. It transpired that he was at Carlisle, so a message was left, simply asking him to call at the local police station. When his mother passed the message on to him he remarked, 'I know why they were here.' He went to the police and startled them by confessing to be the Pollokshields East murderer. And so he was. Subsequently he was sentenced to death.

Since then he has become a textbook case for medical psychologists. He had been making good progress as a locomotive fireman—his superintendent said he was 'well above average'. He was a pacifist but, being in a reserved occupation, he had not been required to join the Services. He was kind and generous, good to his mother. He had been one of the first subscribers to the fund for the relatives of the victims of the Pollokshields East murders.

He was fond of gangster films and had seen *Scarface* five times. He delighted in swing music and had been in London to buy a white whip-cord jacket such as Frank Sinatra wore. He did not smoke or drink. He had no girl friends, but he often went to parties where he would occasionally pretend during games to be a gangster.

Among the many facts that emerged about Charles Brown was that his nose had been broken in a scuffle when he was 14—he was vain about his appearance—and that at about this time his father, an engine driver, had been killed in a railway accident. His first job on leaving school at 14—after a promising start as a pupil he had fallen behind—was as the boy in the office at this Pollokshields East Station.

Why did such a youth commit the worst crime in recent Glasgow history? Was he just play-acting, but this time with a real gun? How and why did he get the gun? And what led him to give himself up after he had completely avoided detection for many months?

No Longer The Second City

In 1951 Glasgow lost its right, maintained for almost 150 years, to be called the Second City of the Empire. The census returns gave the population of Birmingham as 1,112,000 and that of Glasgow as 1,090,000. Twenty years before, Glasgow had led by a short head.

Victorian and Edwardian Glaswegians would have viewed this with dismay—they had even been charged in the past with manipulating the city's boundaries to bring in a few more people. The modern Glaswegian seemed quite unconcerned. Perhaps the Empire meant less to him than to his fathers. Perhaps he was less convinced that he 'belonged to Glasgow'. He might have supposed that, now Glasgow was over the top, he should seek a job somewhere else. In Birmingham, for instance.

At the turn of the century Glasgow had a notion that it might have grown to be the third city in Europe. It is certainly not anything like that now. It has slipped down the table so far that there is doubt about its being in the first twenty. However, authorities have pointed out that population totals can be misleading. Both Sydney and Montreal, which claim to be the second city of the Commonwealth, are counting the whole 'conurbation'. The population of Greater Glasgow, including such neighbouring towns as Paisley, Clydebank and Kirkintilloch, as well as the Lanarkshire industrial towns—where does the line stop?—approaches two millions.

However, there is not much comfort for Glasgow in this argument. A marketing survey based on the last census (1961) gave the five largest conurbations as: London, 8,172,000; Manchester, 2,427,000; Birmingham, 2,344,000; Glasgow, 1,802,000; and Liverpool, 1,386,000. This probably comes nearest to the real size of the principal British cities.

The population of Glasgow does not matter so much even within Scotland itself; it is more than the combined populations of the other three large cities, Edinburgh, Aberdeen and Dundee. But Edinburgh has acquired a new vigour. Not only has it captured the spotlight with its Festival, but Prince Philip, by choosing to be called the Duke of Edinburgh, has given that city fresh glamour in the world's eyes. Continentals, when talking about Scotland, are incredulous when told Glasgow is the larger place. They knew better in the past.

Some people brush such considerations aside. Does a decrease in size really matter? Perhaps it does not, and might even be advantageous if carried out voluntarily and with understanding. But the population of Greater Glasgow has not remained stationary in this century intentionally and by design. Business people are disturbed when they see an undertaking, big or small, declining. It is not regarded as a good sign and that goes for towns too.

The End of the Post-War Era, 1951

The Labour Government retained its majority at the General Election in March, 1950, but the margin was narrow. The brightness of the post-war years was wearing off and Mr. Attlee's Cabinet was not expecting a long life. There were some glorious moments to come, however, with the Festival of Britain, 1951, although the spirit of the Great Exhibition of a century before was not wholly recaptured. Much of the effort was concentrated on the South Bank site in London, but many places arranged events, mostly enjoyable, of local if not national significance.

Glasgow had one of the major ventures, a spectacular exhibition of Industrial Power being located in Kelvin Hall. It was opened by Princess Elizabeth. The designer's conception was imaginative and the staging spectacular. But light-hearted entertainment was singularly lacking, and during its twelve weeks the attendance was 282,000—only half the minimum specified to the organizing committee. During 1951 the University celebrated its Fifth Centenary and this too was a notable occasion. So Glasgow did not lack pleasing distractions in an otherwise grim year, overshadowed by the Persian Government's nationalization of its oil industry, largely British-owned. Nothing brought home to the British people (and to other Europeans) so vividly this country's declining prestige. Glasgow business men with their many interests in Asia were particularly alarmed at these developments and foresaw other disasters to come.

The post-war era ended in October, 1951, when Winston Churchill regained the Prime Ministership. His majority was not large, (Conservatives and allies 321, Labour Members 295). Glasgow, as usual, made few changes. The chosen Members were: Bridgeton, James Carmichael (Lab.); Camlachie, William Reid (Lab.); Cathcart, John Henderson (Con.); Central, James McInnes (Lab.); Gorbals, Mrs. A. Cullen (Lab.); Govan, J. Nixon Browne (Con.); Hillhead, T. G. D. Galbraith (Con.); Kelvingrove, Walter Elliot (Con.); Maryhill, W. Hannan (Lab.); Pollok, T. D. Galbraith (Con.); Scotstoun, J. R. H. Hutchison (Con.); Shettleston, John McGovern (Lab.); Springburn, J. C. Forman (Lab.); Tradeston, John Rankine (Lab.); Woodside, W. G. Bennett (Con.).

A Second Elizabethan Age

George VI died in February, 1952. When his young daughter, Elizabeth, was proclaimed Queen, the people of this country, and particularly the younger generations, now conscious that a *malaise* was afflicting the nation, hailed the opening of a new age. Parallels were drawn with the reign of the Tudor Elizabeth.

They were not to get much satisfaction out of the rest of the nineteen-fifties. Indeed, Great Britain was to receive two of the worst humiliations in her history. In 1956 the Suez adventure brought Sir Anthony Eden's Premiership to an end; and our coyness over joining the Common Market in earlier years was to lead to our exclusion at the behest of Charles de Gaulle. Furthermore, stresses were becoming more noticeable throughout the world—in Cyprus, Tibet and Cuba, for instance. It became clear too that the troubles with Mau Mau in Kenya were indicative of the spreading hostility to the British throughout Africa and Asia.

The country remained prosperous and full employment was maintained in most parts; in Scotland, where the total of people out of work ranged from 50,000 to 100,000, the majority lived on Clyde-side. Except for a brief period in the second half of the war Glasgow has had a persistent unemployment problem for close on half a century.

Nevertheless, most Glaswegians earned good wages during the nineteen-fifties and the political slogan which was in effect to keep the Conservatives in power for 13 years—'you never had it so good' —was, in fact, true of a large number of people in the west of Scotland.

Perhaps the most significant revolution in social habits for many years began in 1953, at the time of the Queen's coronation. Almost everyone in Glasgow saw the procession and the ceremony itself as televised quite brilliantly by the B.B.C. and a great many sets were installed in homes during the following months—mostly procured by hire purchase or rental. Four years later a second channel became available to central Scotland through Scottish Television (S.T.V.), and after that there were few people in the district who could not see the programmes in their own or a friend's home. Indeed, a fair proportion of families had two sets, in different rooms so as to avoid disputes about the programme to be selected.

Television did many things for Glaswegians. It brought the world into their homes and made the country's leading figures (and many others) living personalities to them. But some consequences were negative. For instance, fewer bought newspapers. Both the *Evening News* (1957) and the *Bulletin* (1960) stopped publication.

The public, especially those over 25, went out to evening entertainments less often. Theatres and cinemas suffered most (fire contributed to the loss: the Queen's (1952); the Royalty (1953) renamed the Lyric; and the Metropole (1961) all being destroyed). A courageous but unsuccessful attempt to convert the Empress (after it had been damaged by fire) into the Falcon, a theatre for audiences with discriminating tastes, did not succeed. The only survivors by the early nineteen-sixties were the Alhambra, Citizens', Empress (itself now renamed the Metropole), King's and Pavilion. The Royal had been taken over by S.T.V. for studios and offices. The closure which shocked Glasgow most was probably that of the Empire (1962). It was the largest music-hall outside London and seemed to be attracting good, if occasionally uproarious, audiences. The music-halls in the districts, such as at Bridgeton, Gorbals, Govan and Partick, vanished from the map.

It was in the suburbs that the cinema was most badly hit. The only losses in the centre were the New Savoy (1958), converted into a dance-hall, and the gallery closed at Green's Playhouse (so de-priving that cinema of its distinction of being the largest in Europe). Attendances at many other gatherings dwindled too—church services, lecture meetings and football matches. All fell away, often disastrously.

Dancing continued to be popular, perhaps because young people are unwilling to stay at home in the evenings. Presumably the public that supported the bingo halls—a strange phenomenon of the late

RAPHAEL TUCK

Many street scenes were photographed in the last days of the tramcars. To some this marked the end of an era of Glasgow's greatness. Here is Renfield Street.

257

The last week of 'The Empire'
was greatly regretted
as it had been
the leading music–hall
in Great Britain outside London.
Its closure was much criticized.

The Glasgow pantomime season
used to mean much to the city.
Only a few years ago no fewer than eight pantomimes
were presented in Glasgow.
Cartoons from the press
showing some of the stars of yester year
are gathered together in this picture.

258

nineteen-fifties—were drawn from less intelligent members of society, particularly women. The marked increase in dining out was more difficult to explain, but it certainly indicated that people had more to spend. It seemed that many were inclined to go out for a meal rather than for a show. In contrast to the opening of new restaurants was the disappearance of tea rooms and smoke rooms, for long features of Glasgow city life. Rising costs had greatly reduced their profitability. The James Craig restaurants were particularly affected, the Gordon and Union Street buildings being converted into shops and offices in 1955, and the Rhul in 1958. The Ca'doro and Cranston's were other establishments greatly altered during the decade.

Club life was changing too. The Constitutional Club did not re-open after the war and is now almost as forgotten as the Liberal Club. The Western and the New amalgamated and then moved to a smaller building.

Several other blocks in the city besides the Western Club, the Empire and Lyric theatres were demolished to make way for tall office buildings. The Corn Exchange, in Hope Street, was one of them. But the city's greatest loss was caused by fire—the complete destruction of St. Andrew's Halls in 1962. However, advantage is being taken of this disaster to erect new St. Andrew's Halls (although not, apparently, under that name) to seat 2000, a theatre, smaller halls and an art gallery, in a cultural centre on the site of the Buchanan Street goods station.

'The Most Modern City in Europe'

Since the first world war Glasgow Corporation have cleared many sites and have built 170,000 houses. Twenty-nine areas were earmarked for redevelopment. They cover five square miles and include not only over 100,000 obsolete tenement and other houses, where families lived at densities of as much as 450 men, women and children to the acre, but also 2,500 commercial and industrial concerns and small family businesses.

The Comprehensive Development Areas include, in the city centres, Anderston Cross, Woodside, Cowcaddens, Townhead, Royston, Laurieston-Gorbals, and Kinning Park. Others are Govan and Partick. There are also several rehabilitation areas, such as the Meadowside district of disused shipyards and the Springburn–Sighthill district associated with former steam locomotive works.

The Inner Ring Road, $4\frac{1}{2}$ miles long, will provide a fast by-pass route for half the traffic that would otherwise cause congestion in the city. The North and West flanks are already in use, including the magnificent Kingston Bridge, opened by the Queen Mother in 1970. With fewer motor vehicles in the city Buchanan Street and parts of Sauchiehall Street have become pedestrian ways.

There are also outer ring ring roads and associated radial motorways. In 1972 preliminary work began for four of the latter, an enlarged Great Western Road, the Maryhill–Lomond motorway, the Stirling motorway and the Pollock–Ayr motorway.

Many of the fine old buildings which gave the city dignity and character have been preserved. Indeed, 300 of them are listed for retention.

The Clyde Tunnels, between Whiteinch and Govan, with their two-lane carriageways (suggested as long ago as the

eighteen-forties) are now actualities and form an integral part of the new network. Over 100 million vehicles have already passed through them.

Not only are Glasgow's internal transport arrangements being greatly changed but so are the ways of entering and leaving the city. Dual carriageways are being constructed north, south, east and west of the city. Renfrew Airport has been transferred to Abbotsinch, planned for 6,000,000 passengers a year. The railways are being re-grouped, although this has one aspect viewed with mixed feelings, the closing of St. Enoch and Buchanan Street stations. The electrification of the local railway services with the introduction of fast diesel locomotives is, however, most acceptable. So is the reduction of the travelling time between Queen Street Station in Glasgow, and Waverley Station in Edinburgh, 45 minutes.

Smoke Control Orders are being applied district by district, and

These tall flats, designed by Sir Basil Spence, form part of the Gorbals— Hutchesontown development.

TOP▶
The new road system, already partly built, is among the most ambitious attempted in Europe. The centre of the city is 'ringed' and motorways come in from north, south, east and west.

FOOT▶
Charing Cross as it was envisaged in the official book about replacing Glasgow.

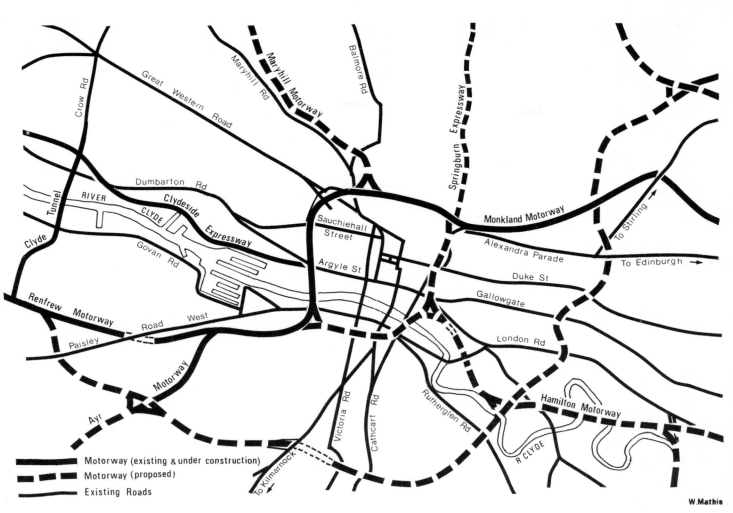

Motorway (existing & under construction)
Motorway (proposed)
Existing Roads

W.Mathie

virtually embraced the city by 1970. By then the three rivers,
Clyde, Kelvin and Cart, were much cleaner than for a very long time.
Salmon have come up the Clyde as far as Govan and the Kelvin, and
some smaller rivers have been restocked with fish.

Overspill is proceeding at a rate of 10,000 people a year, the
intention being that 60,000 families (200,000 people) should move to
the 52 towns (including the new towns) with overspill

When this drawing of the proposed 'Townhead Interchange' was published in the 'Highway Plan for Glasgow' it was treated as very imaginative. But so was the Charing Cross section—and it is now a reality.

Glasgow Cathedral is in the centre of the section on this page, showing how it and High Street might be affected.

So the construction of the Eastern Flank of the Inner Ring Road has proved to be much more controversial than that of the Western Flank.

CORPORATION OF GLASGOW

agreements. These agreements provide for nominated tenants being rehoused in these towns, the latter receiving a grant from Glasgow Corporation for doing so. The overspill towns extend from Stranraer to Wick, but most of the people are not going far away from Glasgow. The population of Glasgow may fall to 900,000, but it is doubtful if the population of Greater Glasgow will fall by very much, if it falls at all.

Ending on a Proud Note

Administering Glasgow is 'big business'. Already it costs £100 million, part being recovered from undertakings, such as transport, that earn revenue. The city's area is 40,000 acres and the boundaries now include places as far apart as Lambhill, Nitshill, Yoker, Queenslie, Penilee and Drumchapel. No fewer than 180,000 children have to be looked after for most of the waking hours of their impressionable lives, and 'further' education provided for 100,000 others. The city employs 8,000 teachers.

Relatively a larger proportion of students take full-time day courses in Glasgow than in any other large city in the Commonwealth. There are 20,000 of them. Glasgow has two large universities. The University of Glasgow, which expects to have 11,500 students by 1976, has been joined by the University of Strathclyde, which is creating places for 6,000 students. Several other colleges are affiliated to or associated with these two universities, but some still preserve their independence, such as the Glasgow School of Art and the Royal Scottish Academy of Music, in which the College of Dramatic Art is housed. The teachers' Training College of Education at Jordanhill is, incidentally, the largest in the Commonwealth.

There is much else of which Glasgow is proud—for instance, of having the largest library service in the British Isles, the finest municipal art collection, and quite the cheapest and most abundant water supply. In former years it also claimed to have the best city-

EVENING CITIZEN

Bill Tait's famous post-war cartoon 'Come on, get off'. This has also been transcribed as 'Cumoangerraff'.

THE SCOTSMAN

The last main thoroughfare in which trams ran was Argyle Street. This photograph was taken when the first buses put in an appearance there.

264

transport system in the world. In the nineteen-twenties the passenger could travel one mile by tramcar for a halfpenny and up to 16 miles for twopence. In that decade, however, the Corporation began to use buses for new routes and, although Glasgow built better and better types of tramcars, the substitution of tramcars by buses on established routes was under way in the years after the second world war. On 4th September, 1962, a sad day for many Glaswegians, the last tramcars were withdrawn, and became museum pieces, abroad as well as in this country.

A Greater Glasgow Transportation Study is intended to co-ordinate the various travel systems to meet the needs of over two million people. This will probably mean that some railway lines will be expanded and closed stations will be renovated.

Another indication of the public services in Glasgow was given in statistics issued by the Western Regional Hospital Board. They showed that the Board was responsible for the care of no fewer than three million people. Admissions to hospitals in 1964 totalled more than 352,000. The out-patient attendances were 4,335,000.

The Duke of Edinburgh, who in his career with the Royal Navy came to know Clydeside well, once remarked that 'Glasgow is a great city in every sense of the word'. No one from the erstwhile Second City will take issue with him on that pronouncement.

But the Victorians who built and re-built the city paid their way. They did not leave posterity to foot much of the bill. Maybe the new Elizabethans are fully warranted in doing so; but there are disturbing aspects. A recent survey showed that almost two-thirds of the factories in Glasgow employing over 250 people are now owned by companies

The largest turn-out of Glasgow people since V.J.-day saw the end of the world-famous tramway system. Along the whole route people were weeping and elderly men holding up their grandchildren to touch the last tram.

265

A splendid photograph of the Clyde taken in 1964 from one of the Gorbals tall flats.

which are not Scottish and do not have their head office in Scotland. It is not really a healthy state of affairs to rely on other people for your new businesses.

In June, 1970 the last General Election under the old Register took place and all but two of the city's seats were held by Labour. The local M.P.s were:

BRIDGETON	*J. Bennett (Lab.)*
CATHCART	*E. M. Taylor (Con.)*
CENTRAL	*T. McMillan (Lab.)*
CRAIGTON	*B. Millar (Lab.)*
GORBALS	*F. McElhone (Lab.)*
GOVAN	*J. Rankin (Lab.)*
HILLHEAD	*Thomas Galbraith (Con.)*
KELVINGROVE	*Dr. M. S. Miller (Lab.)*
MARYHILL	*W. Hannan (Lab.)*
POLLOCK	*J. White (Lab.)*
PROVAN	*H. D. Brown (Lab.)*
SCOTSTOUN	*W. W. Small (Lab.)*
SHETTLESTON	*Sir Myer Galpern (Lab.)*
SPRINGBURN	*R. Buchanan (Lab.)*
WOODSIDE	*N. G. Carmichael (Lab.)*

'What Like is the Glasgow Man?'

That is a more difficult question to answer than it would have been 50 or even 25 years ago. National television and national newspapers have ironed out many idiosyncrasies. So have holidays in England and abroad, and cheap air-flights. Perhaps now he does not differ very much from a Birmingham or a Manchester man. Maybe he has grown to be more like an Edinburgh man.

266

When discussing the Glasgow man in *The Second City*, published
in 1946, a list was given of prominent men who had been born or
brought up in the Glasgow district, or who had become so closely
identified with it that they could be said to 'belong to Glasgow'.
Many of them have since died and others are, alas! not so prominent
as then. But here was the whole list:

Sir Steven Bilsland, the Archbishop of Canterbury Dr. Cosmo
Lang, Sir John Cargill, Sir Patrick Dollan, Sir Andrew Duncan,
Arthur Henderson, Sir Robert Horne, General Sir Archibald Hunter,
Tom Johnston, Sir Alex. B. King, Sir James Lithgow, Sir Robert
McAlpine, Lord McGowan, John Maxwell, James Maxton, Philip
Murray (the American labour leader), the Countess of Oxford (Margot
Asquith), Lord Reith, Emanuel Shinwell, Lord Weir, Sir Cecil Weir,
and John Wheatley. And, as this selection might seem made from
too confined circles, we added the men and women of letters and
arts, such as Sir Muirhead Bone, James Bridie, John Buchan, Sir
D. Y. Cameron, A. J. Cronin, Sir Kenneth Clark, Cowan Dobson,
John Grierson, James Gunn, Frederick Lamond, Muir Mathieson,
Edward A. Wilson (the American book illustrator) and the
Zinkeisen Sisters; the men of the press, such as James Bone,
Sir William Crawford, Sir John Hammerton and Kennedy Jones;
the inventors and scientists, such as J. L. Baird of television, Sir
Alexander Fleming of penicillin, Professor Ian M. Heilbron of
organic chemistry, J. R. Gregg of the shorthand system, and Lord
Boyd Orr of nutrition; the music-hall comedians, such as Sir
Harry Lauder and Nellie Wallace; the film actors and actresses, such
as Andy Clyde, Deborah Kerr, Anna Neagle, Stan Laurel, Donald
Meek—a gardener, incidentally, who cultivated a new rose in
California and called it Glasgow Glory—and perhaps the illustrious
Greer Garson, who, although from the North of Ireland, has close
associations with Glasgow; and, to add even greater variety, Ella

267

s

Logan, the American singer, and Muriel Angelus, the
American musical-comedy star. They all belonged in the mid-decades
of the 1900s to Glasgow and thereabouts.

Drawing up a comparable list for the present time immediately
presents a problem. A hard fact has to be faced. There are not so
many eminent Glasgow men and women to pick from. Perhaps a
similar problem would be encountered if a selection were being made
in Manchester or Birmingham—perhaps in London itself. But one
feature does emerge. No contender is yet in sight for the honour of
being Glasgow's third Prime Minister of this century.

Business provides famous names, such as Fraser, Goldberg and
Woolfson. But there are no captains of industry of stature comparable
to the three Glaswegian men—Lord Weir, Lord Invernairn
(Sir William Beardmore) and Sir James Lithgow—who were so
influential after the first world war in creating the Federation of
British Industries. A dozen or more men could be mentioned who
are chairmen or managing directors of large industrial groups in
England but their names are better known to readers of the
financial pages of the national newspapers than to the general public.
The oil industry has brought some others back to Scotland.

Clydeside continues to provide Fleet Street with journalists—
Alastair Hetherington of *The Guardian*, Ian McColl of the *Daily Express*,
J. B. Junor of the *Sunday Express*, and James Cameron for instance—but
few really top rank novelists or playwrights. James Bridie in spite of
strenuous efforts never found his successor, and the best book written
about Glasgow for many years, Cliff Hanley's *Dancing in the Streets*, is
not widely known outside Scotland. The Glasgow representation in the
cinema world continues to be strong. It is even stronger in television
which has given several potential playwrights opportunities which they
have taken. But proportionately their numbers are no greater than would
be expected from any district of two million people. An exception is
provided by young women singers. Moira Anderson, Lulu, Lena
Martell, Annie Ross and Margaret Savage all come from Glasgow.

One of the characteristics of the Glasgow man is that he wants to
'get on'. He can still be said to be diligent, painstaking, thorough,
attentive to detail. Like John Carrick of the Ship Bank he is imperturb-
able, keeping calm in a crisis. In matters concerning his own interest
he can be, like Kennedy Jones, an opportunist with his eye on the
main chance. He has a good understanding of his fellow-men and
can usually be depended on, as Sir John Moore was when carrying
out the re-training of the British infantry soldier, to concentrate on
what really matters while handling those under him humanely. He
drives the men in his charge, but mixes with them and is never
'stand-offish'. He detests pretentious formality.

He likes to be alone, is reticent, and does not mix so
readily with his fellow-men as the Englishman does—the Glasgow
pub has been a dismal place, lacking the warm geniality of the London
pub—but he can be, nevertheless, the better host. Scottish hospitality
has a world-wide reputation, and the American and Dominion
troops, who spent their leave in this country, made it no secret that
they were better looked after in the north than in the south. Yet
the Glasgow man is short on the social graces—he is reluctant to say
please, thank you, I'm sorry, or excuse me—and he is apt to push
people out of his way crudely and often pointlessly.
The percentage of Clydeside people who seem disposed to
do the opposite of what is suggested to them, is on the high
side. As a recent Medical Officer of Health for Glasgow remarked,

'the people of Glasgow are inclined to be thrawn'. They want the one brand of toothpaste not in stock, to ride on the crowded bus rather than on the empty one behind, to go among the Celtic supporters at a football match and cheer for the Rangers. Their predilection for jay-walking in busy streets is probably the most unfortunate feature of their social behaviour. Believing that he has a prior right on the roadway to automobiles, the Glasgow man expects them, even if the traffic lights are in their favour, to make way for him. He will walk scowling in front of motor-cars, daring their drivers to knock him down. Thus he makes visiting motorists ill-disposed towards his city on their first contact with it. Incidentally, local drivers can be no less perverse.

Perhaps this unreasonableness has its origin in the Glasgow man's endeavour to preserve his individuality. It has good and even fine phases. In integrity, for instance. The reputation of the Scottish insurance companies in the United States is still high because, unlike some American companies, they did not haggle over claims at the time of the San Francisco earthquake. And it is worth noting how often the Glasgow man who has had a business failure succeeds in meeting his creditors in full. Sometimes his children do it for him, years after his death. In comparison with the extraverted southern Englishman or Lancastrian, the Glasgow man is self-concious. He is, for instance, shy about singing in public and, as J. H. Muir remarked, he would not for his life lower himself to be seen in a bus blowing his child's nose. But he might give him the better start in his vocation.

The Glasgow man has the reputation of being stubborn, and wits tell stories about the awful spectacle when two Glasgow men push their chins in each other's faces, both maintaining inviolate principles. Much of this misrepresentation is nonsense, although the Glasgow man does not have the Londoner's sense of compromise, and the lack of it is apt to be a handicap in the conduct of his affairs. Yet he often derives great moral force from his principles—witness, for instance, the courage of the Covenanters and the sacrifices made by many who took part in the Disruption of the Established Church. He came out of his stand against professionalism in sport with more dignity than his opposites in England.

Whether the Glasgow man is more intelligent than most people in Great Britain is debatable. He thinks he is, and speaks about the intellectual limitations of some others, including the Cockney, quite patronizingly. Perhaps he has the tidier mind and the greater capacity for grasping a logical argument. His methods are the more direct, and he has a commendable dislike of fuss, sham and humbug. He does not waste time. Indeed, the stigmata of the Glasgow business man used to be—besides the turned-up trousers, the 'hard hat' and the umbrella—that he was always in a hurry.

It is sometimes said of the young Glasgow salesman that, if left to 'pick up his job', he does badly, because he resents having to be servile. He gets irritated with and argues with difficult customers. Yet Glasgow men have become some of the finest salesmen in the world. A reference was made in the discussion on John Buchan to his 'iron discipline of self, the simplicity of habit, the methodical ordering of his own and other affairs'. It was a sound but rather one-sided analysis. The successful Glasgow man can become, even if nature has not built him that way, the warmest of men. The best chairmen at social functions and the wittiest after-dinner speakers are often London Scots, and many of them are Glaswegians.

The same point can be made about the Glasgow man as a factory operative. He has the reputation of being difficult to handle, and team work undoubtedly comes less naturally to him than to some others. But, if well led, there are few people who march so steadily in step with their fellows as the Glasgow lads. The fact that the Glaswegian is an individualist must always be recognized; but although the characteristic feature of the Glasgow man's play in most sports is individualism—at soccer, for instance, he likes dribbling because of the satisfaction he derives from getting the better of his opponents by his own endeavour—the part he played in making rugby a team game should be remembered.

His caution—as well as his attitude of mental superiority—makes him a difficult man to entertain and to amuse. His attitude to comedians is, 'You say you're funny. Go on, make me laugh.' The Glasgow man's face at an English knock-about farce, with the audience rocking over what is to him sheer inanity, is often worth studying. But producers and authors of witty plays would prefer to have them tried out in Glasgow because they know that fewer of the really good points will be missed.

Like most people whose political views are radical, the Glasgow man is inclined to acquire, particularly as he grows older, some highly conservative tendencies. There have to be set against all of his pioneering efforts, more than a few wasted opportunities—wasted largely, so the younger men of the city allege, because their elders resisted change, and strove to maintain the *status quo ante*. Glasgow has unfortunately acquired the description of the home of lost industries. Neil Munro tells a story which has perhaps had its counterpart more than once in the history of Glasgow's commerce. In the early twentieth century some sound Glasgow business men met to decide the future of 'the old-established and famous waxwork establishment, MacLeod's of the Trongate'. Although advised that moving pictures were sweeping the United States—one of their number had brought them startling reports from New York—they decided that the cinema was a novelty of the moment. The public would, they thought, stick to their old favourite the waxwork. So they went ahead, to 'reconstruct MacLeod's as a waxwork on modern lines'.

However, the elderly Glaswegian's longing for the Brave Days to come again is not in any way novel to present generations, and it has its quaintly humorous sides. J. O. Mitchell, for instance, told a delightful tale of two worthies, Professor John Burns and John Duncan, who resisted the new fashion of wearing trousers, and kept, throughout much of the Victorian era, to knee-breeches and cambric frills on their shirts.

Many of the characteristics which have been attributed to the Glasgow man could be applied to Lowland Scots in general. Where he differs most from them is in having a larger proportion of Celtic, as distinct from Nordic, blood in his veins. Indeed, it is open to question whether he is rightly described as a Lowlander, for Glasgow is at the foot of the Highlands. The man who lives in north-west Glasgow might well suppose that the Highlands begin in his back-garden, and that the Highlander rather than the Lowlander is his nearer relative. The Glasgow man derives some outstanding qualities from his Celtic ancestors. For instance, his sentimentality. He might be a little rough at times in his dealings with other people, but he is rarely cruel or vicious. He does not have the grim mouth, the stolid face, the phlegm of the east coast man. He is, if 'worked up', very demonstrative. If, by chance or by design, he drinks too much, he is more likely to become maudlin than truculent. His sky is often grey but Glasgow is not a grey city. It has too many brilliant flashes of colour for that. And, although the Glasgow man and his wife dress plainly, when they think that a particular occasion calls for something out of the ordinary, they achieve startling and possibly exotic effects.

The outlook of the Glaswegian, like that of the southern Englishman, is thoroughly democratic; yet democracy has evolved in Glasgow along the same lines as in New York, rather than along those to be observed in London. It is more egotistical, less well-mannered. Authority is less readily accepted, but, when accepted, this is done thoroughly rather than compromisingly. Important, perhaps, before all else, is that the youth, no matter the circumstances of his parents, can still make his way to the top. And, when the Glaswegian's good points are being weighed against his bad points, that is something which, in itself, inclines the balance in his favour.

The old and the new in Glasgow.
This photograph was taken recently
when the ship (over 300 years old) on the spire of the old Merchants' House in Bridgegate was being repaired.
A similar ship was placed on the dome of the new Merchants' House in George Square almost 100 years ago.
In the background are some of the tall flats of the Hutchesontown-Gorbals development scheme.

271

Much of the information used in preparing this book came from magazines and newspapers. We are not attempting to identify them here, but would mention that the *Glasgow Herald*'s yearly index, begun in the early 1900s, can be consulted in several libraries. It enables happenings in this century to be pinpointed and people to be identified. The appropriate references in the newspaper can then be readily consulted.

The Glasgow Room in the Mitchell Library has hundreds of volumes on its shelves about the city. They have been card-indexed.

By 1700 Glasgow had become aware that it was a place of importance. The first newspaper, the *Glasgow Courant*, made its appearance in 1715 and just over 20 years afterwards, in 1736, the first history of the city was published. It was written by an odd character, John McUre, and is interesting today because almost everyone who has written a history of Glasgow since has derived some information, perhaps unwittingly, from this old man.

Later in the century, in 1777, another history was published. Its author, John Gibson, is a more clearly defined person than the shadowy John McUre, and we are indebted to him because he included in his book a contemporary account of Glasgow's commerce and manufacture at the end of the tobacco era.

There is no question about the chief reference source for historians covering the period 1770–1830. It is *Glasgow Past and Present* by Senex (Robert Reid), with contributions by Alquis (Dr Mathie Hamilton) and J. B. (John Buchanan). There are three volumes, and they have an absolutely splendid index prepared by David Graham.

Robert Reid (1773–1865) was the son of a well-to-do merchant and served his apprenticeship in one of David Dale's muslin weaving factories. Subsequently he engaged in various manufacturing businesses and, as he lived into his nineties, he was regarded in the 1850s as Glasgow's link with its past. He could recall stories told about, for instance, Bonnie Prince Charlie's seizure of Glasgow. He wrote many reminiscent pieces for the *Glasgow Herald* in a 'racy style', and these were gathered together by James Pagan when taking over the editorship of that newspaper.

The volumes were published in the 1850s, but the best-known edition appeared as late as 1884, and included an informative chapter by John Carrick on the progress of Glasgow as seen at this period of Glasgow's greatest prosperity.

The Superintendent of Public Works, Dr. James Cleland, and one of the leading figures in the city, wrote several books in the post-Napoleonic War period. *The Rise and Progress of the City of Glasgow* (1820) was very statistical and matter-of-fact but included illuminating details and was, as might be expected, well indexed.

James Pagan had written *A Sketch of the History of Glasgow*, which was published in 1847. It contained much personal material and had chapters on such subjects as Prison Discipline and The Early Social Condition of Glasgow. Unfortunately this book was not indexed.

Many students of Glasgow life believe that the most important books of the nineteenth century were written by Peter Mackenzie, particularly perhaps the three volumes of his *Reminiscences* (1865). Mackenzie was a journalist and much closer to the people of the city than others who wrote in the smug Victorian era. He edited Reform weeklies and other radical periodicals read at Bridgeton Cross rather than Charing Cross. Examples of the titles of his chapters are The

Bibliography

Fatal Doom Of the Glasgow Butcher, The Dram-Drinking Case and The Great Meal Fraud.

A year earlier the City Chamberlain, Dr. John Strang, had written a well-remembered book about Glasgow. It was called *Glasgow and its Clubs*, and contained many delightful stories about members of these clubs, ranging from the Anderston Club (1750) to the Crow Club (1832).

George MacGregor, who wrote *The History of Glasgow* in 1881, adopted a chronological sequence instead of dividing his work into different sections. Each chapter covered a number of years, often a decade. This makes the book invaluable to later writers when describing the city's evolution. So is *The Lord Provosts of Glasgow (1833–83)*, published by John Tweed. It contains much more than a biography of each Lord Provost and devotes several pages to events during their periods of office. Another reference book of the period is Andrew Aird's *Glimpses of Glasgow* (1896), rather sanctimonious but informative.

Glasgow in 1901 has been described as the best book written about the city. It is attributed to 'J. H. Muir', with illustrations by Muirhead Bone. Behind the pseudonym were two young men, James Bone and A. H. Charteris. The enchantment of this warm book came from its fresh viewpoint. The authors were fond of their home town as well as proud of it. They were entering the new century full of expectation, little realizing the disappointments ahead. Indeed, both subsequently left Glasgow, James Bone to become one of Fleet Street's personalities and Archie Charteris to occupy a law chair in an Australian university. Muirhead Bone stayed closer to Glasgow, but his reputation too was international rather than local.

J. O. Mitchell's *Old Glasgow Essays* were not published until 1905 but he belonged to an older school. A Glasgow University graduate of the 1840s he was intended for law but entered business and was a partner in a leading firm of leather importers, Schrader, Mitchell and Weir. His interests are disclosed in the titles of some of his other works, such as *Old Country Houses near Glasgow* (1878) and *One Hundred Glasgow Men* (1878). His book contained a table of dates in Glasgow history, from 560 to 1901. It was also splendidly indexed.

The Depute Town Clerk, Dr. Robert Renwick, published his *Glasgow Memorials* in 1908. They were written for the *Glasgow Herald* and the *Evening Times* and were described as 'bearing on such aspects of Glasgow and its institutions as seemed to me to be worthy of elucidation and likely to be acceptable'.

Although Neil Munro's autobiographical *The Brave Days* did not appear until 1931, most of his recollections were of earlier years, from his arrival in Glasgow as a Highland lad to his years as editor of the *Glasgow Evening News*. They were written, after his retirement, as a series for the *Daily Record* and make delightful reading.

Glasgow Corporation had long been interested in a proposal that an official history of the city should be put in hand. Three volumes were published: *The Pre-Reformation Period* by Dr. Robert Renwick and the Town Clerk, Sir John Lindsay (1921); *From the Reformation to the Revolution* by George Eyre-Todd (1931); and *1688 to 1833* also by George Eyre-Todd (1934). The series then lapsed.

In the early 1930s J. J. Bell wrote two books recalling his boyhood in the Hillhead–Kelvinside district during the 1880s and 1890s. They were called, *I Remember* and *Do You Remember?* They brought a good deal of satisfaction to people raised in the West End who regretted the nineteenth century's passing.

Glasgow has been the setting for many novels and countless magazine stories. In recent years several have been distasteful and obsessed with sordid aspects. The name of one district, Gorbals, has become disreputable. Formerly, however, much of the fiction written about Glasgow was humorous and sentimental. Some books are of great interest to social historians. Frederick Niven was the author of almost a score of novels, beginning shortly before the first world war and continuing for over thirty years. Most of them were about Glasgow people and some, such as *The Staff at Simpson's* (1937), give a documentary account of the men and women who worked in the city's warehouses, shops and offices towards the end of the Victorian era.

Guy McCrone wrote close on a dozen novels about the same period, but he was concerned with a different stratum of society. One of his books, *Wax Fruit* (1947), became a best seller, particularly in the United States under the title *Red Plush*, and was translated into several European languages. The leading characters, successful warehousemen in the Glasgow Cross district, are readily identifiable.

Several books about Glasgow have been published since the second world war. The original version of *The Second City* came in 1946. Five years later James Cowan wrote his *From Glasgow's Treasure Chest*. He had worked in a city warehouse for many years and spent part of his 90-minute lunch breaks seeking out information on forgotten and overlooked details. He recorded them in articles for the *Evening Citizen*, under the pseudonym Peter Prowler. The book contains a selection from these articles and is very well indexed.

In 1956 J. M. Reid completed his book on *Glasgow*. It is planned along traditional lines, giving particular attention to buildings. It would have been a model for earlier writers.

Jack House's *The Heart of Glasgow* (1965) is arranged in quite a different way. He goes into the various streets of Central Glasgow, describes buildings, relates incidents, and delineates characters who used to frequent these parts. The smoothness of Jack House's journalistic style conceals the extent to which this book is based on a great deal of carefully detailed research.

During this year, 1965, Andrew Maclaren Young edited his architectural handbook, *Glasgow At A Glance*, which gives invaluable information about the city's many Georgian and Victorian buildings.

In 1958 Clifford Hanley wrote an autobiographical account of his boyhood in Glasgow, *Dancing In The Streets*, during 'the exciting days of the 1930s in a city which never fails to give off an over-plus emotional response'. The book, which had a considerable circulation, did much to restore a sense of proportion by showing the people of Glasgow as they really are: untidy, good-natured, fun-loving, unpretentious, determined and indomitable.

Architecture of Glasgow by Andor Gomme and David Walker (1968) is the definitive book on the subject. Describing Glasgow as essentially a Victorian city with a recognizable local style of architecture, it gives a detailed account of every notable building. Intended for architects, historians, students and others interested in the environment, it contains 250 illustrations, mostly reproductions of superb photographs by David Wrightson and from the Scottish National Buildings Record. A remarkable index begins with a chronological table followed by a genealogical table, an alphabetical list of architects with the buildings, an alphabetical list of streets with their buildings, and ends with a sequence of street maps.

Dr. Tom Honeyman's *Art and Audacity* (1971) is principally

concerned, as its title applies, with art and artists. But it contains many pungent and usually good humoured comments on various aspects of Glasgow life, particularly the Corporation's administration, the theatre and tourists.

Portrait of Glasgow (1972), one of Robert Hale's series of Portrait Books is, as would be expected of Maurice Lindsay, Director of the Scottish Civic Trust, particularly strong on architectural subjects. He is a man of letters too, and makes greater use of poems and novels about Clydeside than any other author in this century. He has also spread his enquiries into other aspects of Glasgow, such as the city's administration and the rise and decline of its industries. He goes into details and these, along with a good index, turn this into a valuable reference book.

a

Abbotsinch Airport . 205
Aberdeen . 3, 47, 73, 84, 198, 247, 255
Accountancy . 95
Adams, The . 33ff, 53, 86
Admiralty . 159ff, 218, 224, 236, 246, 249
Agriculture . 6, 100, 122
Air Force, Royal . 220ff, 227, 249
Airports . 205, 251
Air Raids . 178, 226, 246ff
Aircraft Construction . 224, 238, 239, 251
Aird, Andrew . 80, 274
Airdrie (see also Lanarkshire) . 160ff
Airships . 205, 206, 239
Alexander, J. H. . 37
Alexandra Parade and Park . 93, 259
Alhambra Theatre . 207, 228, 257
Alison, Sheriff Archibald . 39, 103
Allan, Dot . 233
Allan, John R. . 234
Allan, William . 97
Allan Glen's School . 35
Allan Line . 80, 165, 170
'Alquis' . 15, 273
Amateur Theatricals (see also Theatres) 143
Amateurism in Sport . 134, 137
American Wars . 20ff, 48, 65, 78, 106, 109
Anchor Line . 79, 165, 170, 202
Anderson, the Wizard . 103
Anderson, Martin . 157
Anderson's College (see University of Strathclyde)
Anderson's Polytechnic . 177ff, 186, 232
Anderston (including Finnieston) . 9, 13ff, 19, 24, 33, 123, 124, 142, 259
Anglo-Persian Oil Co. . 111
Anthony, Jack . 258
Architecture . 56, 95, 182, 188, 189, 200ff, 203ff, 209ff, 275
Ardrossan . 61, 174
Ardeer . 174
Argyle Street . 11, 12, 16, 23, 32, 33, 51, 56, 102, 121, 129, 142, 145, 177, 186, 187, 188, 191, 232, 237
Argyll Arcade (see also Buchanan Street) . 145, 189
Argyll Car . 205, 211
Arkwright, Sir Richard . 25
Army (see also First and Second World Wars) . 68ff, 111, 130ff, 194, 218
Arrol, Sir William . 169
Art Club . 148, 155
Art Galleries . 116, 154, 155, 182, 209ff
Arthur, J. W. . 221
Arthurs, The . 178
Assemblies (see also Dancing) . 16, 24
Assembly Rooms . 13ff, 15, 33, 53
Athenaeum, The . 34, 36
Athletics . 132, 137, 211
Australia . 75, 251, 255
Authors, Glasgow (see also Books) . 38, 157, 231, 234, 267ff, 273
Automobile Club, Royal Scottish . 148
Automobile Engineering . 205, 211, 224, 229, 238, 239
Aviation . 149, 205, 212, 239, 245ff
Ayrshire . 38, 48, 59, 61, 160, 162, 171, 174, 197, 221, 227

b

B.B.C. . 159, 229, 247, 257, 268
Babcock and Wilcox . 168
Bailie, The . 96, 229 (also illustrations from)
Baillie, Joanna . 39
Baird, John . 42
Baird, J. L. . 267
Bairds, The . 160
Ballantyne, Dugald . 33
Bank Restaurant . 145
Banks . 10, 21, 56, 98, 106
Barclay, Curle and Co. . 73
Barr and Stroud . 168
Barrie, J. M. . 157
Bath Street . 34, 191, 229
Bathgate . 75
Beardmores . 162, 206, 224, 237, 241, 268
Bee, The . 96 (also illustrations from)
Beer . 73, 102, 146
Belfast . 27, 78
Bell, Henry . 28, 165
Bell, H. G. . 39
Bell, John . 27
Bell, J. J. . 140, 144, 145, 146, 157, 231, 274
Bellahouston Park . 214ff
Beresford Hotel . 190
Biles, Sir John H. . 149
Bilsland, Lord . 254, 267
Birmingham . 2, 26, 90, 98, 161, 174, 198, 246, 255, 266, 268
Biscuit Manufacturing . 74
Bishop, T. G. . 181
Bishop's Palace . 1, 22, 116, 182
Bishopton . 251
Black, Joseph . 86
Black Bull Hotel . 15, 100, 101
Blackie and Son . 73, 74, 175
Blake, George . 201, 220, 233, 237
Bleaching Powder . 29
Blythswood Shipbuilding Co. . 236
Blythswood Square . 34, 56, 59, 100
Boer War . 132, 192, 210, 233
Bolitho, William . 201
Bombay . 78, 79
Bone, James . 140, 267, 274
Bone, Muirhead . 156, 223, 267, 274
Bonnie Prince Charlie . 5, 6, 75, 137, 273
Books and Booksellers . 16, 19, 38, 102, 119, 151, 157, 175, 177, 194, 231ff
Boswell, James . 39
Botanic Gardens (see also Great Western Road) . 193
Bothwell Street . 182, 191
Bough, Sam . 103, 153 (also illustrations by)
Boulton, Matthew . 26ff
Bowls, Game of . 138
Boys' Brigade . 120, 221
Brewster, Rev. Patrick . 50
Bridge Building . 169
Bridges (see also by name) . 2ff, 11, 64, 88
Bridgeton . 33, 123, 153, 169, 172, 257
Bridie, James (see also The Mavors) . 157, 230, 235, 267, 268
Bristol . 6
Britannia Music-Hall . 191
Britannia Pottery Co. . 73, 142, 176
British Broadcasting Corporation . 159, 229, 247, 257, 268

Index

British Linen Bank . 9, 56
Broomielaw . 4, 28, 31, 54ff, 78, 107, 122 (see also Clyde)
Brown and Polson . 177
Brown and Co., John . 70, 73, 166, 224, 237
Bryant, Arthur . 61
Buchan, John . 151, 157, 232, 267, 269
Buchanan, Archibald . 27
Buchanan, George . 243
Buchanan, Jack . 143, 208
Buchanan and Bros., John . 74
Buchanan Street and Station . 34, 64, 121, 122, 123, 126, 145, 186, 188, 189, 222, 259
Buck's Head Hotel . 23
Building Industry (see also Architecture) . 200ff
Bulletin, The . 230, 257
Burgh Status . 3
Burghs, Reform of . 43, 154
Burma . 77, 111
Burnbank Sports Ground . 120
Burns, The . 69ff, 78, 103, 119
Burns, J. G. . 144
Burns, Robert . 38, 75, 193, 197
Burrell, Sir William . 154, 254
'Bursts', The . 144, 208

c

Cabs . 124, 135
Ca'doro Restaurant . 259
Calcutta . 78, 79
Caledonian Railway (see also Railways) . 50, 61, 64
Cameron, Sir D. Y. . 156, 267
Campbell, Colin . 80
Campbell, Daniel . 4
Campbell, R. W. . 207, 232
Campbell, Richard . 42
Campbell, Thomas . 38
Campbell-Bannerman, Henry . 178, 179, 195ff
Campbells, The . 178, 195
Canada . 20, 67, 75, 79, 178, 195, 231, 240, 251, 255
Cargills, The . 111, 267
Carlaw and Co., D. . 168
Carnegie, Andrew . 151, 203
Carpet Making . 73, 171ff
Carrick, John . 56, 268, 273
Carrick, Robert . 21
Carron Company . 29

Carswell, Catherine . 233
Cassell Cyanide Co. . 174
Castle Street . 6, 22
Cathcart Circle (see also Railways) . 124
Cathedral, The . 1ff, 11, 18, 21ff, 37, 52, 81, 86, 87, 91, 119, 221, 222
Celtic Football Club . 134ff
Central Station and Hotel . 62, 64, 191, 250
Chalmers, Dr. Thomas . 81ff, 145
Chalmers, Tom . 221
Chamber of Commerce . 22, 110, 184, 185, 221, 239
Charing Cross . 94, 131, 186, 191, 216, 259ff
Charity Societies and Trusts . 52, 69, 96ff, 154, 240
Charlotte Dundas, The . 28
Chartism (see also Radicalism) . 50ff
Chemical Industry . 29, 73, 173
China . 31, 77
Choirs . 159
Cholera . 32, 92, 102, 119
Choral and Orchestral Union . 144, 158, 191
Christmas Cards, Making . 175
Churches . 80, 84, 111, 113, 119, 160, 182, 197, 257, 269
Churchill, Winston (see also First and Second World Wars) . 242, 249, 252, 256
Cinemas . 145, 152, 206, 207, 228, 247, 254, 257, 268
Circuses . 103ff, 141, 142, 152, 191
Citizens Theatre . 254, 257
City Chambers (see also Corporation of Glasgow) . 183ff
City Hall . 36, 56, 100, 114, 143, 144, 158
City Improvements Acts . 59, 199
City Line . 71, 165, 170
City of Glasgow Bank . 98, 106, 113ff, 240, 245
Clan Line . 79, 165, 170, 224
Cleland, Dr. James . 34, 47, 273
Climate . 1ff, 45, 102, 132, 133, 138, 140, 210, 214, 226, 253, 270
Clough, Mary Ann . 119
Clubs . 7, 13, 14, 19, 102ff, 148, 155, 217, 259, 274
Cluthas . 128, 129
Clyde and the Port Authorities . 2ff, 8, 31, 70ff, 89, 92, 128, 138, 164, 169, 174, 223, 239, 247, 262
Clyde Fortnight . 138
Clyde, Lord . 80
Clyde Paper Co. . 73
Clyde Steamers . 104, 105, 156
Clydebank . 73, 162, 168, 170, 224, 225, 237, 248, 255
Clydesdale Club . 133, 134, 136
Coaches, Stage . 14, 15
Coal . 29, 59, 61, 75, 93, 140, 160ff, 174, 227, 239, 253
'Coast, The' . 95, 99, 104, 138, 156, 227
Coatbridge . 64, 160ff
Cochran, Andrew . 6, 7, 19, 21, 22, 77
Cochran Street . 12
Cocker, W. D. . 143, 198
Coffee Rooms (see Smoke Rooms)
Coliseum Theatre . 207, 208, 229, 230
College of Dramatic Art . 264
Collins and Co., Edward . 73
Collins and Sons, William . 73, 175
Colquhoun, Patrick . 22
Colvilles, The (see also Iron and Steel) . 162

Comet, The . 28, 165
Comprehensive Development Areas . 259ff
Condie, John . 27
Confectionery Manufacture . 74
Confederation of British Industries . 268
Connals, The . 79
Conservative Club . 148
Corn Exchange and Restaurant . 56, 145, 259
Cooper and Co. . 130, 181
Co-operative Movement . 25, 97, 98, 182
Corporation of Glasgow (the Town Council) . 4, 12, 35ff, 41, 43, 44, 57, 82, 90, 91, 92, 103, 124ff, 130, 138, 193, 199, 201, 204, 221, 244, 274
Cosmo Cinema . 228
Cotton . 23ff, 28, 40, 50, 65ff, 78, 97, 106, 170, 204, 238, 239
Courts, Police . 14, 185, 200
Covenanters . 269
Craig, James . 259
Cranstons, The . 146ff, 185ff, 207, 259
Cricket . 102, 133, 134
Crime and Punishment . 14, 42, 50, 51, 185, 200
Crimean War, The . 68, 71, 80, 130
Cronin, Dr. A. J. . 157, 234, 267
Crosland, T. W. H. . 202ff, 235
Cullen, William . 19, 86
Cunard, Sam, and Line . 70, 79, 165, 166, 237
Cuninghame, William . 7, 54, 77
Curran, Jimmy . 144
Cycling . 176, 211
'Cynicus' . 157

d

Daily Express, Scottish . 230
Daily Record (see also *North British Daily Mail*) . 96, 229, 274
D'Albert, Eugene . 159
Dale, David . 23ff, 66, 86, 97, 273
Dalmuir (see also Clydebank) . 224
Dalrymple, James . 220, 222
Dancing . 13, 16, 37, 99, 140, 144, 158ff, 206, 226, 227, 254, 257
Daphne disaster . 117
Darien Scheme . 4
Denmark . 103
Dennistoun . 144, 191
Dennys, The . 68, 164, 166
Depressions, Business . 21, 24, 25, 41ff, 66, 78, 98, 106, 193, 204, 212, 224, 227ff, 235ff, 239
De Quincy, Thomas . 157
Dickens, Charles . 36, 157
Disruption of the Church (see also Churches) . 82ff
Dixons, The . 29ff, 159
Dobbie, McInnes . 168
Dobson, Cowan . 157, 267
Docks (see Clyde)
Donaldsons, The . 77, 79, 170
Douglas, O. . 232
Doyle, Conan . 217
Drunkenness . 22, 96, 102ff, 147, 187, 188
Duke of Edinburgh . 255, 265
Dumbarton . 4, 149, 160, 166
Duncan, John . 124, 164
Dundee . 75, 209, 235, 255

Dunlop, J. B. . 176
Dunlop Rubber Co. . 29
Dunlops, The . 21, 29ff, 159
Dunns, The . 177
Dunoon . 104, 138, 249
Dyer, Dr. H. . 166

e

East India Company . 31, 78
East Kilbride . 253
Edinburgh . 3, 5, 12, 15, 17, 32, 38, 47, 59, 84, 86, 95, 131, 136, 141, 157, 171, 176, 203, 208, 226, 229, 232, 247, 248, 254, 255
Education (see also Universities) . 19, 34ff, 84ff, 97, 107, 149, 203, 264
Eglinton Toll (see also Port Eglinton) . 192
Egypt . 66
Elder, David . 71
Elder, John . 71, 165, 166
Elder-Dempster Line . 165
Electricity . 121, 130, 149, 168, 181, 212, 253
Elliot, Walter . 244, 245
Emigration . 67, 79ff, 195, 201, 203, 253
Empire Music-Hall . 142, 190, 191, 208, 228, 257, 258
Empress Theatre . 207, 257
Engineering . 65, 75, 152, 167ff, 204, 223ff, 245
Engineers and Shipbuilders, Institute of . 152
English and Scotland . 4, 18, 26, 135, 148, 190, 202, 203, 208, 209, 246
Evening Citizen . 96, 230, 275
Evening News . 230, 257, 274
Evening Times . 96, 164, 230, 231, 274

f

F. and F.'s (Ferguson and Forrester's) Restaurant . 145
Fair, Glasgow . 103ff, 124
Fairfield Shipyard . 72, 166, 167, 224
Fairy Queen . 28, 165
Falcon Theatre . 257
Falkirk . 29
Fellowes, Horace . 142
Fenians, The . 107, 119
Ferguson and Co., Alexander . 74
Ferries, Clyde . 128, 129
Fighting (Pugilism) . 102, 132
Fighting, Street . 38, 52, 103, 104, 118, 187, 225
Film Society . 228
Finlay, Alec . 228, 258
Finlays, The . 27, 30ff, 78, 111
Finnieston (see Anderston)
Fires . 29, 101, 140, 141, 142, 172, 183, 193, 240, 241, 257, 259
First World War . 80, 193ff, 202, 207, 218ff, 230, 231, 232, 238
Foodstuffs, Manufacturing . 176ff, 239
Football (see also various Clubs) . 133, 254, 257, 269
Fort William . 61
Forth and Clyde Canal . 28, 48, 59, 61
Foulis Brothers . 14, 19, 153
Foundry Boys' Religious Society . 119
Frame, Robert . 123

Frame, W. F. . 144
France . 4, 6, 9, 10, 25, 41, 106, 111, 130, 155, 162, 194, 218ff, 219, 236, 237, 252, 254
Fraser, Lord . 268
Fraser, Mrs. Kennedy . 158
Frazer, Sir James G. . 157
Freedom of the City . 42, 84, 180, 226
Friendly Societies . 99
Fyffe, William . 209, 258

g

Gaiety Theatre . 141, 142
Gallacher, William . 243
Gallowgate . 12, 15, 33, 53, 59
Gambling . 7, 13, 137, 139
Gangsters . 46, 52, 135, 187, 240ff, 255
Garden of Eden Music-Hall . 146
Garment Making . 74
Garroway, R. and J. . 173
Gas . 26ff, 42, 75, 92, 95, 106, 119, 130, 253
Gaumont Cinema . 146, 207
George Square . 14, 33, 34, 40, 43, 53, 75, 90, 110, 184, 185, 242
George V Bridge, King . 89, 191
George V Dock, King . 251
Germany . 75, 106, 111, 130, 159, 166, 186, 192, 193, 194, 218ff, 227, 236
Gibson, Alexander . 159
Gibson, Scott . 197, 198
Gibson, Walter . 4
Gilmour and Pollok . 76
Glasgow Academy . 35, 136, 143
Glasgow Cross . 5, 12, 18, 42, 43, 50, 57, 62, 124, 129, 186, 187, 239, 259
Glasgow Green . 33, 40ff, 50, 53, 55, 93, 104, 106, 112, 134, 138, 171, 197
Glasgow Herald . 56, 96, 102, 103, 104, 109, 130, 193, 218, 221, 222, 223, 226, 242, 246, 273, 274
Glasgow School of Art . 184ff, 264
Glasgow School of Painters . 154ff, 231
Glasgow and S.W. Railway (see also Railways) . 61, 64
Glassford, John . 7, 9, 21
Glassford Street . 12, 39, 51, 185, 245
Glen, William . 39
Glovers, The . 102, 104ff
Golborne, John . 4, 31
Golden Bough, The . 157
Golf . 137ff
Gorbals . 31, 34, 57, 89, 195, 257, 259, 260, 266, 271, 275
Gordon, Harry . 258
Gordon Street . 7, 145, 182, 186, 188
Govan . 9, 28, 72, 73, 90, 129, 134, 142, 162, 194, 198, 257
Graft, Charges of . 241
Graham, David . 204
Graham, Prof. Thomas . 75
Grand Hotel . 131, 253
Grand Theatre . 141, 142, 191, 208
Gray, Dunn & Co. . 94
Great Western Road . 94, 115, 123, 133, 134, 181, 259
Greenock . 4, 11, 25, 31, 47, 59, 73, 169, 227, 237, 248, 252
Green's Playhouse . 228, 257
Grierson, John . 228, 267
Grosvenor Restaurant . 145
Gunn, James . 156, 267
Guthrie, James . 155

h

Haig, Earl . 226
Hamilton (see also Lanarkshire) . 48, 208
Hamilton, David . 182
Hamilton, Robert . 86
Hamilton, William . 158
Hammerton, Sir John . 187, 235, 267
Hanley, Cliff . 268, 275
Hardie, Keir . 42, 197
Harley, William . 34
Harte, Bret . 157
Hassall, John (also illustrations by) . 231
Hawkie . 119
Health (see Public Health)
Heavy Industries . 29ff, 159, 238, 239
Henderson, Arthur . 244, 267
Henderson, Patrick . 79
Hengler's Circus . 141, 142, 152
Henry, George . 155
High School, The . 34, 80, 195
High Street (see also Cathedral and University) . 5, 6, 12, 14, 32, 33, 57, 59, 64ff, 150
Highlanders in Glasgow . 5, 15, 16, 55, 131, 134, 137, 201, 222, 233, 270
'Highway Plan' . 262ff
Hill, David O. . 60
Hillhead (see Kelvinside)
His Lordship's Larder . 145, 146
Holland . 6, 25, 32, 138, 176
Hollins and Co., William . 172
Hong Kong . 76
Hope Street . 186, 191
Horne, Sir Robert . 151, 232, 242, 244, 267
Hornel, E. A. . 156
Hosiery Manufacture (see Knitwear)
Hospitals (see also named Hospitals) . 81, 86ff, 265
Hotels (see also named Hotels) . 6, 15, 43, 53, 101, 110, 145, 185, 190
Housing Conditions . 12, 18, 32, 41, 51, 55, 57, 59, 92, 102, 198ff, 207, 227, 243, 253, 259ff, 268
Houston and Co., Alexander . 10
Howard Street . 180
Howard and Wyndham . 141, 206
Hudson's Bay Company . 75
Hungry 'Forties . 52ff, 67, 99, 179, 240
Hunter, Leslie . 156
Hunterian Museum . 35, 62
Hurd, Archibald . 224
Hutcheson's Hospital . 11, 32, 52, 182
Hutcheson's School . 232
Hutchison, Francis . 19

i

Ibrox disaster . 134
Ice Cream Saloons . 202
I.C.I. (see also Chemical Industry) . 174
Imperial Tobacco Company . 11
India . 31, 77, 78, 79, 111, 198, 239
Ingram, Archibald . 9
Ingram Street . 7, 12, 15, 33, 52, 53, 141, 178, 185
Inner Ring Road . 259ff
Institute of Engineers and Shipbuilders . 152

Insurance . 27, 99, 269
Inverness . 222
Ireland and the Irish . 18, 50, 52, 55, 67, 83, 95, 99, 107, 119, 135, 179ff, 193, 194, 201, 202, 218, 240, 241
Iron and Steel . 29ff, 59, 73, 77, 159ff, 174, 238ff, 251, 253
Iron Ring, The . 195, 204, 238
Irrawaddy Flotilla . 79, 111
Italy and the Italians . 201, 210, 227, 236

j

Jacks, William . 77
Jackson, John . 37
Jail Square (and Bridge) . 42, 104
Jamaica Street (and Bridge) . 64, 70, 88, 89, 90, 127, 145, 177, 180, 181, 186, 191, 234
Japan . 79, 111, 162, 227, 236, 252
Jardine, George . 86
Jardine, Dr. William . 78
Jarvie, Bailie Nicol . 25, 68
Jean's Worthies . 178
Johnston, Tom . 243, 244, 267
Jones, Sir Henry . 232
Jones, Kennedy . 235, 267, 268,
Juvenile Problems . 43, 102, 119, 187, 199, 241

k

Keir Hardie, J. . 42, 197
Kelly, William . 27
Kelvin Hall . 173, 209ff, 229, 254, 256
Kelvin, Lord . 130, 149, 168
Kelvin, River . 9, 13, 94, 116, 172, 173, 210ff, 262
Kelvingrove Park . 93ff, 116, 123, 124, 144, 154, 172, 209ff, 218
Kelvinside (and Hillhead) . 126, 140, 150, 157, 182, 198, 229, 231, 232, 243
Kennedy, John . 28
Kettle, Robert . 145
Kilmarnock . 171, 227
Kilpatrick, J. A. . 157
King Billy's Statue . 8, 15, 43, 45, 109, 129
King Edward VII . 107, 116, 151, 165, 203
King Edward VIII . 226, 227
King George IV . 42
King George V . 89
King George VI . 244, 256
King's Theatre . 207, 228, 257
Kingston Dock . 170
Kirk, Dr. A. C. . 164ff
Kirkcudbright . 28
Kirkwood, David . 241, 243
Knitwear . 173, 239

l

Labour Party (see also Members of Parliament) . 194, 197, 241ff, 252
Laissez-Faire . 19
Lamond, Frederic A. . 159, 267
Lanark (and New Lanark) . 25, 97
Lanarkshire (see also various towns) . 25, 29, 48, 59, 61, 64, 66, 77, 92, 97,

131, 137, 159, 160ff, 176, 197, 208, 238, 255
Lang's Restaurant . 146, 147
La Scala Cinema . 207
Lauder, Harry . 145, 208, 219, 258, 267
Lavery, John . 156
Law, A. Bonar . 195ff, 242
Leather Industry . 73, 175
Lewis's Stores . 178, 186
Liberalism (see also Members of Parliament) . 42, 50, 55, 80, 96, 107, 160, 197
Libraries . 16, 203ff, 254, 264
Linen Industry . 8, 23ff, 66
Lipton, Sir Thomas . 179, 180
Lister, Lord . 87
Literature in Glasgow (see also Books) . 38, 157, 231ff
Lithgows . 73, 267, 268
Liverpool . 6, 52, 59, 61, 76, 78, 170, 181, 201, 249, 255
Livingstone, David . 84
Lloyd George . 241ff
Lobnitz and Co. . 251
Locarno Dance Hall . 190, 227
Lockhart, J. G. . 39
Loch Katrine Scheme . 91ff, 131
Loch Lomond . 124
Lockheed Aircraft Corporation . 251
Locomotive Building . 162, 224, 239
Logan, Jimmy . 258
London . 23, 58, 61, 109, 170, 181, 198, 202, 204, 211, 235, 269
Long, Harry A. . 119
Lorne, Tommy . 228, 258
Low, Peter . 86
Lucknow, Relief of . 80
Lyceum Theatre . 142, 208
Lyons and Co., Joseph . 181
Lyric Theatre . 142, 190, 257ff

m

MacBeth, Allan . 159
McColl, R. S. . 135
McCorquodale and Co. . 175
McCunn, Hamish . 159
MacDonald, Hugh . 103
Macdonald, J. C. . 143, 208
McDowall, Col. Wm. . 9
Macewan, Sir William . 87
Macfarlane and Co., Walter . 163
Macfarlane, Lang and Co. . 74
McGill University . 20
MacGregor, Duncan . 123
MacGregor, George . 113
MacGregor, W. Y. . 155
McInnes, Helen . 234
Macintosh, Charles . 28
MacIntyre, Dr. John . 87
McIver, David . 69ff
MacKenzie, Agnes M. . 66
MacKenzie, John . 76
MacKenzie, Peter . 42, 83
Mackintosh, Charles Rennie . 147, 185ff
MacLean, Sir Donald . 76
MacLehose and Co., Robert . 175
McLellan Galleries . 154
MacLellan and Co., George . 74
MacNair, James . 55
McPherson, Jessie . 216
Macrae, Duncan . 258

Malabar, Old . 119
Maley, William . 135
Manchester . 2, 5, 28, 29, 29, 59, 74, 75, 225, 266, 268
Maps of Glasgow, Early . 17, 32ff, 47
Markets . 14
Maryhill . 127, 137, 145, 198
Mavors, The . 130, 168, 223
Maxton, James . 243, 267
Maxwell, John . 228, 267
Maxwells, The . 21
Mechanics' Institutes . 35, 203
Medical School, Glasgow . 86
Members of Parliament . 44, 107, 194, 243, 244, 252, 256
Menzies, Andrew . 123, 212
Merchants' House . 3, 7, 9, 11, 14, 43, 56, 68, 82, 110, 154, 184, 185, 271
Metropole Theatre . 142, 191, 208, 257
Middle Class in Glasgow . 96, 111, 139, 158, 198, 199, 207
Middlesbrough . 238
Miller, George . 50
Miller, Robert . 27
Miller, William . 39
Milliken, James . 9
Minstrels, Amateur . 144
Missionaries, Church . 84
Mitchell, J.O. . 270, 274
Mitchell Library . 203, 261, 273
Mitchell, Stephen . 73, 204
Monteiths, The . 24, 41, 66, 90
Montreal . 79
Moore, Dugald . 39
Moore, Sir John . 40, 43, 80, 268
Morgan, Tommy . 258
Morison, J. L. . 151
Morton, Thomas . 171
Mossman, J. . 103
Motherwell . 160, 227
Motherwell, William . 39
Motorways . 261
Muir, John . 243
'Muir, J. H.' . 146, 148, 188, 269, 274
Mulberry Harbours . 251
Mumford's Geggie . 142
Municipal Buildings (see City Chambers)
Munro, Ian S. . 221
Munro, John . 130, 204
Munro, Neil . 147, 155, 157, 191, 233, 235, 270, 274
Murders . 100, 216, 254
Murdoch, William . 26ff
Murray, Gilbert . 232
Mushet, David . 29
Music-Halls . 55, 102, 140ff, 206, 228, 270
Musicians, Itinerant . 140, 141

n

Napier, David . 68, 165
Napier, Robert . 69, 90, 162, 164, 165, 166
Napoleonic Wars . 10, 30, 40, 82, 96, 109
Nasmyth, James . 27
Navy, Royal . 159ff, 218, 224, 235, 246, 249ff
Necropolis . 81, 82, 91
Neilson and Co., John . 28
Neilsons, The . 27, 30, 77, 162

Nelson Monument . 33, 93
New Savoy Theatre . 257
New Town, Glasgow's . 56, 93, 94, 123, 124
New Year's Day Observance . 44, 144
New York . 79, 202, 271
New Zealand . 76, 79
Newcastle . 2, 47, 182, 237
Newsome's Circus . 141
Newspapers (see also by name) . 14, 16, 48, 52, 96, 115, 175, 192, 202, 217, 229ff, 235, 252, 257, 266, 273
Night Clubs . 227
Niven, Frederick . 233, 275
Nobel, Alfred . 174
Normal School . 85
North British Daily Mail . 96, 109, 192
North British Hotel . 43, 110, 185
North British Railway . 61, 111
Nurses, Education of . 87

o

O'Connor, Daniel . 50
O'Connor, T. P. . 195
Ogstons, The . 175
Oil Industry . 176
Oils, Distilling . 75, 111, 248
Old Age . 52
Olympia Music-Hall . 208
Omnibuses . 49, 94, 122, 123ff
Orchestral Concerts . 158ff
Orpheus Choir . 159
Oswalds, The . 10, 44
'Overspill' . 259, 262
Owen, Robert . 25, 97

p

Pagan, James . 38, 57, 61, 74, 273
Paint and Oil Industry . 74, 176
Paisley . 20, 48, 49, 50, 66ff, 177, 198, 227, 255
Palace Theatre . 208
Panopticon . 143, 208
Panorama . 142, 146, 191
Pantomimes . 99, 101, 141, 142, 206, 208, 258
Paper Making . 73, 175, 176, 239
Park, Stuart . 156
Park District . 94, 234
Parkhead . 126, 162
Parks, City . 93
Partick . 9, 13, 90, 129, 133, 136, 141, 194, 198, 237, 257
Paterson, James . 156
Paterson, William . 4
Paul, Robert . 11, 15
Pavilion Theatre . 207, 208, 228, 257
Pearces, The . 73
Penny Geggies . 142
Perry, Dr. Robert . 87
Picture House . 207
Pilcher, Percy . 149
Plagues . 32, 51, 92, 102
Planning, Street . 33, 201, 259ff
Plaza Dance-Hall . 227
Plymouth . 2
Poets (see also Books) . 38ff
Poland . 75, 202

Police . 41, 52, 67, 68, 106, 118, 200, 217, 240, 254
Polloks, The . 76
Pollokshaws . 9
Poloc Club . 133
Population Increases . 9, 23, 31, 113, 195, 198, 201, 255, 263
Port of Glasgow (see Clyde)
Port Dundas . 62, 74, 122
Port Eglinton . 122, 124
Port Glasgow . 4, 73
Postal Deliveries . 12, 14, 15, 16, 33, 50, 53, 79, 90, 130, 204, 250
Potteries . 73, 176, 238, 239
Poverty . 82, 83, 85, 96, 97, 118, 120, 199, 207, 240, 273
Power, William . 231
Preston, J. B. . 143
Prestwick Airport . 251
Prime Ministers (Glasgow) . 178, 195
Prince's Dock . 170
Prince's Theatre . 102
Princeton University . 20
Pringle, J. Q. . 153
Printing Industry . 19, 73, 175, 239
Pritchard, Dr. Edward . 100, 216
Provand's Lordship . 6
Provosts (Lord) . 6, 24, 42, 44, 90, 114, 198, 220, 226, 242
Public Health . 14, 18, 32, 38, 41, 51, 57, 58, 92, 99, 129, 198ff, 227, 262
Public Houses . 13, 14, 22, 41, 96, 102, 139ff, 147, 188, 189, 202, 268

q

Quarrier, William . 119
Queen Elizabeth, The . 237
Queen Margaret College . 151, 229
Queen Mary, The . 237
Queen Street and Station . 37, 59, 61, 145, 148, 178, 248
Queen Elizabeth . 256ff
Queen Victoria . 91, 107, 131, 132, 137, 191, 210
Queen's Dock . 170
Queen's Park . 93
Queen's Park Club . 134ff
Queen's Rooms . 144
Queen's Theatre . 142, 257
Quiz . 96 (also illustrations from)

r

R.34 . 205, 206
Radcliffe, Jack . 228
Radicalism . 40ff, 50, 55, 95, 97, 106ff, 112, 113, 194, 197, 241
Radio . 229, 247
Railways . 48ff, 50, 56, 59ff, 77, 95, 96, 109, 129, 162, 175, 211
Rainfall (see also Climate) . 1, 17, 25
Rambles around Glasgow . 103
Ramsay, Sir William . 149
Ramshorn Kirk . 4, 11, 34, 82, 119
Randolph, Charles . 71, 151, 165
Rangers Football Club . 134ff
Rangoon . 78, 79, 111
Rankine, Macquorn . 149
Rating Procedures . 200
Redevelopment . 259ff

Reform Movements . 4, 41ff, 77, 82, 97, 106ff, 111, 194, 227, 253, 273
Regal Cinema . 142, 152, 190, 228
Rehabilitation Areas . 259
Reid, J. M. . 238, 275
Reith, Lord . 267
Religious Intolerance . 52, 55, 274
Religious Societies . 120, 135, 177, 231
Renfield Street . 59, 191, 257
Renfrew and Renfrewshire . 4, 11, 20, 25, 31, 34, 48, 50, 59, 66ff, 73, 95, 168, 175, 198, 227, 237, 248, 251, 252, 255
Renfrew Street . 189
Rent Restriction . 253
Repertory Theatre . 193, 206
Restaurants . 64, 101, 102, 139ff, 146ff, 189, 207, 225, 259
Rigby, William . 27
Riots . 41ff, 55, 152, 193, 230, 242
Ritchie, James . 7, 21
Ritchie, William . 27
Roberton, Sir Hugh . 159
Roberts, Earl . 218
Roche, Alexander . 156
Rodger, Alexander . 39
Rolls Royce . 251
Roman Catholicism . 55, 112, 135
Romans . 2
Rothesay . 104, 227
Rothesay Dock . 170
Royal Crescent . 123
Royal Exchange . 7, 40, 42, 54, 57, 77, 146, 161, 179, 182, 254
Royal Glasgow Institute of Fine Arts . 153, 155
Royal Infirmary . 81, 86, 89ff
Royal Mail Line . 165
Royal Princess's Theatre . 141, 191, 208
Royal Scottish Academy of Music . 159, 264
Royal Technical College (see University of Strathclyde)
Royal Theatres . 37, 101, 103, 140, 141, 142, 191, 206, 207, 208, 228, 257
Royalty Theatre . 141, 142, 191, 206, 207, 257
Rubber Manufacturing . 28, 74, 176
Rugby Football . 134, 136, 270
Rum . 9, 41
Russell, Dr. J. B. . 199
Russia . 80, 111, 130, 148, 194, 210, 218, 252
Rutherglen . 162, 198

s

St. Andrews . 3, 82, 84, 138
St. Andrew's Church . 11, 12, 57
St. Andrew's Halls . 149, 158, 178, 182, 191, 218, 225, 259
St. Enoch Square and Station . 16, 64, 122, 127, 130, 140, 145, 146, 188
St. George's Church . 34, 57
St. Mungo . 96 (also illustrations from)
St. Mungo Prize . 254
St. Rollox . 29, 174
St. Thenew . 16
St. Vincent Street . 40, 57, 93, 110, 148
Safety in the Streets . 27, 42, 46, 52, 102
Salmon . 13, 28
Salon Cinema . 207, 219
Salvation Army . 113
San Francisco . 269
Saracen's Head Hotel . 15, 101

Saturdays . 122, 127, 132, 144, 145, 186, 187, 188, 225
Sauchiehall Street . 62, 100, 130, 131, 139ff, 142, 145, 151, 181, 186, 187ff, 219, 227, 235
Savings Bank . 98
Savoy Theatre, New . 257
School of Art, Glasgow . 184ff, 264
Schools (see also Education) . 25, 34, 81, 82, 83, 84ff, 97, 136, 195, 221, 264
'Scotch Comics' . 143ff, 208, 228, 259, 270
Scotia Theatre . 142
Scots Pictorial . 229 (and illustrations from)
Scott, Gilbert . 150
Scott, Michael . 39
Scott, Professor W. R. . 243
Scottish Amateur Athletic Association . 137
Scottish Artificial Silks Case . 240
Scottish Co-operative Wholesale Society . 25, 97, 182
Scottish Film Council . 228
Scottish (National) Orchestra . 158
Scottish Television . 141, 257
Scotts of Greenock . 73
'The Second City' . 3, 32, 61, 212, 255, 265
Second World War . 193, 198, 214, 224ff, 226ff, 237, 239, 240, 242, 245ff, 268
Sellars, James . 182
'Senex' . 17, 177, 273
Service, R. W. . 157
Sewage Disposal . 92, 129
Shanghai . 78
Shanks and Co. . 73
Sheffield . 162
Shinty . 139
Shinwell, Emanuel . 198, 243, 253, 267
Shipbuilding . 28, 66, 68ff, 148ff, 164, 174, 186, 223ff, 235, 242, 259
Shipping . 5, 28, 31, 78ff, 164ff, 170, 178, 202, 224, 239, 242, 249
Shopping in Glasgow . 13, 15, 29, 50, 74, 121, 123, 124, 132, 177, 186, 188ff, 232, 259, 269
Sillitoe, Sir Percy . 240
Simson, Professor Robert . 14, 19
Singer Manufacturing Co. . 168
Skating . 151, 152, 206
Slater, Oscar . 216ff
Slave Trading . 10
Sloan's Restaurant . 145
Slums (see also Public Health) . 14, 32, 38, 41, 51, 57, 59, 64
Smith, Adam . 14, 18
Smith, George . 79
Smith, Madeleine . 100, 216
Smith, Sir William . 120
Smoke Control . 262
Smoke Rooms . 146ff, 259
Smollett, Tobias . 39
Snodgrass, J. . 27
Snowfalls (see also Climate) . 2, 61, 83
Soap, Manufacturing . 174
Social Life . 9, 12, 18, 34, 46, 53, 99ff, 122, 140, 158, 206, 250
Soup Kitchens . 83
South Africa . 174, 178, 233
'South Side, The' . 130, 133, 144, 198, 232, 243, 254
Spain . 160
'Special Areas' . 240
Spiers, Alexander . 7, 21

Sports . 132, 137, 211
Stage Coaches . 14, 15, 43, 46, 49, 50, 51, 61, 119
Star Theatre . 141
Steamers, Clyde . 104, 105, 156
Steel, Manufacturing (see Iron)
Stephen and Co., Alexander . 73, 117
Stephen, Campbell . 243
Sterne and Co., L. . 168
Stevenson, Macaulay . 156
Stewart Memorial Fountain . 91, 212
Stewart, William . 243
Stewarts and Lloyds . 161
Stirling . 48
Stirlings, The . 9, 17, 234
Stock Exchange . 90, 116, 148, 222
Stow, David . 85, 107
Strang, William . 156
Strong, Mrs. . 87
Street Characters . 102, 119, 207
Street Games . 85, 132, 133
Streets, State of the . 17, 18, 122
Strikes . 41ff, 50, 66, 72, 97, 241ff, 252
Suez . 79, 193, 256
Suffragettes . 193, 194, 226
Sugar Growing and Refining . 6ff, 20, 77
Sunday Newspapers . 230
Supply, Ministry of . 251
Sweden . 236

t

Tait, Thomas S. . 214
Tamson, Spud . 207, 232
Tate and Lyle . 11
Tea, Importing . 77, 180
Tea Rooms . 146ff, 182, 185ff, 259
Telephone Development . 121, 204
Television . 141, 257, 266, 267
Temperance Movement . 50, 80, 103, 112, 135, 144ff, 196
Templeton and Co., James . 73, 171, 223
Tenements . 56, 93, 95, 198ff, 259
Tennant, Charles . 29, 62, 75, 173, 174, 195
Tennent, J. and R. . 15, 73
Territorial Army (see Volunteers)
Textile Manufacturing (see Cotton, Linen and Woollen Industries)
Textile Printing, etc. . 9, 17, 66
Theatres (see also names) . 37, 99ff, 103, 139ff, 191, 206, 235, 247, 254, 257
Thieving . 38, 52, 59, 118
Third Lanark Club . 136
Thomson, 'Greek' . 183, 249
Thomson, J. and G. . 70, 73, 166
Thrift, Habit of . 98
Timber Yards . 76, 79
Tivoli Theatre . 142
Tobacco . 6ff, 20ff, 73, 204, 231, 239
Tod and MacGregor . 69, 73, 165, 166

Tolbooth Buildings . 5, 11, 12, 15, 53, 109, 125, 129, 239
Tollcross . 29
Tontine Hotel . 6, 12, 15, 16, 18, 22, 24, 42, 45, 51, 57, 59, 107, 129, 188
Toronto . 75
Trade Unions . 50, 97, 98, 194, 197, 242
Trades House . 3ff, 33ff, 43, 51, 154, 185, 221
Tradeston . 60
Trading Companies . 76ff, 79ff
Trams . 121, 124, 189, 190, 211, 220, 225, 226, 231, 234, 237, 242, 247, 248, 257, 264, 265
Trongate . 5, 8, 11, 15, 18, 23, 33, 43, 45, 59, 109, 122, 125, 145, 186, 187, 188, 241, 270
Tron Church . 56, 81, 125
Tullis, D. and J. . 168
Tunnel, Clyde . 128, 129, 259
Typhus . 32, 87, 92
Tyres, Rubber . 176

u

Underground Railways . 90, 129, 130
Unemployment . 41, 55, 95, 98, 177, 197, 227, 239ff, 257
Union of Parliaments . 4
Union Street . 12, 191
United States . 10, 20, 55, 66, 67, 70, 98, 100, 103, 106, 137, 145, 151, 162, 164, 168, 179, 180, 193, 202, 206, 227, 240, 249, 251, 253, 269, 270
United Turkey Red Co. . 9
University of Glasgow . 11, 12, 18, 26, 39, 62, 64ff, 82, 84, 107, 116, 119, 130, 133, 137, 149ff, 168, 172, 173, 183, 194, 195, 196, 209, 211ff, 218, 222, 230, 231, 232, 256, 264
University of Strathclyde (also Anderson's College and Royal Technical College) . 35ff, 150, 203, 221, 264
Urie, John . 103

v

Vale of Leven . 9
Vancouver . 75
Verrefield Pottery . 176
V.C.'s, Glasgow . 223, 252
Victoria Infirmary . 87
Victoria Park . 137
Virginia Street . 7
Volunteers, The . 40, 107, 120, 130ff, 194, 218, 219, 245

w

Wages, Rates of . 50, 55, 66, 67, 72, 95, 98, 226, 257

Wallace, Arthur . 95, 107
Wallace, Edgar . 217
Wallace, Nellie . 258, 267
Walsh, P. . 197
Walton, E. A. . 156
Warehouses . 74, 178, 275
Wareing, Alfred . 206
Washing Greens . 43, 52
Water Supplies (see also Public Health) . 13, 34, 66, 87, 90ff, 131, 180, 231
Waterloo Rooms . 145, 207
Watson, G. L. . 138, 139
Watson, Robert . 90
Watt, James . 25ff, 71
Wee MacGreegor . 231, 242
Wee Willie Winkie . 39
Weir, G. and J. . 168
Weir, William (Lord), . 226, 267, 268
Wellington . 29, 54, 80
Wellington Arcade . 189
Welsh, Dr. David . 82
'West End, The' . 57, 59, 188, 206, 231, 253
West Indies . 6, 9ff, 41, 90
West of Scotland Cricket Club . 133, 136
West, George . 258
Western Bank Failure . 106
Western Club . 56, 148, 162, 259
Western Infirmary . 87
Wheatley, John . 243ff, 267
Whisky Distilling . 9, 41, 73, 239
White, J. and J. . 74, 173
White, James . 168
Whiteinch . 128
Whytock, Richard . 171
Willis, Dave . 228, 258
Wilson, Alexander . 19
Wilson, John . 39
Wizard of the North, The . 38
Wood and Co., John . 28, 69
Woolfson, Sir Isaac . 268
Woollen Textiles . 75, 170, 223
Wotherspoon, John . 20

y

Yachting . 138, 148ff, 164, 179, 180
Yarrow and Co. . 235, 236
Young, G. M. . 83, 106
Young, John . 212
Y.M.C.A., The . 78
Young, 'Paraffin' . 75

z

Zoo, Glasgow . 191